Canadian Environmental Policy:
Ecosystems, Politics, and Process

Canadian Environmental Policy:

Ecosystems, Politics, and Process

EDITED BY
Robert Boardman

Toronto Oxford New York
OXFORD UNIVERSITY PRESS
1992

Oxford University Press, 70 Wynford Drive, Don Mills, Ontario M3C 1J9

Toronto Oxford New York Delhi Bombay Calcutta Madras Karachi
Petaling Jaya Singapore Hong Kong Tokyo Nairobi Dar es Salaam Cape Town
Melbourne Auckland

and associated companies in
Berlin Ibadan

Canadian Cataloguing in Publication Data

Main entry under title:

Canadian environmental policy

Includes index.
ISBN 0–19–540774–1

1. Environmental policy—Canada.   2. Environmental
protection—Canada.   I. Boardman, Robert.

HC120.E5C3 1992   333.7'0971   C91–095110–1

Printed in Canada by Gagné Printing

Contents

Figures and Tables

Preface

The growth of the literature on environmental policy and politics in recent years, and the rise of environmental questions to prominent positions on the agendas of the federal and provincial governments, present the authors and editor of a volume such as this with difficult choices in the selection of topics and approaches. The common theme of the contributions is the character and significance of the politics and processes that underlie policy-making on the environment.

In the first part, the focus is on government, and particularly on the current complex constitutional and legislative framework, policy processes in the federal bureaucracy and Cabinet, including the role played by environmental advisory groups, the working of federal-provincial relations on environmental issues, and the expanding role of the courts. The second part explores the impact of pressure groups, the responses of the party system to environmental questions, and shifts of public opinion and values. Two chapters also examine respectively the rise of an environmental industry in Canada and the beginnings of a policy in this area, and the various ways in which the news media have dealt with and adapted to environmental issues and the environmental movement. Finally, we turn to the international context of policy, by means of discussions of Canadian-American relations, and Canadian approaches to multilateral developments. This third part closes with a comparatively based assessment of Canadian environmental policy performance.

At Oxford University Press, the project was encouraged from the outset by Richard Teleky, then Managing Editor, and steered through to publication by Olive Koyama. Thanks are also due to Paulette Simard, who helped to keep things on line at the Dalhousie end.

ROBERT BOARDMAN
CHESTER BASIN, JULY 1991

Introduction

———

ROBERT BOARDMAN

The environmental policies and programs of Canada's governments take diverse forms and have many sources. At one level they can be seen as a product of political calculation, a response to the moral crusading of some and the ingrained hostility to government regulation of others, or a means of balancing appeals to scientific truths with appreciation of the skills of governance. They may reflect great expectations. Particular programs may be judged outside government in relation not only to the specific problems ostensibly addressed — protection of threatened habitats, safer handling of toxic materials, cleaner air — but also to a putative requirement of transforming Canadian society. Special lenses may also be needed even to detect 'environmental' policy, of which abstract definitions are legion, as opposed to programs in a variety of more neatly discrete and manageable areas, from sewage to sulphur dioxide, from orioles to ozone. The topics covered by the term environmental policy are already abundant. The cast grows still larger if we take account of the many others, hovering in the wings, that at any time may be being coached by friends and agents for their hour in the spotlights.

Thus older environmental agendas centring on approaches to specific instances of pollution, or to the preservation of endangered species of wildlife and the protection of threatened natural areas, have been criticized as inadequate underpinnings of alternative agendas that take environment-economy linkages as their main focus.[1] This tack became increasingly common in Canadian policy debates from the mid-1980s. Questions as diverse as urban renewal, transportation, and energy supply have been incorporated into some definitions of environmental policy in western countries.[2] Clashing ideological perspectives complicate the picture still further and affect the placing of issues on environmental or sustainable development agendas. Environmental issues can also be viewed as members of larger families of questions. Green agendas characteristically link these with peace, international development, multiculturalism, and feminism;[3] by the early 1990s many Canadians were increasingly detecting important environmental dimensions to questions of national security.[4] Environmental issues may also be seen as part of a larger cluster of issues of risk in contemporary society, along with questions such as workplace safety, traffic accidents, and smoking.[5]

Connections with broader processes of ideology formation have been a distinguishing feature of environmental politics. Attempting to define the common ground of the 'central value assertions of environmentalism', Robert Paehlke has noted such elements as the idea that 'the complexities of the ecological web of life are politically salient', humility in relation to other species, a global view, a preference in political arrangements for decentralization, an extended time horizon, a commitment to 'sustainable' bases of societies and economies, and an 'aesthetic appreciation for season, setting, climate, and natural materials'.[6] Environmentalism is interpreted as an evolving ideology to assist the transition from industrial to postindustrial society, 'much as liberalism, conservatism, and socialism saw us through the formation of a new society during the Industrial Revolution'.[7]

Other writers have drawn attention to central elements of environmental thinking that influence the formation of public policy, and that distinguish these kinds of issues from others on contemporary agendas. Drawing primarily on the United States experience, Daniel Henning and William Mangun identify such features as the fact of ecological complexities, the crisis orientation of many environmental issues, the concern for future generations inherent in approaches to these questions, and the intangible nature of many environmental values.[8] Similar themes recur in environmental policy arguments. The need to think in the long term, for example, or at least in a longer frame than seems feasible for politicians with minds set on the next election, is a key element of environmental thought. Environmental policy, in a word, is policy designed to escape from the 'tyranny of the immediate'.[9] Similarly, it has been argued that since the ecological complexities at the root of policy problems are often difficult to grasp intellectually, the issues themselves may be ignored.[10]

The linkages that are formed in this fashion between environmental and other issues often serve in practice to define their character. The free-trade issue in the late 1980s and continued evaluation of the progress of the Canada-US economic relationship, for example, has been a central question in many environmental debates of the last few years. It led among other things to criticisms by a number of environmental groups that Canadian sovereignty over water resources was being compromised by emerging Canadian policy positions.[11] Free trade has also been identified as one of the leading culprits behind the issue of bison slaughter in Wood Buffalo National Park.[12]

Whether environmentalism has as a result begun to constitute an alternative philosophical foundation for late twentieth-century industrial societies remains to be seen. Though environmentalism can indeed be defined in ways that transcend older left-right dimensions, critics have nonetheless claimed to discern older and more characteristically left-oriented anti-private sector stances behind the approaches of some environmentalists to prominent issues. Environmentalist critiques of industry's role in relation to the constraints standing in the way of effective pollution control, or of unsustainable resource development practices in the forestry sector, have been taken as examples. The media's allegedly one-sided handling of environmental questions has also been cited.[13] Companies for their part have had a healthy suspicion of environmentalism as inherently, and excessively, regulatory. Strategies of resistance, Ted Schrecker has noted, have included job blackmail and adopting a greenish tinge as a means of deflecting criticism or averting more intrusive regulatory norms in the future.[14] There has traditionally been little prospect of a sustained and productive dialogue between the view that the corporate role is irrevocably self-serving and anti-environmental, and the notion that environmentalism is an irredeemably anti-growth philosophy. Discussion of alternative market-based approaches to environmental policy, such as tradeable effluent permits, has also been weakened as a result.[15] Even so, there was increasing evidence during the late 1980s and early 1990s of more private sector readiness to participate in joint forums, particularly following the impact on Canadian environmental debates of the Brundtland Report of 1987 and the progress of the Round Table experience at both federal and provincial levels.

Supporters and critics alike, however, have traditionally somewhat overstated the degree of common ideological ground present in environmental advocacy. There is also a considerable amount of diversity. Protection of species and natural habitats, for example, a staple of environmental conservation philosophies in Canada from the late nineteenth century, has been criticized from the more radical deep ecology perspective as an ethically objectionable form of incarceration in which national parks feature as the functional equivalent of prisons.[16] Variety and a lack of internal coherence is present in much ecological thinking.[17] The origins of this diversity can perhaps be found in the varied character of the environmental movement itself. Historically this has encompassed a wide range of groups with viewpoints varying from a traditional concern for the protection of species and wild spaces to critiques of the fundamental value systems of Canadian society. Different mixes have arisen in different countries. In some (as in continental Europe) the anti-nuclear movement played a catalytic role in fostering the emergence of an environmental movement, while in others, among them Canada, the US, Australia, and New Zealand, the politics of wildness has arguably had a more formative impact.[18]

The processes by which environmental issues emerge on Canadian agendas, and the ways these are handled by governments and groups, defy simple description. Public opinion, and shifts of taste and ideas, play a part. Public concern over environmental pollution problems rose sharply, especially in Ontario, during the late 1960s, and, following a lengthy period of ups and downs at lower plateaux as other issues took the lead, re-emerged in the mid-1980s with even more force and with a wider range of issues at its focus. Objections on free market grounds to the deepening of regulatory structures implied by environmentalism have likewise been a recurring and countervailing tendency, particularly in the context of arguments that modern governments were already overburdened with demands from largely ungovernable contemporary societies.[19] This has reinforced the reluctance of governments to interfere with existing jobs-environment mixes, possibly to the point of tolerating excessive pollution.[20]

Government institutions have figured in these debates in a number of ways. Some writers have suggested that the character of environmental policy problems, particularly their inherent complexity, interconnectedness, and transboundary nature, means that conventional structures of government are likely to be found increasingly ill-equipped to handle the tasks of the 1990s.[21] The theme is echoed in environmentalist critiques of Canadian federalism as an overly tolerant system which too easily accommodates provincial government departures from desired policy norms. Steven Kennett has argued that this kind of territorial and political fragmentation, combined with sectoral fragmentation inside government, makes for significant externalities in the case of water resource management.[22] Environmental policy is also marked by some blurring of the lines between processes inside and outside government. As Kathryn Harrison and George Hoberg have shown in their study of environmental agenda-setting, for example, policy entrepreneurs, whether in government agencies or interest groups, play a vital role in getting environmental issues on to regulatory agendas.[23] The significance of different actors may vary over time, as well as in relation to different kinds of environmental issues. One of the most important developments of the late 1980s was the expanded significance of the courts in relation to environmental problems, a changing role graphically demonstrated in the Alberta (Oldman River) and Saskatchewan (Rafferty-Alameda) dam cases.

Ten years ago one political scientist observed in relation to the study of environmental issues that, apart from occasional contributions by economists and students of public administration, 'by and large, the work of social scientists in this realm lags far behind that of their colleagues in the natural sciences'.[24] The last decade, and particularly the last five years, have witnessed impressive strides forward in the volume and quality of scholarly attention to these matters by political scientists and their colleagues in related disciplines. The chapters which follow address these issues in three main sections: first, through examination of processes operating primarily at the governmental level; second, by means of study of political activity on environmental issues outside government; and third, with the aid of international and comparative perspectives on Canadian environmental policy.

PART I

Policy Process and the Environment

CHAPTER 1

Canada and Environmental Protection

Confident Political Faces, Uncertain Legal Hands

———

DAVID VANDERZWAAG
AND LINDA DUNCAN*

Canadian politicians and bureaucrats have prided themselves on being international leaders in supporting sustainable development and forging new institutions and laws to protect the environment. When the Canadian Environmental Protection Act (CEPA)[1] was first released as a draft bill in December, 1986, the then Minister of Environment, Tom McMillan, called it the most comprehensive piece of legislation in the western hemisphere and said it constituted the nation's first environmental bill of rights.[2] In a preface to *Canada's Green Plan* of 1990, the Minister of the Environment, Robert de Cotret praised the Plan as 'the most important environmental action plan ever produced in Canada'; more than a hundred initiatives would be supported with $3 billion in new funds over five years.[3] Referring to the proposed Canadian Environmental Assessment Act, he boasted of a process which 'is more powerful in its impact on decision-making than any other environmental assessment legislation in the world.'[4]

While Canadian governments struggle to strengthen their institutional and legal capacities to protect the environment,[5] constitutional tensions and legislative uncertainties raise doubts over their ability to attain a sustainable environment. This chapter begins by highlighting the unstable constitutional foundation for environmental management and the sources of federal-provincial conflict. We next summarize the potential strengths of three broad-reaching federal laws—CEPA, the 1984 Environmental Assessment Review Guidelines Order,[6] and the Fisheries Act[7]—and note the uncertainties in application stemming from interjurisdictional wrangles, political compromises, and citizen suits. The potential for the Charter of Rights and Freedoms to impact on environmental protection is discussed, together with the environmental implications of entrenching aboriginal rights in the constitution.[8] The chapter concludes with a look at the parallel trends of co-operative federalism on the environment and provincial approaches to environmental bills of rights.

CONSTITUTIONAL POWERS: READING BETWEEN THE LINES

Division of Powers

The Canadian Constitution makes no direct reference to the environment. Unlike the constitutions of many states,[9] Canada's provides no enshrined guarantee to a clean, healthy environment. No clarification is provided on which level of government bears environmental responsibility. Resolution of the matter is made complex by the distribution of powers between federal and provincial governments in a myriad of areas or fields of power which potentially touch on the matter of environmental protection and sustainable development.

Section 91 of the Constitution Act, 1967,[10] establishes various federal levers of power relating to aspects of environmental protection. The federal power over sea-coast and inland fisheries (s. 91[12]) enabled the federal government to enact the federal Fisheries Act.[11] The Navigable Waters Protection Act[12] is enacted under the power to control navigation and shipping (s. 91[10]). The Arctic Waters Pollution Prevention Act[13] and Northern Inland Waters Act[14] are enacted pursuant to federal powers to regulate activities affecting federal lands and waters. The Canadian Environmental Protection Act, based on the peace, order, and good government (POGG) power (s. 91 preamble), was enacted to establish nationally consistent standards for the control of toxic substances. This Act also expands the scope for federal regulation of environmental impacts on federal lands.

International obligations also fall under federal authority. Enactments under this power include the Migratory Birds Convention Act[15] and the International River Improvements Act.[16]

By far the largest collection of environment enactments are promulgated by the provinces. For the most part these laws have been enacted under the section 92 provincial powers over local works and undertakings (s. 92[10]), property and civil rights within the provinces (s. 92[13]), and matters of a local or private nature (s. 92 [16]). The provinces are also assigned authority over provincially owned lands and resources (ss. 92 [5]; 109). The latter is especially significant as most lands outside the Territories are provincially owned.[18]

Pursuant to a 1982 amendment, section 92A, the provinces are also assigned exclusive jurisdiction over the development, conservation, and management of non-renewable resources in the province, including forestry and hydroelectric facilities. Each province has created its own pollution control and environmental assessment regulatory regime.[17] Some have enacted separate statutes controlling water use and quality, air pollution control, and waste management. Others have chosen a more holistic or consolidated approach.[18]

The Canadian courts have established flexible principles of interpretation for determining the proper scope and application of these respective federal and provincial powers. Because the federal government and the provinces are empowered by sections 91 and 92 to 'make laws in relation to matters that come within enumerated classes of subjects', the subject matter of a contested law must first be characterized.[19] Second, it must be determined whether the subject matter of the law comes within any of the s. 92 levels of power. If not, a provincial law would be *ultra vires* (beyond its power), since sections 91 and 92 give jurisdiction over the residue of classes of subjects not mentioned in section 92 to the federal government; a federal law, however, would still be valid.[20] Both federal and provincial laws may operate concurrently unless they are in direct conflict, in which case the doctrine of 'paramountcy' would give federal law precedence and provincial law would be inoperative to the extent of the conflict.[21]

With the exception of fisheries there are only sparse legal precedents on the validity of these myriad laws. There is even less judicial guidance in the interpretation of powers incorporated in laws which are yet to be exercised. For example, while no judicial ruling has yet been made on the validity of the federal powers exercised in the enactment of CEPA, constitutional challenges are anticipated as federal authorities move to enforce the act.

Three areas stand out as potential battlegrounds for federal-provincial relations.

Scope of Federal Treaty Powers

Entering into and giving domestic legal effect to international environmental agreements is likely to be one of the federal government's major routes of jurisdictional expansions within the next few decades, for example in relation to the conventions on biodiversity and global climate change coming before the 1992 UN Conference on Environment and Development.[22] Canada has also pledged to contribute to the development of a global forestry convention, called for by the Group of Seven Summit Countries.[23] In May 1991, Canada hosted an international panel of experts to develop a global agreement to protect the marine environment from land-based sources of pollution.[24]

Unfortunately, the Canadian Constitution provides no clear answer to the scope of modern federal treaty-making powers. Section 132 of the Constitution Act, 1967, gave the federal government both treaty-making and treaty-implementing powers, but the section only expressly considered Canada's powers in relation to Empire Treaties, that is, treaties entered into by Great Britain on behalf of Canada. Section 132 reads:

> The Parliament and Government of Canada shall have all Powers necessary or proper for performing the Obligations of Canada or of any Province thereof, as Part of the British Empire, towards Foreign Countries, arising under Treaties between the Empire and such Foreign Countries.

Case-law interpretation of the federal treaty power has left doubt whether the Canadian government could unilaterally implement through national legislation treaty obligations that fall under provincial heads of power, for example, forestry conservation provisions. In the well-known *Labour Conventions* case[25] the Privy Council held that the federal Parliament, which had given domestic effect to three conventions prepared by the International Labour Organization, had exceeded its powers. Treaty-implementing power would have to be treated in the same manner as all other imputed constitutional powers, namely, by respecting the heads of power in sections 91 and 92 and by determining whether the treaty matter fell under one of those heads. Thus it would be up to individual provinces to decide whether or not a treaty should be implemented if its subject matter falls within provincial jurisdiction.[26]

In a more recent decision, *MacDonald vs Vapor Canada Ltd,*[27] the Supreme Court of Canada hinted the federal government might not be so restricted. Independent treaties, like Empire treaties, might encroach on provincial jurisdiction and bypass provincial implementation, provided the federal legislation implementing the treaty clearly showed an intent to implement the treaty and stayed within the limits of treaty obligations.[28] The Court refrained from ruling on the issue since the federal trade mark legislation in question did not expressly state it was implementing the Convention on Industrial Property.

Strong arguments exist for finding both general treaty-making and treaty-implementing powers to be within federal jurisdiction. The federal government must be able to pursue a coherent and consistent foreign policy.[29] The Vienna Convention on the Law of Treaties does not allow states to be excused from international obligations because of internal conflicts.[30] Federal action in the international arena, however, can trigger provincial legislative action on environmental protection. Thus Ontario beat the federal government out of the gate in enacting new laws for control of chlorofluorocarbons (CFCs).[31] This action was prompted by Canada's front-line role in formulating the Montreal Protocol on Substances that Deplete the Ozone Layer.[32] Ontario's move also breached a federal-provincial agreement to move simultaneously on regulating CFCs.

Federal 'Water Powers'

Federal powers over sea-coast and inland fisheries and navigation and shipping have come into conflict with provincial powers over natural resource exploration and development, and courts have recognized a broad role of federal management. In *The Water Powers' Reference,*[33] the

Supreme Court of Canada indicated the federal government may severely restrict, perhaps even prohibit provincial water developments, in order to preserve federal navigation rights and fisheries rights.[34] Another Supreme Court case lends support to the federal right to protect the marine environment in the name of the sea-coast and inland fisheries clause. In *Northwest Falling Contractors Ltd vs The Queen*,[35] the Court upheld a federal prosecution under the Fisheries Act against a company which had spilled oil into a British Columbia inlet. The Court rejected the defendant's argument that the subject of pollution fell under provincial 'Property and Civil Rights' power and found pollution regulation, so long as restricted to activities harmful to fish, to be *intra vires* (within the power of) the federal Parliament.[36]

However, a number of cases have closely circumscribed federal use of the fisheries power to protect the environment. In *Fowler vs The Queen*,[37] the Supreme Court found section 33(3) of the federal Fisheries Act (which prohibited placing logging debris into any waters) beyond the power of the federal Parliament, for logging regulation came under provincial power over 'Property and Civil Rights'. The decision seemed to hinge on two major rationales. First, the federal government had failed to show timber debris to have a specified deleterious effect on fish.[38] Second, section 33(3) was overbroad. It specified no standard concerning the amount of debris; it covered not only water frequented by fish but water flowing into such water; and it, in fact, covered the whole spectrum of logging operations.[39] In *R. vs MacMillan Bloedel Ltd*,[40] the British Columbia Court of Appeal struck down the conviction of MacMillan Bloedel for disrupting fish habitat contrary to the Fisheries Act because the remote stream where alleged disruption had taken place was not a 'fisheries water' where commercial or sport-fishing occurred.

A possible question awaiting resolution is the effect of section 92A on provincial-federal powers over environmental impacts of provincial development projects. Since section 92A grants provinces the right to exclusively make laws in relation to 'development, conservation, and management' of non-renewable resources, forestry resources, and electrical energy sites and facilities, the provinces may argue for a broader say in environmental approvals and conditions. However, given the continued existence of federal powers touching on environmental quality (particularly fisheries), the federal government may argue that the basic distribution of powers is little changed.[41]

The POGG Power

In 1988, the Supreme Court of Canada in *R. vs Crown Zellerbach Canada Ltd*[42] bestowed on the federal government a potentially strong arm for regulating environmental pollution. In upholding the federal prosecution of a defendant who, without a required permit under the Ocean Dumping

Control Act,[43] had been found guilty of depositing logging debris in the provincial waters of Beaver Cove, British Columbia, the Court breathed new life into the Peace Order and Good Government power.[44] The case indicated that not only would the federal government be able to intervene in national environmental emergencies, but also on the basis of the two-pronged national concern doctrine: the federal government may legislate and regulate concerning new matters not existing at the time of Confederation, as well as matters originally considered of a local-provincial nature which evolve as national concerns.[45] Even though no actual environmental harm or direct impacts to fisheries or navigation were shown from the defendant's deposit, the Court upheld federal control of marine pollution because of its predominantly extra-provincial, as well as international, character.[46]

However, the Court still left considerable uncertainty as to when the national concern doctrine may be invoked and as to its effect on provincial jurisdiction. Rather vague parameters were established for determining whether a matter qualifies as a national concern. The matter must have a singleness, distinctiveness, and indivisibility that clearly distinguishes it from provincial concern,[47] and the scale of impact on provincial jurisdiction must be reconcilable with constitutional distribution of powers.[48] While a finding of national concern might grant Parliament exclusive and plenary jurisdiction to legislate, including intra-provincial aspects, the Court indicated provinces may, through concurrent jurisdiction, protect coastal waters as an aspect of local jurisdiction.[49]

Following the Crown Zellerbach case, the federal government enacted CEPA, partly basing this on the POGG power in the Preamble, which refers to 'the presence of toxic substances in the environment' as 'a matter of national concern'.

UNCERTAIN LEGISLATIVE/REGULATORY HANDS:
WRANGLES, COMPROMISES, AND CITIZEN SUITS

Federal and provincial decisions about the exercise of jurisdiction have been more a matter of balancing political powers than proper legal interpretation. The translation of constitutional powers into legislative action may be more accurately characterized by friendly federal-provincial relations than an exercise of control over environmental impacts. It has been viewed as federal abdication of regulatory power and delegation of administrative or enforcement authority to the provinces.

The overriding political agenda to co-operate with the provinces is even planted within legislation establishing the Department of the Environment. The Department of the Environment Act,[50] in section 7, allows the Minister of the Environment, with the approval of Cabinet, to enter into agreements with provincial governments or agencies respecting the carrying out of programs for which the Minister is responsible.

While federal environmental laws do contain potentially strong legal teeth, a wavering and uncertain compromise mentality has operated in practice, as shown in the following discussions of the Canadian Environmental Protection Act (CEPA), the Environmental Assessment Review Guidelines Order, and the Fisheries Act.

The Canadian Environmental Protection Act

CEPA, the federal government's legislative framework for managing toxic substances from 'cradle to grave', contains many strengths. The Act allows the Ministers of Environment and Health and Welfare broad powers to gather detailed information about toxic or potentially toxic substances from manufacturers, importers, transporters, distributors, and users.[51] The Act requires the compilation of a Priority Substances List[52] of 'suspect toxins' for which assessment priority must be given and assessment reports prepared, with the intent of control by national regulation. If the Governor-in-Council adds the names of toxic substances to the List of Toxic Substances in Schedule I,[53] the Governor-in-Council is granted broad regulatory power to control all aspects including manufacture, import, export, packaging, labelling, transportation, and storage.[54] Every person who fails to give required information or who fails to comply with regulations is liable on conviction to up to a one-million-dollar fine or up to three years imprisonment, or both.[55]

The most obvious limitation in the legislation is the broad ministerial discretion to name substances to the Priority List and to recommend regulatory action. With 30,000 to 40,000 chemicals estimated to be manufactured or imported into Canada,[56] it may be highly controversial as to what constitutes a manageable number of chemicals for assessment priority. Where a substance has been on the Priority Substances List for five years and not yet assessed, any person may request a board of review,[57] but the resultant report would be recommendary.[58] As of August 1990 only twelve substances had been listed under Schedule I and subject to very limited regulation.[59]

Although the Preamble to the Act declares that 'national leadership' is required to protect the environment, reading more carefully into that text one encounters numerous hurdles to speedy or unilateral action. Before regulations for toxic substances are imposed by Cabinet, a federal-provincial advisory committee must have an opportunity to tender its advice.[60] If the Minister of the Environment and the government of a province agree in writing that provincial and federal regulatory provisions for a toxic substance are equivalent, and both governments have similar investigative provisions, the Governor-in-Council may make an order declaring that the federal regulatory provisions are non-applicable in the province.[61] The application of the equivalency concept continues to be controversial and as yet no such agreements have been entered into.[62] The Minister, with Cabinet approval, is also allowed to enter into agreements with provincial governments concerning administration of the Act.[63]

A number of reasons may account for the delay in implementation. Among them is provincial reticence to admit to any federal authority in the area, coupled with an overriding concern with the capacity for control through the POGG power. There is also a lack of any significant federal regulatory or enforcement actions which would provide the impetus for negotiated agreements.

The ability of the federal government to unilaterally control international air pollution is also circumscribed in the Act. Where there is reason to believe an air contaminant in Canada is creating air pollution in another country or violating an international agreement, the Minister of the Environment may recommend regulatory prohibitions or controls. However, other than for federal works or undertakings, the Minister is not allowed to make a recommendation unless consultation occurs with the provinces or province of pollution source as to whether regulatory steps may be taken under provincial laws. The Minister must endeavour to bring about provincial prevention or control if possible.[64] Any federal regulation passed to control international air pollution may be made inapplicable to a province where equivalent provisions and investigative procedures are in place.[65]

Environmental Assessment and Review Process Guidelines Order

In June, 1984, the federal government gave a new legal foundation for the federal environmental assessment process through an Order-in-Council. The Guidelines cast a potentially broad net of proposals subject to federal review.[66] Proposals located on federal lands, involving a federal financial commitment, environmentally affecting an area of federal responsibility, or undertaken by an initiating federal department would all be subject to review.[67]

However, numerous legal cracks were latent in the Guidelines. These allowed for further interdepartmental and federal-provincial political manoeuvrings and opened the door for environmental lip service to be paid in the name of economic progress. Initiating departments[68] were to 'self-assess' proposals to see if environmental implications were significant and, if so, they would have to refer a proposal to the Minister of the Environment for a public review.[69] While public concern about a proposal was to be grounds for a full public review, the Guidelines appeared to leave the initiating department as the ultimate judge of whether public concern made a public review desirable.[70] Initiating departments, being required to screen or assess proposals, were left the discretion to find environmental effects mitigable with known technology and thereby to allow a project to proceed without a formal public review.[71] If an environmental assessment review panel were appointed to hold public hearings, a panel would have recommendary powers only.[72] Finally, duplication of public reviews were to be avoided where a proposal was subject to environmental regulation independently of the process.[73]

That interjurisdictional wranglings and compromises led to environmentally leaky deals and decisions to be made is demonstrated in the decision-making processes surrounding the Rafferty and Alameda dams on the Souris River in Saskatchewan, the Oldman River Dam in Alberta, and the Point Aconi coal-fired energy project in Cape Breton, Nova Scotia.[74]

(i) Rafferty and Alameda Dams　'Hands off, leave environmental reviews to the province' aptly describes the federal government's initial attitude towards the Saskatchewan government's proposal to construct two dams on the Souris River rising in Saskatchewan and flowing into North Dakota and then northward to Manitoba. On 4 August 1987, the Souris Basin Development Authority, a provincial Crown corporation, submitted an environmental impact statement to the Minister of the Environment for Saskatchewan. Following public hearings as part of a provincial environmental review, the Minister of the Environment granted approval on 15 February 1988 for the project to proceed. Even though the environmental impact assessment prepared in Saskatchewan did not assess impacts on North Dakota or Manitoba, on 17 June 1988 the federal Minister of the Environment issued a licence pursuant to the International River Improvements Act, allowing the project to go ahead.[75]

In a lawsuit brought by the Canadian Wildlife Federation the federal government's regulatory reluctance became clear.[76] The federal Crown argued that since the project was a provincially funded initiative, located on provincial lands and subjected to a formal review by the provincial Department of the Environment and Public Safety, a federal environmental assessment review would be an unwarranted duplication.[77] The Court, however, declared the Order to be binding on the federal government, quashed the license, and ordered compliance with the Guidelines Order.[78] Regardless of this clear judicial opinion of the binding nature of the EARP Order, the federal assessment as ordered was conducted without formal public hearings and the licence was reissued. A public hearing panel was appointed only following further litigation by the Canadian Wildlife Federation to obtain a court order for its appointment.[79]

Political dealings and wranglings followed, further shaking the credibility of the environmental assessment process. In late January, 1990, the federal Minister of the Environment and Saskatchewan reached an agreement for construction to be postponed. Ottawa would pay Saskatchewan $1 million a month for up to ten months to cover the extra costs of halting the project during a formal review.[80] On 4 October 1990, the environmental review panel, established in response to the court ruling in December, wrote to the Minister of the Environment that the panel's terms of reference were being violated by Saskatchewan's initiation of channelization downstream of the dam and proposed tree-clearing above. On 11 October Premier Devine instructed the Souris Basin Development Authority to begin or resume construction on all aspects of the Rafferty-Alameda project. On 12 October the panel tendered its resignation.[81]

Federal respect for the environmental assessment process was also called into question by the Government of Canada's signing an agreement with the United States in October, 1990, assuring the US of dam completions. In return for approximately $41 million (US) the Government of Canada agreed to 'expeditiously provide' the US with flood control storage from the Rafferty and Alameda dams and pledged to ensure the dams would be designed to have a hundred-year project life.[82] The Canadian Government was subsequently severely criticized for not itself referring the agreement for public process and hearings.[83]

(ii) Oldman River Dam   Alberta's proposed construction of a dam at the Three Rivers site on the Oldman River followed a similar scenario, with federal deference to provincial environmental reviews and a litigative forcing of federal action. Following various provincial environmental reviews the Alberta government proceeded with construction of the dam, and by the end of March 1989 the dam was already 40% complete.[84] As in Saskatchewan, the federal government issued approvals without conducting the necessary environmental assessment or referring the project to public review under the EARP Guidelines Order.[85]

Federal deference to Alberta's environmental jurisdiction was made clear in a statement by Raymond Robinson, then Executive Chairman of the Federal Environmental Assessment Review Office, to the House of Commons Standing Committee on Environment on 11 May 1989:

> [W]e do have an agreement with Alberta; it is the only province with which we do have an agreement on environmental assessment. Under the agreement, each party is to rely upon the other to take account of the interests of the other when dealing with a project that falls under the first party's jurisdiction. There is no question that these projects fall under provincial jurisdiction.[86]

The Federal Court of Appeal held otherwise. In a court action by the Friends of the Oldman River Society, the Court, on 13 March 1990, found evidence of potential detrimental environmental effects on areas of federal responsibility including fisheries, Indians, and Indian lands, and ruled that federal legal obligations under the EARP Guidelines Order had not been met.[87] Although the Navigable Waters Protection Act did not explicitly require an environmental assessment, the Minister of Transport was found to have a 'superadded' duty under EARP to require an environmental assessment review. Even though the project proponent did not seek an authorization to disrupt fish habitat, the Minister of Fisheries and Oceans was seen as having a decision-making responsibility by becoming aware of the proposal's potential effects on fisheries. Therefore, the Ministers were also required to comply with the Guidelines Order.

Both levels of government responded. On 16 November 1990 Environment Canada announced the appointment of a six-member panel to review the environmental and socio-economic effects of the Oldman River Dam. Alberta's Attorney General appealed the 13 March decision to the Supreme Court of Canada.[88] That Court's decision will likely establish a significant precedent for future application of federal law over provincially based projects.

(iii) **Point Aconi Power Plant** The Nova Scotia Power Corporation's proposal to construct a $436-million coal-fired power plant using fluidized-bed technology to reduce sulphur dioxide emissions by up to 90% has also been the subject of political manipulations and controversial decisions relating to environmental assessment. The pet project of then Premier John Buchanan, the Point Aconi proposal was given expedited approvals by a provincial Conservative government intent on securing and providing jobs in economically depressed Cape Breton. The project was specifically exempted through legal amendment from review by the provincial Public Utilities Board into the economic merits of the new plant.[89] Following a one-day public hearing by the Nova Scotia Environmental Control Council, the Council recommended approval of the generating station subject to various recommended conditions, including the need for the Nova Scotia Power Corporation to declare a policy of CO_2 emissions reduction and to increase research into CO_2 reduction technology.[90] The Nova Scotia Minister of the Environment announced approval of the Point Aconi project in March, 1990,[91] and preliminary site construction commenced.

The project avoided a full public review under the federal Environmental Assessment Review Guidelines Order through a combination of departmental decisions. The federal government determined that the Guidelines Order did apply to the project, and that the Department of Fisheries and Oceans (DFO) would be designated the initiating department. Following an Initial Environmental Assessment, DFO Minister Bernard Valcourt announced that, since environmental effects could be mitigated with known technology, he would not request a public review. He also announced that authorization under the Fisheries Act would be issued subject to conditions, including measures to control sediment run-off, fish entrainment, and potential effects from chlorination.[92]

When pressed about why the federal Minister of the Environment would not trigger a full public review, given the predicted release into the atmosphere by the Point Aconi plant of 1.5 million tonnes per year of carbon dioxide, the Executive Chairman of FEARO indicated a couple of reasons. Given the lack of specific laws dealing with CO_2 emissions, Environment Canada was viewed as having no decision-making authority. A political judgement as to whether public concern made panel review desirable was already made.[93]

The failure of the provincial environmental process to fully address the issue of carbon dioxide emissions was rationalized by the Nova Scotia Minister of the Environment in these words:

> First, it is important to note that carbon dioxide is only one of at least seven gases that contribute to the greenhouse effect in Nova Scotia. The other major ones are water vapour, ozone, nitrous oxide, CFCs, volatile organic carbons and methane. . . . the other six are far more active in contributing to the greenhouse effect than is CO_2. For example, methane has 20 times more impact than CO_2. Nitrous oxide has 200 times more impact and CFCs have 10,000 times more impact. This variety of greenhouse gases in the Nova Scotian environment provide us with the opportunity to explore a multi-faceted approach to address the greenhouse effect. In other words, we do not need to target one gas and single it out for reduction on its own. A menu approach not only permits significant, quick and cost-efficient reductions in greenhouse gases, but it also offers additional time for research and analysis. We need a better understanding of the complex interactions between all the factors that contribute to the global warming phenomenon.[94]

In a lawsuit launched by concerned residents and environmental groups, Justice Andrew MacKay of the Federal Court, Trial Division, upheld the decision of the Minister of Fisheries and Oceans not to require a public review. He found the Minister did not err in law in accepting the IEE conclusion that potentially adverse environmental effects were insignificant or mitigable with known technology. He also found the Minister acted within his discretion in deciding whether public concern made a public review desirable.[95]

The federal government's tabling of a new Canadian Environmental Assessment Act[96] offers to plug a few major holes in the existing Environmental Review Process. The Act would grant explicit federal powers to prohibit proponents from undertaking construction or development activities until an environmental assessment is completed. Section 42 authorizes the Minister of the Environment to prohibit by order the proponent from doing anything to carry out the project in whole or part[97] and section 48 allows the Attorney General of Canada to seek a court injunction where such a ministerial order is or is likely to be contravened. The Act would grant the Minister of the Environment the independent discretion to refer a project to a panel review or mediation if there are likely to be significant and non-mitigable adverse environmental effects or public concerns warrant it.[98]

However, the proposed legislation still contains numerous potential loopholes for political influences to end-run around or water down the process.[99] Broad exclusion and exception powers are included. The biggest exclusion is the removal of the existing broad requirement to assess impacts of any project which impacts on an area of federal responsibility. This is the key trade-off to the provinces and to federal departments which do not wish to assess their projects. Pursuant to section 6, a responsible authority is allowed to exclude projects from an environmental assessment if the project is described on an exclusion list.[100] The Governor-in-Council is authorized through regulations to exempt projects where environmental effects are likely to be negligible or where it is determined that the contribution of the responsible authority to projects is minimal.[101] The legislation only guarantees assessments of projects[102] and does not expressly require assessment of proposed government programs or policies such as Cabinet decisions.[103] The legislated framework would continue the non-binding, recommendary nature of public reviews.[104] Finally, the discretionary wording of the proposed law would preclude future private actions forcing a reluctant federal hand, as is currently possible under the EARP Order.

The Fisheries Act

Through broad definitions of pollution offences and recently increased penalties, the Fisheries Act is potentially Canada's most powerful weapon in protecting the environment. Section 35(1) makes it an offence for any person to 'carry on any work or undertaking that results in the harmful alteration, disruption or destruction of fish habitat'. Section 36(3) prohibits persons from depositing or permitting the deposit of deleterious substances into water frequented by fish. In 1991 amendments, new maximum fines were provided for violations of either fish habitat or deleterious deposit provisions. First offenders would be punishable on summary conviction by a fine of up to $300,000 and subsequent offences could lead to a fine of up to $300,000 plus imprisonment of up to six months. Maximum penalties on indictment would be up to $1,000,000 for first offences and for subsequent offences up to $1,000,000 plus up to three years in jail.[105]

Enforcement of the Act has, however, been inconsistent and sporadic. Responsibility for enforcement of the pollution control provisions has been divided, and in some cases shared, between Environment Canada, Fisheries and Oceans, and provincial pollution agencies, and rather cumbersome consultative processes have been created.[106] A leaked memo of 14 November 1989, from the head of the Habitat Management Unit,

Fraser River, northern British Columbia and Yukon Division of DFO, highlighted the perceived inconsistencies:

> Over the years many of us have been critical about DFO's inconsistent application of the habitat and pollution provisions of the Fisheries Act. The most obvious past criticisms have occurred on pollution issues. We have been known for charging individuals for spills of deleterious substances (often accidental and less than a few gallons) and then continually ignore the daily discharge of millions of gallons of toxic effluent from a mill next door. This often results in the small guy or minor offense getting prosecuted and the large corporation getting some degree of 'discretionary immunity'.
>
> The reasons for the above inconsistency are obvious but are not defendable. The large continuous discharge, such as the Quesnel pulpmill, can constantly produce a toxic effluent over a 10 year period and not be in fear of prosecution. This is because they have a B.C. WMM Permit and DOE-EP works through that agency.[107]

The tendency to adopt a conciliatory rather than a strict enforcement approach can also be seen in the federal government's approach to pollution from Scott Maritimes Ltd's Abercombie Point pulp and paper mill in Nova Scotia. When a major fish kill occurred in the vicinity of an effluent treatment facility operated by the provincial Department of the Environment on behalf of Scott, Environment Canada recommended that charges be laid. The Department of Justice refused to act on the recommendation and the federal Ministers of Environment and Fisheries and Oceans subsequently developed federal guidelines for future operation of the treatment facility.[108]

Sentencing has also been identified as a major weakness. A Law Reform Commission of Canada study found that of 38 convictions registered under the deleterious deposit provision of the Fisheries Act between 1978 and the end of 1983, only 8 resulted in fines of over $5,000.[109]

CHARTER OF RIGHTS AND FREEDOMS AND ABORIGINAL RIGHTS: FURTHER UNCERTAINTIES

Charter of Rights and Freedoms

The Canadian Charter of Rights and Freedoms, added to the Canadian Constitution in 1982,[110] does not explicitly refer to a right to a healthy environment. However, by recognizing individual rights, such as the section 7 right not to be deprived of life, liberty, and security of the person except in accordance with the principles of fundamental justice, it may provide an opening for individuals to contest governmental actions relating to the environment and public health. Both procedural and substantive rights may be argued. Procedural rights may include the right to receive notice of governmental regulatory initiatives, the right to financial assistance in making one's case, access to the actual decision-maker, and access to information.[111] Substantive rights may include a right to a clean environment or the right not to have one's health unreasonably jeopardized.[112]

The 1989 judgement of the Ontario Court of Appeal in *Energy Probe vs Canada (Attorney General)*[113] demonstrates how creative Charter arguments may be used by individuals and environmental organizations to challenge governmental environment-related legislation. In that case, Energy Probe and other applicants sought a declaration that certain sections of the federal Nuclear Liability Act,[114] including the limitation of liability of an operator of a nuclear facility to $75 million and provision of a maximum limitation period of ten years for bringing suit, were of no force because of inconsistency with sections 7 and 15 (equality under the law)[115] of the Charter. Various section 7 arguments were allowed to go to trial, including the allegation that the Nuclear Liability Act, by shielding suppliers and designers from liability and thereby removing an incentive to maximize safety, was inconsistent with citizen rights to life, liberty, and security of the person. Section 15 arguments, also allowed to go to trial, included the claim that the imposition of a ceiling of recovery and the short limitation period for nuclear victims constituted unequal treatment and discrimination as compared to recovery allowed to victims of other tortious acts.[116]

Numerous hurdles, however, may thwart individual challenges. The Charter essentially applies only to laws and actions of federal and provincial governments and their public agencies.[117] As is suggested in a second citizen challenge to testing of cruise missiles in Canada's North,[118] it may be impossible to establish a causal connection between government action and infringement of individual rights. Even if a Charter right is infringed, the law or action may be upheld under section 1 if 'reasonably and demonstrably justified in a free and democratic society'.[119] Corporate environmental organizations may not be able to argue liberty and security of person denials[120] as section 7 was intended to protect human beings.[121]

Charter arguments may also have a negative impact on environmental protection by granting defendants in environmental prosecutions new grounds for contesting convictions and governmental enforcement procedures. The section 8 right to be secure against unreasonable search and seizure, the section 11(d) right to be presumed innocent until proven guilty, and the section 7 right to life, liberty, and security of the person are particularly apt to give rise to arguments.[122]

Aboriginal Rights

Aboriginal rights, including among other interests the rights to hunt, trap, and fish in traditional ways and the right to certain water uses,[123] may also restrict governmental legislative and regulatory actions with environmental implications. For example, an aboriginal individual or community might challenge a governmental permit allowing an industrial project, having potentially negative effects on traditional lands or uses, to proceed. Aboriginal rights have been elevated to constitutional status in section 35(1) of the Constitution Act, 1982: 'The existing aboriginal and treaty rights of the aboriginal peoples of Canada are hereby recognized and affirmed.'[124]

In 1990, the Supreme Court of Canada, in *R. vs Sparrow*,[125] in its first interpretation of section 35, gave notice of how governmental natural resource management measures may be strictly limited in their relation to aboriginal rights. In that case Ronald Sparrow, a member of the Musqueam Indian Band in British Columbia, had been charged under the federal Fisheries Act for salmon fishing with a drift net 45 fathoms in length, contrary to the 25-fathom length allowed by the terms of the Band's Indian food-fishing licence. In responding to Sparrow's argument that the federal regulatory requirement was inconsistent with a section 35(1) aboriginal right to a food fishery, the Court recognized that constitutional encroachment 'gives a measure of control over government conduct and a strong check on legislative power'.[126]

The Court suggested an analytical process for determining the constitutional validity of governmental actions. First, the aboriginal individual or group bears the onus of proving a prima-facie infringement of an aboriginal right. Questions relevant to that determination would include:

1. whether the limitation was unreasonable (for example, whether the fish catch has been reduced below reasonable food and ceremonial needs of the aboriginal complainant[s]);

2. whether the regulation imposes undue hardship (for example, undue time and money per fish caught is required); and

3. whether the regulation denies right holders the preferred means of exercising their rights.[127]

Second, if a prima-facie infringement of an aboriginal right or rights is established, the Crown then has the burden of justifying governmental regulation. A rather open-ended analytical process was suggested by the Court in weighing governmental justification. First, the Crown would have to establish a valid legislative objective (for example, the need to conserve and manage a natural resource).[128] Second, assuming a valid objective was found, the Crown would have to demonstrate a resource allocation in accordance with the governmental trust responsibility to aboriginals. The Court suggested that Indian food-fishing would have to be given a top priority after conservation requirements had been met.[129] Additional questions to be considered depending on the circumstances would include:

1. whether there has been as little infringement on aboriginal rights as possible;

2. whether, in a situation of expropriation, fair compensation is available; and

3. whether the aboriginal group has been consulted as to the implemented conservation measures.[130]

The case left open the scope of governmental obligation towards aboriginal groups or individuals in the regulation setting process. The Supreme Court noted that at the very least, aboriginal peoples would have to be informed about a proposed or determined regulatory scheme.[131] The Court stopped short of examining the possibilities of shared management arrangements, or aboriginal self-regulation subject to conservation requirements.[132]

While constitutionally entrenched aboriginal rights offer a new creative context for government, recently settled aboriginal land claims and management agreements also specify rights and obligations relating to resource management in affected lands. These comprehensive land claim agreements define powerful roles for aboriginal groups in environmental decision-making processes and are proving to have a profound effect on decisions about environmental impacts. By their application they have created a third tier of government. The James Bay and Northern Quebec Agreement[133] of 1975, negotiated among the Cree, the Inuit, the Government of Quebec, the Government of Canada, and provincial Crown corporations responsible for hydro development in Northern Quebec, provides complex advisory mechanisms for native involvement while authorizing the undertaking of the James Bay Hydro Project and future developments.[134] Separate, but similar, environmental regimes are established for developments both south and north of the 55th Parallel.[135] For developments below the 55th Parallel, an Environmental and Social Impact Review Committee, having both provincial and Cree representatives, is established to review projects involving provincial jurisdiction, and an Environmental and Social Impact Review Panel, with federal government and Cree appointees, is set up to review projects involving federal jurisdiction. The federal government, Quebec, and the Cree Regional Authority may by mutual agreement combine the review bodies. For developments north of the 55th Parallel, an Environmental Quality Commission, appointed by the Kativik Regional Government and Quebec, is the official body for assessing projects within provincial jurisdiction. An Environmental and Social Impact Review Panel, composed of federal and Inuit appointees, is authorized to review developments coming under federal jurisdiction and reviews may again be combined by mutual agreement. Environmental advisory committees are established for both regions to make recommendations concerning the assessment review processes and the adequacy of environmental laws and regulations.

Federal and provincial laws related to environmental and social protection are still applicable in the areas in so far as not inconsistent with the Agreement. While the Agreement recognizes the need to minimize ecological impacts, the Crees and/or Inuit are not to use sociological factors or impacts as grounds for opposing or preventing hydroelectric developments.[136]

In 1984 approximately 2,500 Inuvialuit in the western Arctic entered into a comprehensive land claims settlement[137] and secured a role in onshore/offshore resource management. An Environmental Impact Screening Committee, consisting of three Inuvialuit appointees and three governmental appointees in addition to a mutually acceptable chairperson, is to screen proposed developments for potential impacts on wildlife harvesting. If a project may cause a significant negative impact on present or future wildlife harvesting, the Screening Committee may refer the proposal to a special Environmental Impact Review Board made up of a chairperson, three Inuvialuit appointees, and three Canadian appointees. The Review Board can recommend to the government agency having approval power mitigative and remedial measures to minimize negative impacts on wildlife harvesting. If a development project causes loss(es) to wildlife harvesting, an Inuvialuit claimant is given a right to compensation, without having to prove fault or negligence.[138]

On 30 April 1990, the federal government and the Tungavik Federation of Nunavut (TFN) signed an Agreement-in-Principle covering areas of the eastern Arctic.[139] Besides establishing new institutional structures for wildlife and water management, the Agreement provides for the establishment of a Nunavut Impact Review Board (NIRB) to review ecosystemic and socio-economic impacts of project proposals in the Nunavut Settlement Area. The Board is to determine whether proposals should proceed and, if so, under what terms and conditions.[140]

The potential for new institutional processes to affect proposed resource developments may be glimpsed from the recent episode involving Gulf Canada Resources Limited's Kulluk Drilling Program 1990–92 proposal for the eastern Beaufort Sea.[141] A series of wells were proposed to be drilled by the *Kulluk* floating drilling vessel over a three-year period. The Environmental Impact Screening Committee, created pursuant to the Inuvialuit Final Agreement, determined that the development could have significant negative environmental impacts on present or future wildlife harvesting and referred the proposal to the Environmental Impact Review Board for a public review. The Board subsequently recommended strongly against approval, based on 'a startling lack of preparedness' on the parts of Gulf and government to effectively deal with a major oil-well blow-out in the Beaufort Sea open-water season, and Gulf's inability to provide a liability estimate for a worst-case blow-out.[142] Nine specific recommendations were made, including the need to concentrate counter-measure and clean-up responsibilities in one government agency, preferably the Canadian Coast Guard, and the need to develop guidelines for assessing instruments of financial responsibility.

This decision precipitated the formation of the Beaufort Sea Steering Committee. The Committee, representing the oil and gas industry, the Inuvialuit, the governments of Yukon, the Northwest Territories, and the federal government, was assigned the task of coming up with workable solutions to the issues raised in the Board's report.[143]

TRENDS: CO-OPERATIVE FEDERALISM AND ENVIRONMENTAL BILLS OF RIGHTS

While uncertain constitutional and legal trends, as discussed above, have led to considerable *ad hoc*-ery and conflict, the federal and provincial governments have also forged numerous co-operative agreements and arrangements to overcome jurisdictional tensions.[144] Perhaps the best examples are the agreements between Canada and Nova Scotia,[145] and Canada and Newfoundland,[146] whereby offshore jurisdictional disputes were put aside and co-operative resource management and revenue sharing mechanisms were agreed to.[147]

Various federal-provincial-territorial ministerial councils may play important roles in co-ordinating national actions on the environment. In 1990, the Canadian Council of Ministers of the Environment (CCME) finalized a Statement of Interjurisdictional Co-operation in Environmental Matters which pledged harmonization of environmental legislation, regulations, policies, and programs, as well as timely notification and consultation concerning projects with potential interjurisdictional impacts. The Council is working on draft Co-operative Principles for Environmental Assessment. Other councils deal with wildlife, parks, forestry, agriculture, and energy.[148]

With growing financial commitments from both federal and provincial governments to implement the sustainable development principles of the Brundtland Commission, Canadian environmental efforts are rapidly shifting from a regulation setting/penalty focus[149] to the forging of new co-operative institutions and programs. For example, in 1988 the Canadian Council of Ministers of the Environment agreed to develop a comprehensive ten-year federal-provincial management plan to control nitrogen oxides (NO_x) and volatile organic compounds (VOC) emissions, and the federal government is committed to negotiating individual agreements with the provinces setting emission targets for the year 2000.[150] In 1989, the federal and provincial governments agreed to a $250 million, cost-shared, five-year program to clean up abandoned, hazardous waste sites in Canada, and agreements with individual provinces are in the process of implementation.[151] Under co-operative agreements with the seven eastern-most provinces and industry, the federal government has orchestrated measures to reduce sulphur dioxide emissions by 1994 to levels that will be fifty per cent of 1980 emission levels.[152] In a first-of-its-kind $15-million four-year Canada/Nova Scotia Co-operation Agreement on Sustainable Economic Development, Canada and Nova Scotia on 18 March 1991 established a framework for assisting businesses to find solutions to environmental problems, including the development of new environment-friendly products, and for fostering public education.[153]

While near-term provincial trends in environmental laws will likely involve increasing public participation in decision-making processes affecting the environment, including provision of intervenor funding,[154] a potential long-term trend may be the legislative enactment of an environmental bill of rights. In 1990 the Government of the Northwest Territories became the first legislature anywhere in Canada to pass an Environmental Rights Act.[155] The legislation could be at least a partial model for other jurisdictions. The Act bestows a right of every person to obtain access to information from any Minister of the Northwest Territories concerning permits, approvals, orders, and data related to releases of contaminants into the environment.[156] Any two residents of the Northwest Territories, aged 19 years or older, may request an investigation of contaminant releases or likely releases.[157] Any resident may bring a private prosecution of an offence committed under an Act listed in Schedule A and may recover costs of prosecution.[158] Without having to establish the usual common law requirements of legal standing involving a proprietary or pecuniary interest, any resident may commence a civil action against polluters and seek an injunction and even damages payable to the minister responsible for the environment.[159] 'Whistle-blower' protection is provided for employees who take actions implicating employers.[160] The Ontario government, in its November 1990 Throne Speech, promised to introduce a new Bill of Environmental Rights, and an Advisory Committee representing various interest groups and government agencies has been involved in preparing a draft bill.[161]

CONCLUSION

The Canadian approach to environmental protection can best be described as a direct by-product of the nation's constitutional frailties and diffident approach to federalism. The constitution contains no enshrined rights to a healthy environment, nor does it dictate clear responsibility for effecting environmental protection or sustained management of resources.

The evolution of environmental law and policy closely mirrors the historical balancing act between federal and provincial governments. Apart from early enactments falling under precise federal powers, environmental regulation has been the prerogative of the provinces. Laws evolved as an adjustment to the provincial exercise of their powers to exploit provincially owned resources. Even in those instances where the federal government was responsible for implementing international obligations, the approach has been one of deference to the provinces. Canadian initiatives for resolving transboundary disputes also reflect this demeanour. Where federal intervention was obligated by statute, the power to act has in practice been dealt away by federal-provincial agreement.

In the past few years, however, there have been significant shifts in the accommodative approach because of growing pressure associated with global problems and an informed public forcing the hands of government through litigation and lobbying. Privately inititated court actions have forced federal intervention in areas traditionally left to the provinces, most significantly the environmental assessment of resource development projects. The first brave act by Ottawa was the decision to enact a national law for the regulation of toxic substances under the exercise of its POGG power. A significant break from traditional reliance on the federal criminal-law power, this has however evoked little intrusion into the provincial arena. An important decision which will set the stage for the 1990s will be the decision of the Supreme Court of Canada on the limits of federal jurisdiction to assess impacts of projects on provincial lands. Equally important will be the final form of the federal environmental assessment act. Finally, recently expanded rights accorded to private citizens to participate in decisions about resource development, and to challenge the exercise or lack of exercise of government obligation to protect the environment, will significantly flavour the Canadian approach.

FOR FURTHER READING

C.P. Stevenson, 'A New Perspective on Environmental Rights After the Charter', *Osgoode Hall Law Journal* 21 (1983).

D. Tingley, ed., *Environmental Protection and the Canadian Constitution* (Edmonton: Environmental Law Centre, 1987).

D. Tingley, ed., *Into the Future: Environmental Law and Policy for the 1990s* (Edmonton: Environmental Law Centre, 1990).

M. Valencia and David VanderZwaag, 'Maritime Claims and Management Rights of Indigenous Peoples: Rising Tides in the Pacific and Northern Waters', *Ocean and Shoreline Management* 12 (1989).

Kernaghan Webb, *Pollution Control in Canada: The Regulatory Approach in the 1980s* (Ottawa: Law Reform Commission, 1988).

CHAPTER 2

Organizational Design as Policy Instrument

Environment Canada in the Canadian Bureaucracy

M. PAUL BROWN

Organization design—the use of government reorganization, including the creation of new departmental or interdepartmental structures—has increasingly been recognized as a significant instrument of public policy. Its use rests on the conviction that purposeful organization is an appropriate way of meeting some types of policy problems.[1] The heyday of the use of organizational design for this purpose in Canada was in the 1970s and early 1980s, when a 'ministry system' and 'ministers and ministries of state' were introduced for purposes of horizontal policy co-ordination in a number of areas, such as transportation, science and technology, regional and economic development, and social development.[2] However, organizational design can also combine operational and co-ordinative responsibilities, as in the resort to new organizations as a means of spearheading the attack on regional economic disparities in Canada; the Atlantic Canada Opportunities Agency, created in 1987, is the most recent example.[3]

Purposeful reorganization is, however, in and of itself no guarantor of success in resolving the problem to which it is addressed. As with other policy instruments, the acid test is successful implementation: achieving the assigned mandate. It has also become increasingly clear that it is far easier to effect organizational change than it is effectively to address the policy problem at issue.[4] This is no less true when the purpose of institutional change is to 'bend' the activities of existing structures in a direction represented by the newly designed organization.[5]

As with other types of policy instrument, successful implementation or lack of it through organizational design can depend upon a myriad of factors. In an early review of the implementation process, Sabatier and Mazmanian identified a number of the variables which act as determinants of implementation, many of which are relevant to the use of design as a response to policy problems. They point out, for example, that much depends upon the *tractability of the problem*, including such factors as the extent and degree of behaviour change required of the target group. *Non-statutory variables* such as the degree of media attention, public support, and ties to the 'sovereign' (executive support), can also work to either facilitate or frustrate implementation.[6] Finally, the *statutory underpinning* of the process — including such variables as the clarity of policy directives, financial resources, and the degree of hierarchical integration within and among implementing agencies — is also crucial. In fact, the causal nature of the relationship between these variables ought to be stressed. For example, the perceived tractability of a problem could well influence the degree of public support for proposed solutions. Similarly, the degree of public support clearly has an impact on the level of support accorded a problem, and hence a response through organization design, by the 'sovereign', and that in turn will impinge on the strength of policy directives and the hierarchical ordering of implementing agencies.

These dynamics of organizational design as policy stand out in sharp relief in the case of Environment Canada.[7] Created in 1971 as part of Ottawa's response to the demand for greater environmental protection, Environment Canada represented the use of the design instrument in several respects. First, it brought together a variety of existing agencies having responsibility for various aspects of environmental protection and renewable resource management — including sea-coast and inland fisheries, forests, migratory birds and other 'non-domestic flora and fauna', water, and meteorology — and thus provided greater focus to and visibility for the federal government's response to 'environmental concern'.[8] Second, it featured an entirely new Environmental Protection Service (EPS) which was to spearhead Ottawa's effort to combat pollution, and thus protect and enhance water, air, and soil quality. Third, it was by statute to 'co-ordinate programs of the Government of Canada . . . designed to promote the establishment or adoption of objectives or standards relating to environmental quality, or to control pollution';[9] in other words, it was to achieve its conservation and protection objectives by 'influencing and co-ordinating the activities of other departments'.[10]

Environment Canada's experience in the Canadian bureaucracy has not, however, been as its designers might have envisaged. Indeed, the department has historically been criticized for its ineffectiveness, particularly in its co-ordinative role with respect to ensuring consideration of environmental factors in sectoral decision-making at the federal level. The low point came shortly after the Mulroney administration came to power, when Environment Canada was under attack from all sides, including within. Its own Minister, Suzanne Blais-Grenier, slashed a quarter of the person-years in the Canadian Wildlife Service. The 1986 Nielsen Task Force on program review criticized 'successive federal

Ministers of the Environment' for 'making maximum use of environmental incidents and new worrisome scientific assumptions and findings to draw governments' and the population's attention to environmental concerns',[11] while an essay in *Probe Post* condemned the department for not doing enough and called for 'an alternative'.[12]

This situation has since changed dramatically. In recent years Environment Canada has moved from the periphery to the centre of decision-making in Ottawa, to the point where it has in some respects taken on the role of a central agency, with a mandate to ensure environment-economic linkages across the full range of national decision-making, both in Ottawa, and, increasingly, in the regions.

This chapter explores Environment Canada's role within the Cabinet and the Canadian bureaucracy. It first identifies the factors which have historically frustrated the purposeful organizational change embodied in Environment Canada. Next, it details how recent changes in these variables have led to a reaffirmation of the original design and ushered in a period of re-design, still under way, to the point where Environment Canada's function nowadays bears more and more the hallmarks of a central agency.

THE FRUSTRATION OF DESIGN

The role of public support in the frustration of the purposeful design embodied in Environment Canada deserves first mention, because public opinion was by all accounts a critical determining factor in the decision to establish the new department. Between 1967 and 1970 there was a dramatic surge in public concern about pollution. By 1970, for example, some 69% of Canadians in one national survey indicated that pollution was a 'very serious' problem, and another survey found that Canadians ranked pollution as the issue most deserving attention by government.[13] The subsequent development of opinion as revealed in the Gallup Poll suggested, however, that this concern was short-lived. For example, the number of respondents indicating that pollution was a 'very serious' problem fell to 52% by 1975 and to 51% by 1985. Similarly, 56% of respondents indicated in 1970 that pollution was a problem in their area, but this fell to 53% by 1975 and to 46% by 1985.[14] Though representing half the population, these numbers were not the stuff of which powerful bureaucratic or political mandates could be built.

It is tempting to see these results simply in terms of Anthony Downs's famous 'issue-attention' cycle,[15] but in Canada they spoke more precisely to the tractability of the problem of pollution and environmental sensitivity. Job creation has historically been the leading policy issue in the minds of Canadian citizens as measured by public opinion polls. Even with the upsurge of concern about the environment there was uncertainty about what addressing environmental problems would mean for other, economic, goals in society. In particular, according to André Raynauld, Chair of the Economic Council of Canada, there was 'some apprehension that relatively severe pollution control measures will result in a serious slow-down of economic growth, a high degree of unemployment and, at least for a time, a decrease in income levels'.[16] The advice from economists and environmentalists on this score was less than reassuring. Raynauld could only offer that 'neither in Canada nor anywhere else should the costs of environmental protection be so burdensome that they will compel *drastic* sacrifice of the other objectives of society'(emphasis added). Such comments seemed to occasion a 'mix of concern and resignation'[17] in Canadian attitudes, and, in the crunch, a pronounced if reluctant preference for jobs. Accordingly, support for environmental protection has tended to rise and fall with the performance of the economy.[18] Politicians have typically followed these tides of opinion, and economic players outside government,[19] as well as the bureaucracy within government, have used them to frustrate the application of more stringent environmental protection measures, including a more powerful role for an environment department.

The extent of public concern with the environment is inextricably linked to another non-statutory variable, the level of 'sovereign' or executive support. In the case of Environment Canada, the link to sovereign support could until 1986 be couched almost entirely in negative terms. No government dared politically to eliminate 'environment' from the federal departmental nomenclature, but neither did any feel obliged to give it other than perfunctory attention.

The signs that Environment Canada did not enjoy executive favour were many. Most obviously, environmental quality faded as a policy priority as the environment receded as a public concern, making it difficult for Environment Canada to 'exert a continuing and vital influence on national decision-making'.[20] Instead, the department was subjected to the organizational shuffles and ministerial rotations usually reserved for the more inconsequential of agencies. With respect to the former, Environment Canada sank to the status of a junior ministry of state under a Minister of Fisheries and Oceans by 1977, and thus drifted to the very periphery of federal decision-making. Though it became a separate department again in 1979, its status remained distinctly lower-tier in the Cabinet pecking order. By 1986 Environment Canada had had no less than ten ministers, some genuinely committed but many of them lacklustre, culminating in the disastrous appointment of Montreal MP Suzanne Blais-Grenier, who lacked 'commitment to environmental issues'.[21] Thus condemned to the political back-burner, Environment Canada offered ministers little of what Scharpf would call 'career opportunities and political visibility'.[22]

The ambivalence in Canadian attitudes towards the environment and executive disinterest also set the tone for the action of the statutory variables identified by Sabatier and Mazmanian. Chief among these was 'ambiguity in policy directives' with respect to Environment Canada's co-ordinative responsibilities for environmental quality protection and pollution control, a weakness which in turn had direct implications for Environment Canada's efforts to co-ordinate other federal agencies and secure resources.

The operative phrase with respect to Environment Canada's statutory clout was the restriction of its Minister to those 'duties, powers and functions . . . not by law assigned to any other department, branch or agency of the Government of Canada'. The residual nature of this operational mandate reflected the determination of the Trudeau administration, guided by what the Nielsen Task Force referred to as 'its own system of government and culture', that 'the maintenance and enhancement of environmental quality responsibilities in sectoral departments, including relevant scientific activities, [was] key to a fuller integration of environmental and economic factors in decision-making over time'.[23] The environment department was thus not to be a superministry in an operational sense. It was given the co-ordinative responsibilities similar to those of other horizontal portfolios created in this time frame; however, the imprecision of its mandate left it with considerable difficulty when confronting sectoral development agencies armed with specific legislative powers.

In addition to these internal statutory constraints, Environment Canada was also hamstrung in its interactions with other federal departments by the 'division of jurisdiction over environmental management between federal and provincial authorities'.[24] The need to step gingerly when dealing with the provinces, and to seek their co-operation in the institution of practices and conduct leading to the better protection and enhancement of environmental quality, left its officials at a distinct political disadvantage in trying to exert influence over other federal departments whose own constitutional authority was more clear-cut.[25]

In these circumstances, Sabatier and Mazmanian's observation that a 'loosely integrated' system will tend to produce 'considerable variation in the degree of behavioural compliance among implementing agencies'[26] soon proved to be apt. Environment Canada tried to put bite into its co-ordinative role within the national bureaucracy in two ways. First, it secured a Cabinet directive establishing an Environmental Assessment and Review Process (EARP) in 1973. The purpose of EARP was to ensure that 'environmental matters were taken into account by all federal departments and agencies in the planning and implementation of projects, programs and activities that originated with the federal government, that planned to use federal funds, or that required federal property'.[27] Second, it launched a multi-million dollar Federal Facilities Program, which was to deal with environmental aspects of federal operations on Indian reserves. This put particular emphasis on the clean-up of environmental wastes and hazards, and the prevention of environmental damage by means of assessment of projects and improved installations of facilities.

These attempts at co-ordination were soon rebuffed, however. The entire clean-up side of the Federal Facilities Program fell victim to the axe in 1975–76, in the first bout of austerity after Environment Canada's creation. Thereafter, the department was reduced to purely horizontal influence, as in monitoring requirements for wastewater treatment at federal facilities. Even here, however, departments were at best minimally co-operative in responding to requests for information, and Environment Canada lacked the resources to conduct inspections on its own on other than an *ad hoc* basis. Stymied in its effort to set the federal environmental house in order, the department turned its focus to industry, where its authority was more certain and the pollution threat more severe, a strategy which remained intact until the 1990s.

The EARP process fared little better. Indeed, its history to 1986 offers a classic confirmation of Laframboise's dictum that 'there is more to bending programs than obtaining an exhortatory Cabinet Record of Decision'.[28] The principal weakness of EARP in this context was that it left the power of initiative for conducting assessments squarely in the hands of sectoral departments, rather than Environment Canada. Attempts to correct this weakness, as in 1977 and 1984, foundered in the face of fear by other departments that 'a vigorous EARP under the sway of the environment minister would give Environment Canada considerable power over their activities'.[29]

This dispersal of national responsibility for environmental quality protection across the federal bureaucracy established a complex patchwork of programming which persisted well into the 1980s. As of 1984–85 the Nielsen Task Force identified some 82 principal federal enactments having a bearing on the environment, of which Environment Canada had lead responsibility for only 13, fewer even than the Department of Indian Affairs and Northern Development, and little more than Energy, Mines and Resources.[30]

The net effect was to create severe problems of overlap and 'turf wars' in the federal effort to ensure environmental quality protection and enhancement, wars which Environment Canada was on its own ill-equipped to fight. A number of administrative arrangements were introduced to overcome these problems. From Environment Canada's perspective, the principal device was an agreement with the Department of Fisheries and Oceans under which it was able to utilize section 33(2) of the Fisheries Act, which forbade the deposit into water of substances deleterious to fish, as a regulatory instrument for promulgating pollution control regulations.[31] Further, Memoranda of Understanding were developed with Transport Canada covering the hazardous-waste manifest system, and with Agriculture Canada concerning the registration of pesticides. The thrust and effect of these arrangements was, however, to lend Environment Canada a regulatory means of making a mark in the wider environmental context, not to increase its co-ordinative leverage over the other signatories.

The flow of financial resources, another of Sabatier and Mazmanian's statutory variables, tended to follow the channels established by this legislative framework. In essence, Environment Canada simply did not become in terms of expenditures the federal government's 'flagship' with respect to prevention and control of pollution. The Nielsen Task Force admitted in 1986, for example, that the resources traditionally allocated to Environment Canada, and more specifically to EPS, for purposes of preventing, eliminating, or reducing pollutants, were 'relatively limited'.[32] The same was true in other areas. For example, Environment Canada spending on environmental science and technology accounted for less than half of federal outlays in this field in 1984–85, and a similar though less dramatic division of spending was evident in the areas of toxic chemicals management and the long-range transport of air-borne pollutants.[33]

Environment Canada's poor funding status can also be attributed in part to the position that it had been assigned within the process of resource allocation at the federal level. Under the policy and expenditure management system (PEMS), spending was controlled by nine envelopes, one of which was the social development envelope containing the so-called 'quality of life' programs.[34] It was here that Environment Canada was consigned.

The social development envelope proved to be an unhappy home for Environment Canada for several reasons. In the first place, it was by far the largest of the nine envelopes, with health and welfare programs alone accounting for over thirty-five per cent of total federal spending. Environmental and other programs were quite simply dwarfed by these 'big-ticket' items. In addition, many of the programs within the envelope were statutory transfers to provinces or individuals, so the room for give-and-take within the envelope was minimal. More importantly, confinement to the 'social' envelope separated Environment Canada from the major sectoral spenders, and thus denied it any effective opportunity to argue its case in terms of the environment-economy interface. Instead, its minister had to compete with the heads of other social program departments for funds, using appropriate — that is social — envelope language.[35] Finally, social programs as a whole fell from grace after 1980, as the preoccupation at the federal level turned increasingly to the economy and to development. Indeed, after 1980, the social development envelope had no policy reserve to support new initiatives at all, and was expected to lose funds 'not only relatively but even absolutely' to 1985–86.[36]

In short, Environment Canada found itself cast in a social policy mould when the wave of enthusiasm for program innovation in this field had spent itself and was in retreat. Its officials could only look with envy on energy programs, which were a priority for the Trudeau administration after 1980 and for that reason given an entirely separate, steadily increasing envelope 'effectively controlled by the Energy minister, who was the most powerful francophone in Cabinet, and his officials'.[37] It was precisely this kind of contrast which prompted some of Environment Canada's intensely committed officials to engage in the kind of 'advocacy' tactics, or bureaucratic guerrilla warfare, if you will, which the Nielsen Task Force found so objectionable.

Taken together, these variables rendered Environment Canada a less than compelling demonstration of the utility of organizational design as an instrument of public policy by 1986. Lacking a convincing base of public support, condemned to the status of a junior ministry, and hampered by weak legislation and little co-ordinative power in the federal policy and fiscal structure, it instead reflected the frustration of purposeful reorganization. Indeed, the trend line in terms of Environment Canada's performance was distinctly towards what Scharpf would call 'policy failure'.

After 1986 a series of events combined to change this trend. Indeed, an about-face is apparent with respect to virtually all of the statutory and non-statutory variables discussed above. Environment Canada has benefited from these changed circumstances, to the point where organizational 're-design' seems the most appropriate description of the process at work.

TOWARDS RE-DESIGN

Of the changes in the statutory and non-statutory variables which came into play after 1986, the degree of public support merits first consideration, because public concern over pollution gave rise to Environment Canada in the first place and has if anything become an even more powerful determinant since. It will be recalled that the level of public concern about the environment as measured by public opinion fell dramatically after 1970, to a low point in 1985.

As early as 1984, Environment Canada's own sampling of public opinion indicated that a major transition in Canadian values was in the offing. Economic and social concerns, previously seen to be at odds, were coalescing under an environmental umbrella.[38] Movements in this direction were soon reported widely. Gallup results were, for example, little short of dramatic. By 1987, 67% of respondents in a Gallup Poll considered the dangers of pollution to be 'very serious', more than those who felt so even in 1970, just before the creation of Environment Canada. By 1989, this figure had climbed to an unprecedented 72%. Moreover, the number of respondents indicating that pollution was a problem in their area jumped from 46% in 1985 to 54% in 1987 and 67% in 1989.[39] Bakvis and Nevitte note similar results with respect to other questions. When asked their degree of concern about the environment, for example, 67% of respondents in 1989 and 78% in 1990 indicated that they were 'very concerned'. Further, on an open-ended query as to the most important problems facing Canada, the 'environment' became significant for the first time in 1987, when 3% deemed it the most important problem, a figure which increased to 17% in 1989.[40]

More importantly, perhaps, there was evidence of an increasing sense that protecting the environment need not mean sacrificing jobs.[41] On the contrary, the notion that environmental protection was necessary to ensure *sustainable* development, and hence, more employment over the longer term, began to show up in poll results. Media coverage of environmental issues went hand in hand with poll results, to the point where *Time* magazine designated 1989 as the Year of the Earth.[42]

The long-term explanation for this resurgence in environmental values is a matter of considerable academic debate.[43] It may be, for example, that the cycle of economic expansion which began in 1982 provided the kind of economic security which allowed more attention to quality-of-life concerns such as the environment; still others refer to the dawning of post-materialist values, one of which is environmental quality.[44] Whatever the case, a number of well-publicized environmental 'emergencies' in 1986–87 could only have helped to increase the sense of anxiety about the environment. One was the 1986 explosion at the Chernobyl nuclear power plant in the Soviet Union, the fall-out from which spread globally; another was the PCB (polychlorinated biphenyls) spill in Kenora, Ontario. This latter accident appears to have fixed the problem of toxic chemicals management in the public mind, particularly when followed by a major fire in a Saint-Basile-le-Grand PCB storage facility in Quebec in August, 1988.

At the same time, the central tenets of a method of harmonizing environmental and developmental concerns began to take shape. Two events merit particular notice in this respect. In May, 1986, the Brundtland World Commission on Environment and Development, which had been established by the United Nations in 1983, brought to Canada its thematic call for 'a process of change in which the exploitation of resources, the direction of investment, the orientation of technological development and institutional changes are made consistent with future as well as present needs'.[45] In response, the Canadian Council of Resource and Environment Ministers (CCREM) in October, 1986, established a

National Task Force on Environment and Economy to 'initiate dialogue on environment-economy integration among Canada's environment ministers, senior executive officers from Canadian industry, and representatives from environmental organizations and the academic community'.[46] That dialogue resulted in a declaration that 'governments and industry . . . must develop and assume new responsibilities to successfully integrate environmental considerations into economic planning'.[47]

Equally important, the National Task Force offered for the first time a consensus that 'environmental and economic concerns must go hand in hand', and that 'it is not possible to have a sound economy without a healthy environment'.[48] Coming as they did from industry as well as government spokespersons, these notions effectively cut the Gordian knot of uncertainty and apprehension which had plagued Canadian attitudes towards the environment, and thus rendered the problem of environmental quality protection more tractable in Sabatier and Mazmanian's terms.

Taken together, these poll results and reports from inquiries representing a broad spectrum of economic and environmental interests seemed to herald a sea-change in attitudes towards the environment. Indeed, Alistair Crerar, Chief Executive Officer of the Environmental Council of Alberta, pronounced the National Task Force Report 'the beginning of a revolution, a profound paradigm shift, and/or a miracle'.[49] Some academics gave a more cautious appraisal, but, while noting that some recommendations were generalized or 'reprises of familiar themes', Schrecker conceded that a decade earlier it would have been unthinkable for industry 'even to pay lip service' to the worth of many of the ideas which the Task Force espoused.[50]

In short, public attitudes and the run of ideas about the feasibility and methods of ensuring both environmental quality and growth began to run very much in Environment Canada's favour after 1986. The action of other non-statutory and statutory variables soon followed suit, in a pattern which has continued to the present.

The immediate catalyst for change was an improvement in the level of executive support for environmental programming and Environment Canada. The first indication of Prime Minister Mulroney's increased sensitivity to the environment was his ouster of Blais-Grenier in August, 1985, and the appointment of Tom McMillan, the dynamic Prince Edward Island MP and brother of Charles McMillan, Mulroney's Senior Policy Advisor, as Minister of Environment Canada. The intensely negative public and media reaction to the cuts which Blais-Grenier had inflicted on the Canadian Wildlife Service, and sinking support in the public opinion polls, left the Cabinet highly receptive to efforts to reverse this damage, an opening which McMillan and his officials hastened to exploit.

The first breakthrough in terms of policy directives came in the form of legislation. McMillan, primed by his senior policy officials who now had a clear feel for 'where the public was going', immediately announced his intention to bring in a new Environmental Protection Act which would consolidate all of Environment Canada's existing statutes. It did not hurt that the Nielsen Task Force environmental quality strategic review, reporting to Cabinet in February, 1986, thought in the same vein.[51]

A Memorandum to Cabinet soon followed and a draft Canadian Environmental Protection Act (CEPA) was introduced in the House of Commons in December, 1986. The new Act not only consolidated departmental legislation for environmental quality protection, especially through a 'cradle to the grave' approach to management of toxic chemicals, but also, this time in defiance of Nielsen Task Force recommendations, established an enforcement and compliance regime which incorporated section 108 of the Criminal Code and authorized stiff jail terms and fines for polluters. Moreover, in contrast to the insipid 1970 Government Organization Act, CEPA gave the Environment Minister 'authority to regulate emissions and effluents, as well as waste handling and disposal practices of federal departments, boards, agencies and Crown corporations', and power to 'regulate federal works, undertakings and federal lands and waters, where existing legislation administered by the responsible federal department does not provide for the making of regulations to protect the environment'.[52] Time will tell whether CEPA will be effective, but Environment Canada officials clearly believe that the Act's more 'focused' character and regulatory provisions give them at last the authority to ensure environmental sensitivity in all of the federal government's operations.

Strength and clarity in policy directives can encompass more than just legislation, as Laframboise has reminded us. At a summer policy-development 'camp' in 1986, Environment Canada officials, infused with Brundtland concepts and armed with public opinion polls, recognized the need for and an opportunity to establish a commitment to greater environment-economy linkages throughout the federal decision structure. Two further Memoranda to Cabinet were prepared under McMillan's direction on that basis, one establishing a *Federal Environmental Quality Policy Framework*, the other, co-sponsored by the Department of Regional Industrial Expansion (DRIE), a blueprint for *Making the Environment-Economy Partnership Work*. Adopted by the federal Cabinet in December, 1986, and thus 'binding on all federal departments', these 'decisions' became policy directives making the early incorporation of environmental considerations, hence anticipation and prevention, an integral component of the economic policy development process throughout the federal bureaucracy.[53]

The litmus test of Cabinet decisions is the degree to which they are followed. Evidence to date suggests that the Memoranda have indeed spread the message of environment-economy integration to an unprecedented extent within the federal economic decision process, and that Environment Canada's role has been greatly enhanced in the process.

Federal programming for regional economic development, with its thrust to job creation in underdeveloped areas heavily dependent upon natural resource exploitation, is a case in point. Both Memoranda in fact specifically alluded to the need to incorporate environmental factors into the federal-provincial Economic and Regional Development Agreements administered by DRIE. The idea was not new. The Nielsen Task Force observed early in 1986, for example, that the economic and regional development agreements (ERDAs) provided 'a most flexible and integrated planning and delivery instrument for a horizontal and strategic approach to the achievement of environment quality improvements over the longer term'.[54] Moreover, Environment Canada's Regional Office had already begun to lobby to make this happen. In 1986, for example, Atlantic Regional Directorate General (RDG) and Environmental Protection Service (EPS) officials, with full support from the Nova Scotia Federal Economic Development Co-ordinator, successfully negotiated a $45 million Canada-Nova Scotia agreement to clean up the Sydney Tar Ponds. This agreement 'laid the ground work and set the precedent for environmentally-oriented change in federal-provincial economic and regional development sub-agreements'.[55]

The creation of the Atlantic Canada Opportunities Agency (ACOA) in 1987, and with it the development of a new generation of 'Co-operation' agreements to replace the ERDAs, served to institutionalize the environment-economy linkage even further. Senior ACOA officials, most of whom came from the Federal Economic Development offices, appreciated early on, with the help of intense lobbying by Environment Canada's regional officials, that 'sustainability' was a must in a part of Canada which relied so heavily on its renewable resource base. Accordingly, ACOA as part of a new strategic thrust initiated in 1988 included 'the environment' as one of its five key themes for the development of new agreements. All new proposals were henceforth to demonstrate as appropriate that they promoted sustainable development of natural resources and prevention of damage of the environment, provided for environment impact statements at an early stage, made use of less-polluting and more cost-effective technology, and adhered to the 'polluter pays' principle.

Environment Canada's technical expertise has placed it in a highly favourable strategic position relative to the federal economic development departments in the development of these agreements. For example, ACOA guidelines now require that all other federal departments obtain input from Environment Canada when drafting co-operation agreements, and Environment Canada must approve every agreement before Treasury Board authorization for expenditures can be secured.

Most recently, Environment Canada itself has determined that some needs and opportunities on the environment-economy interface have fallen between the cracks of other Atlantic region subagreements, and is developing Sustainable Development Co-operation Agreements with the provinces to address them.[56] Successful completion of these negotiations would see Environment Canada as federal manager and lead agency for the implementation of some $30–40 million worth of federal-provincial sustainable development programs and projects.

As a result of these dynamics, Environment Canada has quickly become a much more high-profile player in Ottawa's regional economic development effort. Once condemned to the periphery of economic decision-making, it now sits front row, centre. The sectoral departments have retained their responsibility for integrating environmental factors into their decision-making, but Environment Canada is now seen by both mandate and expertise to be a key resource in making sure this happens. Indeed, in Atlantic Canada at least, Environment Canada officials now find themselves sought out by economic managers who would have eschewed such contact only a few short years ago.

Since the 1988 election, an increased surge of prime-ministerial support has pushed Environment Canada further into the national bureaucratic and political limelight. Though the topic tended to get lost in the furore over free trade, Mulroney did pledge a major environmental initiative during the 1988 election campaign, and reiterated his commitment in the April, 1989, Throne Speech.

One consequence was yet another legislative initiative, this time the introduction of a new Canadian Environmental Assessment Act (CEAA) to reform and strengthen the insipid federal Environmental Assessment and Review Process. Billed as an attempt by the federal government to get its own house in order, this legislation is intended to 'entrench the federal government's obligations to integrate environmental considerations into all of its project planning and implementation', and thus 'ensure that no policy, program legislation or project of the federal government goes ahead without a proper accounting of the potential environmental consequences'. To that end, the Minister of Environment Canada is authorized to 'initiate public reviews of projects with potentially significant environmental effects'.[57] The introduction of the CEAA in the House is all the more notable because Cabinet and departmental apprehensions about its impact on their decision-making processes and budgets were, as recently as 1989, so pronounced.[58]

As earlier, but this time to much more beneficial effect, resources have followed this evolving legislative framework. In stark contrast with the privation of earlier years, for example, Environment Canada received $5 million and 41 full-time positions to expedite the implementation of CEPA,[59] in a year in which all other departments were being told to 'make do with less'. More recently, the CEAA has come with a promise of '$100 million annually and several hundred person-years beyond current levels . . . to ensure the job is done right'.[60]

More importantly, Mulroney also turned his attention to the place of the 'environment' and Environment Canada in Cabinet structures and processes. The first moves were political. First, in what was billed as a post-election demonstration of the ' "foremost" importance he now attached to the environment ministry',[61] Mulroney appointed Lucien Bouchard, a long-time friend and high-profile Quebecker whom he had personally recruited into federal politics, as Minister for Environment Canada. Second, in what was described by the media as an attempt to 'provide the bureaucratic muscle to back up Lucien Bouchard's growing political clout', he then shifted Len Good, the Deputy Secretary to Cabinet (via Energy, Mines and Resources), from his position 'near the centre of Ottawa's power structure'[62] to Environment Canada as Deputy Minister. Together, these changes lifted Environment Canada from the junior to the heavyweight ranks in Cabinet and the federal bureaucracy.

At the same time, Mulroney moved to give the environment greater visibility in the policy processes of the executive arena. The National Task Force had in fact recommended in 1987 that 'environment ministers ... be members of key economic development and priorities and planning committees of Cabinet, or be closely associated, by appropriate mechanisms, with these committees'.[63] Changes in the Cabinet system announced along with the Cabinet shuffle in January, 1989, went one better.

The centrepiece of the changes was the creation of a new Cabinet Committee on Environment (CCE) chaired by the Minister for Environment Canada. In general terms, the CCE was mandated to 'manage the government's environmental agenda' and ensure that all its activities, and 'priorities, programs and other initiatives' which it might be called upon to support, were 'fully compatible' with its 'environmental objectives'.[64] Further, the Environment Canada Minister was given a seat on the Priorities and Planning (P&P) Committee, and the Operations Committee. Mulroney was thus signalling his administration's 'commitment to strong leadership on environmental issues'.[65]

The significance of these changes insofar as Environment Canada is concerned was greater than might be at first apparent. As part of the reforms, the two large sectoral Cabinet committees, Social Development and Economic and Regional Development, were broken down into four much smaller and more specialized committees — one of which was the CCE[66] — each with a 'more precise focus of responsibility and activity ... of direct and common interest to all members',[67] and each charged specifically with 'development of the government's key initiatives', that is, policy.[68] The membership of the CCE — National Health and Welfare; ACOA; Energy, Mines and Resources; Fisheries and Oceans; Transport; Forestry; Consumer and Corporate Affairs; Labour; and the Ministries of State for Agriculture, Transport, and Science and Technology — thus not only spoke of the breadth of the intended interface of environment and sectoral concerns across the federal bureaucracy, but mandated Environment Canada and its Minister to take the lead role with these agencies in the development of a federal environmental policy which would reflect it.

Bouchard promptly announced his intention to develop an action plan on the environment, and Environment Canada scribes, in particular an 'inner core' policy team assembled by Good from Energy, Mines and Resources, Finance, and the Privy Council Office, set to work. By December, 1990, the Prime Minister was able to announce *Canada's Green Plan*, a \$3-billion commitment to:

1. clean air, water, and land;

2. sustainable use of renewable resources;

3. protection of our special spaces and species;

4. preserving the integrity of our North;

5. global environmental security;

6. environmentally responsible decision-making at all levels of society; and

7. minimizing the impacts of environmental emergencies.[69]

Environment Canada did not, for all this, enjoy a 'carte blanche' in the formulation of the Green Plan. Indeed, Bouchard's original action plan died in the CCE because he failed to consult other federal departments, who worried about the costs they might incur in an environmental regulatory thrust at a time of restraint and feared that an Environment Canada 'grab for power' was afoot, let alone private sector stakeholders, whose behaviour was ultimately at issue. He was as a result forced to undertake an intensive multi-phase, multi-stakeholder consultation process in which a background paper, *A Framework for Discussion on the Environment*, was ultimately transformed into *Canada's Green Plan*. Moreover, as the ostensible client, the CCE itself was far from pliant. It approved the Framework discussion paper, met at least every two weeks as the Green Plan took shape, and, unlike traditional Cabinet policy committees, insisted on vetting the final document word for word.

Nevertheless, the development of the Green Plan carried Environment Canada to extraordinary heights in terms of the objectives underlying its original design. It not only provided virtually all the substantive grist for the CCE mill, but was able to elicit unprecedented interest in environmental themes by other departments.

Whether because of Mulroney's interest or because of the lure of what promised to be generous Green Plan funding at a time of severe fiscal constraint, the embrace of the green theme and co-operation with Environment Canada suddenly became a political and bureaucratic imperative. CCE deliberations, for example, apparently featured a minimum of the political manoeuvring sometimes found in the Cabinet decision process and an earnest attempt to deal with the environmental issues at hand. Similar signs of high-level favour abounded within the bureaucracy. Thus, the Deputy Minister held previously unthinkable regular meetings with his counterparts in the Privy Council Office and Treasury Board on policy and funding. The Clerk of Privy Council himself lent weight to the effort, sometimes chairing deputy ministerial sessions on the Green Plan, a level of interest which was quickly noticed by a bureaucracy ever alert for indications of executive favour. Moreover, after years of barely being able to wedge a foot in the door of sectoral departments, Environment Canada now found it possible to secure the regular participation of up to twenty-six departments on a regular basis in Assistant Deputy Minister (ADM) policy briefings. Down the line, Environment Canada's Atlantic Regional Office was able, on only three days' notice, to secure the attendance of fifty-two of fifty-five Regional Director Generals at the lengthy public consultation sessions.

There was no doubt, moreover, that the Green Plan was primarily an Environment Canada show; it not only had clear responsibility for translating the theme of environment-economy linkage into policy, but increasingly a virtual monopoly of information on progress to that end. Indeed, as funding amounts were discussed a veil of budget-like secrecy was drawn over the process, and Environment Canada's policy and co-ordinative role in the preparation of the Green Plan took on a distinctly central-agency and, for some departments, frustrating character.

Preliminary indications are that Environment Canada will continue to have a quasi-central agency function in the implementation phase of the Green Plan. Though CCE does not have power to allocate monies under the Green Plan, its approval is a prerequisite to Treasury Board approval of any submission, and, as CCE Chair, the Environment Canada Minister is positioned to ensure that new federal initiatives reflect the objectives set out therein. Moreover, all such submissions to CCE have to go through Environment Canada for vetting of programmatic content, and a secretariat has been established to perform this function. This arrangement replicates at the national level the kind of role which Environment Canada now plays in development programming at the regional level, at least in Atlantic Canada. This policy role alone gives Environment Canada the kind of central-agency status enjoyed by the Ministry of State for Social Development (MSSD) and the Ministry of State for Economic and Regional Development (MSERD) in the early 1980s in servicing the Cabinet sectoral committees.[70]

Environment Canada's membership on P&P and Operations committees may be still more important in the longer term. With resource
allocation decisions now centralized in P&P, the Environment Canada
Minister has direct input into longer term resource allocation decisions
reaching beyond the scope of the Green Plan, while membership on
Operations allows input into the management of the overall agenda on a
weekly basis. Environment Canada thus currently has a say in everything
that is going in Ottawa.

Still, none of this should be taken to mean that Environment Canada
has become a superministry. There has been no evident change in the
thinking that sectoral managers themselves should be taking environmental factors into account at the outset of their own decision-making, where
policies and programs originate. Good himself has indicated on behalf of
his minister that Environment Canada is 'not working to be a department
that imposes environmental considerations, but [one that] tries to establish processes which permit environmental factors to be integrated into
decision-making'.[71] If the experience in Atlantic Canada is any example,
any such greening of the decision process will place even greater demand
on Environment Canada for policy advice, and hence only further its
influence within the federal bureaucracy for the future.

CONCLUSION

Environment Canada was a product of organizational design aimed to
provide a co-ordinated federal response to environmental concern in
Canada, and its experience within the Canadian bureaucracy in pursuing
the design objective has been a roller-coaster ride.

The initial leg was a precipitous descent. Between 1973 and 1986,
Environment Canada had to endure virtually all of the factors that can
frustrate policy implementation. Ambivalence in public attitudes towards
the environment and executive indifference translated into ambiguity
in policy directives, limited funding, and a peripheral status in federal
decision-making. The concept of design failure seemed increasingly apt.

Since 1986, however, a remarkable turn-about has catapulted Environment Canada upwards in terms of mandate and status within the federal
bureaucracy. A dawning public and prime-ministerial conviction that
environment protection enhances rather than thwarts the prospects for
sustainable growth has not only reaffirmed the original design, but ushered in an intense period of re-design resulting in a greatly enhanced role
for Environment Canada within the federal bureaucracy. Indeed, the
combination of its policy advisory role to the Cabinet Committee on
Environment, in the context of both the Green Plan and its regulatory
and co-ordinative authority under the CEPA and CEAA, and its policy
and management role in regional development programming has carried

it to a more powerful practical position than MSSD and MSERD ever had.

It is more difficult to assess Environment Canada's future role as a result of these changes. One possibility is that the logic of Downs's issue-attention cycle will assert itself, environmental concerns will be displaced by others, and that Environment Canada's role will wane once again. Indeed, Bakvis and Nevitte present evidence that environmental concerns were less likely in 1990 than in 1989 to be identified as the most important problem,[72] and this was before the 1990 recession had taken hold. It seems more likely, however, that Crerar's allusion to a paradigm shift is more apt, and that the environment-economy interface has become a baseline in policy deliberations at the national level.

It is, of course, too early to talk of the fulfilment of design. The true test will be whether Cabinet and the sectoral departments move towards the greening of their decision processes as called for in the Green Plan, begin to couch all of their initiatives, inside the Green Plan and out, in terms of sustainability, and act on that basis. As things now stand, Environment Canada is by virtue of its expertise indispensable to that effort. The chief impediment in this respect may, ironically enough, be the complexion of its own personnel. Dispensing policy advice in a co-ordinative milieu requires policy skills which most of Environment Canada's personnel have had little occasion to develop—witness the fact that a policy team had to be seconded from without to produce the Green Plan. This problem will clearly have to be resolved if Environment Canada is to reap the opportunity for advancing environment-economy integration which changes in action of the variables affecting implementation have brought about.

Finally, the process of re-design may not yet be complete. Though the full implications of the Green Plan have yet to be worked out, it appears to represent a sustainable development strategy which exceeds in scope the kind of industrial strategy which has been so long and futilely sought in Canada.[73] If so, further changes may be required in both Cabinet decision structures and in Environment Canada. One possibility, for example, is that Environment Canada's new-found policy role could become its principal one, and that its own structures would be re-designed in response. At the very least, this means that organizational design will continue to be an important, and intriguing, policy instrument in the environmental field in Ottawa.

FOR FURTHER READING

Peter Aucoin and Herman Bakvis, *The Centralization-Decentralization Conundrum: Organization and Management in the Canadian Government* (Halifax: Institute for Research on Public Policy, 1988).

F. Bregha et al., *The Integration of Environmental Considerations in Government Policy* (Ottawa: Rawson Academy of Aquatic Science, 1990).

William Block, *Economics and the Environment: A Reconciliation* (Vancouver: Fraser Institute, 1990).

Paul Brown, 'Environment Canada and the Pursuit of Administrative Decentralization', *Canadian Public Administration,* 29, 2 (Summer, 1986): 218-36.

Canada, *Environmental Quality Strategic Review: A Follow-on Report of the Task Force on Program Review* (Ottawa: Ministry of Supply and Services, 1986).

Canadian Council of Resource and Environment Ministers, *Report of the National Task Force on Environment and Economy* (Downsview, Ont.: CCREM, 1987).

G. Bruce Doern, 'Getting It Green: Canadian Environmental Policy in the 1990s', in G. Bruce Doern, ed., *The Environmental Imperative: Market Approaches to the Greening of Canada* (Toronto: C.D. Howe Institute, 1990), 1-18.

Robert Paehlke and Douglas Torgerson, eds., *Managing Leviathan: Environmental Politics and the Administrative State* (Toronto: Broadview Press, 1990).

Douglas Smith, 'Defining the Agenda for Environmental Protection', in Katherine Graham, ed., *How Ottawa Spends 1990–91* (Ottawa: Carleton University Press, 1990), 113-36.

CHAPTER 3

Environmental Policy in a Federal System

Ottawa and the Provinces

GRACE SKOGSTAD AND PAUL KOPAS

Federal-provincial relations in the area of environmental policy are in a process of transition. The harmony that characterized intergovernmental relations throughout the first generation of environmental legislation has been put to the test during the late 1980s and early 1990s. A second generation of federal and provincial legislation, directed toward controlling toxic substances, now supplements the traditional legislation aimed primarily at regulating pollution and waste on land, and in the air and sea.[1] The shift in the focus of environmental policy has created pressures for a change in the policy-making process. As decision-making processes alter, the traditionally relatively closed and collaborative process of policy-making, in which industry and governmental officials at both levels formulated and implemented environmental policy in relative isolation from public opinion and environmental groups' scrutiny, is in jeopardy. A number of factors in the late 1980s and early 1990s have threatened to destabilize this pattern of policy-making. These events include the greater priority of environmental issues on the public agenda as the magnitude of the problem of environmental degradation has become clearer, strong international pressures on the national government to formulate environmentally sustainable policies, decisions of the Canadian courts which have indirectly legitimized a say for citizen groups in determining the appropriateness of resource development projects with environmental ramifications, and other judicial decisions which have implied a greater federal jurisdictional base than Ottawa has traditionally claimed and the provinces have accepted. In short, decision-makers are faced with pressures not only for substantively different policies with respect to environmental matters, but, as well, for a different, more open, participative process of formulating and implementing environmentally sustainable policies.

The concern of this chapter is to examine the traditional pattern of federal-provincial relations surrounding environmental policy, and then to map out how these relations are changing in the early 1990s. Would environmental policy outcomes in Canada be different in the absence of a federal system? Has the federal system stymied more effective regulatory control of polluters? Would environmental policies have more 'bite' if the government of Canada had exclusive jurisdiction to protect the environment?

THE TRADITIONAL PATTERN OF FEDERAL-PROVINCIAL RELATIONS

The traditional relationship characterizing federal-provincial relations on matters of environmental policy has three essential features: federal leadership in proposing national guidelines and objectives; federal-provincial consultation and bargaining to establish regulatory standards; and provincial enforcement. This pattern of intergovernmental relations can be attributed to three factors in particular: first, the lack of clarity as well as the overlap of jurisdictional responsibility for environmental matters; second, a shared set of federal and provincial norms which included a preference to avoid coercive regulation and an underlying belief that economic development and environmental quality were antithetical and that resource/economic development (a matter within provincial jurisdiction) must take priority; and third, the presence of well-established mechanisms to facilitate intergovernmental consultation.

Jurisdictional Ambiguity: Concurrent Legislation

Jurisdiction concerning environmental matters is cloudy, for there is no explicit provision in the Canadian Constitution that relates directly to environmental matters. For its part, the federal government can justify its legislative and regulatory presence in environmental matters by virtue of its authority to make laws for the peace, order, and good government of Canada, trade and commerce (including the regulation of interprovincial transportation and marketing), and criminal law. Additional specific subject headings which give the Government of Canada jurisdiction over sea coast and inland fisheries, agriculture, navigation and shipping, direct and indirect taxes, and the negotiation and signing of treaties can also indirectly authorize a federal environmental presence. Thus, the Government of Canada, by virtue of its legal authority to regulate export and interprovincial commerce, has been ascendant in regulating transboundary pollution and toxic products traded across provincial, provincial-territorial, and international borders. This has entailed federal supremacy in such areas as regulating automobile emission standards, the quality of the Great Lakes water, acid rain, protection of the ozone layer, global climate change, and pesticide registration. However, of its potential bases for legal authority regarding the environment, the Government of Canada's power over fisheries has traditionally been the most significant, constituting the basis for federal involvement in water pollution control.[2]

The provinces' ownership of natural resources within their borders, combined with the presumption that environmental pollution offences are civil (not criminal) law offences, have given provinces a strong jurisdictional base to control land, water, and stationary (not ambient) air pollution. Additional provincial powers over land within their borders, property and civil rights, and all matters of local concern reinforce provincial authority to regulate pollution. Through its ownership of public lands and its legal authority to dictate how its natural resources, including the forestry and hydroelectricity, will be managed, developed, and/or conserved, a provincial government is pivotal in affecting the quality of the environment within its borders.

This situation of some jurisdictional ambiguity and considerable potential overlap of legal authority raises the immediate spectre of both conflict and 'double unilateralism'.[3] The greatest source of potential conflict has been between federal authority with respect to fisheries and provincial ownership of natural resources, including the right to manage and develop forestry resources. More generally, the spill-over of environmental problems across subject matters assigned to the two levels of government creates the possibility for unco-ordinated legislation: that is, each level of government legislating and regulating in many of the same general policy areas. This has happened to some extent; at the same time the government of Canada was responding to environmental concerns in the early 1970s by passing legislation and establishing environmental agencies to regulate the environmental quality of water (the Clean Water Act, the Fisheries Act Pollution Amendments and Industry Regulations, the Clean Air Act), so were the provinces. Thus, provincial water pollution regulations overlap with federal fisheries regulations — both governments have regulations with respect to the prevention of accidents causing environmental damage and the clean-up of contaminated waters — and both governments have been involved in regulating the quality of the air. Federal regulations regarding the use, distribution, and sale of pesticides may be at odds with provincial requirements, with the consequence that companies manufacturing pesticides may find their products licensed federally but restricted from use in certain provinces. (This is especially likely in Ontario where pesticide-use prohibitions are more stringent than those in federal regulations.) And, as recent developments have made apparent, there are overlaps and disparities among federal and provincial environmental assessment review processes.

But the possibility of double unilateralism, with the attendant costs of contradictory federal and provincial policies and duplication of existing policies, has generally been avoided. Dwivedi notes that Ottawa and the provinces agreed at the federal-provincial Constitutional Conference in

1970 to co-operate in managing the environment.[4] The understanding was that Ottawa would assume leadership with respect to international issues, while the provinces took responsibility for the environment within their borders, with the proviso of federal assistance by mutual agreement of the two levels of government. This delineation of spheres of influence has tended to prevail.

Following varying degrees of consultation and negotiation with the provinces, broad legislation setting out national standards has been achieved. The Government of Canada has then delegated to the provinces, through formal agreements and accords, authority to enforce and implement both water and air pollution control regulations.[5] The consequence has been that provinces have tended to exercise responsibility for the actual enforcement of pollution control regulations.[6] Such provincial implementation authority, in conjunction with provincial jurisdiction over water and lands within their borders, has established a paramount role for the provinces in the areas of land and water management.

This pattern of federal standard-setting and provincial enforcement in an area of overlapping national and provincial authority is evident regarding the regulation of pulp and paper effluents. By virtue of its constitutional power to deal with sea coast and inland fisheries (including fish habitat and the water occupied by fish), the Government of Canada prohibits pollution of water frequented by fish under section 36.3 (formerly section 33) of the Fisheries Act. Although the Pulp and Paper Effluent Regulations, which were promulgated in 1971 pursuant to the Fisheries Act, were drafted without appreciable provincial influence,[7] the strength of the provincial claim to exercise constitutional authority over water pollution led to Ottawa's decision to delegate enforcement of the Regulations to the provinces. In 1975 Ottawa negotiated bilateral environmental protection accords (known as 'Accords for the Protection and Enhancement of Environmental Quality') with seven provinces (BC, Newfoundland, and Quebec were the exceptions), under which it delegated responsibility to the provinces to enforce federal regulations pursuant to the Fisheries Act. Under the terms of the Accords, provinces agreed to implement environmental quality objectives that were as stringent as federal requirements, but the federal government retained the right to initiate legal proceedings in relation to the agreements. As well, the Government of Canada retained authority over coastal fisheries and over fish that spawn in fresh waters and later migrate to salt water.

The same pattern of provinces being delegated enforcement powers with respect to federal legislation also applied to air quality control. Subsequent to the passage in 1971 of the Clean Air Act, in which the Government of Canada prescribed national air quality objectives and standards, Ottawa negotiated agreements with the provinces to implement these objectives in provincial legislation and vested provinces with powers to enforce federal standards. Although the Accords have now lapsed, the breadth of federal-provincial co-operation on environmental policy can be illustrated by the fact that there are now in excess of 400 federal-provincial agreements on the environment and hundreds of more informal arrangements.

Shared Norms and Closed Policy Networks

To stress the co-operation which has characterized federal-provincial relations on environmental issues should not blind one to the possibility, and indeed reality, of intergovernmental conflict on environmental matters. Federal concerns for protection of the environment have the potential to jeopardize provincial priorities for resource development — for the harvesting of forests, the production of pulp and paper, oil and gas exploration and development, and the development of hydroelectric power, to cite the most obvious examples.[8] The high dependence of a number of provincial economies on a single natural resource — BC on forestry, Alberta on oil and gas, New Brunswick and Quebec on pulp and paper — and within Atlantic Canada, Quebec, northern Ontario, and BC, the reality of single-industry towns and communities, makes these provincial governments loath to enforce pollution control regulations that could threaten to remove the major source of employment and income. This economic strength, coupled with the high degree of organizational development of most natural resource industries, has meant that the dominant resource industry has considerable leverage over provincial resource/environmental policies. Thus, in Alberta, says Doern, 'environmental policy is energy policy', and in British Columbia, Coleman describes the relationship between the pulp and paper industry and the provincial government as a 'clientelist' one in which the industry's preferred policy options prevail.[9]

That federal-provincial conflict has been largely avoided, at least until recently, can be attributed to two factors. First, polluting industries have enjoyed the same close and influential access to federal policy-makers as they have to provincial authorities. Second, the federal government, holding to the same economic development bias as provincial and industry officials, has been willing to turn a blind eye to provincial failures to enforce regulatory pollution control standards. A closer look at the historical situation surrounding the formulation and enforcement of pulp and paper effluent regulations sheds light upon both the close industry-government policy networks and the prevailing norms of governments.

Regulations placing ceilings on the release of pulp and paper effluents into receiving waters constituted the first major attempt to regulate industrial pollution. A lengthy process of consultation with the Canadian Pulp and Paper Association, representing the pulp and paper industry, 'Canada's largest industrial discharger of water-borne pollutants',[10] preceded the drafting of the Regulations promulgated in 1971. But the draft Regulations themselves were vigorously criticized by the industry, which, like the provinces, had not been involved in their final drafting. In the wake of this negative response, the Department of Fisheries and Forestry struck a Regulations Development Team, consisting of representatives of the industry, and federal and provincial governments, but excluding representatives of other interested publics, like the BC fishing industry. The pulp and paper industry played a critical role on the Regulations Development Team; their technical data and expertise were vital in offsetting the limited knowledge base of the government, and their criticisms of the very need for the regulations at all resulted in a weakening of the regulations.[11] The industry successfully argued that the older mills (those built before 1971 and located principally in Quebec and New Brunswick) lacked the technical and financial capability to meet government-proposed requirements. This consideration, combined with industry and provincial government concern regarding the vulnerability of one-industry towns should the costs of complying with regulatory standards force a mill to close or curtail its operations, secured older mills' exemption from the regulations.[12]

Federal enforcement zeal has been no less lax than that of provincial officials. Giroux notes a sharp decline in the number of federal prosecutions after responsibility for enforcement of section 33 of the Fisheries Act was delegated to the provinces, even in those provinces that did not sign accords to implement federal requirements. In Quebec, where there was no federal-provincial accord and where instances of non-compliance with federal standards for effluents in the pulp and paper industry under the Fisheries Act were highest, there were no federal prosecutions. Until recently, the federal government faced no pressure from the Canadian public, seemingly uninterested in this laxity of regulatory enforcement, and so had no political incentive to engage in a dispute with provincial enforcement authorities, or, for that matter, to be a more vigilant regulator itself.[13]

Institutionalized Forums of Consultation

The amicable working relationship between federal and provincial governments in setting environmental quality standards and overall policies owes much to the existence of long-standing mechanisms of intergovernmental consultation and co-operation among first ministers (of the environment), as well as among bureaucratic officials in federal and provincial departments of the environment. These federal-provincial links are buttressed by advisory committees.

Beginning with the Canadian Council of Resource Ministers in 1964, followed by the Canadian Council of Resource and Environment Ministers in 1971, and since 1988, through the Canadian Council of Ministers of the Environment (CCME), there has been an institutionalized forum for intergovernmental discussion of environmental matters of national importance. The eleven members of the Council are federal and provincial ministers with responsibility for the environment. The two territorial ministers have observer status, but participate fully in discussions and activities.

Acting originally as a forum to provide advice to governments on policies, programs, and agreements, the Council has facilitated the exchange of information, and promoted the consultation and debates that allow for the development of co-operative and compatible policies. In this task, it is aided by a steering committee of federal and provincial deputy ministers of the environment, and by a permanent secretariat of officials. The effectiveness of the Council in providing 'a stable and ongoing forum for ministerial contact and consultation'[14] regarding common problems and possible solutions may be, at least partly, attributed to the distinctive character of its chairmanship. Rotation of the position among the member governments tends to put all governments on an equal footing, as does the sharing of costs associated with the CCME. (Ottawa contributes one-third of the costs and the provinces the remaining two-thirds on a per capita basis.)

In addition to the CCME, other forums have arisen to facilitate dialogue and understanding on environmental matters: for example, the National Round Table on the Environment and Economy and the National Forest Strategy.[15] Significant attempts to develop a National Forest Strategy by federal and provincial forestry ministers, as well as by academics and industry officials, can also be cited as another mechanism of intergovernmental co-operation.[16]

THE TRADITIONAL INTERGOVERNMENTAL RELATIONSHIP AND POLICY OUTCOMES

Canadian federalism, in terms of both the ambiguous and overlapping legal relationship between provincial and federal governments and its political expression in federal-provincial bargaining and predominantly provincial implementation, appears to have affected the scope and substantive nature of pollution control policies in Canada. The ambiguity and imprecision surrounding jurisdictional authority would seem to have undermined the scope of federal environmental policy historically and contributed to a weak enforcement regime. However, the effects of federalism on policy outcomes are difficult to isolate from the impact of other factors, among them the predominance in government and industry circles of a development/production-oriented ideology, and the existence of closed policy networks in which industry and government officials have collaborated in the formulation of policies with environmental implications.

There is evidence that 'perceived provincial "sensitivities" concerning federal intrusion into traditional provincial areas' caused the Government of Canada to exercise self-restraint with respect to both the breadth of its pollution control legislation and its willingness to promulgate pollution control regulations.[17] The Canadian government's decision to regulate pulp and paper effluents under the Fisheries Act, rather than under a proposed comprehensive water management act, was based on the realization that the latter approach, preferred by the Department of Energy, Mines and Resources, would require provincial and local input and co-operation, not necessary for regulations under the Fisheries Act. Later, jurisdictional uncertainties contributed to the federal failure in the late 1970s and early 1980s, first, to implement the extensive and unilateral federal management powers over water quality and quantity in the Canada Water Act, and second, to promulgate regulations under authority of the Clean Air Act to control emissions from all works or undertakings under federal legislative authority.

Federalism has also been implicated in Canada's relatively weak enforcement regime. Lundqvist's comparison of air pollution control policies in Canada, the United States, and Sweden, led him to conclude that Canada's federal structure was partly to blame for both a weaker anti-pollution regulatory regime and its less vigilant enforcement in Canada.[18] 'Key interests' in provinces have been able to influence the provinces to adopt relatively lenient standards, and the national government's acceptance of these lesser standards is owing to provincial jurisdiction regarding the environment and the federal desire to keep provinces on-side. Several others agree.[19] Conway argues that 'uncertainty about federal-provincial jurisdiction', in conjunction with fiscal pressures, made it 'appear logical' for Ottawa to transfer responsibility for enforcement of pollution control regulations to the provinces.[20] And finally, Giroux points to an attitude of 'restraint' in Environment Canada's Environmental Protection Service, 'based on the fear of causing constitutional and political friction with Quebec', as the reason why enforcement was left to the provinces even for pollution sources within federal regulations. Provincial enforcement had the further consequence of creating significant discrepancies in enforcement responses.[21]

These conclusions about the negative effects of political and legal federalism must take account of two other points. The first is that shared jurisdiction is viewed by some to have had beneficial consequences for environmental policy, for instance, by being a catalyst to legislative action. Thus, in the absence of action by the British Columbia government, representatives of fisheries, wildlife, and native interests in BC called on a touring House of Commons Standing Committee on Fisheries and Forestry in April 1969 to urge federal control over pulp and paper effluent and other pollutants. Moreover, Nemetz has argued that regulatory enforcement because of joint federal-provincial activity has been greater than would be the case with unilateral jurisdiction.[22] Concurrent federal and provincial legislative and regulatory activity with respect to water pollution control in British Columbia has resulted, in his view, in more vigorous prosecution of polluters because the federal government's greater information-gathering network and research capability has offset the weak provincial regulatory resources and will.

The second point is that the effects of federalism may be less a determinant of environmental policy than are other factors. In Lundqvist's view, the ideological preference of national decision-makers not to interfere with industrial practices was also important in accounting for Canada's less effective regulatory control relative to Sweden.[23] In agriculture, where shared jurisdiction has been accompanied by some of the most harmonious federal-provincial policy-making, problems of soil degradation can be attributed to the production-oriented bias of governments and producers.[24] While 'insecurity in federal-provincial relations', and a consequent lack of political will, impeded the Department of Environment in making significant progress on environmental protection until recently, Conway cites other factors as also important.[25]

THE ALTERED CONTEXT IN THE 1990s

Environmental policy in the 1990s is being formulated and implemented in a context which differs in some important respects from that of the preceding two decades. First, no longer a matter of concern only to would-be regulated industries and environmental groups, protection and preservation of the environment now appears to be a high-priority concern of the general public. Greater public awareness brings with it a call for meaningful public participation in decisions affecting the quality of the environment. The process of devising environmental policy will be scrutinized as much as its substance; public hearings and consultation are now necessary to create a perception of openness to all stakeholders.[26] The demand for participation on the part of interested publics has been bolstered by recent judicial decisions that have created new opportunities for increasingly sophisticated environmental groups to use the court system to lobby governments on environmentally related economic developments.

Alongside these two developments — the enhanced expectations for more democratic environmental policy-making and implementation, and the existence of the courts as a new forum for influencing environmental policy decisions — a third contextual change is significant. Of great importance is evidence that the Government of Canada is interested in assuming a greater responsibility for protection of the environment, including greater vigilance in enforcement of regulatory standards. Federal leadership ambitions can be traced to the desires to accord with the voting public and to maintain favourable relations with other nations pressing for international action on the environmental front, and to greater confidence in federal jurisdictional authority.

Judicial Decisions

Separate judicial decisions in recent years have strengthened the Government of Canada's legislative authority to regulate water pollution, and have indirectly opened up the environmental policy-making process to the access of citizens.

The Supreme Court of Canada, in *Regina vs Crown Zellerbach Canada Ltd, et al.* (1988), provided a broader authority for the Government of Canada to regulate water pollution than it had enjoyed by virtue of its jurisdiction over fisheries. The Court ruled that Ottawa had a right to legislate to prohibit dumping in marine waters, including provincial marine waters, by virtue of its power to legislate for the 'peace, order and good government of Canada'. Marine pollution is a matter of national interest, said the Court, because marine waters constitute a single, indivisible matter distinct from pollution of fresh waters, and one with inter-provincial and international ramifications. The consequences of the failure of provinces to curtail marine pollution within their waters would spill beyond provincial borders, making federal legislation necessary to ensure effective action.

Speaking for a dissenting minority, Justice LaForest stressed the 'radical' effects of the Crown Zellerbach ruling on the legislative division of jurisdiction. The expanded federal authority to regulate air and water pollution, he argued, could 'completely swallow up provincial power' and 'create considerable stress on Canadian federalism'.[27] Regardless of its legal effects, it does seem clear that the Crown Zellerbach case has given Ottawa an important political resource; it has augmented the national government's political will and bargaining strength *vis-à-vis* the provinces.[28]

The Canadian Environmental Protection Act (CEPA), passed in 1988, not only consolidated a number of federal environmental acts, but also provided for an extension of federal authority into areas previously deemed by the provinces to be in their domain. One such area is regulating and controlling toxic substances, until now predominantly controlled by the provinces.[29] Lucas argues that the Crown Zellerbach ruling was instrumental in this extension of federal authority because a stronger case for federal jurisdiction to regulate toxic substances can be made on the grounds that the matter is one of peace, order, and good government, than can be mounted on the basis of the criminal law power.[30]

Other court cases have also created new openings for a federal role in what has been a hallowed domain of the provinces: natural resource development. Judgements by the Federal Court and the Federal Court of Appeal have determined that provincial resource development projects which may have an environmental impact on an area of federal responsibility, or for which the Government of Canada makes a financial commitment, are subject to a federal environmental impact assessment. In *Friends of the Oldman River Society vs Alberta Minister of the Environment* (1987–1990) and *Canadian Wildlife Federation vs Canada (Minister of the Environment)* (1989), the Federal Court (and the Federal Court of Appeal) quashed provincial licences for construction of provincial dams (already under way) on the grounds that neither had been subject to an environmental impact assessment and review as required by the federal Environmental Assessment and Review Process (EARP) Guidelines Order. The federal impact assessment was necessary in both instances because construction of the Alberta (Oldman River) and Saskatchewan (Rafferty, Alameda) dams affected matters under federal jurisdiction — fish, migratory birds, Indians and Indian lands, and navigable waters. In a related development, a joint federal-provincial environmental impact assessment panel examining the construction of the Alberta-Pacific mill in Northern Alberta in 1990 recommended that construction of the major pulp and paper kraft mill not be approved until further scientific studies were conducted to determine the environmental hazards posed by the mill, including its effects on fish in waters that flowed onto lands under federal jurisdiction (national parks, the Northwest Territories).

The Crown Zellerbach, Oldman River, and Rafferty-Alameda (as the Canadian Wildlife Federation case is popularly known) decisions have expanded the reach of federal authorities on environmental matters. In ruling that the EARP Guidelines are legally binding and that the minister cannot use his/her discretion, but must call for a public review of any proposed development which requires federal permits, funds, or lands and which can be predicted to have significant adverse environmental effects, the Federal Court has made it possible for the federal government to extend the scope of its influence and/or control over environmental matters. The result has been considerable provincial apprehension and federal-provincial tensions.

Competitive Federalism

In the wake of these court rulings and the passage of CEPA, there is a new edginess to relations between the Government of Canada and some provinces. The tensions are most apparent between those provinces whose economic well-being is intricately tied to resource development projects — western Canada and Quebec. Provincial worries about and rejection of the extension of federal environmental authority are couched in terms of an illegitimate invasion of the federal government into provincial ownership and control of natural resources. The national government, some provinces fear, will be able to determine the pace and timing of provincial economic development of natural resources.[31]

Some provinces—Alberta, Saskatchewan, and Nova Scotia—

responded to the court rulings by declaring their intention to ignore them.[32] Quebec and Ottawa became locked in a protracted negotiation concerning the scope and nature of federal authority to review the environmental impact of the James Bay II-Great Whale project.[33] And British Columbia dealt with the uncertainty as to the scope of the EARP by submitting all its proposals for development projects to federal environmental officials in advance.

Confronted by similar public pressures for more effective regulation and citizen input, governments at the two levels have engaged in a certain degree of 'competitive federalism' to obtain public support by providing citizens with the policies they want.[34] A number of provinces have amended existing environmental legislation and introduced new statutes allowing for public participation.[35]

Management of Intergovernmental Conflict

While intergovernmental conflict is elevated, what is significant is the appreciable extent to which it has been managed. Provincial apprehensions have been assuaged and conflict thereby mitigated in two ways. First, federal-provincial bargaining through the forum of the CCME has served to clarify the respective roles of the two levels of government. Second, the federal government has voluntarily restricted its ability to trespass on what the provinces have come to believe is their territory.

(i) Co-operative Federalism The importance of institutional mechanisms of consultation and bargaining in lessening federal-provincial tensions is nowhere more apparent than in the role played by the Canadian Council of Ministers of the Environment in the current era of heightened sensitivities. It has served as the key forum within which to implement CEPA's endorsing of federal-provincial agreements as the means to settle intergovernmental disputes and reach amicable administrative agreements. In 1989, the CCME established a permanent and enlarged secretariat in Winnipeg to enhance its ability to formulate policy. Two committees were struck: one on Strategic Planning with a mandate to advise on strategies to deal with long-term major domestic and international issues, and a second on Environmental Operations, to manage co-operative approaches to current environmental issues. Meetings of the CCME have become more frequent of late, with biannual and even triannual meetings replacing the previous annual conferences. Federal and provincial deputy ministers of environmental departments generally meet four or five times a year; lower level officials, even more frequently.

A Statement, endorsed in principle in November, 1989[36] by federal and provincial environment ministers, defined a central role for the CCME (including the Deputy Ministers' committee and the secretariat) in fostering interjurisdictional co-operation on environmental matters. Among its functions are to contribute to harmonization of environmental legislation and implementation of programs and policies, harmonization of environmental assessment and review procedures between and among jurisdictions, a co-ordinated approach to the strategic management of interjurisdictional environmental matters, and the development of bilateral accords and issue-specific agreements to promote environmental co-operation between and among governments.

While the CCME facilitates intergovernmental consultation and co-operation on *policy* matters, the Federal-Provincial Advisory Committee (FPAC), created pursuant to the passage of CEPA in 1988, exists to advise the federal Minister of the Environment on *regulations* pursuant to federal legislation. It has a key role in advising the federal Minister as to how federal and provincial regulations can be harmonized, thereby avoiding duplication in and conflict between federal and provincial regulatory activity. Since the FPAC, like its predecessor, the Canadian Environmental Advisory Council (CEAC), is composed of individuals broadly representative of territorial and industrial interests, it has a capacity to be sensitive to regional interests.

(ii) Federal Self-Restraint   Provinces were alarmed that the passage of CEPA (1988), with its provision for the Government of Canada to regulate toxic substances from cradle to grave (section 34), portended an extended role for the government of Canada, beyond research, licensing, and regulation of the importing and interprovincial transportation of toxic substances, into the use and disposal of toxic chemicals. Ottawa responded in a number of ways to provincial concerns that it was reaching too far into provincial control over toxic waste management. It has reassured provinces it will not act unilaterally. Moreover, at the suggestion of the provinces, it allowed for equivalency agreements with the provinces. Provinces whose laws provide for standards (of emission, control, measurement, enforcement, and punishment) equivalent to those of the federal government, may be allowed to have provincial laws alone apply. At the time of writing, no equivalency agreements had been struck, as provinces press for greater flexibility in terms of enforcement standards (size of fines) and Ottawa resists on the grounds that CEPA requires the Minister of the Environment to monitor and report to Parliament.

Also on the legislative front, in 1990 Ottawa introduced the Canadian Environmental Assessment Act (CEAA) to replace its Guidelines and to alleviate the concerns of industry and provinces about the scope of federal EARPs and the costliness of duplicate provincial and federal EIAs. The CEAA makes it clear that Ottawa does not intend to use the Court rulings as a way to lean on the provinces; the legislation reduces the scope of federal EARPs from what the Courts have decreed is necessary.[37]

A final initiative is the ministerial Statement on Interjurisdiction Co-operation on Environmental Matters. Regarded as a template for relations between provincial and federal ministries of the environment, the

CCME-drafted Statement recognizes that the two levels of government have authority to regulate matters relating to the environment, and stresses the need for them to work co-operatively. Among the principles of co-operation endorsed are harmonization of environmental legislation, regulations, policies, programs, and their implementation; harmonization of environmental assessment and review procedures; and timely notification and consultation with one another in the event of interjurisdictional impacts. The Statement has been described as reflecting the current state of federal-provincial relations, and the propensity of governments at both levels to seek pragmatic solutions to conflicts, rather than pursue legal clarifications.

ACTIVIST GOVERNMENTS AND POLICY OUTCOMES

The current context thus includes a new measure of competitive federalism co-existing with the traditional co-operative federalism. Whether this two-faceted federalism will prove advantageous or problematic is not immediately clear. It is possible to argue, as Albert Breton does, that competitive federalism does raise the possibility of greater public accountability and democratic policy-making than co-operative federalism which, as Donald Smiley notes, is characteristically secret and preoccupied with the narrow interests of bureaucratic and political officials.[38] One virtue of competitive federalism, then, particularly when it is accompanied by an interested and informed public, is that politicians at the two levels, competing with one another, will have incentives to respond to a broader range of interests than they have in the past.

There are some indications that competitive federalism is already having these effects. Environmental groups, unsuccessful in pursuing their goals at one level, have sought to exploit the division of jurisdiction over the environment by trying to place pressure on the other level of government to act on their behalf.[39] More importantly, simple competition to occupy policy space appears to be resulting in more accountable and democratic environmental policies; the Quebec Minister of the Environment, for example, cited the federal CEAA 'and its implications for James Bay II' as 'forcing the provincial government to strengthen its own review process for fear of inviting federal interference'.[40]

The potential for competitive federalism to broaden the range of interests taken into account by governments in formulating environmental policies would seem to rest upon one contingency in particular: the extent to which the shift of environmental issues from the margins to the centre of government decision-making entails substantive and not merely symbolic policy changes. Recent federal-provincial skirmishes, as well as intra-governmental conflicts, have demonstrated that environment ministers and ministries in both provincial and national cabinets continue to occupy a rung on the ladder below that of their colleagues in resource and central line agencies. Doern argues that the latter have been successful in reducing the scope of federal environmental policy at the national level.[41] At the provincial level, the higher priority of economic development ensures that ministers responsible for resource ministries are able to constrain a shift to environmental management of resources.[42]

The possibility that competitive and activist governments at both levels will ensure responsiveness to a wider array of interests in environmental matters is likely also to be constrained by the continuing high priority placed on co-operative federalism as the appropriate process by which to formulate environmental policy. This can be observed by examining the recent experience of Environment Canada in amending the Pulp and Paper Effluent Regulations. Ottawa sought these amendments for a number of reasons,[43] one of which was to give federal officials more direct access to enforcement procedures. Pursuant to the amendments, Environment Canada will issue separate pollution control permits, accompanying the provincial permit. (Federal-provincial agreements allowed the 1971 pollution control requirements to be incorporated into provincially-issued permits.) The pulp and paper industry prefers a single set of regulations rather than distinct federal and provincial regulations. However, while invited to comment on the initial federal proposals (of August 1989), the industry was subsequently largely excluded from the process of harmonizing federal and provincial regulations. That negotiation took place under the rubric of the CCME and an intergovernmental committee. Pulp and paper industry representatives and environmental group spokesmen were both later invited to comment on the regulatory changes agreed upon by federal and provincial officials. This example may suggest that the 'concertation' that existed between industry and government for most of the past two decades may be giving way to 'contested concertation' as industry groups face an interested and attentive public to which governments need to appear to be responsive.[44] But whether this will make for more effective enforcement remains to be seen. Bonsor doubts that it will; he describes the proposed new pulp and paper effluent regulations as promising 'only a more refined version of the 1971 regulations', regulations which have not been enforced.[45]

Notwithstanding Bonsor's pessimism, it can be argued that the existence of eleven ministries of the environment can raise the level of pollution standards locally and nationally. To the extent that their linkages to other provinces give poorer provinces, such as Nova Scotia and New Brunswick, access to information about new pollution-control technologies, they are better able to offset the bargaining strength of dominant local industries. Provincial standards may thus be raised. Likewise, pressure from a province with a rather restrictive regulatory regime, like Ontario, will cause national standards to rise, rather than reducing them to the lowest common denominator.

If the advantages of competitive federalism are as yet unclear—not least, because one does not know how much of the competition is merely posturing and rhetoric — a situation of governments at both levels actively exploiting their concurrent jurisdiction may have real costs. It raises the spectre of unilateral environmental policy-making, and duplicate/multiple unco-ordinated policies that can work at cross-purposes. Avoiding such legislative jungles puts a premium on co-operation between the two levels of government to harmonize differing standards. This undoubtedly lengthens decision-making and thereby impedes speedy action to redress environmental problems. Policy innovation, as well, is more likely to be frustrated when the agreement of eleven governments must be obtained than when authority is centralized in one government.

Effective redress of environmental problems makes it imperative that the deleterious consequences of concurrent jurisdiction be avoided. Policy co-ordination and harmonization are dictated by the fact that there are clearly local, interprovincial, and international aspects to environmental issues. Moreover, the fact that environmental problems differ significantly from region to region, and within regions from one territorial locality to another, suggests the need for a significant measure of decentralized decision-making. Here, Canada's approach of bilateral, asymmetrical federalism,[46] which has allowed federal and provincial governments to assume different responsibilities across the country, may be ideal for accommodating the diversity across regions in terms of problems and enforcement standards. The possibility of environmental policy asymmetry, in the presence of national standards, is enhanced by the fact that there exist respected forums for federal-provincial co-operation, forums buttressed by statutory and political commitments for harmonization. This makes it likely that national and provincial environmental policies, facing analogous domestic and international imperatives, will move in the same direction, albeit at different speeds, depending upon local economic and political constraints and opportunities. In this sense, federalism, while having contributed to the problem of devising coherent and meaningful environmental policies, can also be instrumental in finding appropriate policy solutions.

FOR FURTHER READING

Alastair R. Lucas, 'The New Environmental Law', in Ronald L. Watts and Douglas M. Brown, eds, *Canada: The State of the Federation 1989* (Kingston: Institute of Intergovernmental Relations, Queen's University, 1989): 167-92.

L.J. Lundqvist, *Environmental Policies in Canada, Sweden, and the United States* (Beverly Hills: Sage, 1974).

J. Owen Saunders, ed., *Managing Natural Resources in a Federal State* (Toronto: Carswell, 1986).

Kernaghan Webb, *Pollution Control in Canada: The Regulatory Approach in the 1980s* (Ottawa: Law Reform Commission, 1988).

CHAPTER 4

Pressures From Inside

Advisory Groups and the Environmental Policy Community*

GREGOR FILYK AND RAY CÔTÉ

Advisory groups are formed on a permanent or *ad hoc* basis to offer guidance on a range of societal issues and activities, including policy-making. The advisory bodies relevant to this study share several common features. All exist to serve the federal government. They are institutionalized organizations, funded by and reporting to the government. They show organizational continuity and stable membership for varying periods of time depending on their mandates; they have knowledge of, and access to, relevant members of the environmental policy community; and they hold distinct mandates, objectives, and operating rules. These features are all characteristics of institutionalized groups as outlined by Pross.[1] Their primary role is to advise; they have restricted, if any, administrative powers. Members of some committees are appointed from outside the government, and they are therefore regarded as providing opinions independent of the political or bureaucratic arena. Other committees consist of public servants or politicians, concerned with legislative, jurisdictional, and interdepartmental aspects of policy. Terms of reference for these advisory bodies vary widely, and their mandates range from partial to comprehensive.

The concept of the policy community has been developed to describe the environment in which public policy decisions are made. Pross defines the policy community as:

> [T]hat part of a political system that — by virtue of its functional responsibilities, its vested interests, and its specialized knowledge — acquires a dominant voice in determining government decisions in a specific field of public activity, and is generally permitted by society at large and the public authorities in particular to determine public policy in that field. It is populated by government agencies, pressure groups, media people, and individuals, including academics, who have an interest in a particular policy field and attempt to influence it. Most policy communities consist of two segments: the sub-government and the attentive public.[2]

To gain influence, a group must target access to appropriate elements of the policy community: the executive, Parliament, and the lead agency, as well as the sub-government and the attentive public. Institutionalized advisory bodies potentially have access to all of these groups. The government agencies that have been delegated authoritative roles in particular policy-making areas wield substantial influence. In the case of federal environmental policy-making, the lead agency is Environment Canada. The sub-government consists of agencies that make routine environmental policy decisions. Many departments and bureaus can be considered part of the sub-government, because their activities have environmental impacts. Central agencies also play a powerful sub-governmental role. These bodies include the Prime Minister's Office (PMO), Privy Council Office (PCO), and Treasury Board. The attentive public comprises any individuals or groups, including other agencies, which are interested in, and try to influence, the policy area, but are not part of the routine decision-making process. Environmental non-governmental organizations (NGOs) fall into this category.

Advisory groups have proliferated in recent decades. The rise of environmentalism in the past twenty years has produced various advisory groups to counsel federal environmental officials. These groups are formed by government because they offer advantages to the policy-making process. By bringing together experts from a wide range of backgrounds and regions, the knowledge represented by the group can serve to address many potentially conflicting objectives, in an independent forum, at relatively small expense. Table 4.1 (p. 62) outlines the main objectives for creating advisory groups.[3]

Several key concepts apply to both pressure groups and advisory groups. The *legitimacy* of an organization is demonstrated by the degree to which it represents, and is supported by, the interest community. Since members are appointed to advisory groups by decision-makers, they cannot claim to have a mandate from the interest community. Instead, any legitimacy of policy advice is determined by the source and quality of that advice. The *constituency* of a group is the number and kinds of people that it represents. Groups can be categorized by interest (e.g., the Canadian Wildlife Federation), by discipline (e.g., the Canadian Society of Environmental Biologists), by region (e.g., the Canadian Arctic Resources Committee), or by sector (e.g., the Canadian Chemical Producers Association). *Collective action* is the ability of a group to use its resources in an organized and concentrated fashion. These resources include knowledge (both substantive and process) and wealth. Since all the institutionalized environmental advisory groups appropriate to this study have their funding, staff, and office space provided by the federal government, they are at least partially dependent on government. However, for those groups whose members come from outside government, the information and

TABLE 4.1   OBJECTIVES FOR ADVISORY GROUP CREATION

Decision-Making Objectives

• Encourage co-ordination
• Find common ground between competing interests; conflict resolution
• Critique existing policy
• Provide new ideas
• Provide independent and alternative opinions
• Perform special studies

Citizen Participation Objectives

• Education of the public and policy interpretation
• Public participation
• Representation of policy interests
• Diffusion of responsibility
• Democratization of the bureaucracy
• Policy legitimization

Political Objectives

• Serve to test public reaction to policies
• Provide a forum for expression of public opinion
• Force controversial issues into an objective arena
• Placate opposition by involving potential expert critics in the decision process
• Provide publicity and support for programs
• Be used for persuasion
• Provide a symbolic response to problems
• Give a false or misleading impression of addressing problems; known as 'window-dressing'
• Delay action
• Serve as patronage instruments

views they provide are independent, and the effective operation of these groups is not tampered with by government. Finally, *access* is the ability of advisers to communicate directly with decision-makers. Access is the principal advantage that advisory groups have over interest groups in influencing policy formation.

The complex and intangible character of advice makes tracing its influence on policy-making difficult. Cause and effect are hard to determine because of the uncertainty of indirect forces, the collaborative efforts often involved, the multiple origins of ideas, time-lags in the process, and impacts that are multidirectional and not contained immediately after the policy is implemented.[4] Several researchers on advisory groups have found the influence of consultative bodies to be modest.[5] However, Guy Steed, a member of the Secretariat of the Science Council of Canada, warns that confining the definition of influence to concrete results underestimates the actual impact of advice:

> The process of policy research is often as important as the product. . . . Observers who focus primarily upon the substantive impact of policy research on legislation miss its much broader impact and uses elsewhere, particularly within the policy-making process, in discretionary decision-making by public servants, in helping to set the policy agenda, in influencing attitudes and behaviour, and in sharpening debate on major science and technology issues.[6]

INSTITUTIONAL ADVISORY GROUPS IN THE CANADIAN ENVIRONMENTAL POLICY COMMUNITY

The main advisory bodies in the federal environmental domain are outlined below, in approximate descending order of hierarchical position. These groups operate at different points and levels in the environmental policy process. They are therefore in unique positions to influence government policy.

1. *The Standing Committee on Environment* — a committee of the House of Commons.

2. *Cabinet Committee on the Environment* — a body formed to discuss and debate environmental issues at the level of Cabinet.

3. *National Round Table on Environment and Economy* — a forum created for discussions between senior government decision-makers, industry, academics, and non-governmental groups on sustainable development.

4. *Canadian Environmental Advisory Council (CEAC)* — an independent advisory group to the Minister of the Environment.

5. *Environmental Impact Assessment Panels* — these committees can be formed to study the environmental impacts of federally sponsored, funded, or administered projects through the Federal Environmental Assessment and Review Office (FEARO). A panel makes its recommendations to the Minister of the Environment.

6. *Canadian Environmental Assessment Research Council (CEARC)* — an advisory group to the chairperson of FEARO on environmental assessment research and implementation.

7. *Environmental Choice Panel* — a group advising the Minister of the Environment on environmentally acceptable consumer and industrial products.

8. *Canadian Council of Ministers of the Environment (CCME)* — an inter-jurisdictional body of federal and provincial Ministers of Environment, formed to co-ordinate policies of the two levels of government.

9. Ad hoc *Boards of Inquiry* — bodies formed at the Parliamentary or departmental levels, pursuant to some legislative authority, to perform a specific study (e.g., Federal Inquiry on Water Policy).

10. *Interdepartmental Committees* — groups operating at the senior bureaucratic level, dealing with specific issues. Currently there exist, for example, Interdepartmental Committees on Water, Toxic Substances, and Oceans.

11. *Sectoral / Special Advisors* — individual advisors to senior management and Services within Environment Canada, such as the Office of the Science Advisor.

12. *Other Institutional Advisory Groups* — There are advisory groups which report to other Ministers, yet occasionally deal with environmental affairs. The *Economic Council of Canada (ECC)*, the *Science Council of Canada (SCC)*, and the *Law Reform Commission of Canada (LRCC)* are independent organizations, created by Parliament to advise on their respective subjects. Each of the organizations has addressed aspects of the resolution of environmental problems.

Table 4.2 illustrates several organizational and structural characteristics of these groups. The federal advisory system is also mirrored at the provincial level. In Nova Scotia, for example, a wide range of advisory groups exist to counsel the Minister on new policies and legislation, and their implementation. These groups include the Environmental Control Council, the Provincial Round Table on Environment and Economy, the Pest Control Products Advisory Committee, and the Environmental Trust Fund Committee, all of which are more or less permanent. In addition, there are *ad hoc* bodies such as Environmental Assessment Panels, the Minister's Task Force on Hazardous Waste Management, the Minister's Task Force on Clean Air, and the Minister's Task Force on Clean Water. The Minister himself receives further policy advice from the CCME, of which he was the Chairperson in 1990–91.

In assessing the influence of advisory groups on federal environmental policy, this chapter examines two particular groups: the Canadian Environmental Advisory Council (CEAC), and the Inquiry on Federal Water Policy (the Pearse Inquiry). Both groups are, or were, composed primarily of experts, and all members are appointed by the Minister of the Environment. The groups report to the Minister, who accepts the advice at his or her discretion. CEAC was formed in 1972, shortly after the creation of the Department of Environment. It is a permanent body, offering

TABLE 4.2   CLASSIFICATION OF INSTITUTIONAL ENVIRONMENTAL ADIVSORY GROUPS IN CANADA

Advisory Group	Duration	Type	Confidentiality	Authority	Membership	Selection	Advice
Standing Committee on Environment	Permanent	General	public	House of Commons	Members of Parliament	Appointed	Optional
Cabinet Committee on Environment	Permanent	General	Private	Prime Minister	Cabinet Ministers	Appointed	Optional
National Round Table on Environment and Economy	Ad hoc	General	Public	Prime Minister	Government, Lay Industry, Experts	Appointed	Optional
Canadian Environmental Advisory Council	Permanent	General	Private / Public	Min. of Environment	Experts	Appointed	Optional
Environmental Assessment Panels	Ad hoc	Specific Task	Public	Min. of Environment	Experts	Appointed	Optional
Canadian Environmental Assessment Research Council	Permanent	Research	Public	Min. of Environment	Experts	Appointed	Optional
Environmental Choice Panel	Permanent	Specific Task	Public	Min. of Environment	Experts, Lay	Appointed	Optional
Canadian Council of Ministers of the Environment	Permanent	Inter-governmental	Private / Public	Not Applicable	Ministers of Environment	By Position	Optional
Ad hoc Boards of Inquiry	Ad hoc	Various	Public	Various	Experts	Appointed	Optional
Interdepartmental Committees	Ad hoc or Permanent	Inter-departmental	Private	Lead Agency	Experts, Civil Servants	Appointed	Optional
Sectoral / Special Advisors	Permanent	General	Private	Lead Agency	Experts	Appointed	Optional
Economic Council of Canada	Permanent	General	Public	Prime Minister	Experts	Appointed	Optional
Science Council of Canada	Permanent	General	Public	Minister of Industry, Science and Technology	Experts	Appointed	Optional
Law Reform Committee of Canada	Permanent	General	Public	Minister of Justice	Experts	Appointed	Optional

general advice on environmental matters. By contrast, the Pearse Inquiry existed for eighteen months, from 1984 to 1985, as an *ad hoc* group. It was charged with the specific task of investigating water policy.

THE CANADIAN ENVIRONMENTAL ADVISORY COUNCIL

The Canadian Environmental Advisory Council provides confidential advice directly to the Minister of the Environment. The main objective of the Council is to provide the Minister with an alternative, but considered, source of advice to Environment Canada and to public interest groups. Its mandate is to provide advice to the Minister as requested, to inform the Minister of public concerns and impending issues and problems, to promote public concern on environmental matters, to give advice on ways of improving the effectiveness of departmental activities, and to provide advice to officials of the Department. Eight to twelve members are usually appointed to Council (although there is provision for up to sixteen members) for three- to four-year terms. They are chosen to provide a range of expertise, backgrounds, and geographic representation. The sixty members appointed over nineteen years have counselled twelve Ministers of Environment. Council meetings are held about every second month. The Chairperson serves part-time, but the position demands regular attention to Council business. Routine administration is handled by the Executive Secretary (now called Executive Director), who heads the Secretariat of four persons. As membership of Council includes people from across the country, the Executive Director is often the only representative of Council permanently based in the Ottawa/Hull region. Until the autumn of 1990, the Secretariat was located in the Environment Canada headquarters in Hull, Quebec. Council is now located separately from the Department, in commercial office space in Ottawa. Funding is provided by Environment Canada, from the Department budget administered by the Deputy Minister. In 1990/91 the Council operated on a budget of $550,000.

The Council's main purpose is to provide private advice to the Minister. Letters of correspondence between the Council and the Minister are the most frequent means of communicating advice. Personal meetings between the Minister and the Chairperson, or with the full Council, are a second method of communication. The Council also publishes occasional reports. These are released publicly after consultation with the Minister, and may also play a role in influencing the development of government policy.

There are many factors which influence the effectiveness of advice. These factors include organizational characteristics and relationships with different groups, as well as the designated role of the advisory group in the policy process. Some characteristics, such as group decision-making dynamics, are generally within the control of the group itself. Other factors, such as resources provided by the department, involve agencies and forces commonly outside of the group's control. These factors, individually and collectively, play an important role in determining the group's influence on the policy-making process. The group may be in a position to plan for different eventualities, but in some circumstances it may simply be forced to react.

Organizational Characteristics

CEAC has shown strong organizational effectiveness. While the quality of advice *per se* is not an issue in this chapter, the advice can be inferred to be of a generally high calibre. Many of Canada's leading environmental experts have served on the Council, as have other well-qualified and accomplished individuals. The advice generated tends to reflect the make-up of the group, described by one former member as the 'grey-haired' environmental set. In other words, Council members tend to be appointed from the élite of well-established professionals. As a result, the Council is inclined to favour balanced and practical approaches, rather than radical solutions to environmental problems. Nevertheless, according to respondents, CEAC provides progressive and reform-minded advice, valuing consultation, interdisciplinary thinking, and scientific evidence.

The two principal positions on Council are Chairperson and Executive Secretary. The five chairpersons and six secretaries who have served CEAC are all respected by their contemporaries. The Chairperson plays an extremely important role in the success of the group. The Chair leads the group during meetings, serves as the spokesperson for Council, delivers advice to the Minister, and steers the direction and demeanour of the group as a whole. The qualities which the Chairperson must possess are an interest and knowledge of the environment, combined with an appreciation of government process and decision-making. The individual must be a good communicator, and understand the pressures and circumstances operating on the Minister.

The Executive Secretary plays a facilitating role, and is the main source of continuity for the group. Aside from ongoing administrative matters, the Secretary can greatly enhance the effectiveness of the group by building a communications network at various levels of the Department, and with other members of the policy community. Presence within the departmental organization permits the Secretary to relay current bureaucratic information and 'gossip' to the members, allowing the group to follow the informal, but real, status of policy. Recalling Steed's assertion that advice is often found in subtle changes in behaviour and attitude, and in discretionary decisions along the policy process, the Secretary can assist the Council through carefully targeted promotion of the group's opinions.

Group dynamics are a consideration in any type of organization. Interviews with former and current members indicated that discussions are considered to be of high quality, with tolerance for the diverse opinions represented. The heterogeneity of backgrounds leads to a presentation of many sides of an issue. Final decision-making is made through consensus, which is considered an effective means of achieving high quality, 'common-sense' advice to the Minister.

Relationships

Advisory groups exist to serve decision-makers. In the final analysis, then, the relationship developed between the group and the decision-makers whom they advise is the essential determinant of influence. The dominant factors which ultimately dictate the relationship with decision-makers, and the influence wielded by CEAC, are access, confidentiality, and constituency.

Access allows CEAC the opportunity to influence policy. Council has access to one of the most important decision-makers in the environmental policy community, the Minister of the Environment. Council also has access to Department officials, and to confidential material unavailable to other external groups, such as documents, reports, draft proposals, memoranda, and minutes of meetings. The close association with the Department allows the Council an intimate knowledge of the power structure within the Department, of details on Department process and operations, and on ways of influencing policy. Advice can therefore address existing environmental problems with an appreciation for the *realpolitik* of environmental administration.

Confidentiality is a trade-off to the privilege of access. In order to maintain access and offer advice, Council must accept the confidential nature of its role and forgo many relationships with the broader environmental community. Thus CEAC must eschew publicity and work within the system as defined by the government. Public communication is normally viewed as an important instrument for an advisory group. Since Council has no power to implement its advice, the only potential means of coercing the government to action is the threat of embarrassment by public disclosure. Without this threat, the Council depends completely on the goodwill and motivation of others when offering advice.

The constituency of a group is the body of people it represents. A group with a large constituency will have a potentially greater opportunity to influence political decision-makers, because it speaks for a large number of affected individuals or interests. CEAC members are appointed, not elected, from the environmental élite. They therefore have no mandate from the wider policy community. Information is not widely circulated, and few participate in the advisory process. CEAC information and advice flows in a relatively closed feedback loop: members, the Minister, and top Department officials. The Council relies primarily on its members

and contract researchers for information. Aside from occasional participation in workshops, there is little input from the sub-government or
attentive public in deliberations. The public at large never contributes to
Council activities. Finally, there are growing numbers of environmental
groups, at the institutional and grass-roots levels, which claim to represent
various interests. Therefore advice is available to decision-makers from
other sources.

Funding for the group comes from Department budget allocations,
for the Secretariat staff, office space, and administration expenses. The
budget for CEAC has remained virtually static over the years. The first
annual budget in 1972/73 was $175,000. The 1986/87 budget was $206,300,
about eighteen per cent more than the initial funding allotment. Over
the first fifteen-year period the average provision was $182,547. Recent
budgets have improved somewhat to $300,000, $300,300, and $550,000 in
the last three years. Thus, despite current improvements, the Council has
experienced declining funds relative to inflation. The decreased resources
to carry out the mandate of the Council results in a lack of research
staff, relatively low stipends for members, forgone project opportunities,
concentration of effort on a limited number of subjects (often those of
immediate interest to the Minister), and a lack of financial stability for
future planning. It is the Deputy Minister of the Environment, not the
Minister, who controls the departmental budget. Historically, Council has
not fared well in the competition for scarce resources in a Department
that traditionally has not received government funding priority.

Independence is another factor associated with CEAC's relationship
to the Department. Independence is best separated into two components.
On the one hand, Council is dependent on the Department for its budget,
with the consequences outlined above. The relationship obviously makes
the group's activities vulnerable. On the other hand, the vast majority of
members state that Council is independent of the government when
giving advice. Indeed, the membership consists of academics, consultants,
environmental advocates, and others who would not tolerate interference
in Council business. This expert autonomy and integrity is critical to an
advisory body, lending it the legitimacy that as an appointed body it
otherwise lacks. In effect, Council operates independently within a
restricted range of areas.

The influence of Council hinges on the relationship with the Minister
of the Environment. This relationship is not balanced. The Minister
has legal and authoritative control of Council. Moreover, the Minister
effectively has control of most other aspects of Council: the individuals
selected for membership, its size, the schedule of meetings with the
Chairperson or full Council, the direction of research, involvement in
policy, and publication of reports. The Minister controls the fate of advice

by forwarding it to Departmental officials for comment, passing it to Cabinet colleagues for their consideration, or using it in personal decision-making. The Minister is under no obligation to accept advice, nor even to meet with Council. Finally, the Minister can dissolve Council at any time. Therefore, having direct ties to the Minister on the organizational chart does not guarantee access in reality. The onus is on Council and its representatives, the Chairperson and Secretary, to gain access to the Minister. It is crucial for Council to establish a good working relationship with the Minister in order to influence policy.

This subordinate relationship means that each change of Minister affects the fortunes of the Council. Judging by respondents' comments, few Ministers have been inclined to pay special attention to CEAC. This may not be surprising when one considers the circumstances facing the relationship of the Minister and Council.

First, Ministers commonly enter their portfolio without substantive knowledge of the subject matter under their jurisdiction. Even those acquainted with the environment must learn about the workings of the Department, jurisdictional limitations, legislation, and policies. CEAC will be a minor element of a large organization which the Minister must come to understand. Second, Ministers have many pressures on their time: Departmental decisions, for example, Parliamentary schedules, meetings, speeches, constituent concerns, representation of the Department and government, and party obligations. Third, Ministers receive advice from many sources. The Deputy Minister and Senior Management of the Department are the main sources of advice on the environment. The Minister cannot afford to rely too heavily on a small group of outside advisors, and effectively ignore the collective effort of the thousands of civil servants working in the Department. This would show a lack of faith in those employed to protect and enhance the environment. At the same time, the Minister is counselled by his political staff and Cabinet colleagues. Environmental pressure groups, the media, and the public at large also comment on the Minister's initiatives and performance.

A fourth factor is that CEAC has no power to coerce the Minister into action. Political decision-making must consider the effect of decisions on a variety of interests. In general, a Minister will give more credence to a group representing a public voice than to one providing expert opinion. As demonstrated above, Council does not have a large constituency. Ignoring Council does not have the same negative consequences for the Minister as ignoring or contradicting the Department, pressure groups, or public opinion.

Fifth, each Minister is a unique personality. Some personalities are open to accepting advice from a variety of sources, some value expertise, while others are uninterested in or suspicious of advisory groups. This is an important yet completely unpredictable variable. The Council can offer sound authoritative advice; the Secretary and Chairperson can work to facilitate the acceptance of that advice in a number of ways; but, if the Minister is unwilling to entertain advice, Council has virtually no recourse to other channels.

Sixth, Council cannot transfer the goodwill built up between itself and a Minister to the next Minister. (Of course, this can be advantageous in those cases where relations with the Minister were poor, and a new Minister offers the opportunity for a fresh start.) The historically rapid turnover of Ministers adds a further complication. Accepting advice depends on confidence and trust, built up by successful relations over time. A frequent change of Ministers does not permit adequate time for a productive advisor/decision-maker relationship to grow. Thus, every year and a half to two years (the Minister of the Environment portfolio has changed twelve times in nineteen years), the Council must start again in its relationship to a new Minister.

Complicating all of this is the fact that environmental policy is not the exclusive mandate and jurisdiction of Environment Canada. The programs and activities of most other federal agencies affect the environment, while jurisdiction over a range of matters is shared with provinces, who can develop environmental policies independent of the federal government. An advisory group to an historically weak Ministry, in terms of Cabinet hierarchy, cannot easily exert a great deal of influence on government policy because the recipient of advice is itself not in a strong position to implement policy.

The Council can, and does, advise the Departmental Senior Management, particularly the Deputy Minister. Indeed, there are several advantages to advising the bureaucracy instead of the Minister. The Department and Council share similar objectives, i.e., the creation of positive environmental policy. Individual Department staff evaluating substantive policy come from the same scientific/environmental background as many Council members. These officials will likely respect the expertise represented on Council. Senior officials, such as the Deputy Minister, can profit from the advice of an independent group. Policy initiatives arise from many sources, but many, if not most, originate in the bureaucracy. Policy development typically takes years of departmental discussion before implementation. The bureaucracy is more stable than the political level, where as we have seen Ministerial turnover is a frequent occurrence.

Regardless of the fact that advice is given to the Minister of the Environment, its ultimate fate is often determined by the Department and other elements of the sub-government. Confidential advice to the Minister is generally discussed with the Department. Council does provide alternative advice to that of the Department, though a Minister will not usually act unilaterally without conferring with Department officials and political advisors. Therefore, advice is usually evaluated and assimilated by the bureaucracy. The same forces that limit the influence of Council on the Minister also limit its impact on the Deputy Minister: the lack of reward or punishment for heeding Council's advice, when other information sources are available.

The Impact of CEAC

While factors outside its control limit the use of Council, the latter has played a valuable role at times. It is by providing alternative advice to the Minister, contributing to the policy debate, criticizing policy throughout the process, serving to gauge public reaction, and occasionally introducing new initiatives into the Department, that the Council has its greatest impact on the process of policy-making.

Despite its modest use by the Minister, CEAC has made several noteworthy and substantive contributions over the years. Council acted to facilitate discussion between the government and environmental interest groups in the 1970s, during a period when there was little interaction between the two solitudes. Eventually, the Canadian Environmental Network was formed to orchestrate the various environmental advocacy groups. CEAC is given credit for assisting in the creation of the Network. Council has organized workshops, prepared discussion papers, and contributed important recommendations in several areas. These include policy reform (e.g., the Environmental Assessment and Review Process), legislation (e.g., the Canadian Environmental Protection Act), Departmental positioning on issues (e.g., PCB destruction), and informative publications (e.g., State of Environment Reporting).

The influence of Council at any one time defies prediction, because of the Minister's dominant position and discretionary capacity to accept recommendations. Under one Minister the Council was threatened with disbandment. The following Minister consulted regularly with the Council, and involved the group in substantive policy discussions beyond its normally passive advisory role. In general, however, Ministers have made limited use of Council advice. CEAC is simply one input amongst many in the policy field. With the advent of Round Tables and the various stakeholder processes, its influence may be further diluted. Given the external factors operating on Council, it should not be surprising that the group appears to have had only a modest impact on federal environmental policy.

THE INQUIRY ON FEDERAL WATER POLICY

The genesis for an inquiry on water policy came from within the lead agency itself, the Inland Waters Directorate of Environment Canada. According to several Departmental officials the federal government policy *vis-à-vis* water quality, quantity, and management prior to the Inquiry was inadequate. Problems were growing and new issues were rising, such as acid rain and water export. While a department would normally conduct its own policy review, it was felt that a public inquiry would be more useful. Such a process would provide an external perspective, and avoid the perceived bias often associated with an in-house study.

Once the idea for a public inquiry was accepted in the Department, the then Minister of the Environment, John Roberts, sought to establish a Royal Commission under the Inquiries Act. The government refused his request. Despite the initial setback, and following a great deal of discussion and effort, the formation of a committee to study federal water policy was announced on 26 January 1984 by the succeeding Minister of the Environment, Charles Caccia. The original title for the three-member group was the Advisory Committee on Federal Water Strategies. The authority for the appointment was the 1970 Canada Water Act, section 26. This section allows the Minister of the Environment to create advisory committees to advise and assist him in carrying out the Act. This was the first committee established under the section. At the request of the members of the Inquiry, its name was later changed to the Inquiry on Federal Water Policy.

The *ad hoc* committee was asked to produce a final report eighteen months after initiation, and was provided with a budget of $1.5 million. The mandate of the group was to report and advise on emerging water issues and specific strategies to address these issues, identify existing fresh water supplies and future needs, assess the need for scientific expertise in water management, and perform the study in consultation with government and non-government agencies, industry, the academic community, and the public. The three members of the Inquiry were Chairperson Dr Peter H. Pearse, James W. MacLaren, and Françoise Bertrand. Geographic representation was considered; the members came from British Columbia, Ontario, and Quebec respectively. Experience is important for credibility, effective running of the process, and production of a report of quality. Pearse and MacLaren were well known in their respective fields, resource economics and hydrological engineering. Bertrand's field of expertise was in administration, communications, and education. The Secretariat was located in an Ottawa office, physically separate from Environment Canada. The Department provided the resources for the Secretariat, including the budget, Executive and Research Directors, and staff.

The Process

While appearing relatively simple, providing advice on water policy is a complex task. First, numerous federal departments have authority on water issues. A committee advising only Environment Canada would therefore be of limited utility. Prior to the Inquiry, discussions were held with other departments by Departmental officials, and during the Inquiry by the members themselves. The objective was to gain the co-operation of Ministers and senior officials with jurisdictions over water, to increase the likelihood of their accepting eventual recommendations. The Inquiry members also felt that they had to convince some departments that the process was not controlled by Environment Canada. In general, the other departments concerned with water were supportive of the Inquiry initiative, according to a Cabinet paper on the issue. In addition, several departments later made formal presentations to the Inquiry, and were involved with the post-Inquiry task force reviewing the recommendations.

The second complexity was the jurisdictional overlap with the provinces, who actually control most of Canada's water resources below the sixtieth parallel. The commission members spent much of the first few months explaining the objectives of the Inquiry to the provinces. The provinces were concerned with federal infringement on areas of their responsibility, and with possible expansion of federal control. Provincial support for the Inquiry was mixed. The less supportive provinces were those already having conflicts with the federal government over resource and other issues. Alberta had reservations about the National Energy Board; Newfoundland was fighting for offshore oil rights; the government of Quebec was represented by the Parti Québécois at the time, and was not generally interested in co-operating in federal initiatives. Nonetheless, most of the provincial opposition was erased by the start of the Inquiry. Those familiar with the committee's history give much of the credit for this development to Dr Pearse. He reassured the provinces that provincial ownership and primary management responsibility of water resources was recognized by the Inquiry.

The Inquiry relied on two sources to generate information: research papers and public hearings. Research papers were commissioned to stimulate debate, and to gather detailed and objective information on specific topics. The public hearings were held in seventeen cities across Canada, in all provinces and territories. Two hundred submissions were made before the committee, and one hundred supplementary documents were received. The public hearings did not necessarily develop many new ideas, but were important in reinforcing recommendations, and giving them support, according to one Inquiry member.

Many different interests made representations at the hearings stage. Several major federal departments with partial jurisdiction over water presented briefs to the Inquiry. These departments included Agriculture Canada; the Department of Energy, Mines and Resources; External Affairs; Health and Welfare; Transport Canada; the Canada Mortgage and Housing Corporation; and Environment Canada itself. Two federal departments were represented by their Ministers: John Fraser (a former

Minister of the Environment) for Fisheries and Oceans, and David Crombie for Indian and Northern Affairs. Five provinces and one territory made presentations through appropriate Ministries: New Brunswick, Manitoba, Nova Scotia, Ontario, Prince Edward Island, and the Northwest Territories. The non-governmental organizations (NGOs) represented a broad spectrum of interests and regions. Amongst the NGOs were fish and game groups, general and specific environmental groups, regional watershed protection organizations, concerned citizens groups, and conservation councils. The professional associations were likewise varied. They included water technicians and professionals, resource interests such as forestry, agriculture, and electricity, engineers and biologists, trade unions, and industry associations. The only political parties making submissions were the Green Party and the Communist Party of Canada.

The position of Minister of the Environment changed several times during the Inquiry. John Roberts was the Minister when the idea for a study on water policy was first discussed. The formal establishment of the Inquiry was announced under Charles Caccia. In 1984 the Liberal government was defeated and Suzanne Blais-Grenier became the Minister of the Environment in the Progressive Conservative government. By the time the final report was released, Tom McMillan held the ministerial portfolio. Two other Ministers, Lucien Bouchard and Robert de Cotret, have since inherited the legacy of the report.

The provinces were asked by McMillan to provide comments on the final report. The provincial responses were generally supportive. The provinces recognized the need for co-operative approaches between the provincial and federal jurisdictions. They stressed the need for provincial consultation in any federal initiatives. Flexible regional approaches were generally preferred over a uniform national program. At the federal government level, an Interdepartmental Water Policy Task Force was created, which included the main water departments. They had two tasks, one to advise the government on the recommendations of the report, and a second to actually develop a federal water policy for consideration by the government. The study committee divided the review into twenty-five issues. Each department took the lead on issues of particular importance to itself.

The review took twenty-six months. The result was a package of twenty-five statements on water policy, contained in a document entitled 'Federal Water Policy', released in 1987. The contents apply across all agencies and departments of the federal government. A proposal to further develop water policy into comprehensive water legislation, as suggested by Pearse, was approved by Cabinet. A committee was created within Environment Canada, known as the Water Legislation Group; in contrast to the development of the water policy, other departments were not involved. The proposed legislation, the Canada Water Preservation Act, focused on regulation of water exports, which at the time had become a controversial subject in connection with the Free Trade debate. It was tabled before the House of Commons, but died on the Order Papers as Parliament was prorogued for the 1988 general election. Since that time work has continued towards development of legislation in the Department, but a Bill has yet to be reintroduced.

Assessment

The Inquiry was created by a government department to address present and anticipated problems in water policy because there was an acknowledged policy vacuum at the federal level. Institutional arrangements made a co-ordinated approach difficult. Much authority for water policy lies under provincial control, but there were areas of uncertainty about jurisdictional roles. Complex questions were evolving, without a clear means towards resolution. Unlike the United States, a major Canadian national study on water had never been carried out.

As a policy-making instrument, the inquiry process offered several advantages to Environment Canada. First, water policy has little political and public profile. It is not normally controversial, and is generally taken for granted. The group most interested in policy change, the Inland Waters Directorate of Environment Canada, had to convince others that change was necessary. A public inquiry could stimulate interest in the issue of water policy, a first step towards policy reform. The fact that so many disparate agencies and groups participated in the Inquiry shows that concern over water was indeed widespread. Second, it was thought the effort could act as a catalyst, building the consensus and momentum needed for policy reform. The Inquiry focused attention for a period of time on a specific set of issues, and allowed the government an opportunity to escape from the bureaucratic inertia and institutional resistance which make policy initiatives difficult to implement. Third, federal water policy change can only occur if agreement is reached between many different departments. All interests must have confidence in the process, and be given the opportunity to contribute ideas. A credible, independent panel could reassure other parties that the study would be both unbiased and potentially useful. Fourth, water policy is primarily under provincial jurisdiction. Any attempt by the federal government to consider policy change is viewed with suspicion by the provinces as a possible encroachment on their areas of responsibility. At the same time, the federal government does have a legitimate role in water policy, and some issues are best addressed at the national level. From Environment Canada's perspective, an independent committee could examine the issues in a manner acceptable to both the provinces and the federal departments.

A fifth calculation was that any public hearings process increases public participation and forms a constituency. If recommendations emerge from a broad consensus, they can be viewed as representative of the many interests taking part in the debate. Even if no consensus arises, knowledgeable people have given advice based on careful review of substantive research and the opinions of the interested public. The fact that hearings are open to the public increases confidence in a fair process. This serves to legitimize efforts at policy reform, because decision-makers are acting on recommendations which have considered the range of stakeholder opinions.

Sixth, there was little risk to the Department of a negative outcome. The status quo was recognized as a problem in many quarters of the policy community. The major stumbling block was obtaining a co-ordinated institutional effort directed towards change. One of the main achievements of the Inquiry was simply getting the various jurisdictions to work towards a common goal. Although the Department could not predict the outcome of the Inquiry, it could be reasonably confident that many of its concerns would be addressed. This was not due to direct manipulation of the Inquiry, but the belief that many of the problems in water policy are institutional rather than substantive.

Finally, the Department and government could exercise indirect influence on the Inquiry. By controlling the selection of Inquiry members, and by providing office space, budget, and administrative staff, the Department had some impact on the process. Selection of panel members is perhaps the most important means for the recipient to influence a committee's outcome. Decision-makers pay a great deal of attention to the philosophy and expertise of their advisors prior to their appointment. The government and sub-government can subtly influence the direction and acceptability of a committee through the selection process.

Political acceptability, particularly of the Chairperson, was certainly a criterion in this case. Several respondents made nonchalant observations that selections for the Chair position were between Liberal supporters, implying that a political appointment was either acceptable or expected, or both. This was not an issue with respondents, for a number of reasons. The experience of the two principal committee members, Pearse and MacLaren, gave them considerable respect, such that they were laudable choices. Pearse's outlook and thinking were known from previous work. If it mattered, their different political orientations, the one Liberal, the other Conservative, served to counterbalance one other. The process was conducted in a non-partisan manner. The fact that Pearse was not a member of the water community meant that he could examine it from an external perspective; the fact that MacLaren was a member of the water community gave the panel insights into the opportunities and realities of the situation. The commission had an arms-length relationship with the Department. The Inquiry was independent in its own operations and decision-making. The members decided on an agenda for study, chose researchers, conducted hearings, had access to Department information, debated and wrote the text and recommendations for the final report. The overwhelming opinion amongst respondents is that the Inquiry was conducted in an independent manner. Finally, the government had changed by the time the report was released, so that it was a Conservative Minister of the Environment who accepted the Inquiry's recommendations.

As an *ad hoc* committee performing a special study, the group did not advise the Minister on an ongoing basis. Instead, advice was presented in the final report at the end of the Inquiry. This is one of the problems often cited with *ad hoc* committees, that they dissolve upon completion of the final report. Without a body to support and promote the committee's recommendations, advice can be easily ignored. In the case of the Pearse Commission, the Department was prepared to consider the Inquiry's recommendations seriously and take on the task of promoting reform. In addition, both Pearse and MacLaren were contracted to act as representatives for the Inquiry after the final report was released.

Organizational factors were important to the outcome of the Inquiry. Judged by the results of the Inquiry, and the acceptance of its report, the committee performed well. The committee was able to amass, synthesize, and analyse a large amount of qualitative and quantitative data in producing their report. Those respondents who attended public hearings generally felt that they were conducted in a professional manner. Prior to the final report, a number of documents were published to inform the audience of the panel's deliberations. The final report has generally been complimented for its style and content, accessible to both expert and layperson.

A means of overcoming the small constituency represented by three members is to include others in the process. By expanding the circulation of information, the Inquiry was able to do this. Experts in various water-related issues contributed to the debate either through contracted research papers to provide substantive information, or through participation in the public hearings to provide subjective opinion. During the hearings phase, three hundred individuals and groups, representing a wide range of interests and geographic concerns, expressed their opinions. An interesting feature of the public hearings is that their utility lies more in determining stakeholder opinions than in gathering facts. After three hundred submissions, from all sides of the debate, the panel was reasonably assured that it had received an exhaustive and comprehensive range of perspectives on water policy. From this input, the committee was able to build support for its recommendations and consensus for reform.

It is generally agreed that the Inquiry report was a pragmatic document, aiming more at acceptability rather than radical change. Whether this was an appropriate orientation is debated by participants in the process. On the one side are those who believe recommendations ought to be controversial, to advocate a strong position, and to demand major reform. On the other side are those who think a cautious, pragmatic approach is needed to fit recommendations to political realities. The Inquiry favoured the latter approach, perhaps because its Chairperson had experience with prior inquiries into natural resource policies. It is likely that the pragmatic approach was indeed appropriate, given the context of the report. The Inquiry had the support of the Department. The government and provinces had been consulted and were generally amenable to the panel's objectives. A large constituency towards reform had been formed by the creation of a public inquiry. The decision-makers were therefore favourably predisposed to change. However, given the conservative nature of the bureaucracy, and with so many institutions involved, any change would inevitably be incremental rather than revolutionary.

The Inquiry built relations with all four elements of the policy community: lead agency, executive, sub-government, and attentive public. This wide network of associations created a climate in which policy reform could be addressed. The broad constituency, developed through consultation with stakeholders, lent legitimacy to the Inquiry. The examination of specific issues gave focus to substantive problems.

Once the committee had completed its report and made its recommendations, it was up to the Minister of the Environment to determine the fate of the advice. McMillan recognized the value of the inquiry process and the consensus for reform that had evolved. He added the necessary ingredient for recommendations to pass from advice to implementation: political will. McMillan asked his provincial counterparts to review and comment on the final report. At the same time, an interdepartmental committee was established at the federal level to update water policy.

The publication of the Federal Water Policy in 1987 is evidence that the Inquiry did influence policy reform. In his introductory remarks, Minister McMillan explicitly acknowledged the committee's work: 'In all cases, we will be guided by the report of the Inquiry on Federal Water Policy.' The new policy introduced five overall strategies and twenty-five specific statements on water policy. The majority of the fifty-five recommendations contained in the Inquiry report were partially or fully included in the policy paper. Further, the Federal Water Policy added a number of issues not dealt with by the Inquiry recommendations. Examples of such additions are statements on wetlands preservation, hydroelectric development, heritage river preservation, native water rights, international water relations, drought, shoreline erosion, climate change, and technological needs.

The report continues to be a viable document, although the political will to implement further change has slowed since the release of the Federal Water Policy. New legislation on such issues as water exports and drinking-water quality has yet to appear. Equally important, no new funding has been allocated for water research or water-related programs. Without adequate financial support, the positive initiatives of the Federal Water Policy will not be realized. As well, although the Inquiry acted to catalyse some policy reform at the federal level, it did not generate the necessary support for creating a national water policy. Unfortunately this state of affairs points out one of the shortcomings of *ad hoc* advisory committees or task forces. The lack of continuity of an external monitoring and evaluation body has hampered the effective implementation of the recommendations and reduced the opportunity for scrutiny by the policy community and the general public.

CONCLUSIONS

Institutional advisory groups are formed to discuss issues and to counsel government decision-makers. In the complex world in which public decisions are made, there will always be a need for people with substantive and impartial expertise to participate in the public process. They bring valuable insights and criticism on the long- and short-term effects of policy proposals, make credible predictions, and offer alternative viewpoints from representative communities, all at relatively small expense.

   The two groups examined in this chapter, the Canadian Environmental Advisory Council and the Inquiry on Federal Water Policy, demonstrate that many factors determine the influence of a particular group. It is difficult to compare the two advisory bodies directly, since they were formed for different purposes and play different roles. For example, one of CEAC's main strengths is advising on internal Department policies and directions. While important, this role has no public profile, nor does it receive a lot of credit from the Department. In contrast, the Inquiry was established, in part, to attempt to develop a public consensus for policy reform on a specific issue, with significant support of the Department. It is clear that the greater the communication between a group and members of the policy community, the greater the opportunity for an advisory group to influence substantive policy change.

   The environmental policy community, and the advisory system, have evolved over the past three decades. Beginning as think-tanks of experts in the 1960s, advisory groups later extended representation to several areas: gender, language, region, sector, and discipline. More recently, several national environmental non-governmental groups have developed, capable of offering advice of equally high calibre. Not only have new groups and government agencies been created, but existing bodies have been given expanded environmental mandates. For instance, the

House of Commons Standing Committee on Fisheries and Forestry became the Standing Committee on Environment and Forestry, and has now emerged as the Standing Committee on Environment.

The more influential people in Canada's environmental policy community actually comprise a relatively small cross-section of the population. Increasingly, many of these same individuals can be found on different advisory groups at both the federal and provincial levels. This is not necessarily bad in view of the concurrent jurisdiction of the two levels of government over environmental matters. But it is increasingly important, as Canada moves from an emphasis on environmental protection towards the broader perspective of sustainable development, to expand that community across sectors, disciplines, and regions. This is beginning to happen with the Round Tables on Environment and Economy, suggesting that there is a recognition that the constituency must be broadened to develop appropriate policies for the future. The composition of the new advisory groups also suggest that relationships are shifting from independence to interdependence.

As the policy community has grown in numbers and sophistication, however, there is the possibility of overlap and duplication of effort. Each group has its niche, in terms of role, philosophy, interests, expertise, constituency, access to decision-makers, and visibility to the public and media. However, the multiplicity of advisory groups, and especially their proliferation in the past five years, suggests that access to senior officials and particularly Ministers is being diluted. Indeed the current situation is such that there is a risk of alienating existing and potential members of advisory groups who contribute substantial time and effort to the development of environmental policy in Canada. In cognizance of the potential cacophony of advice from so many disparate and sometimes conflicting voices, an ongoing review of mandates and relations is needed by policy community members to ensure that the advisory process as a whole is rational and effective.

FOR FURTHER READING

David S. Brown, 'The Public Advisory Board as an Instrument of Government', *Public Administration Review* 15 (1955): 196-204.

——— , 'The Management of Advisory Committees: An Assignment for the '70's', *Public Administration Review* 32 (1972): 334-42.

William Coleman and Grace Skogstad, eds, *Policy Communities and Public Policy in Canada: A Structural Approach* (Mississauga: Copp Clark Pitman, 1990).

Thomas E. Cronin and Norman C. Thomas, 'Educational Policy Advisors and the Great Society', *Public Policy* 18 (1970): 659-86.

Philip L. Gianos, 'Scientists as Policy Advisers: The Context of Influence', *The Western Political Quarterly* 27 (1974): 429-56.

Norman N. Gill, 'Permanent Advisory Committees in the Federal Government', *The Journal of Politics* 2 (1940): 411-25.

Mort Grant, 'The Technology of Advisory Committees', *Public Policy* 10 (1960): 92-108.

A. Paul Pross, *Group Politics and Public Policy* (Toronto: Oxford University Press, 1986).

Thomas B. Smith, 'Advisory Committees in the Public Policy Process', *International Review of Administrative Sciences* 43, 20, (1977): 153-66.

Cassia Spohn, 'The Role of Advisory Boards in the Policy Process: An Analysis of the Attitudes of HEW Board Members', *American Review of Public Administration* 16 2 / 3 (1983): 185-94.

Guy P.F. Steed, 'Alerting Canadians: The Scope and Use of Policy Research in the Science Council of Canada', *Technology in Society* 10 (1988): 165-83.

George T. Sulzner, 'The Policy Process and the Uses of National Governmental Study Commissions', *Western Political Quarterly* 24 (1971): 438-48.

Michael Whittington, 'Environmental Policy', in G. Bruce Doern and V.S. Wilson, eds, *Issues in Canadian Public Policy* (Toronto: Macmillan of Canada, 1974): 203-27.

CHAPTER 5

Of Invisible Beasts
and the Public Interest

Environmental Cases and the Judicial System

——

TED SCHRECKER

The existence of the deadly yet invisible creature in Ambrose Bierce's magnificent tale 'The Damned Thing' (*The Collected Writings of Ambrose Bierce*, New York: Citadel, 1946) could be inferred from the presence of its mutilated victim and the fact that its silhouette blotted out the stars at night. The idea of the public interest in the environmental policy field is rather like that creature. We know it's there—it *has* to be there—yet it maddeningly eludes precise description or delineation. 'If pressed, most decision-makers would have considerable difficulty in arriving at an acceptable definition of this fundamental concept.'[1] Studying changing conceptions of the public interest, the contexts in which the idea has been implicitly relied on and explicitly invoked, and the way its interpretation has corresponded to changing distributions of economic and political power provides a useful framework for considering the role of judges, courts, and quasi-judicial institutions in environmental policy.

As illustrated by the Federal Court of Canada's recent redefinition of environmental assessment law at the federal level, the increasing severity of sentences for environmental offences in some jurisdictions, and the possibility of some form of environmental bill of rights in Ontario, the role of the Canadian judicial system in environmental policy is changing rapidly. Public concern about environmental protection is such that it is unlikely in the near future to lose its salience as a political issue. Neither is the debate about the proper role of the judiciary in this policy area, and the appropriate scope of unreviewable administrative discretion, likely soon to be resolved.

THE COMMON LAW CONFRONTS INDUSTRIALIZATION

Well before the passage of twentieth-century statutes to control environmental damage,[2] the common law provided a number of possible grounds on which someone affected by it could seek redress, either in the form of an injunction or in the form of an award of compensatory damages. Most of these grounds (like much of the common law) had to do with the protection of property owners and the rights that came with ownership. *Nuisance* denoted the unreasonable and unnecessary interference with the enjoyment of property. *Riparian rights* protected downstream owners of property bordering a body of water against interference with the flow or quality of water by upstream users. *Trespass* simply referred to unauthorized entry or damage to property, and *strict liability* made individuals liable for damage done by the escape of dangerous materials from their property, whatever precautions they might have taken to prevent the escape.[3]

As it was interpreted in the first part of the nineteenth century, the common law provided a powerful legal basis for resisting the environmental encroachments of the day. However, those interpretations also presented substantial barriers to industrialization, many of whose characteristic activities (such as the construction of mills and dams, the building and operation of canals and railways, and the running of factories of various kinds) simply could not be carried out without imposing on third parties the kind of damage, injury, or inconvenience today's economists refer to as a negative externality. Morton Horwitz argues that many areas of US legal history are best described in terms of a pattern in which both courts and legislatures, starting as early as the end of the eighteenth century, reinterpreted a variety of existing common law doctrines to reduce the role of property rights and liability rules as potential legal obstacles to rapid industrialization. He concludes, for instance, that:

> At the beginning of the nineteenth century, the law of nuisance provided an almost exclusive remedy for indirect interferences with property rights, and courts were prepared to award damages for injury to property regardless of the social utility or absence of carelessness of the actor's conduct. By the time of the Civil War, by contrast, American courts had created a variety of legal doctrines whose primary effect was to force those injured by economic activities to bear the cost of these improvements.[4]

The effect was the subsidization of economic growth through the legal system as a variety of its costs were assigned to third parties, usually without compensation.

Some aspects of Horwitz's argument are contentious. Several critics have convincingly argued that the transitions identified by Horwitz were neither as clear-cut nor as identifiable with specific historical periods as he would have us believe.[5] These critiques do not seriously lessen the general importance of Horwitz's argument for the purpose of this chapter. Numerous examples from his work indicate a shift away from a common law preoccupied with a concern for individual entitlements to one considerably more willing to countenance the partial abrogation of those entitlements in favour of a public good, public purpose, or public interest that was strongly identified with rapid economic growth and the industrial and commercial activities necessary to bring it about.

In the definitive study of nuisance law during the roughly comparable period of Canadian economic development (1880–1930), Jennifer Nedelsky finds that Canadian courts, rather unlike their US counterparts, 'followed traditional nuisance law and were generally unwilling to modify substantive rules or rights in order to accommodate the demands of industry'.[6] They were willing to make concessions to a public good identified with industrialization, but those concessions tended to take the form of awarding compensatory damages rather than issuing injunctions. The extreme case of this approach in the early twentieth century is the case of *Black vs Canadian Copper*, in which the court held that:

> Mines cannot be operated without the production of smoke from the roast-yards and smelters, which smoke contains very large quantities of sulphur dioxide. There are circumstances in which it is impossible for the individual so to assert his individual rights as to inflict a substantial injury upon the whole community. If the mines should be prevented from operating, the community could not exist at all. . . . The Court ought not to destroy the mining industry — nickel is of great value to the world — even if a few farms are damaged or destroyed; *but in all such cases compensation, liberally estimated, ought to be awarded*.[7]

Courts would also often offer stays of injunctions in return for abatement of the nuisances in question[8] — an intriguing precursor of the bargaining which characterizes contemporary enforcement of environmental statutes and regulations. However, Canadian courts could not always be relied on to avoid issuing injunctions against environmentally damaging activities.[9] 'The cases do not suggest that the Canadian courts ever systematically refused injunctions to protect industry' during the period in question.[10]

In cases involving riparian rights, this pattern persisted well after the period studied by Nedelsky. The most familiar instance occurred in 1948 when the Ontario Supreme Court issued an injunction, subsequently upheld by the Supreme Court of Canada, restraining the discharge of noxious pollutants by the K.V.P. paper mill in Espanola, Ontario.[11] This case also provides an excellent example of governmental willingness to assert the primacy of industrial development objectives when courts were reluctant to do so. The Ontario Legislature first passed an amendment to the relevant provincial legislation 'requiring the courts to weigh the economic and public interest factors when deciding whether or not to grant an injunction', then dissolved the injunction against K.V.P. by legislation.[12] In 1956, it took similar action to dissolve injunctions against municipal sewage treatment plants. In fact, the legislation immunized all such plants against common law actions based on riparian rights as long as they were operating under licences issued by the newly established Ontario Water Resources Commission.[13] In both situations, legislative action proceeded despite the fact that the court that issued the injunction had temporarily stayed its application to permit the defendants to find alternative means of waste disposal.

Causes of action at common law could also be dissolved by governments in a systematic rather than a case-by-case fashion. In 1919, for example, riparian rights in Nova Scotia were legislatively expropriated and assigned to the provincial government 'without compensation or recourse to the courts'.[14] This represented the culmination of a pattern of statutory removal of common law obstacles to water-related development common to many provinces,[15] typified by the Ontario government's response to 'the apparent threat posed by judicial attitudes to the aspirations of the legislature for economic progress and expansion' with legislation authorizing abrogations of riparian rights by electric power producers for ' "the public good," a concept not defined apart from its relation to the purposes of the legislation'. Similar legislation protected lumbermen using streams to transport logs against injunctions sought by riparian landowners, even when their improvements had made the streams more valuable for purposes of transport.[16] Most of these conflicts did not involve environmental damage in the contemporary sense. They are valuable rather as illustrations of the pattern in which, as applications of the common law to conflicts involving economically important natural resources were recognized as inimical to economic development, governments sought to redefine them as involving a public dimension as well as the competing claims of private resource users. They did so largely by removing the resolution of such conflicts from the judiciary and establishing it instead as a prerogative of the political executive, either directly or through the creation of administrative agencies subject to greater or lesser degrees of visible executive control.

This is not as dramatic a transition as it might seem. In one crucial area of common law (the distinction between public and private nuisances) the discretion of the political executive to define the public interest as it sees fit has been entrenched since before the Industrial Revolution.[17] A public nuisance is one which affects a large number of people in a similar way, without simultaneously interfering with a private right of some other sort (i.e., other than the 'right' not to be afflicted with a nuisance). Courts have generally held that individuals affected by the creation of a public nuisance do not have standing to sue for an injunction or damages unless they have suffered some special damage above and beyond that suffered by the other members of the community. Only the Attorney-General, who is formally and in theory responsible for 'the vindication of the public interest', may bring such a suit.[18] 'The usual rule is that the Attorney-General's discretion here is unimpeachable and not subject to judicial review.'[19]

There is obvious scope for judicial creativity in applying the distinction between private and public nuisances. Horwitz argues that US courts used this opportunity to shield not only public authorities but also private firms (for instance, the operators of railways) from lawsuits.[20] Canadian courts were slower to move in this direction; in 1922 the Supreme Court (in the case of *Canada Paper vs Brown*) refused to deny standing to the original plaintiff (Brown) to sue for relief for pollution damages, even though it was not claimed that the 'nauseating and offensive odours and fumes' emitted by the paper mill in question afflicted him differently or more severely than they did his neighbours.[21] This expansive interpretation of the 'special damage' requirement for standing in cases of public nuisance was not always reflected in subsequent lower court decisions. It was implicitly (but decisively) rejected in a widely cited 1971 decision of the Newfoundland Supreme Court, which denied commercial fishermen's claim that they were entitled to damages as a result of destruction of a fishery by pollution from the defendant company, on the grounds that the rights in question (i.e., the right to fish in Placentia Bay) '[w]ere held in common with all Her Majesty's subjects and can only be vindicated by . . . an action of the Attorney-General in the common interest of the public'.[22]

Judicial deference to the political executive in the area of public nuisances is one of the key reasons that in the early 1970s, when environmental concerns intruded themselves inescapably on public policy, many of the handful of lawyers directly involved with such issues felt that traditional common law doctrines, although theoretically promising, were practically irrelevant to most situations in which citizens might seek protection from environmental damage. Wrote one commentator: 'Forget the private lawsuit as a major strategy!'[23] In the intervening years, at least two further sets of complications have made this seem, if anything, even better advice.

First, convincing demonstrations of the causal connection between a particular pollutant or effluent, from a particular source, and the injury suffered by a plaintiff can be extremely difficult. In the contemporary context these connections are likely to involve not smoke damage to crops or laundry, but the relation between exposure to a substance which is emitted by a number of plants or industries and cancer, birth defects, or other health effects which can usually be attributed to a multitude of factors.[24] (This difficulty was one of the major reasons the Ojibway native people of the White Dog and Grassy Narrows reserves in northern Ontario agreed in 1986 to mediated settlement of a lawsuit claiming that mercury poisoning had resulted from consuming fish contaminated with mercury pollution emitted by the Reid Paper mill in the 1970s.[25]) Ideally, the adversarial setting of the courtroom has great potential for effective scrutiny of scientific evidence.[26] In practice the result is likely to be a battle of (very expensive) expert witnesses. (Recall that this problem exists even assuming that the standing barrier has been overcome.)

Second, litigation is costly, and losing plaintiffs in Canada may be faced with paying not only their own substantial legal costs, but those of the defendant as well. When a group of Cape Breton landowners failed in a 1983 bid for an injunction against planned phenoxy herbicide spraying on adjacent forests, partly as a consequence of the evidentiary problems just described, they were faced not only with their own legal costs but also with an award of costs against them (estimated at more than $200,000) for the lawyers and expert witnesses employed by the corporation they were opposing.[27] The firm eventually agreed to waive these costs (partly in response to a public outcry against its Swedish parent company) but it was under no legal obligation to do so, and the chilling effect on potential future litigants was probably substantial.

FLEXIBLE REGULATION, DISCRETIONARY ENFORCEMENT

Concerns with the application of common law doctrines to environmental questions in an industrializing Canada focused on their potential to inhibit industrial development. The regime of regulation which supplanted those doctrines was much less ambiguous in manifesting 'the tacit pre-eminence accorded the right to despoil the environment over the right to a clean environment'.[28] There are a number of reasons for this outcome, of which only those most directly relevant to the operations of the judicial system (and to its exclusion from certain categories of policy decisions) can be dealt with here.

With the exception of environmental impact assessment legislation, most postwar federal and provincial environmental statutes passed before and during the 1980s were and are enabling in character. Earlier statutes authorized federal and provincial political executives to permit certain specific uses of resources, such as watercourses for the purpose of discharging sewage. Later ones conferred broader authority to make regulations with the objective of protecting the natural environment (or a specific subsystem such as air or water). For the most part, specific policy objectives were not clearly defined in legislation. To provide just one example, the Environment Minister of the day referred to the federal Environmental Contaminants Act of 1975 as 'our main approach' to the problem of toxic substances in the environment.[29] However the Act did little more than confer discretionary powers to regulate, and only a handful of substances were regulated under the Act before its consolidation with other federal statutes in 1988 as the Canadian Environmental Protection Act.[30] As with most other environmental protection statutes, under the new legislation the political executive is not required to take any specific steps to achieve environmental protection objectives; it is merely empowered to act in certain ways.

The discretionary nature of such power was decisively established in a 1978 Supreme Court of Ontario decision[31] involving amendments to

Ontario's Environmental Protection Act, passed in 1976, which empowered the Lieutenant Governor in Council (meaning, as in all such cases, Cabinet) to make regulations 'providing a schedule for the regulation and the prohibition within five years of the use, offering for sale, or sale in Ontario of nonrefillable or nonreturnable containers for any beverage'. Such regulations were to be 'filed under the Regulations Act not later than the 1st day of July, 1977'. When no regulations were filed, 'because of the expected loss of employment among people engaged in the manufacture of nonrefillable or non-returnable containers', a researcher with Toronto's Pollution Probe sought a court order requiring the Ontario Minister of the Environment to issue the regulations. The court ruled such regulations could be made, or not made, at the discretion of Cabinet. 'The provision . . . that the regulations must be filed by July 1, 1977 does not impair that discretion as the words "if enacted" must be read into the section.'[32]

Under US federal environmental law, in contrast, highly detailed objectives and timetables for achieving them are often specified in legislation. A senior federal official has explained this contrast with the argument that:

> Canadian regulatory officials are directly subject to the authority of Parliament's leadership in Cabinet. Thus it is unnecessary for Parliament to spell out legislative intent in great detail or to provide for outcomes which are inconsistent with its expectations. This is in contrast to the American context where social regulation was written with the explicit objective of denying discretion and flexibility to the regulators.[33]

Leaving aside for the moment the merits of this presumption of accountability, the point is that addressing environmental protection by way of enabling statutes reduced the discretionary authority of the courts to resolve conflicts over resource uses, and drastically increased that of the political executive.

Paradoxically, the exceptions to the rule of enabling legislation prove the rule by demanding even more pervasive exercise of administrative discretion. If read literally, the most dramatic of these exceptions, section 14(1) of Ontario's Environmental Protection Act and section 36(3) (formerly s. 33) of the federal Fisheries Act, could be read as prohibiting the discharge of almost any form of pollution, anywhere, at any time, except as specifically authorized by way of permits or regulations.[34] Routine or systematic prosecution under such statutes, were judges to interpret the legislation literally, would be even more destructive of economic activity than a pre-industrial interpretation of a variety of common law property rights and liability rules.

Paul Emond has pointed out that the shift from common law to enabling legislation did not broaden access to decisions about the allocation of the costs of industrial activity in any meaningful way. 'The common law substantially limits participation to the propertied class', by way of its preoccupation with property rights and proprietors' interests. 'The legislation limits it to polluter and government agency. In both cases a relevant and important segment of the public is effectively precluded from contributing to the decision-making process.'[35] The regulations which give content to enabling legislation tended (and still tend, in many jurisdictions) to be developed on the basis of private consultations with the affected firms or their representatives, in the absence of any legislative requirement for public involvement.[36] There are some partial exceptions, such as British Columbia's process of conducting public inquiries as a basis for setting appropriate environmental objectives, but even there '[t]he objectives are not binding on individual pollution sources until they become a provision of a permit or approval issued by the Director of Pollution Control'.[37]

Much the same is true in Ontario, where until recently environmental objectives normally became binding only as part of an instrument known as a Control Order, nominally imposed by the Ministry but in practice negotiated between the Ministry and the firm in question.[38] Control orders are really permits or licences: under Ontario's Environmental Protection Act as long as a firm is operating under the terms of such an order it is immune from prosecutions relating to the activities described in the order. Reliance on control orders rather than on regulations was not a function of the legislative framework, but of political decisions: the Act clearly provided the authority to issue regulations. However, only in 1985, after the election of a new government, did the province's Ministry of the Environment embark on an ambitious effort, still far from completion, to replace the regime of non-binding objectives and source-specific control orders with a set of regulations applying to all municipal and industrial sources of pollution, developed on the basis of consultation with environmental organizations as well as the affected sources.

The allowable level of pollution specified in a permit or regulation dealing with a particular pollution source or a class of sources is meaningless unless we know whether enforcement policies dictate the achievement of that objective today, two years from now, or at some point in the indefinite and constantly receding future. Here again, unfettered executive discretion is the rule, and environmental enforcement policy has conformed rather closely to the last of these patterns.[39] Ontario governments for many years pursued a policy of virtually indefinite renegotiation of the terms of control orders issued under its Environmental Protection Act, while the licensing function of the control order process precluded successful private prosecution. This policy was particularly conspicuous in situations involving firms in the resource industries, especially pulp and paper, which tended to be the principal employers in their communities.[40] This fact enabled them to use 'job blackmail'[41] as part of the bargaining process which has been described as 'the essence of the environmental regulatory process as it is practised in Canada'.[42]

In 1987 the Canadian Environmental Advisory Council (CEAC), an advisory group to the federal Minister of the Environment, identified a pattern of almost two decades of systematic non-enforcement of the antipollution provisions of the Fisheries Act in Quebec, despite the existence of 'a number of land-based sources of continuous discharge of highly toxic substances which seem to enjoy complete immunity from prosecution'.[43] A study of Fisheries Act enforcement carried out for the Law Reform Commission of Canada suggested that the pattern was not confined to Quebec and Ontario, but was characteristic of provincial jurisdictions across Canada to which Fisheries Act enforcement has been delegated under federal-provincial accords.[44] An internal memorandum by a Department of Fisheries and Oceans official leaked in December, 1989, was bitterly critical of the federal 'negotiate and compromise at all costs philosophy' of non-enforcement of Fisheries Act violations against a number of large firms in British Columbia.[45]

A further set of factors serves simultaneously to protect governments' discretionary authority, and to create disincentives for aggressive enforcement. In order to obtain a conviction under environmental statutes, the elements of an offence must be proved beyond a reasonable doubt, much as in criminal cases. The difference, of course, is that whereas most criminal defendants are impoverished or nearly so, potential defendants in environmental cases are often large and wealthy firms which are well able to finance protracted litigation, and for whom even the substantial costs of such delay may be small when compared with the costs of compliance.[46]

Given the limitations on common law actions, private prosecutions are sometimes the least unviable way of bringing an environmental case before the courts. They are the only way of challenging a policy commitment to non-enforcement or flexible enforcement, and even then the challenge can only be developed on a case-by-case basis. However, under Canadian law, '[t]he Attorney General enjoys the exclusive right to stay proceedings', i.e., to intervene in a court case to halt the conduct of a private prosecution, 'without any check on his exercise of this discretion';[47] provincial Attorneys-General have in fact done this in some private prosecutions under the federal Fisheries Act.[48] Even in the absence of such direct interventions, the relevant officials, having themselves declined to prosecute, may be actively hostile to private prosecutors, yet the evidentiary requirements for successful prosecutions present a formidable barrier to entry which private prosecutors will have great difficulty in overcoming without governmental assistance.[49]

Regulation-making and discretionary enforcement in the environmental field have both reflected identification of the public interest with industrial and commercial growth. Until recently, fines levied following conviction on charges arising from environmental damage were generally far smaller than the maxima provided for by statute, and were almost certainly trivial when compared with the cost savings associated with continued noncompliance.[50] This phenomenon may reflect the widespread perception that because environmental offences normally involve the effects of activities whose job-creating and wealth-generating consequences are desirable,[51] they are 'morally ambiguous'.[52]

'In one celebrated case' brought as a private prosecution, 'the defendant's massive effluent was proved to be instantly lethal to fish. Nevertheless, the fine imposed was only $1' for the resulting violation of the Fisheries Act,[53] because of what the judge called 'a multitude of mitigating circumstances', including the poor quality of the existing fishery, the fact that the effluent was being deposited with the approval of the Ontario Ministry of the Environment, the fact that the company claimed to have spent millions of dollars on pollution abatement with the result that the problem would be corrected by 1984, and the fact that '[a]ny shutting off or closing of the Cyanamid pipe on March 23rd, 1981, or at any other time might require the shutting down of the factory with a loss of jobs and dire and severe financial consequences to Cyanamid and to many, if not all of its employees'.[54] This is admittedly an extreme example, in terms both of its explicit concern for economic impacts and its deference to administrative discretion. Indeed, in a few instances judges hearing cases brought by private prosecutors under the Fisheries Act have been strongly critical of governmental policies of non-enforcement.[55] However, it is probably the case that, on the whole, judicial policies of levying inconsequential fines and administrative policies of infrequent prosecution have each served to justify the other.

In many jurisdictions, those trends have continued. A study released in 1989 found that fines levied by Quebec courts for pollution-related provincial offences between 1984 and 1988 averaged just $667.16 per conviction.[56] It is interesting to contrast the Quebec pattern with that which has emerged in Ontario, Canada's most populous, urban, and industrialized province and the one whose citizens are probably less affected than other Canadians by the jobs-versus-environment trade-offs which constrain environmental policy in general. In the words of a former staff lawyer for the province's Ministry of the Environment, 'media and scholarly attention upon the importance and fragility of the environment now finds its reflection in the courts', in the form of literally dozens of cases where fines for violating the province's environmental laws have run into five figures, and occasionally into six. Judges have been increasingly willing to fine both individuals and their corporate employers, to impose separate penalties for each day an offence occurs (as specifically allowed for by legislation), or to take into account the large numbers of individuals affected by environmental offences.[57]

The available data limit comparisons,[58] but this trend appears with isolated exceptions[59] to be distinctive to Ontario, where over the last decade successive provincial governments committed substantial additional resources to investigating and prosecuting offences,[60] and enacted legislative amendments which raised the maximum penalties for violations of the province's Environmental Protection Act, even though the previous maximum penalties had rarely if ever been imposed.[61] Provincial parties since 1985 have explicitly incorporated environmental protection into their electoral packaging; increased maximum fines were part of the package. Environmental protection is not, of course, the only area in which a pattern of increasing severity can be observed in sentencing decisions; the sentences now handed down to intoxicated drivers, especially those involved in accidents causing injury or death, constitute just one additional illustration. Both examples raise the question of the extent to which sentencing patterns respond, and should respond, to perceived shifts in public opinion or 'community standards'. They also suggest that judicial decisions may be indirectly affected by the efforts of governments or government agencies, acting as policy entrepreneurs, to influence public perceptions of the seriousness of particular offences.

ENVIRONMENTAL ASSESSMENT

Both common law and regulatory or quasi-criminal approaches to controlling environmental damage are almost entirely reactive.[62] Legislation can anticipate the hazards of a new industry or a new technology; it may authorize regulations to control their impacts or even prohibit their introduction; but before the courts become involved, damage must be done. (There is a partial exception in the form of the *quia timet* or anticipatory injunction at common law, of the type sought by the plaintiffs in the Nova Scotia herbicide case, but courts are extremely reluctant to grant these, since doing so presupposes that damages cannot provide an adequate remedy.[63]) In contrast, environmental assessment legislation is explicitly prospective in orientation. In some jurisdictions at least, the conduct of environmental reviews has been assigned to quasi-judicial bodies at least formally independent of executive control, 'as an alternative to litigation in the courts'.[64] In others, the judiciary has played a critical role in defining the content of environmental impact assessment requirements.

Ontario's Environmental Assessment Act[65] requires the preparation and internal review of environmental assessments for all provincial government undertakings before they proceed, unless they are exempted by Cabinet. (Sections of the Act extending its application to the private sector have not been proclaimed.) The Act also created an Environmental Assessment Board (EAB), which holds public hearings on the adequacy of such assessments in certain cases,[66] and also holds hearings with a more restricted mandate on certain kinds of approvals under regulatory legislation. The Board operates as a quasi-judicial tribunal; its rulings are authoritative, in the first instance, with respect to undertakings considered under the Environmental Assessment Act; and its powers extend to the imposition of terms and conditions on project proponents.[67] However, there are important limitations to its power. Cabinet can exempt any undertaking from the provisions of the Act 'in the public interest';[68] Cabinet may reject or vary a Board decision under the Act;[69] and the holding of public hearings on a project, even though it has not been exempted from the provisions of the Act, is at the discretion of the Minister of the Environment.[70] The importance of this last provision became apparent when a hearing was refused on the contentious Red Squirrel logging road in the Temagami region, despite protests by environmental groups bitterly opposed to further logging in the area, on the basis that holding a hearing would result in 'undue delay in obtaining access to timber stands, jeopardizing the economic viability of the local forest industry and threatening job layoffs'.[71]

During the early years of their existence the Act and the Board were trivialized by Cabinet exemptions of environmentally significant projects, which became almost routine,[72] and by the fact that 'the central strategy of . . . the Ministry as a whole appear[ed] to be to avoid hearings' under the Environmental Assessment Act.[73] More recently this strategy has been modified, although not (as the Temagami example shows) abandoned. The Board is now holding lengthy hearings on a 'class environmental assessment' of Ontario's timber management policies on Crown lands. It will shortly begin hearings on the Ontario Waste Management Corporation's proposal to construct a major toxic waste disposal facility in southern Ontario,[74] and on an Ontario Hydro long-term system plan which involves the construction of numerous additional nuclear power plants in Ontario over the next 25 years. Just as significantly, in a pathbreaking socialization of the costs of environmental litigation, an intervenor funding program established by legislation has made literally millions of dollars available to finance interventions in EAB hearings.[75]

Particularly as the Board's role expands to include programmatic or policy assessments like those involving timber management and electrical generation, in order to reconcile conflicting priorities and fundamental beliefs about resource use it will have to develop and apply a definition of the public interest in the absence of useful legislative guidance. It remains to be seen how coherently and explicitly it will do so, and the extent to which its definitions will conflict with the political priorities of the day. The latter question arises because, despite the statutory framework within which EAB operates, the current role of the Board (and, by extension, much of the structure of Ontario's environmental assessment process) have been permitted and even facilitated by the political execu-tive rather than mandated by the judiciary.[76]

In this respect, Ontario stands in striking contrast to the United States federal jurisdiction, whence the concept of environmental assessment as a distinctive activity originated. The National Environmental Policy Act (NEPA) passed both houses of Congress by large margins in 1969. NEPA's so-called action-forcing provisions required federal executive agencies to incorporate environmental considerations into their decisions by way of a 'systematic, interdisciplinary approach ... in planning and in decisionmaking which may have an impact on man's environment'. Agencies were directed, *inter alia*, to develop procedures 'which will insure that presently unquantified environmental amenities and values may be given appropriate consideration in decisionmaking along with economic and technical considerations'. This consideration was to take place by way of the preparation of environmental impact statements on proposals for all 'legislation and other major federal actions significantly affecting the quality of the human environment'.[77]

Legislators seem to have given little thought to NEPA's implementa-tion.[78] No special tribunal or board was established;[79] neither was any provision for public hearings. Litigation has emerged as virtually the only mode of public participation in the environmental assessment process, and NEPA's implementation has relied almost entirely on judicial deci-sions in cases where environmental organizations challenged executive agencies' decisions not to prepare impact statements, or argued that the quality of such statements was too poor or superficial to satisfy NEPA requirements. This result, in turn, came about only because of federal courts' general willingness to grant standing to sue for judicial review of administrative action.[80]

Judicial interpretation of NEPA has established that it superimposes an environmental mandate on federal agencies,[81] but one that does not extend beyond considering and publicizing the environmental conse-quences of proposed actions. 'Other statutes may impose substantive environmental obligations on federal agencies', the US Supreme Court ruled in 1989, 'but NEPA merely prohibits uninformed—rather than unwise—agency action'.[82] Judicial enforcement even of that prohibition has enabled NEPA to emerge (according to many observers) as a signifi-cant vehicle for administrative reform, if only because it 'has made it less practical for [congressmen] to urge projects so environmentally "bad" that exposure through the NEPA process would almost certainly cause their demise',[83] rather than merely an eloquent statement of good environ-mental intentions.[84]

NEPA, and the preliminary US experience with its implementation, inspired many of the recommendations of a Canadian interdepartmental task force on environmental impact assessment. Its report, completed in 1972, recommended legislation under which an independent Environmental Review Board would be established to administer environmental impact assessment procedures. Pending the passage of such a law, the working group recommended setting up an interim environmental impact assessment program by Cabinet directive.[85] No legislation was forthcoming. Instead of an Environmental Review Board, Cabinet established the Federal Environmental Assessment and Review Office (FEARO), with far more limited responsibilities; rather than proposing legislation, Cabinet established a set of guidelines known as the Environmental Assessment and Review Process (EARP), outlined in administrative directives in 1973 and 1977. The most recent description of the process was published in the *Canada Gazette* in July 1984, and has come to be referred to as the Guidelines Order.[86]

EARP was widely criticized as ineffectual on a number of grounds. Perhaps the most important were its reliance on self-assessment of environmental impacts of specific projects by the departments promoting them, without any external oversight (of the kind provided by the judiciary under NEPA). This meant, among other things, that those departments alone made the decision to hold public hearings. In the limited number of cases where they were held, hearings under EARP were purely advisory in nature and were conducted by review panels whose membership and terms of reference were both decided on a purely *ad hoc* basis. As Emond has noted: 'If the various federal departments were as rational and environmentally conscientious as is implied by such discretion, then EARP [would be] unnecessary.'[87] They weren't, and it wasn't. Most departments and agencies to which EARP applied treated the process as entirely discretionary; it thus could not supply the impetus for administrative reform provided by NEPA.[88] Interestingly, this problem was anticipated by the 1972 task force, which considered the possibility that in order to overcome Canadian courts' restrictive interpretation of standing requirements:

> [I]t may be desirable . . . specifically to confer status on all individuals and groups who participate in the assessment process to initiate judicial review of procedural requirements. . . . *The very possibility of this type of judicial review would undoubtedly contribute to the effectiveness of the environmental impact assessment policy and process.*[89]

As a direct consequence of judicial action, the legal status of EARP changed, dramatically if perhaps temporarily, in late 1989 and early 1990. In response to lawsuits brought by environmental organizations in two separate cases, the Federal Court of Canada ruled that because the 1984 EARP procedures were set out in a regulation, they imposed a judicially enforceable obligation on the federal government to conduct environmental reviews of its 'undertakings' (the word used in the Guidelines Order).[90]

These rulings were made despite the acknowledged constitutional primacy of provincial jurisdiction in the area of resource management, and despite the fact that both suits involved provincial government projects. However, Saskatchewan's Rafferty-Alameda Dam required a federal licence under the International River Improvements Act, and the Three Rivers Dam on Alberta's Oldman River involved damage to fish habitat proscribed by the Fisheries Act as well as requiring a licence under the Navigable Waters Protection Act.[91] The decision of the Federal Court of Appeal in the Three Rivers Dam case suggests that the Guidelines Order obliges the federal departments involved to apply the prescribed stages of EARP to any undertaking which falls under an area of federal jurisdiction (in this case, Fisheries) even when the proponent of the initiative has not made a request for a federal licence or approval,[92] thus subjecting to environmental assessment a vast range of discretionary decisions not to take regulatory action against environmentally damaging activities. In addition, departmental conclusions about the 'significance' of environmental impacts (a crucial threshold, since this determines whether projects must be referred to review panels for public hearings under the Guidelines) appear now to be subject to judicial review.[93]

The Federal Court rulings did not go as far as they might have done. The Saskatchewan government took advantage of the fact that the Court had allowed construction of the Rafferty-Alameda Dam to continue while a review panel established by court order carried out its work to complete much of the project, arguably rendering the panel's work irrelevant.[94] The court likewise did not order a halt to the construction of the Three Rivers Dam. Since the Alberta government has appealed the decision mandating compliance with EARP in that case to the Supreme Court of Canada, on both constitutional and other grounds, the long-term policy impact of the decisions in both cases will not be settled until the court hands down its ruling (if then). Nevertheless the rulings are important as indicators of an unwonted reluctance on the part of the federal judiciary, conceivably related to the influence of the Charter of Rights and Freedoms, to defer to the discretion of Canadian governments in implementing their own stated environmental policy objectives. Anticipation of further such rulings led directly to the establishment of a joint federal-provincial review panel to evaluate the impacts of a proposed Alberta pulp mill,[95] and to a decision by the National Energy Board to incorporate explicit attention to environmental impacts into its consideration of energy export applications.[96] Such anticipation also led Cabinet to hasten the introduction of a long-promised bill (Bill C-78) which would provide a statutory basis for environmental impact assessment at the federal level. Ironically, if perhaps predictably, the bill as introduced would drastically limit both the scope of federal environmental impact assessment requirements, as compared with the provisions of the 1984 Guidelines as interpreted by the Federal Court, and the extent to which discretionary decisions about their applicability would be judicially reviewable.[97] At this writing, its fate is uncertain.

ENVIRONMENTAL RIGHTS?

Bill C-78 exemplifies Canadian governments' commitment to maintaining their broad discretion in the environmental policy field, and to exercising a high degree of control over the extent to which the judiciary will play a role in environmental policy. In response to this pattern, environmentalists speak with increasing vigour and eloquence about the need for 'environmental rights'.[98] Their arguments normally involve two closely related elements: a legally guaranteed right of access to the deliberations which result in environmental policy decisions, whether the making of regulations or the conduct of environmental assessments, and a substantive legal right to environmental quality, with judicially enforceable access to remedies against both government and private sources of environmental damage in cases where the courts find the right to be infringed.[99]

The key statement of the case for environmental rights in Canada, a 1981 article by lawyers John Swaigen and Richard Woods, argued that a substantive right to environmental quality 'need not be absolute. However, it must have the same prima-facie weight as a property right. This would give it substantial clout both against actions of the State and against private property rights.'[100] This claim, in turn, relied heavily on a point made a decade earlier by Joseph Sax in the US context. Individuals seeking to enforce property rights go before the courts as claimants asserting a legally defined interest, but the citizen seeking protection of the environment is little more than a 'supplicant, requesting that somehow the public interest be interpreted to protect the environmental values from which he benefits'. Effective protection of the environment, argued Sax, required the legal recognition of 'public rights' which, like private property rights, could not safely be left 'to some bureaucrat to vindicate when, and if, he determines them to be consistent with the public interest'.[101]

These proposals seem at first merely to demand the revival of a number of pre-industrial common law causes of action, albeit in a contemporary guise. In fact they go considerably further, for an additional element is the elimination of the common law requirement that an individual be able to show damage (or, in the case of public nuisance, special damage) before being able to assert environmental rights.[102] Swaigen and Woods argue that a substantive right to environmental quality 'must be a function solely of the citizen's rights as a citizen. When an individual is able to bring an action without regard to any specific personal injury, financial, or property loss, and with a prima-facie claim to environmental protection, he will have a truly substantive right.'[103] The effect is to introduce notion of a public trust in the protection of environmental quality,[104] making it something in which every citizen has an interest that is cognizable at law.

The issue of environmental rights and the role they imply for the judiciary is more than strictly academic, since one province's Minister of the Environment (Ontario's Ruth Grier) is now publicly committed to an environmental bill of rights. It is therefore worth examining in some detail the private member's bills she introduced in 1986 and 1987,[105] which started from the premise that 'The people of Ontario have a right to clean air, pure water and the preservation of the natural, scenic, historic and aesthetic values of the environment.' (Section 1 of the bills contained a remarkably expansive definition of 'environment' as including social, economic, and cultural conditions as well as the more conventional biophysical factors.) The proposals clearly entrenched the public trust doctrine in statute, defining that trust as 'the collective interest of residents of the province of Ontario and the protection thereof and the heritage therein for future generations'. The bills provided that:

> Where an activity has contaminated or degraded or an activity is likely to commence, is commencing or is continuing that threatens to contaminate or degrade the environment, any person may commence an action in the Supreme Court of Ontario, without having to show any greater or different right, harm or interest than that of other members of the public or any pecuniary or proprietary right or interest in the subject-matter of the proceedings, against,
> (a) any person who is responsible for the activity; and
> (b) any Minister responsible for regulatory, fiscal or proprietary control of the activity.[106]

This provision applied even in the absence of demonstrated violation of a permit or regulation.

Courts were empowered to inquire into and establish substantive standards of environmental protection where these had not been established by government, having regard to:

> (a) the right of the people of Ontario to the protection of the environment and the public trust therein against contamination or degradation;
> (b) the fulfilment of the widest range of beneficial uses of the environment without contamination or degradation; and
> (c) the achievement of a balance between population and resource use that will permit high standards of living and a wide sharing of life's amenities.[107]

In the absence of standards, once the existence or prospect of environmental contamination or degradation had been established, onus would shift to the defendant 'to establish . . . that there is no feasible and prudent alternative to the defendant's activity and that such activity is in the best interests of the public having regard to' the preceding factors.

Where standards had been established, compliance would constitute a defence against an action 'unless the plaintiff can establish, on a balance of probabilities, that the activity has caused or is likely to cause severe or irreparable contamination or degradation to the environment'. (Interestingly, the term 'standard' was used repeatedly in the Bill, but was nowhere defined.) The proposed legislation further eliminated defences based on the claim that 'the defendant is not the sole cause of the alleged or potential contamination or degradation', or on inconclusive scientific evidence of cause and effect relations 'where the effect on the environment is of a nature consistent with the contaminant or source or degradation being the total or partial, immediate or mediate cause'. Thus, both problems of standing and crucial evidentiary barriers to common law actions to protect the environment were to be effectively eliminated by statute. The licensing function performed by governmental standard-setting was partly safeguarded, but exercises of administrative discretion in its performance were nevertheless exposed to judicial review based on conformity with legislative objectives.

Courts were empowered to grant injunctions, make orders for the remedying of environmental damage, award damages, 'impose conditions on the defendant or make such other order as the Court may consider is necessary'. Courts were also given the option to refer 'any question or questions, except the final determination of the issue in question' to the EAB, which was also to administer a hearing assistance fund for litigants and intervenors involved in proceedings under the Act. Equally far-reaching were the proposed changes in the areas of access to information and public participation outside the courtroom. The bills provided extensive entitlements to information about pollution sources, albeit with the customary safeguards for allegedly proprietary information and for Cabinet confidences; appeals from Ministerial denials of disclosure were to be held by EAB. All environmental licences and permits under a variety of statutes were to be subject to a 30-day notice and comment period, with public hearings to be held on request except when 'the request is not made in good faith or is frivolous or is made only for the purpose of delay'.[108]

In addition, EAB was directed to hear applications for the review of existing permits, licences, and regulations 'having regard to the adequacy of the instrument to protect the environment and the public trust therein, especially in the light of technological advances that can be applied to the Province of Ontario' as long as 'a prima facie case [had] been made' by the applicant 'that the instrument should be amended or revoked'. It was further directed to review all the province's environmental regulations every five years, with regard to the same criteria. However, EAB reports would be subject to variance by Cabinet, like the conclusions of environmental assessment hearings (but unlike court decisions on applications under the environmental rights provisions of the bills).

It remains to be seen whether, or in what modified form, such legislation will be enacted. The concept of an environmental bill of rights in Ontario has a long history of support from politicians in opposition. Grier's bills were 'identical, except for a few grammatical changes, to a 1982 bill' introduced by a Liberal member of the Legislature who became a senior minister following the 1985 provincial election.[109] Indeed, the Liberals had been introducing similar private member's bills since 1979.[110] In government, they declined to pursue such legislation. After the NDP election victory in 1990 Grier indicated that such a bill would be introduced, but only following extensive consultation.[111] If her earlier proposals survive relatively intact, they will create the potential for a dramatic erosion of the discretionary authority of government; hitherto unreviewable regulation-making and permitting decisions (and of course non-decisions) will be exposed to judicial (or at least quasi-judicial) scrutiny.

Perhaps for that reason their survival seems unlikely, at least if past experience with Canadian governments' general aversion to increased judicial involvement in this policy field is a guide. That aversion is particularly apparent from the history of the Canadian Environmental Protection Act (Bill C-74), which was described by the federal Environment Minister of the day (Tom McMillan) as 'in effect, *if not technically*, this country's first "Environmental Bill of Rights" '.[112] Numerous environmental groups, as well as CEAC and its legal consultant, pointed out that it was nothing of the sort.[113] It contained no actionable rights, and only modestly expanded opportunities for public participation in the federal regulatory process.[114]

More significantly, the Minister himself went to great lengths to repudiate the concept of legally entrenched environmental rights before the Parliamentary committee studying the legislation. At the start of its hearings, he argued that such rights would be subject to interpretation and: 'Inevitably, the interpretation is going to come from the courts, not from politicians who are accountable to the people. We would in effect abdicate to the courts decisions affecting the environment, and the courts are not accountable.'[115] Near the end of the committee's deliberations he reiterated this argument:

> I am not sure it is in the public interest, and I am sure it is not in the environment's interest, to have law unduly made by judges as opposed to by politicians who can be held accountable at the ballot box and in other democratic ways. . . . .
> [T]he committee should reflect long and hard before it embraces with undue haste the principle of an environmental bill of rights that simply

takes a whole area of public policy, puts it on the laps of the courts, and tells the judiciary to sort it out.

The Minister went on to warn against the prospect of entrenching various kinds of rights in statute: 'Cumulatively, it could very well undermine the capacity of elected and therefore accountable people to represent the public interest as they see fit.'[116]

In this argument he was supported by at least some members of the business community. Even though Bill C-74 fell far short of actually entrenching environmental rights, one business spokesman claimed during hearings on the bill that its public participation provisions 'opened the door to individual citizens to bypass the normal political process in this country'[117] and another that: 'The powers of injunction and denunciation as well as revision of the regulations are too easily accessible to the ordinary citizen.'[118] Business has generally been very well served by existing patterns of consultation and negotiation with government. Indeed, one of the principal arguments for environmental rights is that they might serve to counterbalance the political influence, and the exclusivity of access to the decision-making process, that business enjoys by virtue of its economic resources.[119] Consequently, even stronger opposition can be expected to serious efforts to entrench environmental rights, likewise making improbable the survival of the Ontario proposals in their undiluted form.

THE FUTURE OF JUDICIAL INVOLVEMENT IN ENVIRONMENTAL POLICY

Several questions must be raised in conclusion — and it should be emphasized that they are questions rather than answers. If a right to environmental quality of the type proposed in Ontario is not to be absolute, where and how are its limitations determined? To how much environmental quality, and where, are people entitled? How can, and how should, courts resolve trade-offs between environment and development of the kind involved with (for example) banning nonrefillable containers, prosecuting polluting industries even at the risk of their closure, or restricting logging activities in wilderness areas?

In a remarkable departure from past Canadian environmental law and practice, the Ontario proposals could assign to the courts the task of making these choices. This is not to imply that the 'floodgates of litigation' would be opened as a result,[120] or that the enactment of such a bill of rights would necessarily change the content of environmental policy substantially. It might well have no such effect. Courts might adopt extremely high standards of proof of environmental degradation or contamination; they might simply defer to the executive with respect to the proper 'balance between population and resource use' in situations where standards do not exist. Conversely, the judiciary might respond to the spread of 'postmaterialist' values within government and among the population;[121] the trends in sentencing in environmental cases discussed earlier in the chapter lend tentative, preliminary support to this hypothesis. Thus the courts might in time address the vexing question of economic hardship in the way proposed by John McLaren two decades ago:

> If in the final analysis, the practical result is the shutting down of the offending operation, then . . . that has to be faced by the polluter and the community with what fortitude they can muster. It can well be argued that in the contemporary scale of social values endeavours to improve the state of the environment are more important than the continued existence of marginal or struggling industrial concerns. Apart from anything else it is not beyond the ingenuity of society and particularly governments to compensate for the adverse community consequences of the demise of a local employer.[122]

The issue is not one of judicial activism or interventionism versus judicial restraint. In a devastating critique of the conventional dichotomy in analysing constitutional interpretation, Cass Sunstein has demonstrated that neither category makes sense except with reference to specific sets of 'baseline assumptions' about the natural or normal state of affairs in civil society and about its proper relation to the state and the legal system.[123] The value of incorporating such assumptions into the analysis of judicial decisions is not confined to constitutional cases. Judges do not, of course, interpret the law in a vacuum, but rather within the constraints established by a body of statute, convention, and precedent. However, in an extremely broad and important range of cases these may not yield determinate answers. Even Ronald Dworkin, the philosopher most closely identified with the argument that there are 'right answers' to legal questions, concedes that judges' decisions about the meaning of particular legal rights will be contingent on such background assumptions.[124]

Environment Minister McMillan's argument that judges, unlike elected officials, are not accountable for such decisions is a familiar one. A certain degree of cynicism is in order about the invocation of this distinction. If accountability were a genuine concern, it could be argued that governments would seek to ensure informed decision-making, in the words of the US Supreme Court, by way of comprehensive and readily enforceable requirements for environmental impact assessment and provisions for the dissemination of the available information. Bill C-78, however, moves in exactly the opposite direction. For that matter, Canadian government in general is characterized by a degree of secrecy that Douglas Hartle has called 'inordinate, indeed obscene' and 'one of the most pernicious and serious flaws in the Canadian political system'.[125] However, not all governments, at all times, necessarily merit the same quotient of cynicism, and two serious lines of response to McMillan suggest themselves.

The first of these is that the accountability of Cabinet-parliamentary governments, in particular, derives from the fact that they can be replaced at elections rather than from any correspondence between the public's policy preferences and governmental decisions. There seems little reason to alter Dahl's verdict of more than thirty years ago that 'in no large nation state can elections tell us much about the preferences of majorities and minorities' with respect to specific policies, and that: 'What is true of elections is even more true of the interelection period.'[126] In Canada the strength of party discipline and its facilitation of full-line forcing as an instrument of partisan strategy are among the factors which add to the applicability of this conclusion.[127] As for the interelection period, it is hard to improve on the classic reminder: 'The flaw in the pluralist heaven is that the heavenly chorus sings with a strong upper-class accent. Probably about ninety per cent of the people cannot get into the pressure system'[128] so crucial to interelection policy decisions and to the agenda-setting function itself. There may be reason to dispute the figure; neither is it clear (as it once might have been) that inequalities in the distribution of political resources necessarily generate a tendency toward weaker rather than stronger environmental law. However the basic importance of those inequalities remains.

This is not an argument against democracy, but rather a warning against the facile assumption that governments necessarily act in the public interest. As illustrated by McMillan's argument, such claims quickly become circular: the public interest is what the government of the day says it is. This suggests a second line of response. It is precisely the isolation of certain kinds of decisions from the political calculus that the entrenchment of legal rights seeks to achieve. From this perspective, the biases created by the unequal distribution of resources and the agenda-setting resources of politicians combine to make 'accountability' the problem, rather than the solution. Given a specified statutory framework and a broader background of understood norms for the making of legal decisions, we (whoever 'we' are) trust judges to make certain kinds of decisions more than we trust elected officials and those who do their bidding – or, perhaps, we mistrust them less. Stephen Holmes has referred to such choices as 'precommitments'.[129] The most basic (and most difficult to alter) of these are rights which have been given a constitutional status. Many legal rights in Canada, however, have no constitutional status and can be extended or abrogated with relative ease by way of a simple amendment to the relevant statute.

There is vast scope for debate about what kinds of policy decisions ought to be constrained by legally entrenched rights. However, the choice of the judicial system as a primary forum for resolving certain kinds of conflicts is not an inherently perverse, irrational, or undemocratic one. Individual mobilization of the legal system can be viewed as a valuable and much neglected form of political participation, albeit one which (like most other forms of participation) is not equally accessible to all citizens.[130] Indeed, it is hard to imagine a liberal society, in the broadest sense of the term, that did not rely on the judicial system in the first instance with respect to some, possibly quite limited range of policy choices and resource allocations, such as those involving certain property rights. Perhaps the deficiencies of Canadian political decision-making, the severity of environmental problems, and the limited scope of existing remedies do not provide a definitive case for the expanded involvement of the judicial system in the environmental policy field, but the case is certainly not a frivolous one. Indeed, the strongest argument against environmental rights may involve the potential effect were judges to adopt the perspective suggested by McLaren. Workers in affected industries and the communities they support could conceivably face the loss of their livelihood without any legal recourse and (quite probably) without the political resources to put forward an effective demand for compensation.

FOR FURTHER READING

D. Estrin and J. Swaigen, *Environment on Trial* (Toronto: Macmillan, 1978).

M. Jeffery, *Environmental Approvals in Canada: Practice and Procedure* (Toronto: Butterworths, 1989).

T. Schrecker, 'The Political Context and Content of Environmental Law', in T. Caputo et al., eds, *Law and Society: A Critical Perspective* (Toronto: Harcourt, Brace, Jovanovich, 1989).

J. Swaigen, ed., *Environmental Rights in Canada* (Toronto: Butterworths, 1981).

J. Whitney and V. Maclaren, eds, *Environmental Impact Assessment: the Canadian Experience* (Toronto: Institute for Environmental Studies, 1985).

PART II

Policy and Politics

CHAPTER 6

Green Lobbies

Pressure Groups and Environmental Policy

JEREMY WILSON

Any composite portrait of Canadian environmental groups must describe
not only the long list of issues groups pursue, but also the wide array of
political methods they employ. The list of issues includes wildlife and
forest conservation, wilderness preservation, pesticide and herbicide use,
air and water pollution, energy conservation, farmland preservation,
recycling, and waste reduction. Each of these categories encompasses
dozens of specific concerns. In the water pollution area, for example,
groups across the country are involved on hundreds of fronts, dealing
with matters ranging from municipal waste disposal and industrial effluent
discharges to offshore dumping and the regulation of oil tanker traffic.

The range of political strategies employed is as disparate as the catalogue of the movement's concerns. Groups prepare research papers,
produce press releases, hold news conferences, and provide reporters
with reaction to events. They write letters, meet with government officials,
launch suits, intervene at regulatory hearings, and present briefs to legislative committees. They publish books, operate resource libraries, and
produce magazines, newsletters, factsheets, videos, and radio shows. They
march, sit-in, and blockade.

As well as being a manifestation of the number of government policies
and agencies environmental groups deal with, this diversity of political
approaches is a product of the movement's composition. Groups draw
from across the social spectrum, pulling together activists with a wide
range of political aptitudes and dispositions. And in another respect,
tactical diversity is a reflection of the fact that many environmental groups
are part pressure group and part 'new social movement'.[1] Many groups,
that is, practise a kind of dual politics, mixing the pressure group's prag-
matism with the social movement's commitment to the goals of societal
transformation and its sensitivity to the dangers of co-optation. This
dualism is evident in the approaches adopted. Most groups devote considerable attention to 'within the system' policy work, often accepting certain
trade-offs and constraints in order to advance bargaining relationships

with public officials. They engage in what we will call direct lobbying. But most groups also invest heavily in measures designed to transform societal thinking about environmental issues. They pursue public-oriented lobbying approaches.

The movement's diversity is a main source of its strength, a strength, however, that has translated most readily into successes in public-oriented lobbying. The Canadian environmental movement's impact on public consciousness concerning the environmental effects of development has not been matched by an equivalent impact on government policy. Groups and their allies have been very effective in putting environmental issues on the agenda. Their direct lobbying attempts to extract firm policy commitments from the country's governments have met with less success.

Environmentalists might be justified in drawing optimistic projections from the movement's trajectory to date; one might contend that, having helped to transform public consciousness regarding the environment, groups are now poised to translate these gains into fundamental and far-reaching changes in government policy and process. An analysis of the movement's record, however, also provides plenty of grounds for gloomy prognoses. The movement's gains have been proscribed by fundamental features of Canadian political-economic reality, most notably the continuing economic importance of resource extraction, and the continuing political strength of concatenations of public-private power premised on 'business as usual' exploitation of natural resource wealth. Much of the history of the Canadian environmental movement has revolved around struggles against coalitions such as those which draw forest companies, government forestry agencies, and their allies together in support of long-term plans to liquidate old-growth forests, or those which link various industries and development-oriented government departments in opposition to measures that would disrupt long-standing waste disposal practices. All of these alliances are propelled by considerable momentum. Some have been slowed or diverted onto safer tracks by environmental opposition, but many have rolled along, providing regular reminders of the obstacles faced by the movement.

ENVIRONMENTAL GROUPS: STRENGTHS AND WEAKNESSES

The environmental movement's greatest resource is its large, varied, and highly committed membership. Environmental groups, that is, are very effective mobilizers of volunteer (and minimal-pay) energy.

The Canadian environmental movement comprises at least 1,800 groups; inclusion of small grass-roots organizations such as neighbourhood recycling committees and school clubs would increase this number by several hundred.[2] Groups vary in size from small, local ones with a few dozen members to large national groups like Greenpeace with over 300,000 members and the Canadian Wildlife Federation (CWF), which claims 620,000 'members, supporters, and affiliates'.[3] In between these poles we find major national groups like the Canadian Nature Federation (CNF) with 36,000 members and the Friends of the Earth (FOE) with 25,000, along with large provincial and regional organizations such as the Western Canada Wilderness Committee (WCWC) with over 25,000 members and Pollution Probe with 20,000.[4] There exists no reliable estimate of the total membership of the country's environmental groups, but taking into account the size of the large organizations and the rapidly burgeoning number of small ones, it seems safe to conjecture that over one million Canadians belong to at least one group. This estimate may in fact be conservative; the nine per cent of Canadian adults who told Angus Reid pollsters in mid-1989 that they belonged to an environmental group would translate into nearly two million individuals.[5]

It is impossible to talk with any precision about the intensity of member support. But the movement's success in mobilizing volunteer labour provides clear proof of the high level of commitment. For example, the WCWC reports that it draws on the volunteer help of over 100 individuals each week, and that just one of its recent projects—the construction of a trail into the Carmanah Valley—absorbed over 8,000 hours of volunteer labour in two years.[6]

This is not the place to explore in depth the genesis of environmental activism, but it is apparent that the high level of membership commitment derives largely from intense concern over issues. What are referred to in the interest group literature as 'selective' and 'solidary' incentives play some part in members' decisions to devote energy to groups; that is, some individuals are influenced by the opportunity to receive benefits unrelated to the group's policy goals (such as magazines or access to courses and field trips) or by a desire to cultivate contacts or friendships.[7] For some, participation also no doubt serves an expressive function; involvement is a way of defining oneself to significant others. 'Purposive' incentives, however, provide the main motivation for participation: 'the intrinsic worth or dignity of the ends themselves are regarded . . . as justifying effort'.[8]

Any attempt to describe the movement's diversity by categorizing types of groups is quickly revealed to be an exercise in pounding square pegs into round holes. There can, however, be no mistaking the movement's breadth. Groups with multiple-issue orientations co-operate with those focused on specific issues. Moderate, reformist groups with a preference for quiet lobbying or scientific homework campaign alongside of those that are more radical and/or more disposed to emotional appeals. Advocacy groups drawing most of their support from a broad constituency of environmentally concerned citizens work beside the bird-watchers, hunters, hikers, and others who predominate in naturalist, wildlife conservation, and outdoor recreation groups.

Pluralism and diversity can, of course, bring internecine squabbling, duplication of effort, competition for members, and other counter-productive activities. Some problems of this sort do affect Canadian environmental groups, but far from creating serious difficulties, diversity usually translates into resourcefulness and adaptability, making for a movement that is able to cover a wide spectrum of issues and draw on a broad repertoire of political methods. Whether circumstances demand a presence on the barricades, scientific research, overtures to potential allies in the native, business, media, or labour communities, a concerted telephone blitz of supporters, or any one of innumerable other strategies, some corner of the movement can usually be counted on to come forward.

Tactical adaptability is also a function of organizational characteristics. Like reform-oriented and public interest groups generally, most environmental groups reject complex, formal structures. Decision-making approaches vary, but in many groups budgetary constraints combine with an adherence to the values of participative democracy to produce what can be characterized as benign, open oligarchies.[9] Larger, more established groups tend to be staff-run, with membership participation channelled through annual meetings and/or boards of directors. In most instances, though, members who involve themselves thoroughly in volunteer work soon find themselves participating actively in decision-making. These characteristics make for organizational fluidity, enabling groups to adapt readily in response to evolving political challenges.

Organizational fluidity also contributes to an effective system for channelling volunteer energy and recruiting leaders. In all organizations some resources are wasted because potential activists find that extant groups do not provide scope for what they regard as their talents. This seems to be a relatively insignificant problem here despite the fact that, like the political world in general, the environmental movement attracts some big egos. Since there is no shortage of important work to be done, existing groups usually are able to offer potential activists roles appropriate to their interests and skills. Most groups are open enough that members wanting to pursue a new issue or approach will be able to do so as long as it passes minimal tests of appropriateness. Many groups provide considerable scope for issue entrepreneurship, allowing members to propose new campaigns and tactics. Finally, those perceiving opportunities to be limited in existing organizations often set up their own.

At the other end of the involvement spectrum, environmental groups also provide options for those wanting to participate mainly with their wallets. As Roger Gibbins has described the view of one hypothetical supporter, 'Greenpeace becomes my "hired gun" in the fight against the whalers, and yet no more is demanded of me than the thirty seconds it takes to write a small cheque. This very minimal form of individual participation, when aggregated across thousands of individuals, provides the foundation for an effective political organization.'[10]

Some groups have access to the resources of international affiliates. FOE and Greenpeace, for example, link most of their issue campaigns to broader international initiatives. The benefits of such co-ordination can be illustrated by reference to the extent to which Greenpeace Canada's pulp and paper campaigners have drawn on information and expertise provided by the organization's Scandinavian wing. Noting that Scandinavian pulp and paper operations have remained competitive while adhering to stricter pollution control rules than prevail in Canada, Greenpeace challenges Canadian companies' claims about the impossibility of meeting tougher standards.

Among the movement's weaknesses is the fact that its large and committed support base has not translated into financial strength. A number of groups do control impressive annual budgets. For example, by the close of the 1980s, Ducks Unlimited Canada was spending in excess of $35 million per year developing and operating waterfowl habitat projects, while the World Wildlife Fund (WWF) was budgeting close to $5 million on its endangered spaces, endangered species, and other programs.[11] FOE and the CNF were operating on yearly budgets of $800,000 and $950,000 respectively.[12] Most groups, however, work with budgets a fraction of this size. And even major national organizations like FOE, WWF, or the CNF cannot afford the sort of political initiatives routinely undertaken by corporations. No environmental group is able to pay well-connected Ottawa lobby firms large monthly retainers, or to afford extensive television advocacy advertising campaigns. The movement's large pool of committed volunteer labour does represent a significant compensating advantage. And low-budget tactical alternatives no doubt reflect the values of the environmental movement better than would slick advertising and business-style lobbying. But there can be no question that many of the activities presently funded on shoestring budgets could be more effectively pursued were the revenue base stronger. For example, groups requiring expert research assistance are often handicapped by their inability to pay salaries equivalent to those offered by industry and government. Volunteers frequently find themselves out-of-pocket for expenses incurred participating in regulatory hearings, meetings with allies from other areas, or other routine endeavours.

The movement's financial limitations are not due to unimaginative fund-raising techniques or, in the case of most organizations, to overly rigid attitudes regarding the appropriateness of accepting funds from corporation and government sources.

Membership fees and individual donations are the main source of funds for most groups, accounting for between 50 and 60% of the revenues of major groups like FOE, the CNF, and the WCWC, and for much higher proportions in most smaller groups.[13] To take two British Columbia groups as examples, member fees and donations accounted for 97% of the 1989 revenues of the Friends of Clayoquot Sound, and for 74% of the 1989 funds of the Valhalla Wilderness Society.[14]

Although many smaller groups simply let prospective donors and members find their way to the door, a number of larger organizations adopt more active and systematic fund-raising methods. The WWF, for example, maintains a 'Finance Team' at the staff level, with different individuals responsible for different facets of the organization's $6 million per year (1989/90) fund-raising effort. Greenpeace conducts membership canvasses in ten cities, using canvassers who are paid an hourly rate plus incentives. A few other groups have emulated this system. Greenpeace has also led the way in the use of direct mail, sending out over five million pieces a year. A portion of this total goes to existing members, but large mailings are also directed at names on lists that Greenpeace buys from magazines and other organizations in order to support its aggressive attempts to 'prospect' for new members and financial supporters. These techniques are controversial among environmentalists since they generate what some consider junk mail. Greenpeace defends the practice, noting its use of recycled paper and arguing that most recipients find the mailings informative.[15] It also argues that direct mail provides public interest groups with a cost-effective means of penetrating the mass media haze and reaching an audience of potential sympathizers. In the words of two international Greenpeace leaders:

> For Greenpeace and a myriad of other public interest groups small and large, the home mailbox has become both a sanctuary and a lifeline: a sanctuary for delivering those political views that cannot survive the media's censorship, and lifeline for the growth and preservation of the ... ailing tradition of citizen involvement in public issues .... [D]irect mail creates a community of concerned citizens that can be reached no other way. Large pools of sympathetic people are contacted and cultivated through the mails, shared with other groups, and eventually educated and cajoled into action.[16]

Various means are used to augment money raised from members and individual donors. Many groups retail products that contribute to awareness of the environment. For example, the CWF's mail-order operation brought in over $5 million of the $11.4 million it raised in 1989/90, while the WCWC's sales of calendars and wilderness-related merchandise contributed an estimated $280,000 of its $620,000 budget in 1988/89.[17] Auctions, benefit concerts, and various other fund-raising events are used extensively.

Government and corporation grants and donations make up the balance of the movement's funding. Some groups refuse to accept grants from either source, but most receive at least some government money. The amounts are usually not large enough to engender any real fears of co-optation. Environment Canada has provided about $225,000 per year to underwrite the costs of the co-ordinating services performed by the

Canadian Environmental Network (CEN) and its affiliated regional networks.[18] Although this funding helps maintain rudimentary inter-group links, it is generally agreed that more financial resources would be required to operate a proper system of information sharing. Environment Canada also dispenses money from its Environment Week and Environmental Partners funds, and from various other programs.

In some instances, groups participating in commissions or hearings receive funding, but with a few exceptions,[19] regulatory bodies and other government agencies have been reluctant to support intervenors.

A number of federal and provincial agencies do provide financial support in the form of contracts for special administrative or research tasks. For example, in 1989–90, the Canadian International Development Agency, Fisheries and Oceans Canada, and various provincial government agencies (along with Environment Canada) helped fund WWF projects.[20] In total, government sources provided about twenty per cent of the WWF's revenues. The WWF has also been among a small number of groups that have aggressively sought to tap into corporate sources. In 1989–90 it reported that about fourteen per cent of its revenues came from corporations, and listed Canada Life, Inco, Noranda, and Petro-Canada among those contributing over $100,000.[21] In turn, the WWF makes many special project grants to smaller organizations such as Earthlife Foundation, Canadian Ecological Advocates, and the Alberta Wilderness Association.[22]

ENVIRONMENTAL LOBBYING

The movement's diversity is reflected in the wide range of political approaches employed in a typical environmental campaign. Most environmental goals are pursued by coalitions of groups, with different organizations bringing distinct tactical dispositions to the mix. Most groups are themselves eclectic in approach. Since tactical decisions are usually taken against a backdrop of great uncertainty about what combination of building blocks might produce the desired outcome, the strategies concocted are generally premised on the risk-aversive notion that a range of initiatives should be pursued. Typically, some resources are invested in direct lobbying of politicians and bureaucrats. But most campaigns place greater emphasis on public-oriented approaches. That is, the movement bases much of its political activity on the belief that in order to move politicians, one must first move public opinion. Applying this two-step analysis of the political process, the movement pursues both short- and long-term educational strategies. It uses the mass media along with more direct means of contacting sympathizers to galvanize support for immediate issue objectives while at the same time trying to transform public consciousness.

Our consideration of the initiatives involved in direct and public-oriented lobbying is not meant to provide an all-inclusive sketch of the measures environmental groups utilize on behalf of the environment. A more comprehensive profile would note, first, that many groups take 'do-it-ourselves' approaches to environmental improvement. Here, among other initiatives, we would want to chronicle the efforts of organizations like the Nature Conservancy of Canada to purchase and preserve natural areas, of Ducks Unlimited and the hundreds of clubs operating under the CWF umbrella to improve fish and wildlife habitat, and of a multitude of organizations operating recycling, clean-up, and waste-reduction projects. Second, a full account would emphasize the large amount of energy invested in secondary functions needed to support issue campaigns. In order to achieve its primary goals, a group must devote considerable energy to gathering the information needed to develop its arguments and guide its strategic decisions, to building and sustaining its membership base, and to keeping open lines of communication to key actors throughout the policy system. Third, a comprehensive analysis of environmental group activities would emphasize 'deep education' initiatives such as those involved in the school programs operated by numerous groups. Fourth, a thorough survey would note the role of litigation strategies, discussing legal challenges such as those launched by the CWF over the Rafferty-Alameda Dam project, and by the Ecology Action Centre, Greenpeace, and others over the Point Aconi power plant.

What about direct lobbying? What kind of access to government officials do environmental groups have? What direct lobbying approaches are most effective? Not surprisingly, it is difficult to offer general answers to questions like these. About the only generalization that can be safely advanced is that no Canadian environmental group has resources adequate enough to cover all of the government officials who play significant roles in the typical policy process. Most government policies emerge from processes involving complex networks of departmental bureaucrats, central agency officials, and Cabinet ministers. The kind of obstacles likely to be faced by environmental lobbyists in Ottawa or any of the provinces are summed up in a description of the Ottawa system offered by Elizabeth May after her stint as a policy adviser to the federal Minister of Environment:

> [T]here are powerful gatekeepers throughout the bureaucracy. People near money—Treasury Board and Finance. People near decision-making—the Department of Justice and the Privy Council Office. All those nameless, faceless bureaucrats who advise the chairmen of cabinet committees about which departmental memoranda have achieved sufficient consensus in the 'the system' to be placed on a cabinet agenda .... Cabinet committees were carefully managed and choreographed by the 'central agencies'. An original idea would be as out of place at a cabinet meeting as a Ouija board

. . . . The good idea must first be ground down fine within a department. Then the department in question must conduct 'bilaterals' — in other words, go from one department to another, convincing other bureaucrats that the proposal is not a threat. If another department is not convinced, chances are the good idea will never make it to a cabinet committee meeting. The gate-keepers at the Privy Council Office will see to that. If through some miracle of tenacity and political pressure an idea does make it to cabinet committee for a decision, the ministers around the table will respond, based on the script of criticism advanced by the Minister's own senior bureaucrats.[23]

Clearly any lobbyist trying to work within such a system faces some daunting challenges. In order to be effective, she/he must have reliable information about when, where, and how decisions are being made, along with an ability to penetrate the screening structures set up to shield decision-makers from unwanted entreaties. The successful lobbyist must earn good access not only to decision-makers but to those who supply the information and advice on which decisions are based. It is essential to recognize the power of those who shape Cabinet ministers' perceptions of problems and solutions.

Those environmentalists who do engage in direct lobbying offer common-sense advice about how these challenges are best met:

[An] important principle is the unceasing cultivation of allies . . . . leave no stone unturned. . . . When the door to a new contact does open, make sure that you've done your homework, that you understand your audience and what their potential interest in your issue may be. When lobbying government or professional people, it's a rule of thumb that the higher up the ladder you go, the more valuable their time is and the more limited their attention span can be. So lay out your case concisely, remembering that a handful of explicit photos may save you hours of explanation. . . . Until you understand the hopes and fears of your adversaries, they will remain your adversaries. For the art of successful negotiation requires that you understand what your adversaries value and need as people — and give it to them — before you can get what you want.[24]

It is important to build personal rapport with the people who are sympathetic and to figure out a strategy for building coalitions across parties. . . . And follow-up is critical. You don't burn people. You don't find out a good piece of information from someone and then make the source known. . . . And one of the basic things is remembering to acknowledge when someone does something you've asked them to — when they ask the question in question period or insert the amendment in the legislative committee. . . . It is important, especially when you're talking to the media, to acknowledge someone who has done the right thing. It makes it more likely that they'll be willing to help the next time.[25]

[A]s in any field of social action, you are about as good as your network. After fifteen years I don't frankly find much more sophisticated ways of influencing decisions than knowing the right people and writing a lot of letters. The kind of personal network and rapport you develop is what really counts in terms of access to information and access to decisions. And it is important to understand the way the place works and to be able to put yourself in the shoes of the bureaucracy.[26]

The trick is to get to the bureaucrats who are working on the file. By the time it reaches the political level it is usually too late. . . . But unfortunately, because of our lack of staff capacity, most environmental groups are not able to follow files as closely as we should at the bureaucratic level.[27]

On the question of which arms to twist, the thing you learn when you lobby is that you don't just do one particular one on one day, you do several dozen . . . . I always feel like one of those people who climbs the bell tower and gets the carillons ringing . . . you keep several ropes going at one time because you need the cacophony, you need the whole orchestra or you can't get music. . . . You need groups coming at the political people, you need their own civil servants reacting to them in a positive manner. . . . Lessons? One is that we live in an imperfect world and to expect perfection is just silly. Secondly, if you've got an ally support him or her, give them assistance, move them toward doing something useful. And give them credit when credit is due. Don't say 'now that the minister's done what we said, that's all very nice, but he or she didn't go the last twenty per cent.' The minister is sitting there saying, why do I bother to deal with these people, they're never satisfied, they're always critical.[28]

A survey of direct lobbying efforts indicates considerable variation across both groups and issues in the extent of access to decision-makers, and in the extent to which access translates into influence. Access and influence are generally better where the issue is not perceived to entail major and visible redistributions of scarce resources (including power) among societal groups or government agencies. Wildlife conservation groups, for example, often work closely with officials from fish and wildlife agencies on issues such as habitat enhancement and game regulation, while outdoor recreation organizations are regularly consulted by park officials on the development of park-use plans. But such groups rarely have equivalent influence over decisions about the allocation of forest or agricultural land to wildlife preserves or parks.

A closely related — and equally obvious — generalization is that groups have better access to bureaucracies with environmental protection mandates than they do to central agencies or to development-oriented departments like those responsible for energy or forests. Federal and provincial environment ministers and their officials all consult with leaders of at least some environmental groups. Those perceived to offer a 'balanced perspective' are naturally more likely to enjoy regular opportunities. Access is exchanged for the things groups are able to offer: information, a conduit for communications with a client constituency, assistance with the administration or enforcement of policy, support in bureaucratic turf wars, or help in legitimizing departmental officials and their policies. In Ottawa, for example, there have been a number of meetings between recent ministers of environment and a 'Group of 8' contingent which draws together representatives from some major wildlife and wilderness conservation groups – the CWF, the CNF, WWF, the Canadian Parks and Wilderness Society, Wildlife Habitat Canada, the Nature Conservancy of Canada, the Canadian Arctic Resources Committee, and Ducks Unlimited. Since these organizations spend heavily on the acquisition, enhancement, and protection of habitat, they are able to wield the influence of potential partners on issues such as grasslands protection.[29]

On certain issues groups may establish particularly close working relationships with environment ministers and their officials. For instance, Adele Hurley and Michael Perley of the Canadian Coalition on Acid Rain worked closely with Ontario's environment minister, Jim Bradley, and his staff to develop the province's new acid emission standards.[30] During the latter stages of the campaign to save South Moresby, federal government strategy appears to have been developed by a network including Minister of Environment Tom McMillan, several of his officials, Members of Parliament John Fraser and Jim Fulton, and key park supporters such as Thom Henley, John Broadhead, Colleen McCrory, and Vicky Husband.[31] The minister consulted with this group on a number of occasions during negotiations with British Columbia over boundaries, using these meetings to glean intelligence about the provincial position and to ensure that the park proponents would back his bargaining stance. In turn, these meetings provided environmentalists with the opportunity to stiffen McMillan's resolve to hold out for inclusion of Lyell Island in the park. And on at least one occasion, the park proponents' input had a critical impact on the Minister's decision about what strategy to pursue in negotiations.[32]

Generally speaking, environment groups have not enjoyed this kind of access to ministers and officials from other departments. In Ottawa, the consequences of this limited influence could be seen operating throughout 1990 in the Cabinet-level processes that weakened the government's Green Plan and diluted previous commitments on environmental assessment and global warming. Speaking of the process that unfolded during the final months of the government's preparation of the Green Plan, Kevin McNamee of the CNF diagnosed the situation:

> The environment movement traditionally has focused on the Minister of Environment. Now those decisions are not being made by the Minister of Environment. He's got to convince his cabinet colleagues on an overall agenda for the environment. And I'm 99% confident in saying that as a community, we have done very little work on other ministers – the Epps and Mazankowskis. And it's difficult to start lobbying them now – because

of time, because of access. . . . At the CNF we have tried to work through the consultative process and the Greenprint process to influence the Green Plan. . . . But now it's a new ballgame, and we don't have the resources, the access, the wherewithal to mount a lobbying campaign encompassing those other ministers and their advisers.[33]

For the most part, then, environmental groups operate in the peripheral zones of the policy communities that shape government responses to environmental issues.[34] On specific issues, certain groups may be granted (and choose to accept) the privileges conferred on those in the inner, 'sub-government', part of the policy community—positions on advisory committees, invitations to comment on draft policy, access to inside information, and the like. But, more often, because they are not invited, because they lack the institutional resources needed to sustain 'inner-circle' policy work, or because they fear co-optation, environmental lobbyists remain on the margins of the policy community, prominently placed in what Pross calls the 'attentive public'.[35] This position offers a good base for the movement's public-oriented lobbying strategies.

As noted, this type of lobbying is premised on a two-step approach to influencing public policy. The movement has tried to shift government priorities by galvanizing and focusing societal concern over the environment. Although the impact of this work on policy has often been disappointing, the movement (along with allies in the scientific, educational, and media sectors) can take credit for significant increases in public environmental consciousness. Its efforts here centre on the distribution of information to members, supporters, and those seeking information. Most groups distribute factsheets, newsletters, or magazines,[36] while some operate speakers' bureaus or other information services. Pollution Probe, for example, estimates that it handled over 35,000 requests for information in 1989.[37] Many groups have produced extensive series of books and pamphlets. The Conservation Council of New Brunswick, for example, lists over a dozen publications, including 'Acid Rain in the East', 'The Dump Dilemma', and 'A Soft Energy Path for New Brunswick'.[38] Building on this core educational work, the movement has developed effective strategies for getting its message to a wider audience of potential sympathizers.

The activities of wilderness preservation groups illustrate a number of imaginative and low-cost means of conveying information and images. These groups have done an excellent job of covering both the intellectual and emotional bases, buttressing research-based arguments about poor forestry practices with presentations juxtaposing the splendours of old-growth forests against the devastation of clear-cut logging. Considerable emphasis is put on the power of photographic images. As Ken Lay of the WCWC says: 'Where the vast majority of the people you want to support preservation of an area will never be able to get there, you have to use photographs and other means to build an emotional attachment to that area. Then they will be moved to action.'[39] The same point is made by John Broadhead in his account of the South Moresby campaign:

> Another ingredient . . . was the use of images. It's not a simple matter to describe the impacts of logging on fish habitat, nor the effects that ripple out through associated ecosystems. So, photographers were coaxed to go into the field (most of them simply volunteered) to acquire images equal to the place and the issue. They returned with superlative photographs of wildlife and ancient ecosystems, and devastating shots of landslides and debris-choked salmon streams. It's no exaggeration to say that at least 100,000 photos were examined over the years, and then winnowed down into ever-improving slide shows for public presentation.[40]

The slide show has been the bread-and-butter means of delivering the wilderness message. One of BC's most peripatetic wilderness campaigners, Vicky Husband, presents her 'Vicky's horror show' catalogue of clear-cut logging excesses to scores of audiences each year.

The WCWC has used broadsheet information handouts to publicize areas it seeks to preserve such as the Stein Valley, the Carmanah Valley, and the Tatshenshini.[41] The WCWC publishes several of these each year, with print runs as high as 500,000 distributed free of charge through libraries, outdoor stores, and other sympathetic outlets. Each issue urges readers to express their concerns to politicians, and provides a handy 'tear-off' solicitation form in the hope of generating contributions sufficient to cover production costs. The WCWC also uses calendars and posters to achieve wide distribution of wilderness images. Each year it sells about 45,000 copies of two calendars (a western Canada version and a Canada version) featuring different endangered wilderness areas each month. Its most popular poster to date — of giant Carmanah Sitka spruce over the words 'big trees, not big stumps' — has sold over 21,000 copies.

The wilderness cause has also been advanced through a series of books. The Stein Valley, South Moresby, and Clayoquot Sound have all been richly depicted in plush, photo-filled volumes.[42] Aimed at being 'the kind of book that people would enjoy giving and receiving, that would linger on coffee tables in the living rooms and offices of opinion leaders in Canadian society',[43] each has sold over 10,000 copies. An innovative variation on the photo-illustrated book became an integral part of the WCWC's campaign to preserve the Carmanah. In 1989 it organized an art project in the valley, inviting Robert Bateman, Toni Onley, Jack Shadbolt, and over 90 other visual artists to use a WCWC-catered camp as a base from which to capture images of the valley. The resultant works were exhibited at a number of centres around British Columbia before being sold at an auction which raised over $115,000. Seventy pieces are presented in *Carmanah: Artistic Visions of an Ancient Rainforest*, an award-winning book introduced by strongly worded arguments for creation of a park in the Carmanah.[44] While it is difficult to assess the contribution of such books, there can be no doubt that the political costs of logging an area increase after it is immortalized between the covers of a well-produced and widely distributed volume.

The wilderness movement has also sought to bring interested members of the public to threatened wilderness areas. A number of groups have undertaken extensive trail building and mapping projects in order to make areas like the Carmanah and the Stein more accessible to the general public. The Sierra Club's bus trips to the Carmanah trailhead have attracted hundreds of visitors during the summers since construction of the trail. Other groups have used whale watching tours in much the same way. As St Lawrence beluga whale campaigner Leone Pippard says, the best way to transform the average apathetic Canadian into an environmentalist is to take him or her on a whale-watching tour.[45]

As even a quick perusal of news coverage will attest, environmental groups are usually able to attract the attention of the media. And the media's treatment of the movement is generally quite sympathetic — and also usually quite superficial.

The movement's ability to put forward credible spokespersons allows it to maintain a strong presence in coverage of policy developments in Ottawa and the provinces. Members of the Ottawa press gallery, for example, frequently draw on individuals like Julia Langer and Kai Millyard of FOE, or Stephen Hazell of the Canadian Arctic Resources Committee, for reaction to federal government moves. A number of more proactive approaches are used to inject an environmental perspective into the daily news diet. Groups hold news conferences, distribute briefs and press releases, take reporters on tours, and pass on information crucial to the initiation or development of stories. Groups such as the Ecology Action Centre present regular radio shows.

The movement has also earned a reputation for attracting media attention in less traditional ways. From its inception as the Vancouver-based 'Don't Make a Wave Committee' in 1970,[46] Greenpeace has been guided in its choice of media strategies by the truism that, for the media, news is new. It has continued to devise novel campaign initiatives, while catering in increasingly sophisticated ways to the needs of the media. Greenpeace usually sends its own photographer and video crew to the events it stages, often providing television stations with access to its own videotape.

Greenpeace has also paid increasing attention to the need to put forward expert spokespersons. The following excerpts exemplify a 'textbook' Greenpeace-initiated story, illustrating how the stunt is used to provide a platform for the scientifically authoritative Greenpeace spokesperson:

> Two environmental activists have chained themselves to a railway track inside a booby-trapped box to draw attention to a pulp and paper mill they say is Canada's biggest polluter. Three members of Greenpeace stopped a

shipment of chlorine from entering the Canadian Pacific Forest Products Ltd mill in La Tuque, Que., yesterday and locked themselves into a large metal box that is bolted to the railway tracks leading to the plant. . . . Diane Goulet, a biochemist and Greenpeace activist, said the CP Forest Products mill dumps 102 tonnes of organochlorines into the St-Maurice River daily, more than any other mill in Canada. Chlorine is used to bleach paper, and byproducts of the process, notably dioxins and furans, are believed to cause cancer. Greenpeace has demanded that chlorine bleaching be outlawed by 1993, and that the amount of permissible untreated effluent be cut to zero.[47]

The importance of the international media has not been overlooked. Describing one technique used to put pressure on the BC government and the forest industry over logging practices, Peter McAllister of the Sierra Club says: 'What we have to do is go beyond BC. The rest of the world is becoming appalled at what's happening. . . . You phone *The Traveler* and *Condé Nast, Sierra Magazine, Audubon, Wilderness* . . . periodicals and journals all over the world and you tell them you've got a good story for them, and a lot of them listen.'[48] McAllister goes on to relate how he took an associate editor of *National Geographic* on a trip to the Kyuquot area on northern Vancouver Island. This excursion led to the magazine's publication of a two-page photo of a clear-cut mountainside which earned the province further notoriety in international conservation circles, and caused the BC government further embarrassment within Canada.[49]

Mass media news provides environmental groups with an excellent means of disseminating images of the type that arouse public concern, but a less satisfactory way of educating the public about the systemic causes of environmental problems. Media coverage of the environment tends to confirm Lance Bennett's characterization of media news as dramatized, personalized, and trivialized.[50] The media tend to 'decontextualize' — they shy away from stories that would connect events to root causes or to broader implications. For example, media treatment of the *Exxon Valdez* oil spill was long on powerful images of oil-soaked otters along with speculation about whether the miscreant captain would be brought to justice. But this coverage provided little information about just how much oil was moving across the world's oceans and under what conditions. Nor did it do much to establish connections between the event and issues such as energy conservation.

CONCLUSIONS

During the past 20 years, Canada's environmental groups have elbowed their way into the policy communities that shape government decisions on the environment. In the process, they have transformed traditional decision-making systems. They have expanded the number of policy communities by putting a host of new issues on the agenda, altered the make–up of existing communities by demanding a voice, and added to the number of government officials involved in the process by pressing for the establishment of new environment departments and regulatory authorities.

If the rise of environmental groups has made the job of government more complicated, this is the price we pay for a richer debate over the consequences of our actions and the viability of our goals. Environmental groups have enriched our democracy by articulating perspectives that for too long went unexpressed. Their presence has ensured a truer accounting of the costs, benefits, and risks of specific economic development initiatives, and stimulated a fuller debate over the consequences of economic growth in general. The society's consciousness — its definition of the political — has been expanded.

Gains in public consciousness have translated into only spotty policy advances. The record of successes and failures reminds us that the movement's feistiness and resourcefulness have often not been sufficient to push aside the obstacles it faces. These obstacles remain formidable. Most importantly, the movement faces corporate-government alliances determined to resist fundamental challenges to 'business as usual' patterns of resource development. These powerful alliances continue to respond with measures designed to limit environmentalism's impact, centring their containment strategies on symbolic responses and on variants of what BC wilderness activists refer to as 'talk and log' approaches.[51]

As we said at the outset, diametrically opposite predictions might be drawn from the Canadian movement's record to date. Whichever outlook we adopt, however, there can be no doubt that the challenges at the next stage of environmental politics will be daunting. The movement has done an excellent job of pushing environmental issues to the top of the political agenda. It now faces the more difficult task of extracting (and enforcing) firm, substantive commitments — and timetables for action — from government and industry. This will require increased attention to direct lobbying; groups will need to expand their capacity to monitor and influence policy developments 'inside the system'. Progress in the 1990s will also require continued excellence in the realm of public-oriented lobbying. Through hard work and imaginative educational tactics, environmental groups have won broad public support. If they are to parry the containment strategies devised by their adversaries, groups will need to ensure that they maintain this support as they delve deeper into the complex causes of environmental degradation.

FOR FURTHER READING

Claude Galipeau, 'Political Parties, Interest Groups, and New Social Movements: Toward New Representations?' in Alain G. Gagnon and A. Brian Tanguay, eds, *Canadian Parties in Transistion: Discourse, Organization, and Representation* (Scarborough: Nelson Canada, 1989), 404-26.

David Israelson, *Silent Earth: The Politics of Our Survival* (Markham, Ont.: Viking, 1990).

Monte Hummel, ed., *Endangered Spaces: The Future of Canada's Wilderness* (Toronto: Key Porter, 1989).

Robert Hunter, *Warriors of the Rainbow: A Chronicle of the Greenpeace Movement* (New York: Holt, Rinehart and Winston, 1979).

Elizabeth May, *Paradise Won: The Struggle for South Moresby* (Toronto: McClelland and Stewart, 1990).

Warren Magnusson, 'Critical Social Movements: De-Centring the State', in Alain G. Gagnon and James P. Bickerton, eds, *Canadian Politics: An Introduction to the Discipline* (Peterborough, Ontario: Broadview Press, 1990), 525-41.

A. Paul Pross, *Group Politics and Public Policy* (Toronto: Oxford University Press, 1986).

Jeremy Wilson, 'Wilderness Politics in BC: The Business Dominated State and the Containment of Environmentalism', in William Coleman and Grace Skogstad, eds, *Policy Communities and Public Policy in Canada: A Structural Approach* (Mississauga: Copp Clark Pitman, 1990), 141-69.

CHAPTER 7

Green Politics

Political Parties, Elections, and Environmental Policy*

————

VAUGHAN LYON

> ... what we call necessary institutions are often no more than institutions to which we have grown accustomed ... in matters of social constitution the field of possibilities is much more extensive than men living in the various societies are ready to imagine.
> —Alexis de Tocqueville

Environmentalists are almost unanimous in thinking that political leaders, functioning within our political system, are still failing to deal effectively with the threat to life posed by the ecological costs of industrialization. Instead of providing leadership, governments must be coerced into taking action. Further, many of the coerced actions are more symbolic than substantive. Some despair that public policy-makers will ever be able to meet their responsibilities in this vital policy area. On the one hand, economists like Robert Heilbroner predict that liberal democracies will have to become more authoritarian to bring about the changes in lifestyle and outlook that meeting the environmental crisis demands.[1] On the other, we have those, including some political parties, that recommend dealing with the ineffectiveness of government by permitting citizens, acting for the community, to sue polluters.[2]

The problems liberal democratic governments experience in dealing effectively with environmental issues are, in some respects, typical of those they face in providing strong responsive leadership across the board. But each policy area presents somewhat distinct challenges. The ecological crisis threatens all citizens in direct personal ways. Rapidly increasing numbers register their worries about it[3] and express a willingness to share the cost of environmental programs.[4] The level of concern is reflected in the extent of interest group activity. It is estimated that 2,500 groups are pressing aspects of the environmental cause in Canada.[5] In addition to its universal impact, the environmental crisis is distinctive as a policy issue in that an adequate response may involve far greater intervention in the economy and in the formation of values than previously attempted by liberal democratic governments.

When environmentalists assess the record of the government in dealing with the ecological crisis, the phrase 'institutional failure' keeps reappearing.[6] There seems to be an awareness that government is not failing because politicians are unconcerned but because, even with their concern, they find it difficult to act. But while the failure is noted, there is little analysis of its cause and how existing political institutions contribute. Only occasionally does one find suggestions for new political tools to deal with the environment – such as an environmental ombudsman and regular public assessments of different aspects of environmental performance.[7] Typically, most thoughtful and concerned citizens are totally absorbed in the immediate problem. Creative energy goes into crisis management rather than into analysis and follow-up action designed to alter policy-making structures and processes so that they encourage crisis aversion.

This is surprising, because a strong prima-facie case exists for the proposition that our political arrangements are 'out of sync' with our values and needs. The basic institutional arrangements of the liberal democracies became firmly (rigidly?) established in an era when the commitment to democratic values was relatively weak, populations were more deferential (with good reason, given differences in education and access to information of rulers and ruled), and demands on government modest. The system was rigorously representative – the people were given only an indirect voice (through elections) in policy-making and implementation. The office of 'citizen' remained largely devoid of power or responsibility. In its essential features, the political system has not changed since the nineteenth century. Social and economic conditions and the agenda of government have, meanwhile, changed dramatically.

This chapter will focus on the ability of parties and the party system to adequately articulate the public's environmental concerns and, at the government level, to develop and implement an appropriate policy response to them. Since the parties dominate representative and governmental processes – 'a democratic system is, in practice, a party system'[8] – analysing their performance will bring much of the political system into view. How might the system be strengthened to deal more effectively with ecological and other important but, perhaps, less pressing issues? The environmental challenge is of such magnitude and likely to be felt over such a long period, and the political response to date is so inadequate, that it is worth considering political reforms simply on the grounds that they might enable us to deal more effectively with ecological issues. However, the argument for institutional change and development gains added strength when it is realized that the system also deals inadequately with a host of other less salient issues and problems.

CANADIAN PARTIES – THEIR CHARACTER AND COMMITMENT
TO GROWTH

The Canadian party system emerged because the purposes to which the power of the state was applied, and by whom, were sufficiently important to encourage groups of Canadians to band together and compete for control over it. Tacitly, over time, they agreed to an elaborate set of rules/ conventions determining which of the contenders for office should assume responsibility for governing, and under what conditions.

The forerunners of modern parties were loosely structured factions representing the dominant classes and held together by patronage.[9] Parties became disciplined organizations as the franchise was broadened to include, eventually, all adults. With a larger number of voters, candidates required more organization to reach them. The more diverse range of interests the new voters brought into politics raised the political stakes, making it far more than a game played by the ins and the outs. The need for an organized competitive instrument was reinforced.

It was possible for these self-selected political antagonists to assume a central role in our politics in and outside Parliament because at no time during the course of our evolution from autocratic to representative government were political institutions specifically designed to support the new system and reflect democratic values.[10] No arrangements were made for communities of citizens to come together, discuss issues, and develop a policy on them which would then guide the actions of their elected representatives. It was left to the parties, more or less adequately and democratically, to perform the functions that allowed the system to operate.

While one can be impressed with the way in which the parties have made it possible for liberal democracies to function, it is important to note that they meet the needs of a democratic system only to the extent that doing so serves their own interests. As Kay Lawson observes, 'They are agencies for the acquisition of power, not selfless political versions of the Red Cross, to whom citizens may go crying in time of need.'[11]

The issues a party promotes, and the way it interacts with the public, is determined by its *raison d'être* and by the context in which it operates. In performing an educational role, for example, the parties focus on issues and information that further their objectives. A citizen would get a very limited political 'education' by reading party tracts. A party will mobilize public support for government when its leaders are in office. But when they are not, it may tear down the credibility of both the office-holders and the institution of government itself. In organizing citizens into public life, a party will encourage political participation that is channelled through and serves to strengthen the party. Otherwise, while offering lip-service to the notion of active citizenship, parties in government and in opposition show little interest in opening up the political system.

The self-interested dimension of party performance is acknowledged. However, uncritical supporters of party government argue that if one looks at the larger picture and sees the 'political market' in which several parties, the media, interest groups, and individuals all interact, democratic needs are served in a kind of mysterious way, making new or changed institutions unnecessary. Another 'invisible hand' is at work. The analogy drawn with the economic market is, however, not reassuring when one notes the ways in which the unregulated economic marketplace threatens the public interest. Party governments are able to moderate the behaviour of economic actors but no agency exists that can require them to act on problems in their own 'market'.

The forerunners of today's Liberal and Conservative parties emerged in the nineteenth century, before universal manhood suffrage was established. Both parties primarily represented middle- and upper-class interests and reflected their commitment to free enterprise and only a 'supportive' economic role for government. Growth—the expansion of markets and opportunities for profit-making—is the hormone that keeps a market-based economic system healthy. Since economic 'illness' is quickly reflected in a lack of support for the governing party, the policies of the two parties had to be carefully designed to encourage business activity. In the twentieth century the commitment of the Liberal and Conservative parties to the autonomy of market forces was modified. Both realized, in varying degrees, that the state had a role to play in economic regulation and in providing various forms of social security for its citizens. However, the basic economic system and the parties' 'booster' relationship to it remained unchanged.

The costs and benefits of a market system are distributed very unequally. As the working class became enfranchised, various labour/ socialist parties were organized to press for greater equality. However, it took a long time for this new force, ultimately organized around the CCF/ NDP, to break the Liberal-Conservative monopoly on representation in the House of Commons. It never did convert more than a handful of the working class from free enterprise to socialism. While originally the CCF wanted to 'eradicate capitalism' and substitute social need for private profit as the guide to production, it had as strong an interest in increased productivity as the other parties. Later, when the ideological position of the party shifted to the centre and it accepted a market system, its interest in growth was reinforced because, as government, it, too, could not be successful without a strongly motivated private sector.

There is still, however, a significant difference in the attitude of the parties toward business. The NDP, accepting but unenthusiastic about capitalism, is considerably more sceptical about how much freedom of action and profitability, and how many inducements, the business community requires in order to maintain a desirable level of economic activity. This critical stance toward the corporate sector makes the NDP more sympathetic than the other parties to the environmental movement's message. Further, the environmental movement's sympathy with historically marginalized groups is shared by the NDP.[12]

On the other hand, the NDP has a traditional agenda some of which is at odds with the views of those most strongly committed to environmentalism.

> [E]nvironmentalists appear to have little sympathy with trade unions; they are more likely to prefer unions to have less power; they do not want unskilled classes to be better rewarded for their labour; and they are less likely to interpret the relationship between workers and managers in terms of class conflict.[13]

There are voices within the NDP, like that of Lynn McDonald, urging it to become the environmental party. To date McDonald claims only that the NDP has 'not been worse, generally speaking, than conservative or liberal parties'. For the future she calls on the party to be as far ahead of its time on environmental issues as it was previously on social questions.[14] But making the party 'radical' again might not sit well with leaders who are now serious contenders for power nationally as well as provincially. Further, it would require a quite profound reorientation of the party's traditional mission which would be controversial among many NDP stalwarts.[15] The Greens (see below) are as sceptical of the ability of the NDP to institute adequate environmental policies effectively as the NDP has been of the 'old line' parties' dedication to welfare state programs.

On a more speculative note, it may be observed that the ideological shift of the CCF/NDP to the centre reduced the scope of ideological debate in Canada. No major party was left encouraging Canadians to think in terms of system change. No major party was familiarizing Canadians with the idea that the government might play a much larger role in managing the economic system and organizing citizens' lives — as perhaps it must, to meet the ecological crisis. In this ideological environment, responding to ecological problems with recycling and protecting 'my' neighbourhood from the negative impact of development may be a more common form of behaviour than rallying to support national or provincial governments trying to develop policies which are consistent with sustainable growth.

Until recently, the national parties' commitment to growth led them to an unquestioning acceptance of a wide range of ecological costs. Rather than risk spoiling the climate for investment and the possibility of new jobs, pulp mills were allowed to dump dangerous effluent into rivers, health-threatening workplaces were tolerated, products threatening to their purchaser and the environment were permitted on the market — the dismal story is very familiar. The mind-set of the party leaders and their strategic electoral interests did not permit them to focus on the carnage being wrought on the environment and on the health of citizens. It would be time enough to deal with these problems when they were widely recognized. The life of a messenger carrying bad news is precarious.

With these three parties setting the national political agenda, and offshoots of them or others with similar attitudes toward development in control of the provinces, it is scarcely surprising that official recognition of the ecological costs of development was belated. Finally, however, as environmental problems mounted, concerned citizens outside the party system sounded the alarm and forced the parties to respond.

However, this ability of the public, mobilized and directed by interest groups, ultimately to add issues to the parties' public agenda hardly compensates for the unresponsiveness of the party system. In a 'party' democracy that encourages leaving politics to the politicians, the public is likely to focus on a social problem and organize a response only when it has become obvious and serious. At this point the damage done may be irreversible. Much avoidable human suffering may have taken place. One must wonder about a system which has a well-organized elected government but still must depend on 'volunteers' to galvanize it into action on an issue of the magnitude of the environment. How will such a government respond to the large number of important but less salient issues facing the community? It is all too easy to be so impressed and relieved (finally they are doing something!) by the dramatic activity of politicians engaged in crisis management that one fails to ask whether they shouldn't have been engaged in 'preventive care'.[16]

THE GREENS

With the policies of the established parties perceived as contributing to the ecological problem, a few environmentalists and other politically dissatisfied individuals sought a political vehicle that would be uncompromisingly committed to their issues and, organizationally, would reflect their values. The Greens had their founding national convention in 1983 at Carleton University, and provincial organizations were set up around the same time.[17] Many of those attracted to the Greens were already members of various environmental and peace lobbies but saw opportunities to push their views further through electoral politics. They were encouraged to do so, of course, by the success of the European Greens, particularly the West Germans, in getting representation in parliament and a high-visibility pulpit.[18]

The organization of the Greens may be seen as a normal development in the party/political 'market'. Concern about environmental questions grew in intensity to the point where it could not be represented to the satisfaction of all by the established parties with their broad range of issues. The Greens emerged to meet the modest 'overflow' demand for the articulation of environmental issues, thereby maintaining the equilibrium of the system. However, the organizing difficulties of the Greens, and the few voters its candidates have attracted, show that by and large the major parties are satisfying the public on environmental issues.[19]

A less sanguine, less system-supporting interpretation of the Green phenomenon would stress two points. First, the struggle of the Greens to get established highlights the oligopolistic tendencies of the party system. This tendency means, in the political as well as in the economic marketplace, that the citizen's freedom of choice is constricted. More specifically, it makes it impossible to conclude that the organizational and voting strength of the Greens reflects the amount of support for their position in the community. Second, the emergence of the Greens is a reminder of what a crude instrument of citizen consultation the vote is. To vote Green in order to assert that the environment should be a top priority for policymakers, the individual must forgo the opportunity to choose which party will govern and the expression of an opinion on other issues.

A new entry to the system must compete for votes from people who have long-standing loyalties to existing 'brands'. These loyalties are much less intense than they once were but they are still a formidable obstacle.[20] The existing parties maintain an élitist, non-participatory system. Most voters are uninformed and uninvolved, making them difficult to communicate with and to motivate. The major organizational resources available to parties — business and trade union money and members — are committed to the existing parties. The new entrant must rely heavily on the support of individuals. New parties, lacking the resources needed to advertise and promote, must depend on media coverage to get out their message. However, before they can get serious media attention, they must be close enough to office to make their views newsworthy — the familiar chicken-and-egg situation.

These 'natural' barriers are formidable enough. But just as Adam Smith noted the proclivity of businessmen to conspire to limit competition, so we may note a similar inclination on the part of politicians. They maintain a single-member electoral system which is known to discriminate severely against third parties with dispersed support. Further, as they 'reform' the system by putting themselves on the public payroll, the parties are careful to ensure that only the three largest, those already 'in', will be able to benefit.[21] All the 'natural' advantages, except novelty, flow to the established parties, and they use the power of the state to restrict what they describe as a 'dangerous proliferation' of parties.

One can only admire the ability of the parties to convince the public that this deliberate effort to stifle free speech and the right to organize is done in the public interest. The big three American auto companies would be delighted if they could protect their market as effectively against the 'proliferation' of Japanese cars. It is impossible to tell how much the Green movement might grow in a less repressive environment. However, it is interesting to note that a recent poll suggests that 'Canada is ripe for a Green revolution'. Forty-two per cent of a sample survey of Canadian voters said they would 'seriously consider' supporting . . . a Green party'.[22]

The effect of the party oligopoly is to substantially reduce the pressure on the parties to respond to new social needs. The costs of their unresponsiveness, in terms of damage done and opportunities lost, and in terms of the credibility of politicians and governments, are high. While our dependence on government and its need for our support to do its job in the face of various vested interests increases, it is exposed as an ineffectual and even unwilling defender of the common interest.

The Greens around the world, and in Canada, have compounded their difficulties in electoral politics by promoting a comprehensive, root-and-branch critique of modern life — its politics, economics and social life — as the CCF/NDP did initially. The critique extends to, indeed emphasizes, a rejection of the social hierarchy found, in exaggerated form, in parties. The Greens insist on reflecting their values in their political activity, eschewing the methods which the other parties have found, through time and experimentation, to be successful. This determination to do it 'our way' can be seen as naïve and unrealistic. The voter who does bother to look closely at the Greens is overwhelmed by the challenge the party presents — reforming the world . . . by consensus. The Canadian Greens would undoubtedly do far better electorally if they were to telescope the evolution experienced by the CCF/NDP[23] and adopt a conventional organizational style and a platform which stressed cleaning up the environment rather than fundamentally changing the system that creates the ecological degradation.

However, in going this route, the Greens would be depriving Canadians of their fundamental critique of modern life. In commenting on the moderate, reformist approach, Murray Bookchin states that it must not

> supplant the need to get to the roots of environmental dislocations. Indeed, in so far as they are restricted merely to reforms, they often create the dangerous illusion that the present social order is capable of rectifying its own abuses. The denaturing of the environment must always be seen as inherent to capitalism, the product of its very law of life, as a system of limitless expansion and capital accumulation. To ignore the anti-ecological core of the present social order — be it in its Western corporate form or its Eastern bureaucratic form — is to allay public concern about the depth of the crisis and lasting means to resolve it.[24]

Liberals who believe that a person cannot be truly free unless aware of alternatives, who believe in the free market of ideas, can no more wish that the Greens drop their radical vision than they can wish that the world had never heard of that earlier socialist vision. On the contrary, what a genuine liberal must wish for is a political system that welcomes rather than represses such an important new body of thought.

Traditionally, Parliament in Canada has been seen primarily as a base for governments. At considerable cost to the quality of our public life, Canadians have been deprived of a Parliament that can 'express the mind of the people, teach the nation what it does not know', and 'make us hear what otherwise we would not'.[25] The voices of some groups — environmentalists, women and natives — should be heard more frequently and forcefully in Parliament. If they were, governments would be helped in fostering the attitude changes which are necessary if they are to institute the policies they already recognize as essential.

PARTIES AS REPRESENTATIVE AGENCIES

We have considered why it was citizens and interest groups, rather than the self-proclaimed protectors of the public interest — the parties — who forced the environment onto the public agenda. But now that environment is front and centre on the political agenda and politicians cannot afford the electoral costs of appearing to be indifferent, are the parties effective agencies to carry the concerns of the public to the heart of the policy-making process? Should voters who put environmental issues at the top of their list of concerns be reassured? Should environmental activists, who want to have far more impact on public policy than they can get through voting, flock to join the parties?

If party rhetoric could be taken seriously, the voter, satisfied that all parties shared his or her environmental concerns, could choose a party on the basis of its stand on other issues. But while the citizen knows enough to be sceptical of mere words, it is not easy to determine which party is most likely to act forcefully. Only peripherally involved in politics between elections, the voter is in a poor position to sort out all the information, the partisan claims and counter-claims, buttressed by lots of 'facts', or to weigh the record of the party in office (extolled between elections in propaganda often paid for by the taxpayer) against the promises of the opposition parties. Bakvis and Nevitte, in their study of the public's attitudes on environmental questions, report that 'no party has appeared as the environmental party; the NDP is slightly more likely to be favoured by pro-environment respondents, but by no stretch of the imagination can one say that the NDP, or any other party, has captured the environmental agenda.'[26] If none of the major parties is distinctively identified with the environment, the citizen cannot use a vote for one of them to make an unequivocal statement about the importance of ecological issues.

Even if this hurdle is overcome, there is a very much larger one waiting which limits the ability of the voter to authoritatively mandate the government to adopt effective environmental policies. All the citizen's formal/ authoritative input to government must be compressed into a single pencilled x after a candidate's name on a ballot every four years. With this x the person is, at various times, urged to pass judgement on the performance of the incumbent government, choose the best local representative, express an opinion on various issues before the public, and so on. The citizen trying to use the vote rationally is faced with a bewildering variety of trade-offs that he or she is ill-equipped to make. Small wonder that for most citizens voting is a symbolic act rather than a serious attempt to influence policy.[27]

Campaigning politicians routinely claim to large audiences that a vote for them will be a mandate to enact this or that program or policy. Political scientists, to much smaller audiences, point out how decidedly misleading this rhetoric is. General elections are not single-issue referendums. Given the range of matters motivating the voters, the election result is wide open to conflicting interpretations. It does not put the public unequivocally behind a policy or tie the government to follow through on any particular commitments.[28]

Parties, as organizations with their own political agendas, operating in a highly competitive environment and a rapidly changing world, have a vested interest in restricting the electorate's control of policy and maximizing their freedom of action. Citizens, aware of the enormous impact of government on their lives and with little reason to be deferential, want more influence on policy. Parties will have their way. Joseph Wearing notes: 'The public's increased interest in issues has been accompanied by more activity and professionalization on the part of interest groups, but conversely, the parties exhibit more evasiveness on those issues during election campaigns.'[29] Voting for one or another party's candidate is a valuable but limited way for citizens to express environmental or other concerns.

Most of the important political activity relating to policy takes place between elections. How does the party system serve those citizens who recognize this? Superficially, the parties that are serious contenders for office offer citizens the possibility of a direct 'inside' route into the policy-making process. The concerned environmentalist can join any one of the major parties and find others who share her concerns. Resolutions on the environment will be sympathetically received and, unless extreme, are likely to be endorsed locally and nationally.

Such resolutions may serve to show the public whether the party is attuned to its concerns. However, since they will contain little that is new or informative, they will only influence government policy-makers if they strengthen the hand of those environmentally conscious individuals involved in negotiating the content or implementation of policy. Whether they do this depends on how much clout the opinions of the membership wings of the parties have on their legislative leaders. Wearing observes,

> While all three parties like to think of themselves as being democratic, the problems with intra-party democracy, especially in the area of party policy, are enormous. How can a party convention, attended by several thousand amateurs, realistically determine the party's position on hundreds of issues for the next two years or more over a three-day weekend? It would be an over-simplification—though not so far from the truth—to say that the Conservatives deal with this problem by not having policy conventions, the Liberals have policy conventions but forget the resolutions once the conventions are over, and the NDP leadership makes sure it gets the resolutions it wants.[30]

The NDP leadership, the only one of the 'big three' which is constitutionally bound to follow membership opinion, does occasionally get some resolutions it does not want—a demand that Canada withdraw from NATO, for example.[31] But Wearing's admitted over-simplification does not have to be qualified very much.

It is worth noting that determined efforts have been made to make intra-party democracy work, i.e., to make parties 'agencies that help citizens influence the processes of government'.[32] Over almost a century, the Progressives, the CCF/NDP, the Liberals . . . and now the Greens have attempted, unsuccessfully, to reconcile party and democratic values.[33] Comparative studies of parties in other systems confirm the democratic dysfunction of parties. After asking what the role of parties as agencies of democracy is, Kay Lawson states, 'Most of the conclusions are negative.'[34] But, alas, democrats seem unable to see beyond parties as agencies linking rulers and ruled. Enormous amounts of creative political energy are devoted to what appears to be the impossible task of making parties function in ways that further democratic values.

Ironically, if the membership wing of any of the parties is successful in putting its team into office, it is less likely to have an influence on policy than before. Constitutionally, the party's legislative hierarchy can then quite legitimately claim that its responsibility to 'all the people' must supersede the claims of the party membership. Further, with power comes the importuning of a wide range of special interests (some of whom, through their control of the economy, control the fate of the government) and the bureaucracy to compete with the party membership for influence. The most effective way for the citizen to influence policy through the parties is, perhaps, to help commit a 'serious' opposition party so strongly to a position that, as government, it must act on it, but even this strategy is problematic.

The difficulties involved in influencing public policy through the parties are obvious to citizen activists. As Dalton Camp, no stranger to parties, has observed,

There remains . . . some primordial ambition that lurks in the heart of a few citizens to participate in the formulation of policy through the party apparatus. I would advise them that if they insist on doing so, not to join a political party. The very least they should do is join a parapolitical pressure group. The very best thing they could do is join the civil service.[35]

Characteristically, and understandably, environmentalists shun party membership and join interest groups.[36] That is far from an ideal reaction to the weakness of parties. A rise in the activity level of 'cause' groups, like the environmentalists, will lead to an increase in the activity of groups threatened by them. Governments surrounded by aggressive, and usually antagonistic, groups are unlikely to have either the will or authority needed to provide strong leadership.

One can sympathize with environmentalists who, possessing limited resources of time and energy, heed Camp's advice and bypass parties. On the other hand, parties dominate political life and, however inadequate in many dimensions, cannot be ignored. The advice that Robert Paehlke offers in his influential new study of environmentalism as an ideology is undoubtedly sound: environmentalists should use the parties, and those supporting established parties should play up the 'potential' links those parties have with environmentalism.[37] Recognizing the handicaps under which green parties struggle in North America, Paehlke recommends working through the major parties.[38]

PARTIES AS GOVERNMENT

The dramatically intensifying public concern about the environment faces all three national parties and the public itself with dilemmas. Shifting to a sustainable-growth economy will require major changes in corporate behaviour and in individual life-styles. The task of making this shift is made ever more complex as national economies become integrated into the global economy. The challenge facing the parties, and especially the governing party, is to promote the change while maintaining support. Superficially, it appears that this should not be difficult. Since the citizens demand environmentally sound policies, why would they not reward the party or parties instituting them? Why would strong citizen support not offset any loss of support the parties might experience from the corporations and unions if their policies interfered with the normal growth of the economy, with profits, with jobs? Answering that question takes us to a central weakness of the Canadian political system.

Canadians relate to the political system in two different ways.[39] As citizens, they are concerned about the long-term viability of their nation and world. As private persons living in a competitive and often cold, impersonal society, they are intensely concerned about their own security and standard of living. As citizens, they demand and welcome political action to protect the environment. As private persons, organized in groups, they often bitterly oppose policies, however otherwise desirable, that threaten their well-being.[40] Corporate leaders are even more likely to emphasize their private, as opposed to citizen, interests than most. Their careers are directly related to success in promoting corporate growth and profitability and the autonomy of their group is threatened by environmentally motivated government intervention in the marketplace. Union leaders are subject to the pressure of members fearing a dislocation in their lives.

In the present system it is unrealistic to expect the citizen to understand fully and accept responsibility for the consequences of the policies he or she demands. The party adopting tough environmental legislation may very well be praised by 'citizens' and defeated at the polls by 'private persons'.

Determining how far a party government can move to accommodate citizens without alienating people who vote their private interests is extremely complex. Typically, an environmental problem must become so intense that citizen demands overwhelm personal interests before the government will act, and then the problem is often beyond satisfactory solution. While waiting for this intensity to develop, governments typically meet demands for action with rhetoric and symbolism, which alienates many whose support the state requires.

If a government is to make the tough decisions needed in a timely fashion, without recourse to authoritarianism, and survive at the polls, more individuals must be persuaded to act politically as 'citizens'. This is difficult to achieve in a society that subscribes to liberal individualistic values and has an élitist political system. Both the liberalism and the élitism contribute to a situation where the individual is hesitant to trust the government and is uninvolved in the political process. Further, the highly adversarial nature of the system, at election time and between, discourages 'citizen' responses. The opposition plays out its role with gusto, all too often catering to private interests and undercutting the credibility of government. People become cynical about politics and politicians and less inclined to support the one instrument that has the authority to insist that economic development be consistent with ecological survival.

Aware of the difficulty of mobilizing public support, parties tend to manoeuvre around it. Unpopular government initiatives are introduced immediately after elections. Millions of dollars of tax revenue are used to 'sell' these programs. Popular programs are saved for the run-up to the next contest. In a destructive cycle, governments manipulate the public, the manipulation breeds cynicism and withdrawal, even less capacity or inclination for supporting political leadership, and an even stronger need for the government to manage people in any way it can. The system offers no organized way for citizen activists to become formally involved in making policy and to take some of the responsibility off parties for its implementation.

Parties evolved to advance particular group interests in the political area. They have, however, served the polity well by facilitating the transition from an autocratic to a more democratic form of political life. Parties organized the newly enfranchised masses and channelled social conflict into non-violent, orderly competition at elections and in legislatures. The system of free elections vested party governments with enough authority to perform the modest tasks assigned to them in an earlier period. Competitive conditions in the party system were far from fair but, gradually, the less powerful members of society got more political clout and more equitable life chances as a result of government action.

The role of the parties in facilitating the entry of new voters into the system is finished. Deep social and economic divisions continue to exist and need to be represented by parties or some other agency. However, the issue we now face is whether parties and a competitive party system, as presently constituted, are suitable instruments to deal effectively with the challenge facing the total community of reorienting values and organizing our social and economic life in environmentally sound ways. Parties that rally people to compete for their particular interests and which, as governments, are limited in what they can do by the very negative political attitudes which their behaviour furthers, scarcely seem up to the task. Yes, they can stumble through. But is that good enough?

Reforms in the representative system and strengthening the ability of the government to lead might proceed in two complementary directions. First, changes might be made which will affect the behaviour of parties in desirable ways. Simply exhorting the parties to serve the polity better is largely futile. Second, recognizing the limitations of parties, thought might be given to developing new institutions which would enable citizens and their governments to enter into continuous meaningful dialogue. Let's deal with each in turn.

Two post-war developments have had a positive impact on the ability of parties to represent and govern. We are gradually moving to a system where there will be either full public funding of parties or, at least, where non-government funding will only come from individuals, as is now the case in Quebec. The public funding of parties diminishes the hold that special interests have on them and makes party claims to seek only the public interest, albeit by different routes, slightly more credible.

Coincident with reform of party finance, there has been a change in the character of political careers. In the national Parliament and provincial legislatures, elected representatives are now usually full-time politicians rather than part-timers with one foot in the private sector. The opportunity is there for politicians to deepen their understanding of public questions and to act more independently. Individual members, like Charles Caccia, who has converted his office into the Parliamentary Centre for Environmentally Sustainable Development, can represent interests more forcefully than his party is willing to do. Potentially, Parliament may become a more adequate forum for the sensible discussion of public concerns than it is now. Much remains to be done to further increase the independence of MPs and of parties from special interests and to increase the policy contribution of backbenchers. Significant further movement on this front will probably require external pressure resulting from other changes in the political system.

A more fundamental and controversial reform which would have a significant and, on balance, positive impact on the functioning of the parties, would be the adoption of a system of proportional representation (PR). The general case for PR has been made elsewhere.[41] Looking at the issue strictly in terms of the environmental cause, a PR system, such as that in use in West Germany (not Israel's!), would make the party system more competitive.[42] Committed environmentalists would be able to pool votes now 'wasted' in individual constituencies and elect members to both provincial and national legislatures. From this vantage point, environmentalists could spread their message more effectively and have a more direct impact on government policy.

In addition to making the party system more responsive, a PR system would have an impact on the style of party government. If the political system is to rise to the challenge of reorienting our economy along an environmentally sound path, a community-wide effort will be required. A PR system would seldom if ever produce majority governments in Canada. It would also avoid the very wide swings in party representation which are the result of the present electoral system. Parties would become used to working with each other. There would be much more continuity in the membership of the House of Commons. The result might well be the more consensual style of parliamentary government which is typical of the Scandinavian countries. The policy output of such governments has a better claim to represent the 'will of the people' than that of highly partisan majority governments backed by less, sometimes far less, than the majority of the electorate. The policy may also be more consistent (less 'stop and go') than when there are dramatic shifts in the relative positions of the parties in the legislature.

Improving the performance of the parties is important, but we have to recognize the inherent limitations of parties as representative and governmental agencies, and look beyond them, if we are to have a political system that makes effective political leadership possible. Means must be found to enable governing politicians to apply the formal authority they possess to solving environmental problems. The objections a liberally minded populace has to strong government, and the electoral disincentives inhibiting radical policy-making by such governments, must be met and offset by encouraging people to work with and to become part of government, as far as that is feasible.

The environmental movement has already recognized that it has a strong stake in a more open democratic policy-making process. After a careful review of environmental politics, Robert Paehlke concludes that 'environmentalism cannot be successful in the long run without a continuous enhancement of democratic participatory values and opportunities.'[43] Pressure from environmentalists has resulted in formalized consultative processes being established that allow individuals and groups to be consulted on issues and projects that are particularly environmentally sensitive. What is required now is a more general opening up of the system which will permit government and the politically engaged community to communicate regularly and intensively and to share in the development of the state's political agenda. To allow this to happen we need an institution like a community parliament to make it possible for many more individuals to adopt a 'citizen' role.[44]

Community parliaments would go a long way toward filling the lacunae in our current democratic structures. Suppose, for example, that each constituency, in addition to electing an MP, were to choose a representative assembly of citizens to work with that MP in developing the positions he or she might take in the legislature.[45] To allow these assemblies to function as an integral part of the policy-making process, and not merely as an advisory body or a collector of after-the-fact reaction, the government would be required to introduce its full sessional legislative program (except for emergency bills) at one time. It would immediately be referred to committees for study. After the committee stage and before MPs were asked to commit themselves formally on any items in the government's program, the members would return to their constituencies for an extended informed discussion with their community parliaments on those aspects of the program (including omissions in it) which seemed significant. In addition to providing a forum for discussion of the ongoing business of government, the community parliaments would serve as a sophisticated kind of 'referendum' on issues where government might feel the need to have a clear public mandate. Canadians would not have to depend on the flawed Senate and polls to speak for them.

Community parliament members would be reimbursed for the time they take off work to participate in these deliberations. They would have all the information presented to parliamentary committees available to them. In addition, local experts and interest groups would fuel these constituency discussions of national issues. The MP would not be required to reflect the views of his or her constituency parliament in speeches and voting in the legislature. However, the elected representative and the government would have a strong vested interest in working in harmony with these large committees of local activists. They would effectively counter the influence special interests now have on public policy.

Most now recognize the limitations of representation. It is not adequate for natives and women, to take only two examples, to be represented in Parliament by middle-class white male lawyers. However, the largest omission in our system of representation continues to be the public. MPs are elected from geographically defined ridings inhabited by a sample of the public, but they represent parties which speak for only sections of that sample. The community parliament idea is to take the amorphous uninformed public, give it form and substance, and make it a working partner of government, thereby meeting Schumpeter's reservation about popular power.

> If we are to argue that the will of the citizens *per se* is a political factor entitled to respect, it must first exist. That is to say, it must be something more than an indeterminate bundle of value impulses loosely playing about given slogans and mistaken impressions.[46]

Without reforms in the political/party systems to bring citizens and governments into a closer working relationship it may well be impossible to achieve sustainable growth before enormous ecological damage is done. On the other hand, if the environmental crisis is sufficient to spark an interest in strengthening our political institutions and enabling politicians to be more far-sighted and responsive, benefits may be realized across the whole policy spectrum.

FOR FURTHER READING

Jean Blondel, *Political Parties: A Genuine Case for Discontent?* (London: Wildwood House, 1978).

Alain Gagnon and A. Brian Tanguay, eds, *Canadian Parties in Transition* (Scarborough, Ontario: Nelson Canada, 1989).

Kay Lawson, *Political Parties and Linkage: a Comparative Perspective* (New Haven: Yale University Press, 1980).

———— and Peter H. Merkl, eds, *When Parties Fail* (Princeton: Princeton University Press, 1988).

Vaughan Lyon, 'The Reluctant Party: Ideology versus Organization in Canada's Green Movement', *Alternatives* (December 1985): 3-9.

————, 'The Future of Parties—Inevitable ... Obsolete', *Journal of Canadian Studies* 18 (Winter, 1983–84): 108-31.

Robert Paehlke, *Environmentalism and the Future of Progressive Politics* (New Haven: Yale University Press, 1989).

Charlene Spretnak and Fritjof Capra, *Green Politics: The Global Promise*, rev. ed. (Santa Fe, New Mexico: Bear and Company, 1986).

Joseph Wearing, *Strained Relations: Canadian Parties and Voters* (Toronto: McClelland and Stewart, 1988), 95.

CHAPTER 8

The Greening of the Canadian Electorate

Environmentalism, Ideology, and Partisanship*

HERMAN BAKVIS
AND NEIL NEVITTE

In virtually all western nations the 'green' revolution is a well established fact. More so than any other manifestation of 'new politics', environmentalism is seen as a potent and concrete expression of the underlying shift in values and cleavage structures in advanced industrial societies. In West Germany the Green Party has gained a significant foothold in the party system. In the Netherlands the Greens, as a sizeable lobby, have effectively penetrated the Labour party, and in 1989 the Dutch national election was fought over the issue of the government's environmental plan. Elsewhere, the impact of environmentalism has been more muted, but only relatively so. In both Sweden and Austria, for example, popular sentiment has effectively halted the expansion of nuclear power development.

It is generally assumed that the Canadian public, while slow off the mark, is nonetheless 'greening' roughly in tandem with those in other countries. By one count alone there are in Canada some 2,500 interest groups whose *raison d'être* relates to pollution, acid rain, or environmental concerns of one stripe or another. Public opinion polls point to increasing concern about the environment among Canadians, and the debates surrounding the 1989 Quebec provincial election imply that environmental issues have the potential to shape electoral outcomes. Certainly the Conservative government's environmental plan will likely become a major element in the Progressive Conservative party's next election campaign.

The Canadian evidence on electoral greening is, nonetheless, sketchy. First, while not denying the possible impact of environmentalism in Canada, there are nonetheless grounds for thinking that 'green politics' in this country may be of a rather different hue from that found in other countries, especially West European ones. Hay and Haward, for instance, have argued that environmental movements beyond the European context, especially in Australia and North America, are qualitatively different. Deep and extensive industrialization has been largely seen as being responsible for the 'green' backlash in Europe, in the form of opposition to nuclear power for example, whereas the frontier experience and the perceived need to preserve wilderness has driven environmentalism in North America and Australia.[1] Second, we do not have a clear picture of how environmentalism is linked with broader conceptions of the political world, for example, how it interacts with conventional ideological polarities such as left-right. And while the 'new politics' theme has been broached by a number of Canadian political scientists,[2] significantly there has been no effort to link it directly with environmentalism. Third, we have few clues about how environmentalism is related to partisan identity, electoral behaviour, or other salient domains.

This chapter aims to fill some of these gaps by addressing three sets of concerns. First, we track the rise of environmentalism by examining responses to both open- and closed-ended questions in national election surveys and other polls conducted over the past decade and a half. Second, using the 1988 national election survey, we evaluate some of the more plausible variables that are generally taken to account for support for environmental causes among mass publics. In particular we examine the 'structural' variables identified in 'new class' theories offered by Claus Offe among others, and 'ideological' variables, of which Ronald Inglehart's 'postmaterialist' value change model is the best known. The former set of theories emphasizes changes in social structure and the effects on individuals located therein; the latter emphasizes value shifts at the individual level, shifts that are driven primarily by generational changes. Third, again using the 1988 national election survey, we examine the crucial links between environmentalism, participation, and partisanship. How environmentalism affects the strength of partisan identity and which party is most likely to garner the support of those placing a high priority on environmental protection are the questions addressed in this section.

THE RISE OF ENVIRONMENTALISM

As with any attitudinal syndrome such as racism or religiosity, environmentalism is best examined through a number of different questions, with the aim of establishing the concept's outer limits, content, and underlying structure. Survey data on environmentalism is sketchy, but fortunately the 1988 national election does contain some questions dealing specifically with the environment and, equally important, includes for the first time in a large-scale Canadian survey the full Inglehart materialism-postmaterialism (MPM) index, allowing us to link environmentalism to the broader 'new politics' domain.

The 'green' issue has until recently been of relatively low interest to the general public. Gallup Canada, for example, has been asking the open-ended question, 'What is the most important problem facing this country today?' since February of 1983. As a volunteered response, 'the environment' became significant as a distinct category only in February of 1987. Since then, however, it has rapidly become more consequential. When asked in February of 1990 how concerned they were about the environment as an issue, 78% of Canadians indicated they were 'very concerned', a change up from 67% when the same closed-ended question was asked in July of 1989. Only 'taxation levels', 'illegal drug use', and 'honesty in government' elicited comparable levels of concern.[3] Responses to another Gallup question, asked since 1970, 'How serious do you, yourself, think the dangers of pollution are?' shows a steady, though curvilinear upward trend in the proportion of those who agree that it is a 'very serious' problem. In 1970, 63% thought pollution dangers to be 'very serious'. The proportion of 'very serious' respondents gradually dropped to a low of 51% in 1985; by 1989, however, the proportion was up again, this time to a high of 72%.[4]

When we examine responses to open-ended questions, however, the results are rather different. In Figure 8.1 we present, first, Gallup poll results in response to the question 'What do you think is the most important problem facing this country today?' As noted, it was not until February of 1987 that it elicited environmental concerns for the first time: then 3% of respondents deemed it as the most important problem; by July 1989, 17% deemed it so, though by March 1990 it had declined to 14%. Figure 8.1 also provides data on the question asked in the national election surveys from 1974 onwards: 'What is the most important issue to you personally in this election?' In 1979, only 0.2% of the electorate sampled raised the environment as the single most important issue; by 1988 a full 6% did so.

The open-ended data reveal rapid growth in support for the environment over a relatively short period of time. By the same token, these data also suggest that the issue does not dominate the public agenda. In the case of both the Gallup polls and the national election surveys, the environmental issue is easily outranked by concern with the 'economy/ inflation and unemployment'; and in 1988 the election agenda was dominated by free trade. Clearly, individuals weigh the importance of the environment in conjunction with other concerns. Even as preoccupation with the environment becomes more widespread — as evidenced in the increase of 11% from July 1989 to February 1990 of those 'very concerned' with the environment — the overall priority assigned to the environment may decline, as suggested by the drop from 17% to 14% over the same time period in response to the open-ended 'most important problem' Gallup question.

At the same time, the open-ended questions, or at least the responses

**FIGURE 8.1:   IDENTIFICATION OF ENVIRONMENT /
POLLUTION AS THE MOST IMPORTANT ISSUE**

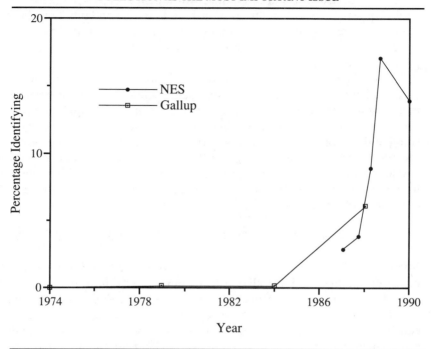

NES: What is/was the most important issue in this campaign to you?

Gallup: What is/was the most important problem facing Canada today?

as coded by the interviewers, or the arrival of singularly important events such as the free trade issue in the 1988 election, may obscure or underrate the importance of environmental concerns, especially in relation to electoral choice. It may well be that many respondents among the approximately 80 per cent who cited 'free trade' as the most important issue in that historic election based their response in part, perhaps even wholly, on environmental concerns. For example, it might be thought that closer economic integration with the US will result in lowering of environmental standards or increasing pressures being placed on wilderness areas for logging purposes. The thinking behind individual responses cannot be established directly, but some indirect evidence casts light on this issue. A forced-choice question in the 1988 survey does ask respondents to agree or disagree with the statement: 'Protecting the environment is more important than creating jobs.' Of the sample, 65.4% mainly agreed with this statement, 20.1% mainly disagreed, and 14.5% expressed no opinion.

Of those who identified an issue other than the environment on the open-ended question, 64.3% still chose the environment over jobs in the forced-choice question. Another question, asking how respondents felt about Americans, reveals that those feeling more positive about Americans were somewhat less likely to favour 'protecting the environment' over jobs.

This evidence is far from definitive, but it does suggest the possibility of a good portion of 'free trade' respondents being animated by environmental concerns. At a minimum, in selecting the most appropriate indicator of environmentalism, the 'environment versus jobs' item is more suitable than volunteered responses to the open-ended issue question in the 1988 survey. Furthermore, given the much smaller number of open-ended 'environment' responses, the 'environment versus jobs' item lends itself more easily to multivariate analysis, that is, to the seeking of antecedent causes of environmentalism.

ACCOUNTING FOR ENVIRONMENTALISM: STRUCTURE AND IDEOLOGY

Much of the literature on environmentalism is focused on Europe, where organizationally and politically environmental groups have been in existence longer and have a stronger presence, and where their activities have struck a much more responsive chord among electorates. This literature can be divided roughly into two camps; these camps are not mutually exclusive in that there is considerable overlap between them.[5] The difference, rather, is one of emphasis. On the one hand are those explanations focused on broad characteristics of advanced industrial democracies and the individual's social location. Specific explanations within this category generally agree that membership in the 'new middle classes' helps generate both sympathy for environmental causes and specific cognitive skills for comprehending the nature of ecological problems. At the same time new middle-class membership is indicative of one's distance and alienation from the core centres of power in society. Robyn Eckersley, for example, stresses the new class's 'relative structural autonomy from the production process'.[6] On a broader plane, Claus Offe has argued that industrial nations are incapable of handling the perverse effects of industrial progress and political modernization: the increasing penetration of the state into the private sphere coupled with the state's decreasing capacity to respond effectively to the by-products of industrial society such as environmental pollution and the continuing lack of equality for women and minority groups.[7] According to Offe, it is primarily well-educated professionals lacking direct vested interests in government or industrial enterprises, health care professionals and teachers for example, who have the skills necessary to identify, understand, and articulate the complex 'contradictions' of modern society. These individuals also have the motivation as well as certain resources (e.g., communication and organizational skills) to support movements intent upon altering established power structures.

While structural theorists emphasize social location, ideological theorists tend to stress individual level characteristics, primarily those related to political values. The best known of these is Inglehart's postmaterialist value thesis. This thesis argues that substantial value change has taken place in advanced industrial states in the course of the last two decades. Further, he suggests that this value change, which is grounded in sustained material prosperity experienced by these states since the Second World War, has transformed long-standing patterns of political discourse and behaviour. It has also re-ordered political agendas and is coupled with the redistribution of political skills between élites and publics. As a consequence, Inglehart suggests, mass publics are increasingly concerned about issues, like environmentalism, that lie beyond the scope of traditional agendas geared to redistributive issues. Because value change has been accompanied by a redistribution of political skills between élites and publics, new issue concerns are promoted not only through conventional political strategies and representative political institutions such as political parties but also through non-conventional strategies such as those employed by direct action interest groups.

To account for these changes, postmaterialist theory specifies two hypotheses, postulating that younger generations are more likely to place a higher priority on the fulfilment of aesthetic and intellectual needs and to display less concern with economic and physical security. The first, the scarcity hypothesis, argues that an individual's priorities reflect the socio-economic environment; one places, according to Inglehart, 'the greatest subjective value on those things in short supply'. The second, the socialization hypothesis, argues that 'one's basic values reflect the conditions that prevailed during one's pre-adult years'.[8] Since conditions of relative affluence and material abundance in relation to the crucial growing-up years have affected mainly younger generations, it is among members of these generations that levels of postmaterialist values tend to be highest.

Considerable controversy exists over the underpinnings and operationalization of Inglehart's theory.[9] Nevertheless, his materialism-postmaterialism (MPM) forced-choice scale has yielded surprisingly consistent results over more than two decades of use and across several countries. The thesis can be rendered as consistent with 'new class' theories. Inglehart notes, for example, that it is mainly members of the middle class, particularly the professional middle classes, who are the primary bearers of postmaterialist values. Nonetheless, he emphasizes that it is early socialization experiences and general societal conditions that lead to the acquisition of basic values, not social location as such. It should also be noted that the MPM divide is not the only important or relevant ideological dimension. The traditional left-right dimension has long been thought important for ideological thinking, providing a basic template for individuals to organize specific views and attitudes into coherent domains.[10] Thus an individual who considers him or herself on the left of the political spectrum is usually thought to have predictable views on matters such as the distribution of wealth and power in society and state intervention into the economy. Environmentalism may be problematical for the left, however, insofar as environmental protection may come at the expense of traditional left concerns such as jobs and increasing material welfare.

Structure

Table 8.1 lists seven common socio-structural variables and their effects on our two indicators of environmentalism: our primary indicator of 'environment versus jobs' and the secondary indicator of 'what is the most important issue in this campaign'. Two of the six independent variables — region and language — are included because of their importance in Canadian political behaviour and politics generally. Rather surprisingly perhaps, the occupational variable has the greatest effect on the spread between the lowest and highest categories (20.4%), surprising in the sense that in Canada occupation and the broader variable of class are not usually thought to have a great deal of impact on voting behaviour. Occupation also appears to account for a fair amount of variation in question 2. Language explains more than gender, but language in turn is superseded by education, the most powerful variable after occupation. The age variable is revealing, primarily for the absence of striking differences between age categories: only the very young stand out for being less supportive of the environment on question 1. In the case of region, the differences are not sharp, at least not with respect to question 1, but interesting nonetheless for two reasons: (1) the general upward trend moving from east to west on question 1;[11] and (2) the manner in which the environmental issue is played out in different provinces. Note how Quebec scores lowest on question 1 but highest on question 2. The almost exact converse appears to be true for the prairies. Depending upon which indicator one chooses, the prairies or Quebec are either high or low in their support of environmentalism. Among other things, these findings suggest that it is probably wise to keep the two indicators separate. Since the environment versus jobs question is somewhat less likely to be contaminated by unique 'one-off' election-related concerns such as free trade, it might be seen as a more reliable overall indicator.

The findings on occupation and perhaps also education are surprising, not only because they are not usually thought of as very potent predictors in the Canadian context but also because recent findings on Western

TABLE 8.1   SOCIO-STRUCTURAL BASES OF SUPPORT FOR ENVIRONMENTALISM

| Socio-Structural Variables | Question 1 | | | | Question 2 | | |
	Env. (66%)	Jobs (20%)	No Op. (14%)	No.	Env. (6%)	Others (94%)	No.
Age							
65+	66.4	20.5	13.1	244	7.8	92.2	372
55 – 64	63.7	21.2	15.1	259	6.1	93.9	423
45 – 54	67.4	20.1	12.5	273	3.6	96.4	466
35 – 44	66.9	18.4	14.7	149	6.6	93.4	803
25 – 34	66.9	18.3	14.8	526	6.6	93.4	960
< 25	59.8	23.3	16.9	219	6.4 ·	93.6	453
Education							
< Secondary	58.0	25.5	16.4	560	4.9	95.1	1074
Secondary	62.5	23.3	14.2	515	5.2	94.8	947
> Secondary	72.4	14.2	13.4	934	7.8	92.2	1505
Gender							
Male	68.0	19.2	12.8	1039	5.9	94.1	1792
Female	63.3	20.4	16.2	979	6.3	93.7	1817
Region							
Atlantic	62.8	24.4	12.8	336	4.6	95.4	562
Quebec	58.5	24.6	16.9	426	11.0	89.0	835
Ontario	67.6	17.8	14.5	545	5.0	95.0	968
Prairies	69.0	17.2	13.8	465	2.9	97.1	818
BC	72.1	14.2	13.8	247	6.8	93.2	426
Occupation							
Prof/Mgr	79.0	7.5	13.6	442	7.6	92.4	748
Tech/Sup	67.2	20.8	12.0	308	6.5	93.5	509
Cler/Sale	62.9	21.3	15.8	847	6.0	94.0	1478
Unsk/Lab	58.6	24.6	16.8	280	3.7	96.3	490
Income							
< $30,000	59.6	22.7	17.7	757	6.7	93.3	1413
$30,000–59,000	68.7	18.3	13.0	769	6.3	93.7	1165
> $59,000	72.5	17.9	9.5	357	5.4	94.6	541
Language							
English	68.3	18.3	13.4	1575	4.8	95.2	2231
French	56.2	25.9	17.9	491	11.0	89.0	691

Question 1: Protecting the environment is more important than creating jobs. (mainly agree, mainly disagree, no opinion)
Question 2: What is the most important issue in this campaign to you?

Europe argue that social class is only weakly associated with support for environmental movements and causes. It was these negative findings that

TABLE 8.2   ENVIRONMENT VS JOBS: IDEOLOGICAL VARIABLES

	Env. (66%)	Jobs (20%)	No Op. (14%)	No.	Env. (6%)	Others (94%)	No.
Left /Right							
Left	80.5	9.4	10.2	128	13.1	86.9	191
Centre	74.5	14.2	11.3	141	7.2	92.8	222
Right	73.9	18.6	7.5	161	4.2	95.8	261
MPM Index							
Materialist	60.2	23.8	16.0	631	5.0	95.0	638
Mixed	65.5	19.6	14.8	1227	5.6	94.4	2745
Postmaterialist	80.5	14.8	8.4	226	15.0	85.0	226

Question 1: Protecting the environment is more important than creating jobs. (mainly agree, mainly disagree, no opinion)
Question 2: What is the most important issue in this campaign to you?

led Rohrschneider to reject 'new class explanations'.[12] With these possible differences between Canada and Europe in mind, let us turn to ideological variables.

Ideology

The classic ideological dimension is left-right. While not noted for having a particularly powerful impact on voting in Canada, it has nonetheless figured in the organization of individuals' views on public policy in a variety of domains.[13] In the 1988 election, survey respondents were asked, first, whether they use the labels 'left' or 'right' and, second, where they would place themselves in terms of left-right. Also included in the 1988 election survey is the scale most frequently associated with the 'new politics' dimension, the Inglehart twelve-item MPM index where respondents are asked to rank-order items denoting either materialist or post-materialist values.[14]

The effects of both variables are displayed in Table 8.2 using three categories for each. One immediate problem in assessing the effect of left-right, however, is that in the 1988 national election survey only 20% of respondents were willing to concede that they used left-right labels and hence were able to place themselves on the left-right scale.[15] This problem notwithstanding, note that with respect to question one, 'environment versus jobs', the spread between left and right is less than 7%; for MPM the spread is more than 20%. In the case of question 2, the open-ended question, the spread is approximately 10% for both scales. Overall, taking into account the fact that there are far more respondents with MPM scores than for left-right self-placement, the postmaterialism index appears to provide far greater purchase on being able to predict support for environmentalism.

Postmaterialism, Age and Education

The spread between materialism and postmaterialism with respect to the 'environment versus jobs' item is comparable to the spread between the high and low categories for structural variables such as occupation. At this level it appears that the main ideological variable, MPM, is at least as powerful as some of the structural variables. Using more elaborate statistical techniques, such as stepwise logistic regression, to assess the relative effects of ideological and structural variables, it is in fact possible to show that MPM constitutes the single most important predictor of the dependent variable, 'environment versus jobs'.[16] At the same time, however, given the likelihood that MPM values are unevenly distributed within populations, we cannot dismiss socio-structural considerations. Furthermore, findings elsewhere generally indicate a strong linear relationship between age and MPM, with younger generations more inclined to favour postmaterial values.[17]

Figure 8.2 amplifies this point, providing a more detailed look at the links between MPM and age and education. The top left-hand figure for the pooled sample shows that while age works in the expected direction, the relationship is weak and uneven. The same holds for education. In contrast, if we examine just those who favour the environment over jobs, the pattern for age and MPM is much more akin to those found in West European settings. Again, the same is true for education. The bottom two figures, using the jobs over environment part of the sample, show the virtual absence of a relationship between MPM and both age and education. These findings suggest that MPM 'works' for the environmentalists, but not for those who opt for jobs over the environment.

THE ATTITUDINAL REACH OF ENVIRONMENTALISM

If support for environmentalism is associated with postmaterialism, as the preceding analysis has shown, then we would expect orientations towards the environment to be linked to the broader 'new politics' agenda. The postmaterialist hypothesis contains a number of expectations in this regard. For example, we would expect environmentalists to be more sympathetic than those preoccupied with jobs to groups that historically have been marginalized in Canadian society. The data presented in Table 8.3 suggest that they are. Environmentalists report significantly more support for women's issues, native peoples, immigrants, and ethnic minorities. Not surprisingly, they are also more likely to feel that it is 'the duty of the strong to protect the weak'.

Second, the postmaterialist hypothesis anticipates significant differences between those promoting the 'new politics' agenda from those following traditional agendas on issues related to class conflict. The data

FIGURE 8.2:   ENVIRONMENT AND JOBS: MPM, AGE, AND EDUCATION

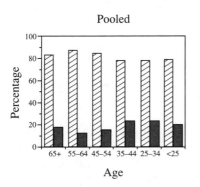

Pooled

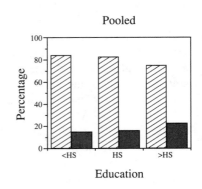

Pooled

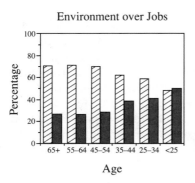

Environment over Jobs

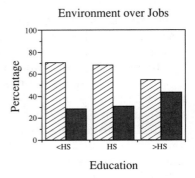

Environment over Jobs

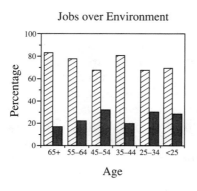

Jobs over Environment

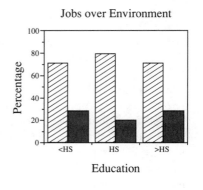

Jobs over Environment

☒ Materialist   ■ Postmaterialist

TABLE 8.3   ATTITUDINAL SPECTRUM

Q: Protecting the environment is more important than creating jobs. (mainly agree, mainly disagree, no opinion)

Attitudinal Variables		Env. (66%)	Jobs (20%)	No Op. (14%)	No.	X^2 (df)	sig.
Rate > feelings about feminist groups:	< 50	66.0	23.0	11.0	652	66.70 (44)	.02
	50 – 79	64.7	19.4	15.9	1088		
	80 – 100	71.9	16.8	11.3	256		
For women, Government should do:	more	61.7	22.8	15.5	843	9.64 (4)	.05
	same	68.4	17.7	13.9	1101		
	less	69.7	20.2	10.1	89		
Rate > how feel about Native people:	< 50	67.0	22.5	10.6	227	83.13 (43)	.00
	50 – 79	69.0	17.3	13.7	1038		
	80 – 100	73.0	14.2	12.8	633		
Native people should be completely assimilated:	agree	66.4	21.5	12.1	991	10.55 (1)	.00
	disagree	74.3	15.6	10.1	716		
New immigrants make Canada better:	agree	72.6	15.8	11.5	771	25.02 (1)	.00
	disagree	62.6	25.9	11.6	874		
Rate > feelings about ethnic minorities:	< 50	61.7	25.7	12.6	261	53.58 (39)	.06
	50 – 79	66.5	18.7	14.8	1142		
	80 – 100	72.1	14.4	13.5	542		
Duty of strong to protect weak:	agree	67.7	19.1	13.2	1585	8.71 (1)	.00
	disagree	62.1	28.3	9.6	240		
How much power should trade union have?	more	61.9	23.0	15.1	265	24.3 (5)	.00
	same	65.4	20.3	14.3	615		
	less	69.2	18.4	12.4	945		
Unskilled workers' wages are:	about right	73.4	16.5	10.1	793	31.16 (2)	.00
	much too low	58.0	25.2	16.8	911		
Workers and management:	enemies	60.7	27.7	11.6	267	13.53 (2)	.00
	same interest	67.1	19.6	13.3	1418		
Do you think people running government are crooked?	quite a few	67.8	19.3	12.9	963	0.23 (23)	.89
	not many	66.3	19.3	14.4	658		
	hardly any	71.1	18.8	10.1	218		
Do you trust Ottawa govt to do right?	about always	50.8	26.2	23.1	65	4.23 (2)	.12
	most of time	66.4	19.7	14.0	946		
	only sometimes	68.6	18.9	12.5	968		
Land & natural resources should be:	privately owned	53.6	31.0	15.5	252	31.25 (2)	.00
	Crown	69.9	19.0	11.1	1286		
Govt. regulation of business:	more harm	68.2	21.3	10.4	469	1.99 (2)	.37
	necessary	67.8	18.6	13.6	1005		
Price Cdns should pay for energy:	market	73.3	17.8	9.0	658	9.94 (2)	.01
	lower	62.8	22.1	15.2	943		
Best way to prevent energy shortage:	cut down use	70.6	17.0	12.4	807	29.88 (2)	.00
	new dams, etc.	59.7	25.0	15.3	953		
People failing at things means:	lazy	67.6	21.9	10.5	571	16.90 (2)	.00
	no chance	59.7	27.2	13.1	375		
Sweeping reform of complicated society:	worth trying	70.1	18.8	11.2	1112	18.11 (2)	.00
	too risky	59.6	26.5	13.9	332		

in Table 8.3 provide some support for these expectations as well: environmentalists appear to have little sympathy with trade unions; they are more
likely to prefer unions to have less power; they do not want unskilled
classes to be better rewarded for their labour; and they are less likely to
interpret the relationship between workers and managers in terms of class
conflict.

Third, the postmaterialist hypothesis also predicts that those who cleave
to the new politics syndrome will be ambivalent about the role of government in society and the economy. That ambivalence is evident in responses
to the question about government regulation of business. Environmentalists are not unduly cynical about government; they are, for example, no
more likely than others to think that 'people running government are
crooked'. But they are slightly less likely than job-oriented respondents
to believe that Ottawa can be trusted 'to do what is right'. Not surprisingly,
environmentalists support greater government involvement, via Crown
agencies, when it comes to the regulation of land and natural resources. At
the same time the data suggest that environmentalists are not inherently
hostile to free enterprise and individualism. For example, they clearly
believe in the Lockean precept that people should 'shift for themselves'
and that market forces should set the price for energy. By the same token,
and again not surprisingly, they are also more likely to prefer conservation
to development as a strategy for preventing energy shortages.

One final aspect of the postmaterialist hypothesis that merits attention
relates to attitudes towards the status quo, towards traditional forms of
political participation, and a preparedness to engage in élite-challenging,
issue-driven, unconventional styles of political action: they take risks.

COGNITIVE MOBILIZATION

The term 'cognitive mobilization' denotes a cluster of political attributes
generally involving the application of well-honed cognitive and communication skills to the task of political action. Thus, according to Inglehart,
postmaterialist segments of the population — generally younger and more
highly educated — are much more adept in engaging in élite directing
activities, activities that frequently involve bypassing traditional political
channels.[18] Table 8.4, enumerating the impact of the environment versus
jobs question on a variety of political interest and participation items,
makes abundantly clear that environmentalists are much more active in
discussing politics, in paying attention to politics generally, and in following election campaigns, and are more likely to belong to a 'concerned'
organization. This high level of activity on the part of environmentalists,
combined with the fact that they are more likely to question the status
quo and to take risks, makes for a potent combination: environmentalists

TABLE 8.4   COGNITIVE MOBILIZATION

Attention / Interest / Activity Variables		Q: Protecting the environment is more important then creating jobs. (mainly agree, mainly disagree, no opinion)					
		Env. (66%)	Jobs (20%)	No Op. (14%)	No.	X² (df)	sig
Discuss politics	yes	69.6	17.1	13.3	1656	57.26 (1)	.00
	no	48.6	32.1	19.3	405		
Help a party	yes	70.4	18.5	11.1	297	0.94 (1)	.33
	no	64.6	20.4	15.0			
Belong to 'concerned' org. (e.g., env.)	yes	74.7	16.0	9.3	257	4.67 (1)	.03
	no	64.2	20.6	15.2	1807		
Attention paid to campaign news articles (before election)	great deal	74.0	13.7	12.3	227	10.92 (5)	.05
	quite a bit	68.7	19.0	12.3	422		
	some	68.1	20.2	11.7	605		
	very little	60.0	22.2	17.8	325		
	none	57.3	23.3	19.4	103		
Interested in federal election campaign	very	74.3	16.2	9.5	588	23.27 (5)	.00
	fairly	65.4	19.8	14.8	928		
	not very	56.0	24.6	19.4	448		
	not at all	59.3	22.1	18.6	113		
Pay much attention to politics generally	very closely	71.9	17.3	10.8	231	22.49 (4)	.00
	fairly close	70.4	17.6	12.0	918		
	not very	61.1	21.9	17.0	782		
	not at all	50.0	27.0	23.0	148		
Interested in federal election campaign (PES)	very	73.1	15.2	11.7	871	46.17 (4)	.00
	fairly	63.6	21.4	15.1	843		
	not very	54.1	26.6	19.3	305		
	not at all	41.9	37.1	21.0	62		

are more likely to engage in élite-challenging activities and to do so with more energy and greater skills than other segments of the population.

PARTISANSHIP AND ENVIRONMENTALISM

The foregoing findings on cognitive mobilization highlight the participation orientation of environmentalists. Does this have any bearing on the relationship between environmentalism and partisanship? The standard literature on partisanship argues that high levels of interest, education,

TABLE 8.5   PARTIES AND VOTING

		Q: Protecting the environment is more important than creating jobs. (mainly agree, mainly disagree, no opinion)			
		Env. (66%)	Jobs (20%)	No Op. (14%)	No.
Membership in	Yes	10.2	8.7	5.7	191
federal party	No	89.8	91.3	94.3	1867
Strength of party	Strong	21.3	24.4	19.5	289
identification	Moderate	51.3	50.9	53.0	686
	Weak	27.4	24.7	27.6	351
Which party?	PC	44.0	45.1	55.4	494
	Liberal	36.9	39.4	32.8	614
	NDP	19.1	15.5	11.8	233
Party vote in 1988	PC	45.2	48.9	48.1	783
	Liberal	29.9	30.8	31.1	511
	NDP	22.0	18.5	19.1	354
	Other	2.9	1.8	1.7	43
Party do not want	PC	37.3	26.7	36.6	381
to vote for	Liberal	22.9	26.7	21.1	253
	NDP	39.8	46.5	42.3	448

participation, and the like are intercorrelated and collectively increase the likelihood of both acquiring a partisan identity and strengthening such an identity.[19] The literature on environmentalism, and more broadly the 'new politics' model, suggests something rather different. Not only are environmentalists disenchanted with the traditional parties, but they also have a pronounced disinclination to develop loyalties to any parties whatsoever. Russell Dalton in his investigation of environmental groups in Western Europe has commented on the a-partisan, even anti-partisan orientation of many group members and predicts that 'the long-term impact of the environmental issue may be less in creating a new stable base of partisan alignments, but in contributing to a more fluid system of West European party politics.'[20]

Table 8.5 illustrates the effects of the environment versus jobs question on a number of party- and voting-related activities. At best, the differences between the environment and jobs categories are limited. Pro-environment respondents are only marginally more likely to be members of a political party and somewhat less likely to acquire a strong partisan identity. They are slightly less likely to vote for the two mainline parties and more likely to vote NDP. Environmentalists are, however, more pronounced in expressing their dislike of certain parties, that is, the parties for which they would *not* vote. Thus the differences are slight but the large majority work in the direction anticipated by the 'new politics' theorists. For example, pro-environmental respondents have weaker partisan ties. The more significant fact perhaps is that no party has appeared as *the* environmental party; the NDP is slightly more likely to be favoured by pro-environment respondents, but by no stretch of the imagination can one say that the NDP, or any other party, has captured the environmental agenda.

There are subtleties relating to partisanship and environmentalism that are worth exploring further. Table 8.6 contains data on some of the same variables examined in Table 8.5, but they are percentaged differently. Strength of partisanship is examined in greater detail as well. Essentially, Table 8.6 draws attention to the effect of partisanship on support for the environment. Note that for Progressive Conservative identifiers strong partisanship is linked with weakened support for the environment. As strength of partisanship declines, support for the environment increases. For Liberals, strength of partisanship makes no difference. Among NDP-ers the relationship is curvilinear: strong identifiers are above average in their support of the environment, moderate identifiers somewhat less supportive, but weak identifiers are most likely to support the environment. These findings perhaps are illustrative of the generally weak linkages between social democratic parties and environmentalism noted elsewhere.[21] They also likely indicate some of the tensions within the NDP, tensions that have been typical of left parties confronting environmentalism in other settings. Those closer to the NDP are somewhat less supportive of environmental issues, and any move towards creating a sharper environmental profile may well be resisted by them. The category of moderate identifiers, incidentally, constitutes almost half of all NDP identifiers.

CONCLUSION

As evidenced by the time series data, there has been a noticeable and measurable 'greening' of the Canadian electorate. As well, using the environment versus jobs question in the 1988 national election survey — the item which most clearly brings into focus the trade-offs between the pursuit of environmental policies and the economic costs involved — it can be shown that pro-environment respondents differ on several attitudinal and behavioural dimensions. On each dimension the difference is not huge, but the cumulative impact of these several differences is significant, including the fact that environmentalists are much more participant-oriented.

Our primary measure of environmentalism (the question 'environment

TABLE 8.6   POLITICAL PARTIES AND THE ENVIRONMENT

| | | Q: Protecting the environment is more important than creating jobs. (mainly agree, mainly disagree, no opinion) | | | |
| | | Env. (66%) | Jobs (20%) | No Op. (14%) | |
Party I.D.	I.D. Strength				No.
P.C.	strong	58.3	24.2	17.5	120
	moderate	63.8	20.2	16.0	307
	weak	64.5	17.7	17.7	186
Liberal	strong	65.0	26.0	9.0	100
	moderate	66.3	20.8	12.9	255
	weak	66.2	20.4	13.4	142
NDP	strong	73.9	17.4	8.7	69
	moderate	68.5	19.2	12.3	130
	weak	82.4	17.6	0.0	34

versus jobs') is not as refined as we would like. Ideally we would have preferred several items tapping different aspects of the 'green' phenomenon. For example, does environmental thinking embrace such issues as animal rights? Opposition to nuclear power? Or are Canadian orientations more specifically focused on such issues as acid rain or waste disposal? Overall, we need to know more about the internal coherence of environmentalism and to what extent there is division within the 'green' community broadly defined. To answer these questions requires much more detailed and specialized survey data of a sort that is usually not available in an omnibus type national election survey. In short, the present dichotomous variable used here may undervalue both the strength and the subtleties of environmentalism.

At the same time, the data in the 1988 national election survey do show that the environmental issue must be seen as part of a larger array of 'new politics' issues. While at first glance environmentalism may be seen as *the* critical predictor, in fact it is the product of a broader underlying dimension, one that produces even sharper divisions in the data. As noted earlier, the materialist-postmaterialist (MPM) index is the single most important predictor of environmentalism. Table 8.7 demonstrates that MPM also has a significant impact on other variables such as partisanship and voting behaviour.

Note in Table 8.7 that postmaterialists are twice as likely to be NDP as Liberal partisans and four times as likely to be NDP as Conservative. The differences in voting behaviour are almost as dramatic. In contrast, there are virtually no differences in strength of partisanship, despite the

TABLE 8.7   POSTMATERIALISM AND PARTISANSHIP

		Postmaterialist (6%)	Mixed (76%)	Materialist (18%)	No.
Party I.D.	PC	2.8	72.3	24.8	990
	Liberal	6.1	75.3	18.6	862
	NDP	12.2	75.1	12.7	393
Party vote in	PC	5.8	66.3	27.9	1049
1988	Liberal	6.6	69.9	23.5	668
	NDP	17.9	68.3	13.8	448
	Other	19.6	62.5	17.9	56
Strength of	Strong	5.0	75.2	19.8	464
party I.D.	Moderate	5.8	73.3	20.8	1147
	Weak	6.2	74.0	19.8	615
Party x	PC – strong	1.5	65.2	33.3	132
strength	– moderate	2.8	65.3	31.9	354
	– weak	5.5	67.7	26.7	217
	Lib. – strong	5.6	69.6	24.8	125
	– moderate	8.5	67.0	24.5	282
	– weak	9.6	65.8	24.7	146
	NDP – strong	15.7	77.1	7.2	83
	– moderate	19.2	62.9	17.9	151
	– weak	17.1	60.0	22.9	35

generally higher levels of education among postmaterialists, a finding consistent with those elsewhere concerning the lack of enthusiasm for traditional party politics on the part of postmaterialists. Among Conservatives and Liberals, postmaterialists tend to be weaker in their strength of partisanship; among NDP supporters there is a slight curvilinear pattern, with postmaterialists tending towards moderately strong partisanship. In short, it is likely that postmaterialism works its effects not only through the 'green' issue but also through other issues, such as protection of minorities and aboriginal rights.

What are the longer-term implications? Some might argue that with the growth of environmentalism will come the creation and eventual success of a Green party, provincially, federally, or both. This is an unlikely prospect, however. As the British experience has already indicated, the problem of the electoral system, including electoral thresholds, makes it very difficult for any new party to gain entry to the established party system.[22] Only an electoral system akin to proportional representation would allow such a development to take place. Robert Paehlke, a proponent of progressive ecological politics in North America, has argued strongly against the creation of Green parties as a viable strategy and instead urges activists to vote for traditional politicians on the basis of acceptance of pro-environmental policies.[23]

To the extent that 'green' voters already consciously pursue such a strategy, and in light of our data, it would appear that the NDP, the smallest and most 'left' of the three traditional parties, is best positioned to capture the support of these voters. The Conservatives would appear least favoured. Yet it was also noted that environmentalists are not necessarily among the NDP's strongest partisans. Once more we need to keep in mind the broader constellation of 'new politics' values, of which environmentalism is but one subset. The findings indicate that postmaterialists are ambivalent about the efficacy of government intervention, are certainly not anti-business, and are less likely to see, among other things, worker-management relations in class conflict terms. In short, they do not cleave to traditional left concerns; in fact they may even be repelled by them. Certainly some of the more radical ecological groups eschew the terms left-right altogether![24] At a minimum, the environment versus jobs division will invariably give rise to conflict within the NDP, something that has already occurred within the provincial NDP in British Columbia.[25]

In brief, it appears that 'new politics' adherents are more likely to vote on the basis of issues and, given their relatively weaker partisan identities, can be persuaded to shift to another party on the basis of perceived strengths in environmental policy and related issues. This relative fluidity in party loyalties would certainly limit the development of a more firmly anchored party system or the dampening of electoral swings. And again, while the NDP may have a natural advantage in the 'green' constituency, internal party structure and interplay of interests will likely prevent the party from offering an optimal package of postmaterialist policy positions designed to maximize support from these voters. A platform containing not only protection of the environment but also proposals to give freer rein to the market and to restrict government intervention would almost certainly be opposed by traditional trade union elements within the NDP.

Finally, the impact of postmaterialist issues generally and environmentalism specifically will depend greatly upon the state of the economy. The priority voters assign to environmental protection at any given time is affected considerably by the extent to which other issues prey on their minds. A downturn in the economy, or a perceived future downturn, combined with the manner in which the issues are presented by the parties, can easily result in the elevation of economic concerns as the deciding factor for many voters in an election campaign.[26] That this can happen is illustrated by a Gallup poll taken during the depths of the 1990–91 recession. While the prominence of the 'environmental' response to the open-ended question 'What do you think is the most important problem facing this country today?' has risen steadily since 1987 — from 3% in February 1987 to 14% in January 1990 — by January 1991 it had dropped precipitously down to only 4%.[27] It is probably not coincidental that at about the same time the federal government quietly placed its Green Plan on the back-burner.

Thus, even assuming that the 'greening' of the Canadian electorate continues apace, the outcome of any given election being determined by the 'green' factor will likely be limited by the state of the economy. At the same time one needs to take into account the more activist orientation of environmentalists, and not just those in organizations but also within the electorate at large. This fact alone, combined with a willingness to use less conventional means in pursuing objectives, will likely mean that this sector of the electorate will continue to enjoy disproportionate influence in shaping the public agenda and in ensuring that the 'green' issue will remain as part of that agenda.

FOR FURTHER READING

Herman Bakvis and Neil Nevitte, 'In Pursuit of Postbourgeois Man: Postmaterialism and Intergenerational Change in Canada', *Comparative Political Studies* 20 (1987): 357-89.

P.R. Hay and M.G. Haward, 'Comparative Green Politics: Beyond the European Context?', *Political Studies* 36 (1988): 433-48.

Ronald Inglehart, *The Silent Revolution: Changing Values and Political Styles Among Western Publics* (Princeton: Princeton University Press, 1977).

————— , *Cultural Shift in Advanced Industrial Society* (Princeton: Princeton University Press, 1990).

Neil Nevitte, Herman Bakvis, and Roger Gibbins, 'The Ideological Contours of "New Politics" in Canada: Policy, Mobilization and Partisan Support', *Canadian Journal of Political Science* 22 (1989): 475-503.

Neil Nevitte and Roger Gibbins, *New Elites in Old States: Ideologies in the Anglo-American Democracies* (Toronto: Oxford University Press, 1990).

Robert Paehlke, *Environmentalism and the Future of Progressive Politics* (New Haven: Yale University Press, 1989).

Robert Rohrschneider, 'The Roots of Public Opinion toward New Social Movements: An Empirical Test of Competing Explanations', *American Journal of Political Science* 34 (1990): 1-30.

CHAPTER 9

Target or Participant?

The Hatching of Environmental Industry Policy

———

M. PAUL BROWN

More than three decades after Lindblom introduced the concept of 'muddling through',[1] how policy develops or emerges remains one the most intriguing questions for analysts. At issue here is what Greenberg and his colleagues refer to as the longitudinal dimension of policy.[2] That is, while some policies seem to appear 'unannounced' or 'grow by themselves',[3] there is 'overwhelming evidence of incrementalism and continuity'.[4] The theoretical problem is to explain the emergence of policy over time, and on that basis to predict the path of future developments.

The search for explanation has focused on a greater elucidation of the dynamics of policy development. Typically, this work has entailed 'historical' analyses of the evolution of policy on a case study basis.[5] The use of the case approach can hardly be questioned, particularly in policy fields about which little is known, but the incorporation of 'similar questions, frameworks, and methods' is of the essence if theory is to be advanced thereby.[6] For example, while readily acknowledging lack of agreement on how to achieve it, Greenberg and his colleagues have stressed the need to 'identify key developmental points in the policy process, such as the beginning point and the point at which it might be said that policy was indeed "made" '.[7]

One attempt to respond to this need has come in the form of Graham T. Molitor's concept of the 'hatching of public opinion'. Starting from the standard premise that 'new policy . . . is not made overnight', but rather emerges 'in an evolutionary process', Molitor argues that policy incubates in the context of an 'issues environment' the parameters of which (insofar as North American jurisdictions are concerned) are leading events, authorities, literature, organizational support, and precursor jurisdictions. The combined influence of these factors over a period of years, he contends, drives a policy 'from initial discussion to enactment'. In particular, when all indicators 'concurrently advance at steep rates of increase, the momentum for public policy action is so great as to be well-nigh irreversible',[8] at which point new policy emerges, or 'hatches'.

In terms of *events*, for example, Molitor argues that relevant policy phenomena occur first as 'isolated events, bits and pieces', but come to take on 'patterns' and through 'documentation of specifics' eventually reach a point where 'codewords for discussing issues . . . are formalized', and some kind of policy action becomes inevitable. Scientific-technical/professional *authorities* or 'visionaries', the 'pre-eminent few in any discipline', including those in policy think-tanks, institutes, and centres, pick up these signals and become the vanguard for change. 'Informal and oral commentaries' on these issues result in a 'written record' or *literature* which reaches a 'point of no return' in the form of influential 'monographs', 'highly specialized' publications, and 'statistical documents'. *Organizational support* in the form of national associations and the like provide a 'responsible cadre for pursuing the issue'. This 'growth of institutional backing for a cause' tends to force 'serious consideration of the issue by policy-makers'. Finally, *precursor jurisdictions* begin to adopt policy responses, and in so doing 'provide an early indication of probable action for other advanced countries'. The policy cycle comes to a close when, a policy response having been achieved, the intensity of the dissonance associated with each of the indicators tapers off.

Molitor is quite specific about the nature of some of these dynamics. With respect to leading authorities, he sees visionary professional advocates getting involved early, before politicians, who tend to 'take up causes' only when a sizeable minority of the people think 'an idea is right'. In terms of precursor jurisdictions, he sees a diffusion pattern running from Europe, and particularly Sweden, to North America, with a two- to ten-year time lag.[9]

One might want to take issue with some aspects of Molitor's model. For example, he gives insufficient recognition to the fact that opportunities as well as problems can be the germinating points for new policy in the 'issues environment'. Moreover, given that 'interaction is endemic to public policy',[10] his independent variables are more likely to be interwoven than stand-alone, aggregated determinants of policy. For example, the kinds of public policy research centres that Molitor classifies as leading authorities also produce the data associated with both the events and literature indicators.

Nevertheless, Molitor's overall approach is very much in the mainstream of approaches to the study of public policy. For example, his innovating authorities sound very much like Mintzberg and Jorgensen's senior public servants, who, having acquired the 'wisdom that comes from living with and experiencing a complex situation first-hand', are seen to be key to development of 'emergent strategy for public policy'.[11] Similarly, the content of both the events and literature indicators bear obvious kinship to the notion of paradigm shift popularized by Manzer and others in Canada,[12] and the notion of organizational support falls well within the rubric of interest-group theory.[13] Finally, the process of policy diffusion to which Molitor alludes has long been recognized in the literature, if primarily in a North American state and provincial context.[14]

On balance, Molitor's model appears to be promising, and deserves testing as a framework for analysing the process of policy development. This chapter applies the model to the 'hatching' of environmental industry policy in Canada. The environmental industry has been defined by Industry, Science and Technology Canada (ISTC) as 'one which provides products and services which have as their effect the conservation, protection, and enhancement of the environment'.[15] In Canada, an appreciation of the presence of the environmental industry, let alone the process of policy development addressed to it, is extremely recent. As of 1986, hardly any policy-makers talked about a Canadian environmental industry, yet the 1989 Throne Speech committed the Mulroney administration to its promotion, and the Prime Minister shortly thereafter announced a $4-million ISTC Environmental Industries Sector Initiative (EISI), spearheaded by an Environmental Industries Division with some twelve person-years.[16]

ISTC officials stress that it is too early to speak of a policy for the environmental industry, since the EISI is a two-phase, three-year undertaking, and the bulk of the work to date has centred on basic data acquisition. In this sense, environmental industry policy is still in process of 'hatching'. Nevertheless, even in this state, the EISI is close to what Greenberg and his colleagues would call the developmental point at which policy is 'made'. Moreover, Phase II of the EISI, the development of a 'set of co-ordinated activities to enhance the international competitiveness of the industry',[17] is clearly on the ISTC agenda for 1992. We are thus provided with a unique opportunity to test the applicability of Molitor's concept not only for explaining the dynamics of environmental industry policy development to date, but, albeit in preliminary fashion, for predicting the shape of policy to come.

THE EMERGENCE OF ENVIRONMENTAL INDUSTRY POLICY IN CANADA

The most obvious 'beginning point' in the emergence of environmental industry policy in Canada was the appearance of the environment as a major item on the national agenda in the late 1960s and early 1970s. As one study for the Organization for Economic Co-operation and Development (OECD) has noted, 'environmental legislation is the most powerful of the various factors that influence specific demands placed on the environmental industry.... [T]here are few cases where significant demands are made on the environment industry without some kind of policy stimulus, however indirect.'[18] Accordingly, the raft of clean air and water acts introduced by most western industrialized countries, including Canada, around 1970 can be seen as both the beginning point stressed by Greenberg and his colleagues and a significant event in Molitor's terms.

Feedback from the implementation of these acts, which involved substantial levels of public- and private-sector spending for both goods and services, gave evidence in global terms of an industry in the making. For example, the world market for 'equipment and services to combat pollution expanded by 86% between 1972 and 1976'.[19] In a North American context, public policy agencies and independent institutes in the United States began to report on the positive macro-economic impact of environmental spending on the American economy. For example, both Data Resources Incorporated (DRI) and the Bureau of Economic Analysis reported significant net employment benefits from spending induced by pollution-control regulations.[20] Such data led Royston to enthuse in 1979 that 'examples of companies finding new growth opportunities through the environment are legion',[21] and Kazis and Grossman to report with respect to the United States that 'the past decade's environmental initiatives have created many new jobs. . . . A dynamic new industry . . . has been created'.[22]

Although this kind of data acted as a catalyst for the immediate development of environmental industry policy in Europe, it did not do so in Canada. In part, this may have been because few if any domestic macro-level data on the economic impact of environmental spending were available. Indeed, not until 1987 did preliminary estimates suggesting that some 125,000 to 150,000 persons were directly employed as a result of environment protection expenditures, with some 10,000 to 15,000 of these being in private activities relating to 'corporate environmental affairs, programs or policies', become available in Canada.[23] In part, too, these early 'signals' may have been missed because Canada's regulatory climate was, at least in the area of water pollution control, relatively lenient compared to that of Europe, so that 'little industrial diffusion of new process technologies',[24] and hence limited growth in the environmental industry, occurred.

More important, however, was the fact that what Molitor refers to as the 'shorthand codewords for discussing the issue' simply had not been formalized and developed in a way that would bring the environmental industry to the fore as a policy issue in Canada. Quantitative data and indicators showing the positive impact on employment of spending for environmental goods and services did not compute with a Canadian business mind-set that saw the environment and anything associated with it in negative terms, as a cost or constraint to development. For example, even though Pollution Probe in 1982 produced a study similar to Royston's on how Canadian companies had been able to 'profit from pollution',[25] their primary focus was on cost reduction rather than on the business opportunities presented by development of waste reduction and recycling technologies and processes. The jargon of the time emphasized the perverse effect of environmental concerns upon business and industry.

The 1986 visit of the United Nations World Commission on Environment and Development changed all this virtually overnight through the power of its sustainable-development message. Brundtland's proposition that environmental quality and economic growth were inextricably linked not only seemed to 'reconcile the irreconcilable', but also 'dramatically altered the terms of the debate',[26] and thus constituted an event of the first order in Molitor's terms. What is more, it induced the Canadian Council of Resource and Environment Ministers (CCREM) to strike a task force on the environment and economy which, reporting in 1987, noted that 'clean technology and the research and expertise which it requires represent an important component of the growing "environmental" economic sector'.[27] Terse though it was, this allusion to an economic sector based on the production of environmental goods and services injected the formal concept of an environmental industry into federal and provincial decision-making at high levels and in a tractable form for the first time. It thus brought Molitor's leading-events indicator to the take-off point with respect to environmental industry policy, particularly when the influence of leading authorities was brought to bear.

Molitor's authorities indicator is quite a broad category. Aside from differentiating between politicians and those with scientific, technical, or professional expertise, Molitor also includes think-tanks, government sponsored research, and, as noted above, 'public policy research centres'. Almost all of these authorities can be clearly identified in the emergence of environmental industry policy in Canada.

Two individuals stand out in this respect, one because of direct contributions, the other because of indirect contributions. To take the latter first, the supporting role of Jim MacNeill, the Canadian who served first as Director of Environment at OECD[28] and then as Secretary-General of the Brundtland Commission, must be acknowledged. As noted, the Brundtland Commission visit constituted a leading event, and MacNeill has been credited with laying 'much of the intellectual foundation for the theory of sustainable development'[29] that Brundtland expounded. In this sense, MacNeill represented the 'statesman' advocate that Molitor anticipated seeing in the push towards recognition of a need for policy in a given field.

A more direct contribution was made by Robert Slater, Environment Canada Senior Assistant Deputy Minister for Policy. Slater is unanimously acknowledged by federal officials working on the environment-economy interface as the first to conceptualize in specific terms the potential for a Canadian environmental industry in Canada. His interest in the demand side for environmental goods and services took shape in the late 1970s when he served as Environment Canada's Regional Director General for Ontario, and intensified when he became the ADM for Corporate Planning in Ottawa.

Taking his cue from the successful privatization of utilities in Europe and from discussion with European officials at specialist trade fairs, Slater in 1986–87 provided the driving force behind a series of Environment Canada initiatives designed to establish the environmental industry as a policy concern. He was, for example, instrumental in Environment Canada's successful attempts to enlist co-sponsorship by the Department of Regional Industrial Expansion (DRIE), ISTC's predecessor, for a Memorandum to Cabinet on 'Making the Environment-Economy Partnership Work', one provision of which was promotion of the environmental industry. It was indicative that within weeks of Cabinet approval of the Memorandum in December, 1986, Slater had commissioned a slew of studies on the environmental industry. He had the Institute for Research on Public Policy (IRPP) prepare a definition of the environmental protection industry, Corpus Information Services make an inventory of firms and preliminary job estimates from environmental spending, Informetrica Ltd present a macro-economic evaluation of employment impacts from environmental protection spending, and other consultants offer economic analyses of both domestic and external market opportunities.

This broad-based engagement of many of Molitor's leading authorities made up for lost developmental time, as it were, and quickly brought this indicator to the point where policy action became virtually irresistible. Taking the initiative in this way, Slater, more than any other actor inside or outside government, lay behind the reference to the environmental industry in the April 1989 Throne Speech, and ISTC's subsequent Environmental Industries Sector Initiative. This was the kind of senior public servant function which Mintzberg and Jorgensen identify as crucial to the development of emergent strategy.

The third of Molitor's indicators, literature, is also very much in evidence as a factor in the development of environmental industry policy, if in a form somewhat different from what might have been envisioned. Molitor saw the appearance of monographs, highly specialized publications, and statistical documents as constituting a 'point of no return' in the development of policy. Though literature, thus understood, might seem to overlap with events as an indicator, Molitor is justified in seeing them as separate analytically. A clear distinction can be made between those elements of the literature which define the nature of a problem or opportunity and those elements which put forward policy recommendations. By their very nature, these kinds of items would be more readily accessed by government officials and opinion-makers than by the general public.

Before 1986, the literature indicator betrayed little evidence of the development of the environmental industry as a policy issue in Canada. However, as with the accumulation of data in the events indicator, this lack of dissonance stemmed more from a mind-set emphasizing the costs of environmental protection than it did from lack of publications. In fact, a variety of commentaries on the employment potential of the environmental industry appeared in Canada in the late 1970s. In 1979, for example, James F. McLaren Limited provided market estimates and a list of suppliers for the Canadian pollution control equipment industry.[30] Allusions to the employment benefits derived from environmental spending also appeared at least once in academic journals by 1982.[31] Within the federal government itself, the most explicit recognition of the commercial potential in the provision of environmental goods and services seems to have been the 1984 report of a Minister of State for Science and Technology (MSST) Task Force on Environmental Technology, which noted that 'the installation of [innovative environmental protection] technologies . . . can provide earnings for those who manufacture them', not only at home, but 'abroad'.[32]

After 1986, more systematic studies couched specifically in terms of the potential of the environmental industry as an entity in itself became much more readily available. By 1988–89, for example, studies of the environmental industry or segments thereof appeared in Nova Scotia, British Columbia, and Ontario, all of them identifying the need for policy initiatives by the federal government, including trade fairs and the like.[33] At the same time, European literature on opportunities in the provision of environmental goods and services, and particularly technology, began to circulate within the government and consulting community.[34] Moreover, by 1988 at least one private opinion poll, which Molitor places at a relatively advanced developmental point on the literature indicator, began to sample Canadian perceptions of the employment benefits associated with environmental protection,[35] and found them highly positive.

The growing written record clearly meets the criteria for Molitor's literature indicator. Whether in the form of IRPP's call for further definition of the environmental industry or the National Task Force's call for 'trade fairs [which] would include special emphasis on environmental technologies and products',[36] it provided supporting evidence for bureaucratic innovators like Slater bent on initiatives in support of the industry. As such, it became a catalyst for change, helping to ratchet the environmental industry higher on the policy agenda to the point of action.

The organizational support indicator presents a less clear picture as a determinant. Molitor perceived that 'growth of institutional backing for a cause — whether measured by number of organizations, persons involved, or resources committed — follows exponential increases which tend to force serious consideration of the issue by public policy-makers.'[37]

At first glance, the performance of this indicator might hardly seem to have been a complement to those mentioned previously as working to 'hatch' policy for the environmental industry. Indeed, as of 1988, it was reported that 'there is no cohesive and well accepted industry association . . . .Thus, the industry has had neither structure nor a united voice.'[38] In that sense, it could hardly be the source of the kind of dissonance which Molitor regarded as critical.

Some movement was nonetheless apparent. While there was no national environmental industry association as such, there was a plethora of the 'highly functionalized, extremely specialized sub groups' which Molitor says denote formalization of a commitment to a cause. For example, the IRPP study listed ten associations as but a sample of the many provincial and national supplier associations based in Ontario.[39] Moreover, in 1988, industry representatives from British Columbia launched an informal national association as an attempt to secure an overall industry voice. This effort bore fruit in the official formation of a Canadian Environmental Industries Association (CEIA) in May, 1989. Not all of the associations representing segments of the environmental industry came together under the CEIA umbrella,[40] and though hardly 'exponential' in character, this sudden growth in attempts at organizational support for the industry nevertheless added to the momentum for policy action.

The last of Molitor's indicators concerns the development of policy by precursor jurisdictions, by which he meant those in Europe. Adoption of policy initiatives in these jurisdictions, he argued, breaks the path of a 'practical and realistic working solution' which North American jurisdictions note and, with a two- to twenty-year time lag, follow.[41]

It is not difficult to find evidence of European path-breaking insofar as environmental industry policy is concerned, although it would probably be more precise to speak in terms of policy instruments. One example was sponsorship of trade fairs to allow the industry to showcase its wares. Here, the causal influence was direct. The National Task Force on Environment and Economy borrowed the idea, and one of Slater's express goals in commissioning studies of the industry was to determine the feasibility of holding a national trade fair similar to those he had attended in Europe.[42]

European jurisdictions used a much broader range of policy instruments to stimulate the environmental industry. Sweden, true to Molitor's expectations, is a case in point. As early as 1970, Swedish enterprises accrued financial subsidies to clean up their pollution, a deliberate means of stimulating the environmental industry, and helping spawn a 'range of specialized companies selling pollution control and recycle technology throughout the world'.[43] This pattern has continued since. For example, with the threat of ozone depletion in the 1980s, Sweden became noted for the tendency of its companies and its government to 'view the development of alternative products and processes as an economic opportunity ... to seize new international markets in a changing global economy'.[44]

Nor was Sweden alone in its policy support for the environmental industry. In 1979, both France and the Netherlands established research programs for the development of clean technologies, and in Denmark and West Germany 'clean technologies' were subsequently 'researched, developed, demonstrated and commercialized through government funded programs'. France, for example, established a Mission for Clean Technologies which provided grants of up to 100% of project costs for innovative approaches that could be used by all companies producing a specific product, and introduced tax changes allowing industries to write off 50% of the capital costs of a waste reduction project during the first year of operation. Denmark established a Clean Technology Fund in 1984, giving grants of up to 100% of the costs of R&D projects that would benefit society or industry in general. The Netherlands promoted clean technologies through a special Committee on Environment and Industry, which by 1988 provided annual funding of $8 million to industry, research institutes, and government agencies for research, development, and demonstration.[45]

Policy initiatives by European precursor jurisdictions were, in short, very much in evidence. As other indicators moved to their own respective 'take-off' points, the presence of workable solutions in Europe provided impetus to the development of policy in Canada.

THE ENVIRONMENTAL INDUSTRY SECTOR INITIATIVE (EISI)

The convergence of these 'structural undercurrents' led, as Molitor predicted, directly to the emergence of environmental industry policy in Canada in the late 1980s. Indeed, policy 'hatched' with an energy exceeding that associated with any of the separate indicators. When ISTC received the Memorandum to Cabinet 'recommendation' for environmental industry promotion in early 1987, the entire federal commitment to the industry as such consisted of a single ISTC official,[46] with what amounted to part-time responsibility, but no funds, for promotion of environmental products for air and water pollution control. By June, 1989, ISTC had secured approval for a $4-million Environmental Industries Sector Initiative (EISI), and the single individual had blossomed into an Environmental Industries and Projects Division, with twelve person-years. This commitment of funds and personnel at a time when both were 'scarce as hens' teeth' testified to the extraordinary increase in prominence which the environmental industry had come to enjoy on the national policy agenda.

The basis of the EISI was ISTC's assessment that the environmental industry faced difficulties which could 'hinder its ability to garner its share' of the 'burgeoning world market for environmental products, services and expertise'. Specifically, it found the industry as a sector to be fragmented, unfocused, lacking in self-awareness, of unspecified size, with relatively undetermined financial, technical, and research strengths and capabilities, and lacking in information on both domestic or export markets, particularly for technologies.[47]

Phase I of the EISI was intended to address these needs. Specifically, it sought to (1) achieve measurable improvement in the statistical and intelligence base for purposes of industry analysis and policy formulation, (2) identify critical technologies and the requirements for their competitive application, (3) create a supply capability profile of the Canadian industry for promising market segments, and (4) identify and provide analysis of the domestic and principal international markets, their competitive environment and requirements for success.[48]

To remedy the lack of comprehensive information, ISTC in 1989–90 funded or co-funded a series of studies on industry economic characteristics, domestic and export markets, and 'critical science and technology'.[49] Moreover, Statistics Canada not only dis-aggregated some of its existing data to better reflect some of the economic dynamics of the industry (as in manufacturing shipments of environmental products), but also agreed to cost-share from its own budget the addition of environmental expenditure questions to its regular industry surveys. To overcome the fragmented nature of the industry, ISTC, in collaboration with Investment Canada and External Affairs and International Trade Canada (EAITC), in 1989 launched an Industrial Wastewater Project, an on-going initiative which, through development and circulation of firm profiles, analysis of business opportunities in France and Japan, and support for attendance at environmental technology fairs, aims to enhance the international competitiveness of small and medium-size firms. Further, and in direct emulation of European precedents, ISTC in 1990 took the lead role in sponsoring Globe '90, a Vancouver showcase displaying Canadian environmental goods and services for domestic and export buyers. Finally, not strictly as part of the EISI but very much in its spirit, ISTC in 1989 launched a $20-million St Lawrence River Environmental Technology Development Program, aimed to develop technology which could be marketed worldwide.[50]

ISTC officials place great stock in the fact that in pursuing the EISI they have eschewed a 'department-centred approach' in favour of one featuring consultation, collaboration, and consensus-building, the better to encourage entrepreneurship and industry awareness even as the strategy develops.[51] It is indeed true that, aside from the divisional nomenclature, one could scarcely discern from ISTC's organizational chart that a major new initiative was under way. Instead, there is heavy reliance on team-building in a 'non-hierarchical environment'.[52] Thus, the EISI organizational structure consists of a Federal-Provincial Committee, a Sector Development Team, and three Working Groups in specific areas (industry structure and economics, marketing, and 'critical science and technology'). As of January 1991, the management team thus assembled included representatives from twelve federal departments, the provinces of Manitoba, Alberta, and Ontario, various businesses, business associations, and research organizations, as well as individuals interested in development of the sector.

There is, of course, the danger that this kind of consultative process matrix, no less than institutionalization through formal organizational change, could slow down the further development of action-oriented responses to the needs of what is a rapidly evolving industry sector. ISTC and Environment Canada officials do seem to be aware of this danger, and determined to see that it does not do so. That alone constitutes a kind of organizational support for the further 'hatching' of environmental industry policy.

FROM EXPLANATION TO PREDICTION IN ENVIRONMENTAL INDUSTRY POLICY

Predicting the future course of environmental industry policy on the basis of Molitor's model is more problematic. Molitor himself suggested that, a policy response once assured, the intensity of the dissonance associated with each of his indicators would taper off and so bring the policy cycle to an end.

That point does not appear to have been reached with respect to environmental industry policy; on the contrary, dissonance continues to build with respect to all of Molitor's indicators. There is accordingly clear potential for a still more dramatic 'hatching of public opinion' in the environmental policy field. The increased documentation of specifics under Molitor's events indicator has, for example, only served to underscore concerns about the ability of the Canadian industry to garner its share of the marketplace for environmental goods and services. For example, a study for the Science Council of Canada in 1989 found that the Canadian share of the sharply expanding domestic market for water resources equipment was only 55% and 'declining'.[53] Canada, and specifically Ontario, has also been found to run a 'significant trade deficit with the US and other countries in control, sampling, and monitoring [CSM] equipment used in environmental protection'.[54] These data confirm the presence of the environmental industry in specific terms, but reveal that its place in the rapidly expanding domestic and international marketplace for environmental goods and services is uncertain. Recognition of this discrepancy is the kind of event which Molitor associates with increasing demand for new policy initiatives.

The authorities indicator is more uncertain. On the one hand, following Molitor's model one would have expected to see more industry and other voices of the stature of MacNeill or Slater appear. They have yet to do so. On the other hand, the Science Council of Canada and the C.D. Howe Institute[55] have joined the IRPP as think-tanks and institutes with an interest in the health of the environmental industry. Their concern alone suggests that the authorities indicator will be a source of increased demand for policy action in support of the industry.

The dissonance associated with Molitor's literature indicator is far from tapering off. On the contrary, some of the recent calls for change reflect demands for policy responses beyond those embodied in the EISI. For example, Fenton's recommendation that Canada combat the decline in its share of the domestic water resources equipment industry by forging increased linkage of 'university and government research laboratories with private firms capable of deriving maximum commercial benefit from research expenditures'[56] speaks to the 'make or buy'[57] controversy which has been a factor in the 'hatching' of Canadian R&D policy generally. It could, for example, lead to an increasing demand for policy action to forestall de-industrialization of Canada in what is the fastest growing area of economic activity on a global basis. In a related vein, a study of the Ontario environmental protection industry found that Canadian branches of multinationals 'have not been given mandates from their parent companies for export operations', and that 'exports to other countries [are] handled by the parent company's larger and generally more efficient production facilities',[58] raising anew the question of the role of foreign ownership in Canadian industrial development. Having perhaps the most promising growth potential today, the environmental industry could well become illustrative of the oft-expressed need for both an industrial strategy and greater government and domestic industry R&D as means to ensuring full Canadian participation in the benefits of the emerging global economy.

The dynamics of Molitor's organizational support indicator are more difficult to fathom. Here the CEIA is the critical factor. On the one hand, its membership as of 1990 included fewer than one hundred of the more than 3,000 firms engaged in provision of environmental goods and services in Canada. On the other hand, serious attempts are under way to turn it into a viable national industry. CEIA held its second annual general meeting in March, 1990, with 'public expression of environmental business concerns through the CEIA' as one item on the agenda.[59] Moreover, as of January, 1991, negotiations were on-going between the specialized groups to establish the CEIA as an umbrella council for the industry. There is reason to expect that these negotiations will be successful, not least because ISTC is actively promoting the development of a national advocacy voice,[60] while trying to avoid establishing it as a 'reverse' group.[61] The CEIA could thus come to represent the kind of national 'peak association' often associated with participation in policy-making in European jurisdictions.[62] Success in current organization efforts could therefore make the new CEIA a significant driving force for further environmental industry policy initiatives.

Finally, the Canadian government's policy responses are far from fully following the policy path broken by precursor jurisdictions in Europe in support of the environmental industry. Government funding for research, development, demonstration, and commercialization of clean technologies in Europe has already been noted. As of 1990, the level of federal funding support in these areas had yet to match that historically available to Canada's competitors in Europe.[63]

More than money is at issue. Of even greater importance is the European tendency to make clean technologies a 'major component of their technological support program', and a thrust to capitalize 'worldwide on their new approaches'.[64] Moreover, the United States has also gotten into this environmental policy act in one area — clean coal technology. According to one observer, 'the collaborative research effort under way to develop . . . clean coal technology has significance beyond the electric power field . . . .US innovation is increasingly the result of collaborative national enterprises that mix public and private resources and risk sharing to build a strong corporate economic base.'[65] In Canada, by way of contrast, the stress until recently has been on public-private sector collaboration short of funding support.

The emphasis may be changing. ISTC's St Lawrence Project is certainly in the same vein, if not in dollar sums, of the kind of support given development of environmental technology in Europe. Moreover, the Green Plan launched late in 1990 declares that the 'environmental technology industry is among the fastest-growing sectors of the Canadian economy' and commits Ottawa to providing 'venture capital, funds, and other support for the demonstration and commercialization of environmental technologies'. Specifically, it promised an Environmental Technology Commercialization Program providing up to 50% of funding for environmental technology demonstration projects.[66] Though still not matching the funding commitments found elsewhere, these initiatives, if fully realized, would carry the thrust of Canadian policy further forward in the path broken by precursor jurisdictions in Europe.

In the case of environmental industry policy, on the basis of our analysis Molitor's model is of less avail for the purposes of prediction than of explanation. Nevertheless, the still dynamic state of Molitor's indicators taken as a whole suggests that public opinion with respect to the environmental industry has not fully 'hatched'. Valuable though it may be in its own right, the EISI is, as ISTC officials appreciate, more a preliminary to than a mature expression of the requisite policy response to industry needs. Prediction, in short, is a perilous undertaking at this stage of policy theory, but it is hard to escape the sense that the current state of dissonance associated with Molitor's indicators will result in a Canadian environmental industry policy with a more sophisticated and better-funded public and private sector collaborative character than is found in many European jurisdictions.

CONCLUSION

Policy analysts have long sought a systematic means of both explaining and predicting the emergence of public policy. Molitor put forward a model of the 'hatching of public opinion' as a possible answer. In any given policy field, he argued, the convergence of 'several big forces' in the shape of events, authorities, literature, organizational support, and action by precursor jurisdictions in the 'issue environment' leads ultimately and inevitably to new public policy. Analysis of the developmental dynamics of these indicators, he suggests, will allow policy analysts to explain, and even predict, the emergence or 'hatching' of policy responses.

Based on this analysis of environmental industry policy, Molitor may well have had good grounds for optimism about the explanatory and predictive power of his model. With some caveats, it is not difficult to link the character of environmental industry policy as expressed in ISTC's Environmental Industry Sector Initiative (EISI) to the dissonance associated with Molitor's indicators. Though they did not ripen uniformly nor to the same extent, it is evident that together they provided a powerful stimulus to the 'hatching' of the EISI. In this sense, Molitor's model may well represent a significant advance towards the long sought systematic means for addressing the emergence of policy. At the very least, the explanatory power of the model deserves further testing.

Even ISTC officials concede, however, that the EISI is not the last word with respect to environmental industry policy. Rather, it represents an approach to determining what shape federal support for the environmental industry should ultimately take — hence the emphasis on consultation, collaboration, and consensus-building.

Here Molitor's claims about the predictive power of his model become germane. It is apparent that the structural undercurrents of pressure for new policy initiatives as represented by Molitor's indicators have far from exhausted themselves. Events in the form of emerging data on the health of the environmental industry in the marketplace, increased interest by such authorities as policy think-tanks, suggestions for financial support for innovation and public-private sector collaboration in technology development in the literature, the appearance of more sophisticated organizational support in the shape of the CEIA, and the still more sophisticated policy responses apparent in precursor jurisdictions — all suggest that the emergence in Canada of an environmental industry policy more closely following the path broken by precursor jurisdictions is at hand. Given the current state of policy theory, being in the position to predict even this is a significant step forward.

FOR FURTHER READING

Stephen Brooks, *Public Policy in Canada: An Introduction* (Toronto: McClelland & Stewart Inc., 1989), Chapter 7, 'Industrial Policy', 201-37.

Bruce A. Fenton, *The Canadian Water Resources Equipment Industry: Opportunities for Research and Manufacturing* (Ottawa: Science Council of Canada, 1989).

William Glenn, 'Jobs and the Environment: Some Preliminary Number Crunching', *Alternatives* 14, 3 (1987): 18-30.

Organization for Economic Co-operation and Development, *The Macro-economic Impact of Environmental Expenditures*. Paris, 1985.

Michael G. Royston, *Pollution Prevention Pays* (Oxford: Pergamon Press, 1979).

Fazley Siddiq and M. Paul Brown, 'The Economic Impact of Environmental Production', *Canadian Journal of Regional Science* 12, 3 (Autumn, 1989): 355-65.

————, 'The Structure and Composition of the Environmental Industry in Nova Scotia', *A.C.E.A. Papers* 17 (October 1988): 45-65.

CHAPTER 10

Mirror or Participant?

The News Media
and Environmental Policy

——

FREDERICK J. FLETCHER
AND LORI STAHLBRAND

Although the direct influence of the news media on public policy is often hard to trace, news coverage has clearly had an important role in promoting concern with environmental issues. There is strong circumstantial evidence that the priorities of policy-makers and the general public are influenced, though by no means determined, by the issues stressed in news coverage. Research in the 1960s and 1970s 'suggests that the mass media . . . played a major role in influencing public concern for environmental issues'.[1] A number of case studies have concluded that sustained media attention forced government action on a particular issue or problem.[2] In addition to mobilizing concern, media coverage influences public perceptions and the responses of politicians by framing issues as economic or social, personal or political.[3]

The media not only raise and lower the profile of issues but also help to determine which voices will be heard in public debate. Their choice of sources and the credibility they accord them help to shape the debate. In the 1990s environmental groups are being accorded much more legitimacy than they were in the 1960s. Many groups have worked hard to establish effective lines of communication with the media, as have industry groups faced with environmental concerns.[4] While today environmental groups have a greater voice than in the past, how much hearing they have obtained for their key arguments remains in question. Earlier studies have found that the media tend to bring to environmental stories an already established narrative line.[5] Where environmentalists wish to link current crises to larger issues of economic and social change, news coverage tends to focus on short-term concerns regarding public health and safety, a focus reflected in public opinion surveys.[6] Environmental coverage remains contested terrain, in which the language used and the interpretations provided are the subjects of a struggle between environmental advocates and economic interests to influence the messages provided by the news media.[7]

In the early 1970s, a brief surge of public concern about environmental issues appears to have been a result of increased media attention to water and air quality, beginning about 1968.[8] By 1970, 65% of respondents to the Gallup Poll in Canada identified pollution as a problem to which government should give priority attention. However, both media attention and public concern declined as energy issues and economic concerns came to the fore. By 1976, the proportion of Canadians identifying pollution control as a government priority had dropped to 35%.[9] Parlour and Schatzow suggest the following sequence of events:

1. advocacy groups, often based in universities, became concerned about pollution issues;

2. they organized or mobilized more broadly based groups,

3. which in turn, using various methods, communicated their concerns to the media, often using 'trigger events';

4. media attention followed and led to increased public concern,

5. until (a) the news agenda was altered by other events (such as the oil price shock of the early 1970s) and (b) government had acted to reassure the public that it had things under control;

6. which led to a decline in public concern.

Remembering this pattern, environmental advocacy groups are concerned that the current high level of concern with environmental issues will also prove to be ephemeral. The level of concern has been growing for more than a decade.[10] Although it is broadly based and covers a wide range of issues—water and air quality, disposal of toxic wastes, landfill sites, the greenhouse effect and the depletion of the ozone layer—it remains fluid and possibly fragile.[11] Many respondents are willing to pay more for goods and to sacrifice some degree of economic growth, but support for dramatic measures declines as the effects become more personal.[12] The extent to which environmental concerns reflect new post-materialist values or a more critical consciousness regarding the economic and political system remains in question.[13]

If concern for environmental issues is fragile, then the role of the media takes on greater significance. If environmental reporting is institutionalized in the large news organizations, coverage is not likely to decline as sharply as it did in the early 1970s. The fact that there are now environmental specialists in many news organizations might be expected to help keep these issues on the public agenda. If environmental degradation is more visible in the 1990s than in the 1970s, audiences will have local referents for the coverage and may thus find it more persuasive. It seems clear that media coverage will be a major factor in maintaining a high level of concern about these issues, but the reasons for the waxing and waning of media attention remain elusive.[14]

We asked a dozen journalists about their perceptions of environmental issues, the focus of their reporting, how they perceived their roles, the sources they tended to use in their reporting, the constraints that they faced, and their own views of their influence on public opinion and public policy. Not surprisingly, we found that their perceptions varied according to medium, news organization, life experience, and personal philosophy.

Because we were not able to define the universe of environmental journalists with any precision, we made no attempt to select a representative sample.[15] Rather, we sought respondents who had considerable experience in environmental reporting (a term that is not itself very precise) representing television, radio, and both the mainstream and alternative press. The fact that we were able to identify more than two dozen journalists, in major news organizations, with an environmental focus suggests that the issue will not fade away as easily in the 1990s as it did in the 1970s. In concluding the analysis, we examine the extent to which the patterns observed by Parlour and Schatzow in their examination of the 1960–1972 period[16] persist into the 1990s.

This essay is inevitably exploratory. Little current work has been done on the influence of the media on public policy or on public opinion regarding environmental issues. We have chosen to focus here on some of the crucial 'gatekeepers' in the process of public debate on these issues. For the most part, we have chosen to let them speak in their own words. We hope that this compilation of views and the patterns they reveal will help others to understand the process and to examine the operation and the influence of the media.

THE ENVIRONMENT AS NEWS

In 1988 the environment suddenly became news, reflecting a new level of environmental concern. During that summer, North America was seized by a heat wave the likes of which only the dust-bowl babies had ever known. Farmers watched helplessly as their crops withered. Urban dwellers quickly bought up all the fans to be had. Then James Hansen, a prominent American scientist, stood up before Congress and told the world about the Greenhouse Effect. He said our cars and industries were spewing so much carbon dioxide into the atmosphere that the earth was becoming a literal greenhouse. The predicted increase in the earth's temperature might bring unprecedented and terrifying changes in weather: floods in some parts of the world as polar ice caps melted, drought and famine in others. Although Hansen was careful to emphasize that these weather patterns were at least several decades away, many of those sweating it through an unusually hot summer were quick to make the connection.

For some, 1988 marked a watershed. 'That was the summer that changed the way we related to the world around us,' says Anita Gordon, Executive Producer of the CBC Radio series *It's a Matter of Survival*. 'It was the first year we didn't just see or hear what was happening to the environment, we felt it. It permeated the pores of our skin. It was a summer that began to haunt us because it was the first time we realized there was something fundamentally wrong.'

Ross Howard is a reporter with *The Globe and Mail* who specializes in the politics of environmental issues and is the author of several books on the subject. He traces the current environmental anxiety to Three-Mile Island in 1979.[17] 'That anxiety turned to dread in 1988 when we discovered the hole in the ozone layer, whales in the St Lawrence River filled with toxins, the PCB fire at St-Basile-le-Grand, etc.'

In the years since, interest in and concern over environmental problems has remained high on the public agenda. Even a downturn in the North American economy has not pushed the environment off the list of most pressing concerns.

THE CHALLENGE OF REPORTING THE ENVIRONMENT

This new level of public concern poses a special challenge to journalists. The emotion, indeed fear, that surrounds so many environmental issues puts a heavy responsibility on the shoulders of those covering this 'beat'. They must find a way to deal with the emotion, as well as the politics and science, of issues that can be extremely complex. The complexity of the issues is exacerbated by the fact they are embedded in well-entrenched economic interests and beliefs.

Although most environmental problems are not new, their new priority in the public mind is forcing journalists to come to terms with their approach to these issues. And as journalists struggle to develop their own policies on how environmental issues should be defined and covered, they must also deal with the implications their work may have for government policy-makers and powerful economic interests.

The relationship between journalists and policy-makers is problematic at best. The stakes are high and journalists are subjected to considerable efforts at manipulation from government, business, labour, and environmental groups. These groups see themselves in a struggle to define the agenda and frame the issues with the media as a major battleground. The choices these reporters make have important implications for other groups.[18] Surprisingly, however, our respondents did not appear to regard these pressures as a major problem in their work.

The scope and implications of the environmental crisis mean that it does not fit neatly into the normal framework of journalism. The standard approach to news, with its emphasis on 'facticity' or the five Ws (who, what, when, where, and why), is not much help in dealing with a fundamental threat to the natural world. The holistic nature of environmental issues makes them hard for journalists, used to presenting reports on small fragments of reality, to deal with.

In the absence of industry-wide norms for dealing with these issues, journalists are charting their own courses. Although they still must negotiate with editors and news directors for work time, resources, space, and air time, they are often given considerable leeway, partly because the issues are so often difficult for non-specialists to understand.

Although 1988 was the year environmental stories broke out of the margins and into the headlines, many of the journalists in these pages have been writing about and struggling with these issues for much longer. Some, such as freelance magazine writer Andrew Nikiforuk and Barbara Rae Robson, an editorial writer with the Winnipeg *Free Press*, have established reputations for solid investigative work in this field over many years. Others, such as Martin Mittelstaedt of *The Globe and Mail*, have come to the beat more recently. In several cases, environmental journalists have also been environmental activists. CITY-TV's ecology specialist, Bob Hunter, is a notable example. He was instrumental in the founding of Greenpeace twenty years ago.

DEFINING THE BEAT

A natural starting point in a discussion of environmental reporting is to define the beat. As various studies of journalistic practice have noted, this is a crucial question. Every news organization has a 'network' of listening posts and sources that determine to a considerable degree what it covers, especially with respect to stories that are not event-driven.[19] It is self-evident that where one looks determines to a large extent what one sees.

It turns out that defining the environment beat is not a simple thing to do. There is no single pattern. 'I don't have any special guidelines,' says Eve Savory, medicine, science, and technology reporter for *The National*. 'I think I just go with my gut. It's a lot like AIDS. That started as a medical story. Then it became a social story and simultaneously a political story.' Ed Struzik, whose offical title is 'science reporter' at *The Edmonton Journal*, put it this way:

> I don't consider there are limits to environmental reporting because everything we do affects the environment. The questions around issues like industrial effluent are important, but so are questions around what we do with our garbage, what chemicals we use to garden, if we choose to drive

a car. Take any major issue today and somehow it will relate back to the environment. As a result, it becomes more a matter of picking and choosing the topics that interest me.

Martin Mittelstaedt agrees. 'I don't see a clear demarcation between what a science or medical reporter would write and what I would write', he says.

Andrew Nikiforuk is a freelance magazine writer and former managing editor of *Equinox* magazine. He has written major stories on such topics as forestry development in Alberta and our system of national parks. He says good environmental reporting has to take an ecological approach. It has to look for connections. He explains his approach this way:

> You have to take a look not only at the effect on the environment per se, but also at the political, social, and economic effects a project or policy might have. Most reporting tends to simplify issues and reduce them. But the effect of that kind of reporting is that it prevents people from seeing the whole picture. I think this is a problem with reporting in general, whether political, economic, or environmental.

Barbara Rae Robson believes that one area that journalists often overlook is the connection between occupational health and safety issues and the environment:

> Workers are like canaries in a mine shaft. They're the guinea pigs for exposure to contaminants. An awful lot of medical and scientific literature on contaminants extrapolates results from workplace exposure. That's where disease first shows up.

Wayne Roberts of *NOW Magazine*, an alternative weekly in Toronto, agrees:

> The link between occupational health and safety and the environment is key. It doesn't take a rocket scientist to understand that a toxin in a plant will soon be a toxin outside a plant. Yet these two areas are often separated and separation diffuses them both.

Roberts says that taken together these two areas are explosive because they have the potential to challenge the structure of society in a fundamental way:

> The environment is inherently a local issue — the water from my river is bad, the air in my plant is bad. It can't be dealt with by bureaucrats at the top dealing with other bureaucrats at the top. As such, it has the potential to play havoc with the rules of the game in politics and coalitions in this country.

Roberts adds that by failing to link these topics, journalists are complicit in denying the connections. Rather than maintaining their objectivity, they become part of the scenario that sees environmentalists played off against workers who are trying to hold on to their jobs.

For the most part, our informants suggest, environmental reporting tends to focus on health or safety concerns. While some were reluctant to see environmental issues in political terms, as will be seen, others tied the issues they covered quite closely to political or public policy issues. Few, however, focused on the political economy of these issues, except for job losses, or on the challenge they pose to established economic systems and life-styles. Others, however, make these connections explicit and, because they challenge conventional wisdom, may be accused of lacking objectivity.

OBSERVERS OR ADVOCATES?

The issue of objectivity is a crucial one when it comes to covering the environment. Although it is generally regarded as impossible to achieve, most journalists still believe it is the goal towards which they must strive. Some consider objectivity to be a loaded term and prefer to use the words 'balance' or 'fairness' to describe their approach. Where journalists place themselves on the spectrum between objectivity and advocacy varies widely and is dependent on a number of factors.

The self-perception of journalists in this respect is determined not only by the expectations of their editors or news directors, but also by the expectations of the public. Journalists are concerned about their credibility. The degree to which they must present their work as 'fact' or 'commentary' depends upon the medium and the role. For example, reporters have less autonomy than feature writers and columnists. Those in the alternative media have greater leeway than mainstream journalists.

'I can't cross over into obvious opinion,' says Ross Howard of *The Globe and Mail*. 'It's part of the pursuit of the myth of objectivity and balance. But I think that's the way it should be. I want to be credible and I want to bring out an informed debate.' Eve Savory believes journalists can be passionate about the environment, but find other voices to express that passion. 'We shouldn't use our own voices in news because people will stop trusting our ability to be fair and to tell them the truth.'

Others are concerned specifically with the moral dimension of the issues but still feel compelled to seek balance in their reporting. Trish Wood is a field correspondent for CBC Radio's daily current affairs program *As It Happens*. Until recently, she was the show's medicine and environment specialist. She says what has attracted her to environmental stories is that 'most of them are a sort of morality play. I like the fact that there is often a clear good guy and bad guy with the truth probably somewhere in between.' These journalists recognize that their own judgements and preferences shape their reports but they choose a format that emphasizes other voices and gives the appearance of 'facticity', as media scholar Gaye Tuchman has put it.[20]

For some journalists, the depth of the environmental crisis has changed the rules of the game forever. 'There are not two sides to this issue any more,' says Anita Gordon:

> The discussion on how to get to a healthier planet is open. Should cars be banned totally? Should we have non-gas vehicles only? But the fundamental fact is that we're going to have to change, to wean ourselves off fossil fuels, and, given the reality that fossil fuels are the engine that drives our economic system, that we're going to have to take another look at our economic system, that is now beyond dispute.

Gordon believes objectivity is a flawed concept from the start. 'We have never been objective,' she says. 'Every story we have done has come from a human-centric point of view. That's not objective. Journalists are the great reflectors of the status quo.' To take this perspective, to view humans as part of nature, involves a shift of perspective that is difficult for journalists. The mass media reflect conventional wisdom more easily than challenges to it. As Joyce Nelson has put it: 'A message in support of the status quo is typically considered to be "neutral", "objective", and "non-controversial", while a message that departs from the status quo position or criticizes it is considered to have a "point of view" or "bias".[21]

Paul Mackay agrees with Gordon. He has specialized in issues around nuclear power and worked as a policy advisor to the Minister of Energy in Ontario's NDP government. He's proud to call himself a social activist, having once spent thirty-six hours atop a hydro tower to protest construction of the Darlington Nuclear Generating Station, and he believes social activism is completely compatible with journalism. 'To me the central focus of journalism should be making the world a better place, and that means yes, you're an activist and there's no such thing as objectivity. You take positions and you're partisan.' But Mackay makes a clear distinction between a personal bias on the part of a journalist and a point of view. 'In most cases the journalist is unimportant and insignificant, but the point of view isn't.' As an example, Mackay cites a story he wrote for *This Magazine* about uranium mining in the Northwest Territories:

> I approached that story not from a personal point of view, but with the intention of revealing something that hadn't been revealed, in particular the social consequences of uranium exploration and development. Many reporters would see this as a great economic story, a story about a development boom. They would call their story objective. But that story would be no more objective than mine. It would be a conventional point of view passed off for objectivity.

Mackay says all too often objectivity simply means following the status quo, fitting into the mainstream political spectrum. But if reporters are to take the demands of environmental reporting seriously, that spectrum is going to have to widen and shift.

Andrew Nikiforuk agrees that journalists usually reflect the cultural and political norm. He says this can prejudice them against the environment:

> Canada has always had this frontier mentality in terms of developing its economy. I call it the 'Hudson Bay Mentality'. We started with fur trapping, which was predicated on the belief that once you'd trapped one area you just march on to the next valley. We took the same approach and applied it to trees, to water, to fish, to every resource in this country. We've created a national mentality, an ideology that precludes conservation. Journalists reflect this way of thinking.

Bob Hunter is as well known as an environmentalist as he is as a journalist. Twenty years ago in Vancouver, his commitment to stopping US nuclear testing on Amchitka Island led him to help found Greenpeace. Today he is ecology specialist for Toronto's CITY-TV. He makes no bones about being an advocate for the environment and has little patience for journalists who believe in the concept of objectivity:

> It's funny. The media accepted censorship and manipulation during a crisis like the Gulf War. We have a crisis on a planetary-wide basis and they don't see the similarity. They say we submit to censorship because we can't be responsible for the death of a soldier if the enemy got the information. But they're going to be responsible for the death of the whole world through their determination to remain objective. So to me, objectivity is an excuse for irresponsibility at this stage.

But Hunter is in a unique position. He is called 'ecology specialist' deliberately. He is not an environmental reporter, but really more of a columnist. He was hired precisely because of his experience with the environmental movement and he says he is given free rein to pursue stories as he sees fit. Hunter's advocacy is compatible with the station's opinionated approach to television journalism.

For Barbara Rae Robson, this is an important distinction to make. While she believes some of the best environmental journalism is done in an advocacy role, she says there is a place for objectivity. But she stresses that objectivity is much more than the old formula 'on one hand this, on the other hand that'. 'You must give evidence its true weight. You can't balance a world expert on an issue with someone who isn't of the same calibre.'

Ed Struzik of *The Edmonton Journal* says that is now a lot easier to do than when he first started reporting on environmental issues a decade ago:

> When I began reporting on these issues, there weren't a lot of informed individuals or organized environmental groups able to act as watchdogs. Sometimes I found after getting the government and industry sides of the

story, it was difficult to find someone else to comment. So I think what happened is that some of the rules changed. I would raise an issue myself, and in a sense I was speaking for people out there. I was presenting a voice that was out there, but wasn't being clearly articulated.

For example, if native people in a small Northern community told me they were concerned because last year they trapped five hundred muskrat and this year they only harvested fifty, I would listen. If I could I would go out with them to see for myself. They might be articulating the problem in a fairly primitive way, but they had something to say.

I think there's been some frustration on the part of industry and government who believe they're providing the expert information, while these people are only giving anecdotal evidence. But to my mind, it would be fair to use the native voices because they didn't have the resources to play the game the way government and industry do.

However, this was not an enviable position for a reporter to be in and I had many discussions with my editors to make sure we were approaching the story in an ethical way. I think that has changed. There are now so many informed people who can state the case for the other side.

Wayne Roberts agrees with this approach, expressing an increasingly common view about science and 'experts': 'I have no trouble using experiential evidence, as long as it's registered for what it is. After all, what we call objective science is a product of the conquest of nature, and as such has an enormous bias built into it.' Roberts adds that in environmental stories, often the 'other side' is nature itself:

There's been a legal question: 'Do trees have standing?'; in other words, does nature get to speak. Investigative reporters and radical reporters are used to speaking on behalf of those who don't have a voice – the poor, immigrants, etc. This is taking that concept one step further in effect.

While the various perspectives on objectivity are idiosyncratic, it is notable that journalists working for the conventional media feel more necessity to adhere to established formats. Those working for the alternative press, CITY-TV, and some CBC programs apparently feel less constrained about the way they raise issues. Nevertheless, these voices and the nature of the issue appear to be bringing about changes throughout the media, increasing the prospects that more fundamental issues will be raised.

WHO GETS TO SPEAK?

Recently, a number of studies have noted the tendency of the media to provide a voice mainly for official sources. Studies have shown that credibility in the eyes of the media is closely tied to official sources.[22] In dealing with the environment, however, reporters have increasingly turned to advocacy groups, although the hierarchy of legitimacy continues to privilege the more conservative, research-oriented groups, rather than the activists. The latter get media attention for their actions but rarely for their arguments.[23] According to our respondents, practices now vary quite widely.

Paul Mackay states forthrightly that he often goes to environmental groups first when he is researching a story:

> I come from that background. In university and beyond I was active in OPIRG [Ontario Public Interest Research Group], and I know there are people in environmental groups, citizens groups, native organizations, etc. who are dedicated. Often they have collected every report and documented case histories. They've thought about the issue, been enraged by it, know the whole thing backwards and forwards. In most cases, unlike government people, they don't go home to a fancy house at night or put the issue on the back shelf on the weekend. Rather they're out giving a good part of their weekend as activists. That's part of the whole activist culture. For these reasons, they can be a profound source of information.

Mackay believes the credibility of environmental groups has increased in recent years:

> Fifteen years ago, anti-nuclear groups in Ontario were getting nowhere. They were laughed out of the paper. They couldn't draw anyone to their news conferences. But then Three Mile Island happened and they gained some credibility. Chernobyl happened several years later and all of a sudden, they were being taken more seriously. Then Ontario Hydro started to find cracks in the rotors of their reactors and the cost of Darlington skyrocketed. Editors could no longer ignore what these groups were saying.

Trish Wood says environmental journalists are becoming more sceptical of the traditional sources of information:

> We're smart enough now to know that the government also has an agenda. I think government is less likely to be completely honest about a situation if policy-makers are going to look bad. The stakes are higher now. That's not to say that Greenpeace or Pollution Probe are pure. They also have an agenda. But we're considering more sources now. That means we're probably doing better analysis.

Eve Savory says often information from environmental groups can be very valuable, but she is put off by political rhetoric whatever its source. She says she draws on years of covering an issue in order to evaluate when she's being fed a line. 'You get some awareness of what the mainstream beliefs are and you grow into the ability to judge as you do a beat.' It is unclear what Savory means by 'political rhetoric', but it often means challenging economic and political orthodoxy. Journalists often define comments as 'political' in order to avoid taking a stand on these larger and more controversial issues. If an environmental problem can be defined as a health or safety issue, the political element can be omitted and controversy lessened.

Feature writers and magazine journalists have the luxury of time, which permits more broadly based research, and a wider range of sources. It takes Andrew Nikiforuk from two to four months to complete a feature article for a magazine. He takes advantage of that luxury of time by speaking to as many independent sources as he can:

> The information I dig out and eventually use is not from any one group. The first source for anything is to go to the local community affected. Then I talk to a variety of scientists. Lastly I will approach environmental groups. But I no more go to environmental groups than I go to government for information. I find they quite often take a narrow view of things and get their facts wrong. I don't think my approach has changed over the years. I'm still very wary of any group.

Journalists are generally wary of being 'used' by advocacy groups of all stripes.

Covering the environment beat has disabused Barbara Rae Robson of the notion that the various levels of government were the guardians of public health:

> I was pretty stunned by the lack of interest I found in those who should be there defending our interests. The way I found out was by noting how often they defended the interests of industry. Asbestos is a good example. Those who claimed there are no health problems associated with asbestos were in Quebec where there's an industry to protect.
>
> I've also learned to be sceptical of epidemiological studies. Sometimes they are designed so that they cannot detect a substance at the level that it's believed to exist. Sometimes an absence of evidence is not necessarily an evidence of absence.

Complex scientific data are a part of many environmental stories. Yet most journalists do not have the academic training to evaluate the data or the interpretations presented by interested parties. It is a challenge to journalists to become 'literate' in the science involved in the issues they report on, especially under deadline pressures. The limited scientific literacy of the general public also presents a problem for journalists, limiting their capacity to provide the full flavour of scientific debate.

Margaret Munro of the Vancouver *Sun* is an exception. Her training is in biochemistry and microbiology. Munro was one of the writers on the Southam Environment Project in 1989, an insert into all Southam papers that tried to deal with some of the larger implications of environmental degradation. Munro says journalists should not be afraid of scientific facts and figures:

> When I'm determining credibility, I tend to go to scientists endorsed by the

United Nations. I tend to query scientists who are working for environmental groups such as Greenpeace more. Perhaps that is because of my indoctrination in the news business. I know what will get by the editors.

For a variety of reasons, the fear of manipulation focuses more on advocacy groups than on official sources.

Anita Gordon notes that the gap between what environmental groups are saying and what industry is saying is narrowing as industries become more conscious of green issues. This makes it more difficult for journalists to evaluate the information coming from various sources. The material presented is more nuanced and more evidence is provided. Gordon says: 'It means really knowing your subject. Maybe the days of the thirty-second clip are over when we're dealing with these issues. Maybe we have to find a new approach.'

With respect to many environmental issues, the 'experts' are divided. The various interests involved have their own experts to make the case for their preferred position. It is difficult for specialist journalists to sort out the competing claims. Journalists are dependent on more dispassionate sources for assistance on such matters; increasingly, however, there are few such sources. Many university-based scientists now have ties with the interests involved.

MEDIA CONSTRAINTS

Gordon's point draws our attention to the nature of the media themselves and how their structures and practices can make it difficult to portray environmental issues fairly and completely. Journalists in all three popular media struggle continually with restrictions of time, space, and resources. It takes time to dig out and evaluate scientific data. It also takes time to explain it properly.

Ed Struzik says the sheer number of environmental stories surfacing now can pose a problem:

> There are so many stories out there that you have to pick and choose. To some extent you become the editor. You decide what the public gets to hear. But often those decisions are based on money. For example, when Tom Berger held public hearings on the Mackenzie Valley Pipeline, everyone followed him. Now, similar hearings attract only a few local reporters because there are so many other issues to cover and not enough reporters to go around.

Limited resources are also a problem for Eve Savory at CBC Television. 'There are so many stories I can't cover because they don't happen in Toronto. I can rarely afford to bring a whole crew even as far as Vancouver.'

Television is oriented towards short, colourful items. It is rarely conducive to communicating complex ideas. Nevertheless, it is the most widely used and trusted source of news for Canadians. In addition, with respect to many environmental stories, it conveys the effects of environmental degradation with a power unmatched by other media. It is probable that the most powerful images that citizens bring to mind when they think about environmental issues are those provided by television: oil-soaked birds, struggling to survive; columns of black smoke from oil fires. It is clear also, of course, that the visual orientation favours some environmental stories over others that may be more important.

CITY-TV's Bob Hunter has tried to turn the limitations of television to his advantage: 'I try to think of an item as a haiku. In three lines you can say a whole poem. I started off as a painter, so I'm actually quite comfortable with this medium because I look for images.' He says with many environmental issues it is no longer a matter of putting a major exposé on the air. Most people know something about the greenhouse effect or ozone depletion. Rather Hunter sees his job as bringing the issue to viewers in a way that will hold their attention:

> They told me right off the bat here that this is the era of the zapper and if I come down as Doctor Doom every evening, viewers will just zap me off because they don't want to hear that. So I deliberately throw in positive stories. That leaves me free to put in a killer piece about once a week, such as one I did about ozone depletion. It basically said our children and grandchildren are going to fry. Thank you. I'm Bob Hunter.

But Hunter has his moments of frustration. 'I still quibble with the fact that I do an ozone story and it shows up twenty minutes into the show, while the lead is a teenager stabbed in North York.'

Ross Howard adds that getting beyond stories about individual environmental disasters can be difficult:

> I try to do the political angle on environmental stories. For example, if there's an oil spill, I'll do stories from Ottawa that look at who's responsible, why tankers are allowed to be built without double hulls, who will compensate the fishermen, etc. But it's hard to get stories about the economics of these issues on page one. They're just not considered sexy enough.

It must be remembered that these limitations are the result not so much of the medium but of the profit-oriented, ratings-driven nature of the news business. 'You have to keep in mind that a newspaper or television broadcast is primarily a means of delivering consumers to advertisers,' says Martin Mittelstaedt of *The Globe and Mail*. 'Every newspaper is chock-full of ads that endorse and reinforce a consumerist society.' Wayne Roberts concurs:

> Media receives major funding from advertisers, among them some of the

major polluters. Advertising is itself contributing to the environmental crisis because it is at the crux of the problem, that we are demanding more of the planet than the planet can give. Advertising is pressure to get people to consume what they don't inherently want. The major vehicle for that is the media.

There is a paradox inherent in the notion that the media can play a major role in environmental education. News organizations are part of their communities and are tied in with the economic interests that may have much to lose from aggressive environmental reporting.

Margaret Munro agrees that it is sometimes difficult for a reporter to cover an issue properly:

> In British Columbia the pressure is on to paint a better picture of the forestry industry. But in fact, I don't think the *Sun* can cover these issues properly. Forestry issues are so complex. Yet we have one little reporter against the whole industry.

Although it is clear that industry has at times successfully brought pressure to bear on news organizations, this is difficult to document. Nevertheless, industries that raise environmental concerns have clearly become increasingly sophisticated in their public relations and more and more willing to demand that their point of view be included in environmental reporting.[24] This is a sure sign that such reporting is having a measurable effect.

One of the most problematic characteristics of the media in terms of environmental coverage is the urge to compartmentalize everything. Anita Gordon says she had to overcome this tendency before she could make any progress on the radio series *It's a Matter of Survival*:

> The media label everything. We tend to assume we understand something once we've given it a name. But the more background reading I did in preparation for the series, the more I realized the environmental crisis has nothing to do with external things called 'acid rain' or 'global warming'. It has to do with us. It has to do with the fact that we are a species that is growing too big for the planet, that we are consuming too much, that we are wasting too much, and that we believe nature is infinite. Once I came to terms with that, everything started to fall into perspective. It was something of a revelation for me.

The dilemma so aptly stated by Gordon reflects a contradiction between the demands of the popular media and the nature of the environmental story. The media operate by fragmenting larger issues into manageable chunks but environmental issues reflect the operation of systems, ecological and political-economic. When 'everything is connected to everything else', in Barry Commoner's famous phrase, conventional journalism finds reporting difficult.

JOURNALISTS AND PUBLIC POLICY

Despite this inherent limitation of the media, Gordon believes fervently that journalists can influence environmental policy. She also believes they have a duty to try:

> We're in the information business and I believe information is empowering. If we understand what we're facing, then we can act on it. That's where the media come in. Normally the way to change a mind-set in society is through education. People can change their point of view and even their value system if they feel threatened, as in times of war. The problem with the environmental crisis is that by the time we understand its full implications, it will be too late. There's no time for the slow process of education. There's only one group that has the power to reach people. That's the media.

Bob Hunter, who combines the roles of activist and journalist, believes that the media have a vital role to play:

> I've believed since my early days as an environmental activist/journalist that the only system big enough to deal with the destruction of the environment is the global communication system. When we started Greenpeace we were always conscious of the power of images and the fact that through the media one person could theoretically address the whole world.

Hunter says that in moments of despair he worries that using the media to get the message across puts an unrealistic burden on the environmental movement to deliver the goods. There is a real possibility that people will believe the problem is being solved simply because they see it discussed on television. Joyce Nelson believes that television news operates by alarming and then reassuring audiences, so that it is not a good vehicle for mobilization.[25] The return of the unflappable anchorperson reassures us that everything is under control.

For Barbara Rae Robson, the role of the media is to disseminate information and in doing so to influence policy indirectly:

> The environment is putting other values on the public agenda than corporate economic values. Each little story adds to that process. Take the issue of asbestos. The science about the dangers of exposure has to be there, but journalists are the ones who get the information out. That encourages victims to come forward, lawyers to launch cases. Sometimes that process can lead to changes in legislation.

Ross Howard agrees that journalists can have some impact:

> They help to bring the public to the point where they can no longer be controlled by government. That's when policies change. I think that happened with the acid rain issue. In that sense the media is a participant in the policy process.

Howard's colleague, Martin Mittelstaedt, believes that an environmental ethic is being incorporated into Western capitalist society and that the media are reflecting that process:

> I think that it would be interesting if concerns about the environment led people to reject consumerism, to refuse to work forty hours a week, to live more modestly. But I don't think that is what's happening. Instead, an environmental sensibility is being incorporated into laws and regulations and production process. This mitigates the problems. It draws us away from the brink. It allows this society to crank up the old jalopy for another spin around the track.

For Paul Mackay, the best of today's environmental journalists are successors to the muck-raking tradition of the first decades of this century, when Sinclair Lewis and Theodore Dreiser were filling the front pages with the horrors of the Chicago stockyards, working conditions in the garment factories, and stories of political corruption. Mackay identified with H.L. Mencken's famous dictum that the purpose of journalism is to 'comfort the afflicted and afflict the comfortable'. The central assumption of muck-raking or exposure journalism is that 'if corruption and inequality are revealed, they will be corrected'.

That assumption is challenged by Wayne Roberts, who argues that information has rarely been the problem. He cites several cases:

> In health and safety, where I have had my most profound experience, people have been aware of the dangers of asbestos since Roman times. The Mad Hatter in *Alice in Wonderland* referred to the effects of mercury on hatters. Cancer of the scrotum was identified as an occupational hazard of chimney sweeps as far back as the eighteenth century. A lack of information is not what prevented these problems from being solved. It was a lack of alternatives. I think that's true with most environmental issues.

Roberts believes in exposure journalism but is not optimistic about its effects. Journalism may tip the balance when government is unsure of its direction but this does not happen very often. In his view, information changes power relations only if 'it can generate or feed into a movement'. Roberts cites the effects of Upton Sinclair's exposure of the exploitation of immigrant workers in the large meat-packing plants in his book *The Jungle* (1905). His dramatic example of a man falling into a machine and being minced with the meat led not to better protection for workers but rather to meat inspection laws, a reform the meat packers wanted to help them compete in European export markets.[26]

Asked to cite cases where their work had had an impact on public policy, most of our respondents were hard pressed to identify clear-cut cases of influence. Nikiforuk cited an article co-authored with Ed Struzik on a plan to license pulp mills on the Peace and Athabaska rivers: 'I think the article may have slowed the project down but it's still going through with virtually no changes.' He noted that his articles on the future of Canada's parks had had no discernible impact. He sees his contribution as raising public consciousness, a long process with only an indirect effect on policy.

Ed Struzik agrees that direct policy effects are usually minimal but argues that sticking with a story over a long period can produce a response. He cites his series of about seventy articles on the impact of resource extraction on Wood Buffalo National Park. He documented how, among other things, clear-cut logging was going on inside the park:

> The day after one of the articles on logging appeared, the federal Environment Minister announced he was going to attempt to buy out the logging company. The two sides are now in the middle of negotiations. I'm fairly confident the negotiations will succeed.

One area where the direct influence of the media has been documented is on question period in Parliament and in the provincial legislatures. The media have considerable influence on the questions and the responses. Ministers are briefed every day on what is in the media.[27] This influence on the theatrical side of politics does not necessarily result in any real impact on policy. Nevertheless, advocates of all stripes remain convinced that the media are an essential part of the process of influence, even though their effects may be longer term or indirect.

CONCLUSION

Although these journalists may well under-estimate their influence, it is clear that they operate within a very real set of constraints and that short-term effects are hard to discern. They remain short of resources, time, and space, and their needs are not fully understood by management. In addition, to the extent that their concerns require challenging conventional wisdom, those in the mainstream media are constrained by the traditional practices and economic interests of their employers.

How have things changed over the last twenty years? In a study based in part on interviews with reporters covering environmental issues in the period 1960–1972, Parlour and Schatzow made several general observations about environmental reporting:

1. the major coverage decisions were made by individual reporters rather than by management;

2. a general lack of understanding of the issues by management often deprived reporters of needed scientific assistance;

3. lack of scientific expertise on the part of media personnel left them at the mercy of experts, unable to assess claims;

4. news operations generally reacted to rather than initiated reports on environmental problems.[28]

In general, our respondents agree with the first three points. The positive side of neglect by management is autonomy. They worried about their own grasp of the science involved but were constrained at least as much by their perceptions of audience background, which they took to be weak. It appears that in recent years, there has been more willingness to take the initiative in reporting the environmental story. Several dailies have produced special supplements to probe the issue in more depth and there have been radio and television features that go beyond event-driven reportage.

In our interviews, respondents showed little inclination to discuss constraints derived from the corporate ties of the media. Critics like Joyce Nelson[29] have suggested that media coverage is substantially manipulated by corporate public relations and is subject to editorial restraint for fear of offending major advertisers or getting 'flak' in response to reports that question the practices of major industries. It is unclear whether these reporters did not feel limited by such concerns or were simply reluctant to discuss them. Although business columnists like Terrence Corcoran of *The Globe and Mail*'s *Report on Business* refer to 'environmental terrorists', the mainstream media provide at best a reformist perspective on these issues, rarely a radical one.

Parlour and Schatzow were concerned that 'while the media were effective in mobilizing concern they appear to have been . . . ineffective in educating the public about environmental problems'.[30] By the end of the period studied, the public still had little grasp of the larger issues and environmental concerns proved ephemeral for many. It seems fair to say that by 1990, the concerns were more deeply entrenched and less abstract. However, analyses of media coverage and poll data both suggest that most citizens and many journalists still have only a limited capacity to assess risk or to understand the trade-offs that must be made in selecting environmental policy options.[31] Perhaps, however, this is too much to ask.

Can and should journalists have greater influence? Anita Gordon contends that what stops journalists from getting to the crux of the problem of environmental degradation is a lack of courage:

> It's going to demand real courage to look beyond the status quo. We've got to step outside of our materialistic civilization and look at it from a distance. *It's a Matter of Survival* was an advocacy program. There was no question about what it was saying. Yet when it went on the air, thirteen thousand people responded. They told us: 'I've been feeling this way for a long time and you have articulated it for me.' That starts to build up a mutual kind of courage.

As the depth of the environmental crisis grows, journalists will continue to play a role in shaping public opinion on these issues. In the absence of clearly defined rules, journalists working in this area will continue to struggle with what that role should be. Andrew Nikiforuk sums up his own views and those of many others:

> My role as a writer is to tell good stories about issues that matter to ordinary people, in language that ordinary people can understand. If these stories get people mad enough to change or influence policy, that's great. My prime goal is to make a difference to the reader.

As for the citizens, we still must rely on journalists' interpretations of the issues for much of our knowledge and understanding.

INTERVIEWS

Interviews with the following present and former environmental journalists were carried out by Lori Stahlbrand in February, March, and April of 1991:

Anita Gordon
Executive Producer
Quirks and Quarks
CBC Radio

Ross Howard
Parliamentary Correspondent
The Globe and Mail

Bob Hunter
Ecology Specialist
CITY-TV

Paul Mackay
Policy Advisor
Ontario Minister of Energy

Martin Mittelstaedt
Environment Reporter
The Globe and Mail

Margaret Munro
Science Reporter
The Vancouver Sun

Andrew Nikiforuk
Freelance magazine writer

Wayne Roberts
Political Columnist
NOW Magazine

Barbara Rae Robson
Editorial Writer
The Winnipeg Free Press

Eve Savory
Medicine, Science, and
Technology Reporter
The National
CBC Television

Ed Struzik
Science Reporter
The Edmonton Journal

Trish Wood
Environment/Medicine Reporter
As It Happens, CBC Radio

FOR FURTHER READING

Michael Greenberg, et al., 'Risk, Drama and Geography in Coverage of Environmental Risk by Network Television', *Journalism Quarterly*, Summer 1989.

Allan Gregg and Michael Posner, *The Big Picture: What Canadians Think About Almost Everything* (Toronto: Macfarlane, Walter and Ross, 1990).

Joyce Nelson, *The Perfect Machine: Television in the Nuclear Age* (Toronto: Between the Lines, 1990).

J.W. Parlour and S. Schatzow, 'The Mass Media and Public Concern for Environmental Problems in Canada, 1960–72', *International Journal of Environmental Studies* 13 (1978): 9-17.

David Taras, *The Newsmakers: The Media's Influence on Canadian Politics* (Toronto: Nelson Canada, 1990).

PART III

Policy in an International Context

CHAPTER 11

The Continental Dimension

Canada and the United States*

—

DON MUNTON AND GEOFFREY CASTLE

The major environmental issue in Canada during the 1960s and 1970s was the alarming condition of the Great Lakes. The huge area of these lakes and their vital importance to Canada's heartland, coupled with the extent of the degradation, made their fate a national interest, not just a regional concern. The single most prominent pollution issue during the 1980s in Canada was that of acid rain. Increasingly recognized impacts on aquatic and terrestrial ecosystems led to widespread concern throughout eastern Canada and the northeastern United States.

These two distinct problems have common roots in the development and growth of modern urban and industrial societies in central Canada and the United States mid-west. They also have a common structure. In both cases sources on the American side of the boundary contributed more to the problem than those on the Canadian side. The transboundary flows of pollutants were, in other words, more south-to-north than north-to-south. The political processes for dealing with Great Lakes pollution and acid rain, moreover, followed common paths. The fact of substantial transboundary flows, which are particularly important in the Canadian context, meant that solutions had to be pursued through not only the instruments of domestic policy, but also, especially for Canada, through the instruments of foreign policy as well. The eventual results of the two Canada-US diplomatic efforts were strikingly similar international environmental agreements — the Great Lakes Water Quality Agreement of 1972, renegotiated in 1978 and amended in 1987, and the 1991 Air Quality Agreement. Both of these reflect the common interests, and the fundamental differences, of the two countries.

THE NOT-SO-GREAT LAKES

Pollution in the Great Lakes was not newly discovered during the upsurge of environmentalism in the late 1960s and early 1970s. The governments of Canada and the United States had twice earlier requested the

International Joint Commission (IJC), created by the Boundary Waters Treaty of 1909, to study pollution problems in the Great Lakes region. Two Commission reports, in 1918 and 1951, had identified serious problems, especially in the Lakes' connecting channels and near-shore areas, but public concern was not much aroused and the response of governments was totally inadequate.[1]

By the early 1960s scientific evidence of serious basin-wide pollution problems was mounting. A much publicized controversy over whether or not Lake Erie was 'dead' highlighted the particularly acute state of the smallest and shallowest of the Lakes. Firm political action was clearly needed in order to translate into practical reality the abstract legal principles of the Boundary Waters Treaty, and specifically its Article IV, which flatly declares that the 'boundary waters . . . shall not be polluted on either side to the injury of health or property on the other'.

Canada and the US formally asked the IJC in October, 1964, to undertake yet another report, this time on the whole of the lower Lakes. Due to the complexity of the problems they were facing, to a lack of staff within the Commission itself, and to the difficulties of borrowing experts from the governments, which were not at this point well supplied with expertise themselves, the IJC's technical advisory group took six years to put together their final report. This massive three-volume, 800-page document was ultimately delivered to the IJC in the early fall of 1969.[2] To no one's surprise, the scientists and engineers unanimously concluded that Lakes Erie and Ontario and the international section of the St Lawrence were indeed being polluted on both sides of the boundary. The report warned of a range of industrial pollutants but emphasized the problem of 'eutrophication', the accelerated aging of the Lakes as manifested in algae formation, and linked this problem to excessive phosphates loadings, especially from municipal sewage. They also presented data showing for the first time the relative contribution of US and Canadian sources of pollution. The bulk of it was from the more heavily populated and industrialized American side. The major recommendations were that phosphate control programs be implemented immediately, that a new set of water quality objectives be adopted for these waters, that additional programs be developed to meet these water quality objectives, and that a new international board be established to co-ordinate both these programs and the required monitoring and surveillance.

During January and February 1970 the IJC held public hearings on the report in eight cities around the Great Lakes. There were heated confrontations between government scientists and detergent industry spokesmen over whether phosphates were indeed the problem and whether controls on phosphate levels in laundry products were needed. The general consensus by the end of the hearings was that the deleterious effect of phosphates had been argued conclusively. The detergent companies were thought to be in retreat. As the IJC itself prepared a special interim report, sent to the two federal governments in April, 1970, the politicians, bureaucrats, and diplomats had already begun to sense growing public demand for a major clean-up effort.

Negotiating the 1972 Agreement

Responding to signs of public concern, the Canadian Parliament approved an array of environment-oriented legislation during 1969 and 1970, including the Arctic Waters Pollution Prevention Act, a new Fisheries Act, and the new Canada Water Act.[3] To the latter, at the eleventh hour, was added a provision requiring reductions in the amount of phosphates manufacturers included in household detergents. This provision was the direct result of the IJC studies on the Great Lakes.

In the US, President Nixon made a point of signing into effect on New Year's Day 1970, the recently passed National Environmental Policy Act (NEPA), which among other things established a Council on Environmental Quality. He followed up this gesture by emphasizing pollution problems in his January State of the Union message, by sending to the Congress in February a Special Message on the Environment, and by creating a new Environmental Protection Agency (EPA). Strong doubts persisted that the White House had become genuinely committed to cleaning up pollution, but it was clear the Nixon administration at least wanted to avoid being left behind by the environmental bandwagon.[4]

The lack of effective action on Great Lakes pollution in the past convinced government officials in Canada that something more than pious rhetoric was necessary. Behind the closed doors of the Trudeau government, the Minister of Energy, Mines and Resources, J.J. Greene, argued strongly that work had to begin immediately toward a co-operative Canada-US arrangement, including a new bilateral environmental agency with some real powers, and probably an entirely new bilateral environmental treaty. Such far-ranging proposals were too grand for the Department of External Affairs. Eventually the two departments agreed to aim for a formal agreement but not to try to establish a new supranational environmental agency. Getting the US government on board was a much more difficult challenge. Through the spring of 1970 Washington remained noncommittal. A series of blunt, highly critical speeches by Greene, a number of them to American audiences, had little effect.[5]

The American government's apparent deafness stemmed not so much from a lack of commitment to environmental causes or lack of responsiveness to a neighbour's concerns, as from an inter-bureaucratic struggle over which agency would play the lead role on the US side in the pollution issue. This tussle spilled over into a mini-battle over who would handle a

Canada-US meeting planned to discuss the expected interim report of the IJC in April, 1970. Genuine reservations soon emerged in Washington, however, about the sort of regulatory actions that would be required if there were to be a serious effort to clean up the Lakes, and about the costs of these actions.

Despite an evident lack of agreement between the officials of the two countries on how to proceed, the first ministerial-level meeting devoted to Great Lakes pollution problems in the history of Canadian-American relations took place in May, 1970. The Canadian ministers, J.J. Greene and Jack Davis, urged the acceptance of the recommendations of the IJC Interim Report and proposed the negotiation of a water quality treaty. They met with no success; the Americans were not yet ready either to approve the IJC report or to begin formal negotiations. The two sides could only agree that transboundary pollution existed, that most of it originated on the United States side, and that such pollution was contrary to the obligations each had under the Boundary Waters Treaty. The Canadian back-up proposal was for a working group to examine the adequacy of the present effort and the need for a possible agreement. This idea was accepted by the US side only after a private discussion between Greene and Russell Train.

White House approval to move came in the early fall with Nixon's signature on the report of a task force chaired by Train. The United States was finally committed to a bilateral approach for controlling pollution in the Great Lakes, but not necessarily to what the Canadian side was seeking.[6] The Canada-US Joint Working Group met in September and quickly agreed on the establishment of and terms of reference for ten sub-groups (covering water quality objectives and standards, institutional matters, environmental legislation, contingency planning, the co-ordination of special programs and of research, and pollution from hazardous materials, from agriculture and forestry, and from watercraft). The sub-groups, involving approximately seventy-five federal, provincial, and state officials in all, each began a series of meetings to draft reports on their particular problems. Their work predictably took longer than expected but for the most part proceeded well. The issues which proved most difficult to resolve included whether or not the US federal government would follow Canada's example and regulate detergent phosphates, the question of an IJC staff unit, vessel waste regulation, and, more generally, the nature and form of the prospective bilateral agreement.

At a second ministerial meeting in June 1971 the representatives of the two governments formally approved the Joint Working Group Report. Hopes were high for an agreement by fall, but the process stalled once again.

First the Canadian officials became preoccupied with the negotiation of a back-up agreement with Ontario. Such an agreement was essential given that the implementation of the pollution control programs envisaged under the agreement would be largely the province's constitutional responsibility.[7] After several meetings, some of which were at least as difficult as any held with the Americans, the necessary deal was made. Ottawa agreed to provide an accelerated $173 million program of loans and grants for new municipal sewage treatment facilities while Ontario, in return, formally agreed to assist in implementing the prospective Canada-US agreement.

The bilateral talks were then further delayed in mid-September when the US government's slow movement toward detergent phosphate controls was abruptly reversed. The Nixon Administration's senior health official publicly announced that there were possible harmful effects to human health from the replacement of phosphates in detergents with the leading alternative, NTA (nitrilotriacetic acid). Despite acknowledging a lack of clear scientific evidence of such dangers, he advised the public to return to the use of phosphates. The administration was immediately and heavily criticized for having capitulated to political pressures from the major soap and detergent companies. This announcement not only sealed the fate of proposals for US federal government phosphate controls but also delayed the bilateral negotiations for months as officials of the newly created Environmental Protection Agency reassessed whether and how the US could reduce overall phosphate loadings into Lakes Erie and Ontario without federal controls on the content of detergents. The alternative means chosen was expensive — the fitting of American cities' sewage treatment plants with the capability to remove the phosphates before they entered the Lakes — and would take more time.

A December 1971 meeting in Ottawa of the two negotiating teams finally began detailed consideration of both sides' draft texts. Much of the discussion proved difficult. The American draft was considerably more qualified and less specific on various key items. To the Canadians, it was particularly lacking with respect to phosphate reduction requirements, implementation programs to attain common water quality objectives, broadened 'watch-dog' responsibilities for the IJC, and creation of an IJC staff office. The first two of these provisions were, of course, intended to ensure the agreement would have some 'teeth'. The latter two points were the equivalent of verification provisions in an arms control agreement; these were essential, in the eyes of Canadian officials, in order to prevent the natural tendency toward backsliding once the accord had been signed.

During subsequent sessions, Canadian efforts to secure as firm as possible American commitments on implementing pollution control programs were only partially successful. During an early February full negotiating meeting in Washington, the Canadians reluctantly accepted an American-proposed wording to the effect that municipal programs 'would be complete *or in the process of implementation*' by 31 December 1975 (emphasis added). The concession was a crucial one. This particular phrase was to become the object of much attention over the coming years when US municipal treatment programs noticeably lagged. But the American negotiators would offer no more. Canadian officials also pushed hard to obtain what they regarded as an adequate schedule of US reductions of phosphate inputs and to overcome apparent State Department reluctance to establishing the IJC office. At the final full negotiating session in mid-March the Canadians accepted the latest American proposals on phosphate reductions, even though these fell short of the 1970 IJC recommendations. The US side then agreed to a provision which authorized, but did not require, the IJC to establish a Great Lakes regional office.

After six years of studies and two years of intensive discussions and negotiations, the Great Lakes Water Quality Agreement was ceremoniously signed into effect on 15 April 1972 by Prime Minister Trudeau and President Nixon during the latter's visit to Ottawa.[8]

The structure of the Agreement was essentially as originally proposed by Canada two years earlier: a set of common general water quality objectives, specific regulatory standards for a variety of pollutants, mutual commitments to implement national programs to achieve these objectives, and procedures for monitoring subsequent progress.[9] It is important to note that while the Agreement specified *common* objectives and water quality standards, and the monitoring of progress was to be *joint*, the pollution control programs were not joint programs but national ones. The programs were to be *complementary* but developed and implemented separately in the various jurisdictions. The Agreement gave the International Joint Commission[10] new responsibilities for the collection and analysis of information on water quality objectives and the pollution control programs on both sides of the Lakes, for the independent verification of data, and for the publication of reports assessing progress toward these objectives. In addition, it gave the IJC responsibility for providing 'assistance in the co-ordination of the joint activities'. The IJC was directed to establish a Water Quality Board, to assist the Commission on pollution control issues, and a Research (later termed, Science) Advisory Board, to advise specifically on scientific issues. The Commission was also empowered to establish a regional office.

While the structure of the accord was in line with Canadian thinking, the substance was less than what Canada had sought. The target date for the municipal sewage treatment works was the end of 1975. The plants did not have to be in operation by that date, however; the target would be met technically even if they were only under construction. The schedules stipulating reductions in overall Canadian and US phosphate loadings into Lakes Erie and Ontario by specific dates were less rigorous than the cuts recommended by the IJC.

For many environmentalists, the Agreement's provisions, if not too late, at least represented no real advance. The Agreement offered new promises but comprised no new initiatives; all of its measures were already to be found in existing pollution control programs. Some problems had proved too complex or too contentious, such as vessel wastes, pollution of the Upper Lakes (Superior, Michigan and Huron), and pollution from agricultural land use drainage (the so-called 'non-point' sources, as opposed to 'point' sources such as the effluent pipes emanating from sewage treatment plants). While identified in the Agreement, these problems were left for future study—and future control programs. Moreover, consistent with the municipal emphasis of the IJC reports, the agreement was rather vague on the whole area of industrial pollutants. It also made but passing reference to such problems as toxic substances and radioactivity in and around the Lakes. At the time, most of these omissions remained virtually unnoticed by the public. But they became dominant concerns of the scientists and governments well before the stipulated joint fifth-year review of the Agreement and its renegotiation began in 1977.

Implementation of the Agreement

The establishment of the Water Quality Board reflected the fact that the job of pollution control, let alone a 'clean-up', had barely begun; the establishment of the Research Advisory Board reflected the fact that scientific uncertainties remained about many other pollutants and much needed scientific knowledge was not yet at hand. These two boards were advisory and co-ordinating bodies only. The Great Lakes Water Quality Agreement did not effect any change in responsibilities for implementing pollution programs; these remained firmly in the hands of the respective governments: provincial, state, and federal. Inevitably, but perhaps necessarily, the political mission to save the Great Lakes had rather quickly become predominantly bureaucratic in character.

The process of developing and implementing policies for controlling pollution in the Great Lakes that evolved in the years following the first agreement was a complex, rather cumbersome one. Each of the two federal, eight state, and two provincial governments (Ontario and Quebec) pursued their respective policies to a greater or lesser extent in the context of the international agreement. The Water Quality and Science Advisory Boards met regularly and every year drew up a substantial report evaluating the progress achieved. These reports were then formally presented to the Commission at a public meeting (though in fact the practice became for the Board members and Commissioners to meet and discuss the reports beforehand). The Commissioners and their staff then prepared and debated an IJC report which was, in turn, eventually presented to the governments. Officials then prepared and politicians approved for each government a formal response to those points in the IJC report to which they chose to respond. The governments—federal, provincial, and state—then, sometimes, made improvements, or at least changes, in their pollution control programs.

Consistent with the 1972 Agreement, the focus was at first largely on the problem of excessive nutrients, especially phosphates, and on the municipal sources which accounted for most of these nutrients. The sewage treatment plant construction program in Ontario, helped along by the federal grants, proceeded smoothly. That on the US side did not. Indeed, Washington's commitment to the US effort, about which there had always been Canadian concerns, was almost immediately thrown into doubt. In November 1972 President Nixon impounded US federal funds already authorized for building municipal sewage treatment plants, including some key ones in the Great Lakes states. The justification was general budgetary constraints. For this and other reasons, the IJC's 1975 report on the Lakes concluded that progress so far had been 'generally slow, uneven and in certain cases, disappointing'.[11] Phosphorus loading reductions from US sources agreed to in 1972 were eventually met in the early 1980s.

As detection instrumentation improved over the 1970s and a better basis of scientific understanding of the dangers of toxins was established, more concern focused on the problem of toxic contaminants in the Lakes. This shift highlighted what was at least perceived to be a lack of will on the part of the Ontario minority Conservative government to pressure powerful industries during a period of economic slow-down. It also highlighted the weakness of Canadian legislation for controlling industrial pollution in comparison with the tough new 1972 US Water Pollution Control Act Amendments. This Act, passed after the Great Lakes Agreement had been negotiated, based pollution abatement on effluent standards, which specify the amount of contaminants allowed in the outflow from a city sewage system or a plant, rather than on general water quality standards, which specify the general conditions of a whole body of water.

By the time the governments came to renegotiate the 1972 Agreement in its fifth year, most of the attention of both scientists and regulators was on the extent and seriousness of industrial and toxic pollutants in the Lakes. As part of the process of reviewing and renegotiating the Agreement in 1977–78, officials on both sides drew up a list of hundreds of hazardous chemicals that were to be eliminated from the Lakes. American officials pressed their Canadian counterparts to adopt the effluent standard approach of the US legislation, but Queen's Park and Ottawa resisted, arguing that there was 'less need' for similar effluent standards in Canada because it contributed less total pollution. The adoption of such standards would also have been politically difficult, as the Americans well knew. It would have meant a significant tightening of industrial pollution requirements in Ontario, and, if these were enforced, the provincial government would have had to confront polluting industries to an uncharacteristic degree.[12] Ontario's Ministry of Environment over the next few years nevertheless slowly began to modify its regulatory structure to include effluent standards.

The renegotiating of the original agreement also introduced a potentially important shift in the framework within which these efforts were to be undertaken. The parties committed themselves to adopting an 'ecosystem approach' rather than trying to attack each pollutant or problem-area individually. The governments also made some changes to the operation of the IJC's Regional Office which had the effect of reducing its independence. The Canadian side of the IJC, particularly its chairman, Maxwell Cohen, protested, but with little success.

The negotiations themselves did not take long and were dominated by technical improvements. Once again, however, as in 1972, the White House's powerful fiscal overseer—the Office of Management and Budget (OMB)—needed much convincing that there were no financial commitments, explicit or implied, in the agreement beyond those already provided for by existing American domestic environment programs. OMB eventually gave its grudging approval. The Great Lakes Water Quality Agreement of 1978 came into effect in November of that year.[13]

While the basic structure of the 1972 document was maintained, the specific substantive changes were in some cases crucial. In its most important departure, the new Agreement called for the discharge of toxic chemicals to be largely eliminated and specified approximately 350 'hazardous polluting substances' to be banned from the Lakes. The two countries also agreed that municipal and industrial pollution abatement and control programs would be completed and in operation no later than the end of 1982 and 1983, respectively. The former deadline was in fact the date by which the much-delayed new sewage treatment facilities for the city of Detroit were expected finally to be on line. Also included was a new surveillance program and revised water quality objectives, including much tougher standards for radioactivity. The new agreement also set out a new, more stringent set of overall phosphorus-loading reductions for each of the Great Lakes, but left the actual division of loadings between the two countries—a highly contentious matter—to be negotiated later.

The revised agreement thus reflected the consensus of officials on both sides of the border that municipal pollution programs were at least under way, that industrial pollutants now represented the major problem requiring attention, and that the Agreement itself had to be expanded to cover a range of problems not previously foreseen or simply not covered in the 1972 version.

Through the 1980s the IJC reports tended to focus on what the Water

Quality Board had come to call 'areas of concern', particularly polluted and degraded areas of the Lakes where remedial action was most needed. One perennial area of concern, for example, is Hamilton Harbour. Another is the complex of chemical industry dumps near Niagara Falls, New York. The infamous Love Canal area, now completely evacuated, its homes bulldozed, and its toxic ground water being collected for disposal, is one of the smallest of these dump sites. The highly contaminated waters of the Niagara River — into which more than 3,000 pounds of pollutants are discharged daily, 90% of them from the US side — are appalling evidence of the scope and severity of the problem. The clean up of these dump sites has long been stalled by the high costs and uncertainties surrounding the optimal set of remedial actions, including who should pay for it. Under a new and separate accord concluded in early 1987, both federal governments, New York, and Ontario agreed to cut these emissions in half by 1996, thus recommitting themselves to commitments already implied under the 1978 Agreement.

In 1984 the Royal Society of Canada and the US National Academy of Sciences undertook a review of the on-going work under the Agreement.[14] The major conclusion of the report was 'that we have the commitment to a basin-wide ecosystem approach, but the approach has yet to be undertaken. There has been a giant step in concept and principle but the implementation is as yet in the exploratory stage.' In short, the ideas were fine but the execution was lagging. Governments seemed to agree.

As required by the terms of the Agreement, they announced their own review process in the spring of 1987, following receipt of the IJC third biennial report. This review was a remarkably open process, in contrast to both 1972 and 1978. (A draft version of proposed amendments to the Agreement was distributed to interested parties.[15]) It was also comparatively quick. The discussions between the two sides during the fall of 1987 were low-key and congenial. What revisions were made consisted largely of up-dating technical references and modifying the detailed annexes. The emphasis was less on the substance of programs than on their implementation. There were no major new initiatives, no significant new spending programs, and no substantial institutional reforms — such as a strengthening of the IJC's independence. Officials on both sides even refused, correctly so, to characterize the process as a 'renegotiation' of the Agreement. The modest amendments to the accord came into effect rather quietly in 1989.

CONTROLLING ACID RAIN

'Acid rain' was first brought publicly to the agenda of Canadian-American relations in June 1977 by then federal Environment Minister Romeo LeBlanc. It was, he warned, 'an environmental time bomb', indeed, 'the worst environmental problem [Canada has] ever had to face'. LeBlanc also suggested that '[we] do not have time to wait for final research before beginning political action' and indicated that bilateral negotiations were expected to commence within 'a few weeks'. These negotiations would 'draw up new rules which could allow one nation to tell the other to turn off the pollution at the source'.[16] The minister was overly optimistic. It would be not weeks but years before serious negotiations began. And it would be almost a decade and a half before any 'new rules' came into effect.

The popular term 'acid rain' has come to stand for a complex set of physical and chemical phenomena by which gases, especially sulphur and nitrogen oxides, are emitted as a result of combustion and other processes. While being transported through the atmosphere, the gases are transformed into acidic compounds and then are deposited by rain, snow, and dry particles on land and water surfaces.[17]

Although it was discovered — and the term 'acid rain' coined — in the 1800s, the phenomenon remained outside the realm of international politics until the 1970s. It was the work of a number of Scandinavian scientists, which served as the basis for a report on acid rain presented by Sweden to the 1972 UN Environment Conference, that provided two key pieces of the acid rain puzzle hitherto missing. One was direct evidence on the long-range atmospheric transport of the pollutant, which was made possible by improved meteorological data and computer models. The second key was direct evidence of acidity trends over time, which was made possible by the continuous operation from the 1950s of Scandinavian and Western European precipitation sampling networks.[18]

Stimulated by the Scandinavian work, and as part of a World Health Organization project, a small-scale Canadian federal government precipitation sampling program was initiated in 1973. Systematic monitoring networks were in operation in both Canada and the United States by 1978. Canadian and American government scientists working in this area began to meet and discuss their mutual efforts during the mid-1970s. Interest was broadened somewhat when IJC studies on pollution of the upper Great Lakes, initiated by the 1972 Water Quality Agreement, found a surprisingly high overall proportion of pollutants entered those lakes from the atmosphere.

It was early clear to Canadian officials that the problem was to a significant extent transboundary in nature. Acid rain, LeBlanc had noted in his speech, came from both the United States and Canada:

> Despite all co-operation that exists between Canada and the United States, I believe we have both been negligent in this area. What we have allowed to happen, innocently enough perhaps, is a massive international exchange of air pollutants, and neither party to this exchange is free of guilt.[19]

Newspaper reports of his speech noted that 'it was estimated' that US sources in fact contributed five times as much air pollution to Canada as

Canadian sources did to the US.[20] This situation with respect to the relative contribution of sources was, of course, analogous to that of water pollution in the Great Lakes. The parallel goes further. In fact, the Great Lakes Water Quality accord has been used by both governments as an explicit model, both in terms of process and of substance, for the ongoing effort to fashion the first ever bilateral air quality accord.

The Carter Administration and Acid Rain

In the months following Leblanc's proposal of bilateral talks little progress occurred on the diplomatic front. Some friendly, informal meetings were held, but the Americans were not ready to negotiate. Indeed, some were not convinced there was anything to negotiate about. While the Canadian side continued to envision an air quality treaty, the US aim was 'to get a picture of the present state of air pollution across the border'.[21] The two governments did agree to establish a joint scientific committee to review the problem which came to be called the Bilateral Research Consultation Group (BRCG).[22] Some pressure for diplomatic-level talks was created in the fall of 1978 when the US Congress passed a resolution requiring the State Department to enter into negotiations with Canada toward an air quality agreement. The key figures behind this unexpected move were a small group of border state Congressmen whose constituents were concerned, not about acid rain, but about possible air pollution from sources in Canada. In particular, the concern was focused on two coal-fired power plants being planned for sites just across the international boundary in southern Saskatchewan (Poplar River project) and north-western Ontario (Atikokan project). Two meetings were subsequently held, but they did not progress beyond the exploratory discussion stage. The initiative soon died in quiet diplomatic fashion.

The report of the BRCG, released in October, 1979, represented a comprehensive and objective compilation of existing scientific informa-tion on the origins, transport, and deleterious effects of acid precipita-tion.[23] It identified thermal generating plants in the US and non-ferrous smelters in Canada as the main sources of emissions.[24] Its emphasis was on the 'irreversible' damage being caused to lakes, rivers, and fish. It also confirmed what Canadian officials had been saying about the two countries' relative contributions; American emissions of sulphur dioxide were estimated to be five times greater than the Canadian ones, and American emissions of nitrous oxides ten times greater. While both coun-tries polluted their own and the other's territory, the US produced overall about 70-80 per cent of transboundary air pollution. The scientists, being scientists, stressed the preliminary nature of their conclusions and the need for the whole problem of acid rain to be studied more thoroughly.[25] Ottawa and Washington requested a further report.

On 13 November 1979, Canada and the US joined thirty-two European countries in signing an agreement calling for the reduction of air pollution, and especially the reduction of transboundary, long-range transport of acid pollutants. This resolution represented a modest result of long-standing but largely unsuccessful pressure by the Scandinavian countries on their neighbours. It also reflected the political resistance put up by the major polluting states, for it did not actually commit its signatories to undertake specific reductions.

The immediate problem for Canada was to put acid rain on the American agenda, and this agenda had some conflicting priorities. In the midst of the preliminary discussions about transboundary acid rain, the Carter Administration announced that it would propose to Congress a $10 billion program to convert oil-fired power plants to coal.[26] As a response to the oil crisis of the 1970s and in the interest of reducing dependence on foreign oil, there would have to be a significant increase in acid rain.[27] As one Environmental Protection Agency official admitted, 'The DoE won at the White House. EPA lost.'[28] To say the least, the news was not welcomed in Ottawa.

The Carter coal conversion plan, however, was not the basic problem. Nor was it the novelty of acid rain. The key problem was that the United States lacked the necessary legislative basis to deal with their acid rain problem. While the 1972 and 1977 Clean Air Acts led to significant improvements in urban air quality and a reduction in smog, there were no provisions specifically designed to combat the problem of long-range transport of air pollutants. In order to obtain reductions in these acid-forming pollutants, significant amendments had to be made to the 1977 version of the Clean Air Act. It was here that EPA, the scientists, and Canadian officials were up against powerful political opposition to stronger air pollution controls in the US.

The core opponents to new controls on the emission of acid pollutants were industrial interests, including coal-mining companies and utilities,[29] and a number of large coal-producer and large coal-user states, most of them in the American mid-west. This area, particularly the Ohio River Valley, is responsible for the bulk of US sulphur dioxide emissions because of a large number of old, unregulated power plants burning locally produced, high-sulphur coal. The economic interests of these 'coal states' alone dictate opposition to sulphur dioxide emission controls, and, because their bedrock and soils are well buffered against acidification, they suffer little from acid rain. In contrast, the major US recipients, especially New York and the New England states, have low bicarbonate soils with little or no buffering capability. (Much of Ontario, Quebec, and the Atlantic provinces is in the same predicament.) The political problem for American federal authorities *vis-à-vis* domestic polluters, therefore, as well as the political problem for Canada *vis-à-vis* the US, is thus compounded because the major source areas are not the major recipient areas, and the former therefore stand to benefit little from costly reductions in their own emissions. The position of Ohio's Governor Rhodes was typical of the regional divisions in the United States. Said Rhodes, 'You're talking about some fish in the northeast, while in Ohio we've got 22,000 unemployed coal miners.'

Toward the end of the Carter Administration the congressional climate worsened. As long-time advocate Senator Edmund Muskie observed in 1980, the 'momentum behind [US] environmental laws . . . is fast running out of steam, I guess'.[30] A Congressional aide agreed. 'Don't expect any Congressional initiatives against acid rain in the near future', he said. 'It's a good time to circle the wagons and protect what environmental legislation we have.'[31]

Canadian Environment Minister John Roberts became increasingly active in making the Canadian case about acid rain to American audiences. In a hard-hitting speech to the Air Pollution Control Association, he noted, 'Some Canadians have spoken darkly about "environmental aggression".' Although the phrase was not his, he could see no reason why

> Canada's ecosystems . . . Canada's people, tourist camp operators, fishing guides, commercial fishermen, loggers, other forest product workers, building owners and tenants and possibly our asthmatics or others with respiratory illnesses . . . should have to pay the price of keeping the electricity rates of those coal-producing middle-western states well below those now being paid along the United States eastern seaboard.[32]

If the Carter Administration was unable to deliver what Canada was asking for, it was at least willing to offer a diplomatic IOU. After more informal talks, it signed with the Trudeau government in August, 1980, a joint Memorandum of Intent committing the two countries to negotiate an acid rain agreement. It not only detailed a technical working group structure and specified procedures and a schedule but outlined the major features of the prospective agreement and committed both governments, albeit only rhetorically, to pursue vigorous enforcement actions under existing statutes. But even as the document was being signed, in the midst of the 1980 presidential election campaign, the US commitment was being put in doubt. 'This all goes to hell,' a senior American official noted quietly, 'if Ronald Reagan gets in.'[33] He did. And it did.

After Carter's defeat at the polls, the lame-duck Democratic Administration attempted to bind the incoming Republican President to reducing acid rain emissions through the use of a little-known section of the Clean Air Act. Section 115 of the 1977 Act authorized the EPA Administrator to order cuts in pollution emissions causing damage in another country, provided reciprocal treatment was offered by the other country. The ensuing years saw an extensive court battle which arrested the section

115 process. Avoiding the merits of the case, the new Administration successfully argued that former Secretary of State Muskie's finding—that US pollution was adversely affecting Canada—was arrived at without following the necessary rule-making procedures.[34] The fight against acid rain was not to be won in American courts.

The Reagan Administration and Acid Rain

The impact of the Reagan White House on relations with its northern neighbour was soon felt. Its list of Canada-US 'irritants', beginning with the Foreign Investment Review Agency and the National Energy Program, was as long as if not longer than that of the Nixon Administration in 1971. Many of the outstanding issues reflect the different and diverging perspectives, philosophical and political, of Reagan's Washington and Trudeau's Ottawa. To be sure, the changes wrought were not solely the work of what Charlie Farquharson once referred to as the then 'encumbrance' in the White House. They were largely the work of the officials put in charge of US environmental policy—a crop of pro-industry figures, aggressive in their pursuit of deregulation and government withdrawal from pollution control and research. Beyond a change in personalities and ideologies, the pressures of slow economic growth and high inflation, which were partly responsible for the conservative shift apparent in the 1980 American elections, contributed to the pressure to reduce environmental regulations.

The Reagan Administration, the president of the National Audubon Society, one of the leading US conservation organizations, soon observed, was 'deliberately undercutting the nation's environmental laws and programs'. Such concerns were by no means restricted to environmental groups. The *Chicago Tribune*, for example, while supporting editorially the president's defence and economic policies, bluntly stated that 'as far as the environment is concerned, Mr Reagan is a menace'. Congressional sources agreed: 'The administration's real position', said an aide to a Republican senator, 'is to do nothing about acid rain.'

So nothing got done. A few Canada-US negotiation sessions were subsequently held but there was no progress. The Reagan Administration, espousing its anti-regulatory philosophy, showed little interest in pursuing the goal of the Memorandum of Intent, and showed even less in considering new pollution controls. The administration's refrain on acid rain became 'more research has to be done'. And in case the research looked a mite too definitive, as it did in the draft second report of the BRCG, senior Reagan political appointees set about re-writing the scientists' conclusions in order to tone them down.[35]

Scientific arguments, evidently, were not going to be enough to sway the Reaganites. Canada's political tactics had already begun to change somewhat, and the process was accelerated by the stalemate in the official diplomatic negotiations. One direction was towards what might be called 'public diplomacy'. Officials in Ottawa and at the Canadian Embassy on Washington's Massachusetts Avenue began to carry their arguments more often and more directly to the US Congress and to the American public. The style was in distinct contrast to the old sacred cows of Canadian-American 'quiet diplomacy'. It was not received well by all who observed the new tactics. It was particularly resented by those against whom it was employed effectively.[36]

A second front in the acid rain war was opened within Canada. Federal environment officials succeeded in slowly patching together an agreement with the seven eastern provinces to reduce Canadian emissions of SO_2 by half. This agreement could not solve Canada's acid rain problem unilaterally, but was designed to ensure provincial action to fulfil Canadian commitments under an eventual Canada-US acid rain accord. (It was thus the equivalent of the 1971 Canada-Ontario agreement reached prior to the final negotiations on the Great Lakes Water Quality Agreement.) The Canadian government had long set as its objective achieving reductions of 50% in US and Canadian emissions in order to control acid rain. The last government to sign on to the federal-provincial agreement — that of coal-producing and coal-burning Nova Scotia — finally did so in late 1987.

The third front was multilateral. Ottawa organized a major meeting in early 1984 of what became known as the '30% club' — a group of western developed states committed to reducing SO_2 emissions within their own territories by at least 30%. The club, needless to say, did not include the United States, although the embarrassed Americans insisted they be invited to the meeting as observers. The meeting was described later by Fitzhugh Green, then one of Reagan's appointees at EPA, as 'a hanging in effigy of the American policy'.[37]

The election victory of the Conservatives under Brian Mulroney in September 1984 led, along with the dismantling of the Foreign Investment Review Agency and the National Energy Policy, to a decline in the Canadian bilateral 'public diplomacy' approach on acid rain. All were out of keeping with new political realities as well as with Prime Minister Brian Mulroney's rhetoric of a new co-operative era in Canadian-American relations. The Mulroney government pursued a much softer line than even the 1979 Conservative government, whose Environment Minister, John Fraser, had worked enthusiastically at raising the public profile of acid rain in the US.

The co-operative rhetoric of this new era was enshrined in the Shamrock Summit of 1985. Although the prime minister had dutifully identified acid rain as a top Canadian concern, it was not that for the United States, and certainly not a concern at all for Ronald Reagan. Destined to make no breakthroughs on this issue, the leader's salvage teams came up with what appeared to many observers as a mere face-saving action—the appointment of two 'special envoys' to investigate the problem for a year.

The envoys, Bill Davis, former premier of Ontario, and Drew Lewis, former transportation secretary in Ronald Reagan's cabinet, reported back as bidden to the following year's summit in Washington. They concluded that acid rain was indeed a problem, not a myth, but did not recommend immediate emission reductions. Instead they proposed a major and long-term $5 billion investment by industry and government into research, development, and demonstration of so-called 'clean coal' technologies. Both the president and prime minister accepted the report.

'Clean coal', however, was more promise than prospect. First, the Reagan Administration was slow to put its share of the promised money into its development. Despite summit promises, it was only after forceful Canadian representations during a visit by Vice-President George Bush to Ottawa the year later that the White House finally sought funding for the 'clean coal' technology demonstration program recommended by the envoys. It soon became clear, however, that decades would pass before such technologies could be adopted and begin to reduce emissions from the major sources of acid rain.[38] At the third annual Reagan-Mulroney summit of April 1987 the President added only a meaningless pledge that he 'agreed to *consider* the Prime Minister's proposal for a bilateral accord on acid rain' (italics added). As evidence of the potential of face-to-face meetings to solve bilateral problems, and the potency of the personal rapport between the two men, this pledge was not much.

It was not even enough to get the formal talks going again in any productive fashion. The next month a team of Canadian officials arrived in Washington for a one-day meeting with American counterparts—the first such formal meeting during the tenure of the Mulroney government. There, and again at two follow-up meetings in the next months, it became evident that the fundamental opposition of the Administration to any sort of new legislated emission reductions remained unshaken. 'Canada', one American official observed, 'got snookered again.'[39]

The duplicity of the Reagan Administration over acid rain may have reached its height in the series of events surrounding the release of the long-awaited National Acid Precipitation Assessment Program (NAPAP) interim report of 1987, comprising over 800 pages, ten substantive chapters, and four volumes. The first of these volumes was an Executive Summary largely written by the White House-appointed NAPAP director, Dr J. Lawrence Kulp, a former energy industry scientist. The report was accompanied by an Administration-prepared press release. In general, the Summary and the press release left the impression that the damage due to acidic deposition is largely unproven, slight and not widespread where proven, and probably not getting worse. Release of the Interim Assessment was greeted with what one industry journal termed 'a crescendo of criticism'.[40] Canadian Environment Minister Tom McMillan reacted quickly, calling a press conference the day after the NAPAP assessment was released, and branded it 'voodoo science'.

The Bush Breakthrough

The American presidential election of November 1988 was remarkable in a number of respects, but certainly for the extent to which the heir of the Reagan legacy, George Bush, sought to outflank his Democratic opponent, Michael Dukakis, in attacking pollution. A bold initiative this was not; it was clear to all that in late 1988 the country's mounting environmental ills were firmly and squarely back on the political agenda. The victorious Bush then symbolically broke with eight years of Reaganism in appointing a well-known environmentalist as Administrator of the EPA, and by committing his administration to formulating a new Clean Air Act, including, most importantly for Canada, provisions to reduce the sulphur and nitrogen oxide emissions that produce acid rain. The new Administration's proposals were forwarded to Congress in the fall of 1989.

Another key political development, this within Congress, was the replacement of Senate majority leader Senator Robert Byrd of coal-dependent West Virginia, an arch-opponent of acid rain controls, by George Mitchell of Maine, a long and strong proponent of such controls. After a careful weighing of the balance of forces, Mitchell and his supporters made a pact with the White House on a set of amendments to the Act with which both sides could live, and proceeded through the early months of 1990 to gain Senate approval for them. Included in the set were requirements for reductions in acid rain of approximately 50% from 1980 levels — a figure which had become accepted by most of the players on all sides of this issue. In May the House of Representatives passed a similar bill. The US Administration now had, at last, the necessary statutory basis for dealing with the acid rain problem and thus for proceeding to negotiate the kind of international agreement which Canada had long sought.

A new round of bilateral negotiations began even before the Congress had completed its work. Formal negotiations proceeded through the fall and winter months. They were concluded in 1991. The new Canada-US Air Quality Agreement included provisions confirming the commitment to emission reductions by both sides, as well as an agreement to establish a research and monitoring network similar to that established by the Great Lakes Water Quality Agreement. It is much too early to assess the implementation of this recent accord. If the history of the Great Lakes Agreement is any guide, and if the history of the 1990 US Clean Air Act is anything like that of its predecessors, implementation will not follow automatically or easily.

CONCLUSION

Canadian-American relations in general have often been characterized by the high degree of 'interdependence' between the two countries. In related fashion, the extent of bilateral co-operation has been explained by reference to common interests, to shared technical information, and to a mutual problem-solving approach. To a certain extent, the content of the 1972/1978 Great Lakes Agreement and of the 1991 Air Quality Agreement reflect these factors at work. And, to a certain extent, the co-operative aspects of the implementation of these agreements also reflects them. Environmental issues, which are often described as 'common property' problems, would seem to fit well then into such a pattern. They do so, however, only on the surface.

What these perspectives cannot adequately explain are the continuing conflicts over environmental issues. An understanding of why these issues arise in the first place and then prove so difficult to deal with lies in the set of factors that we term 'environmental dependence'. The now abundant literature on dependence and *dependencia* emphasizes the extent to which a country's economy is tied to foreign purchasers of goods and suppliers of capital.[41] The crucial factor, though, is neither mere linkage nor even the concentration on a particular purchaser or supplier, but rather the extent of alternative opportunities and the costs of shifting to such new arrangements. Through most of its history, Canada has been dependent economically on a major power, first Britain and then the United States, for its markets and capital. In a similar way, Canada has become increasingly dependent on the United States with respect to the quality of its environment.

Most of the pollutants dumped into the Great Lakes originate on the US side. Most of the sulphur and nitrogen oxides that lead to acid rain originate in the United States. Not all of them, to be sure. But enough that in both cases unilateral Canadian action to deal with the problem would be ineffective. Even drastic controls on the sources of acidic pollution in Canada, for example, would not sufficiently protect the Canadian environment. The only feasible option, therefore, is for Canada to seek American co-operation in mounting programs to reduce emissions. And therefore, on issues such as acid rain and water pollution in the Great Lakes, Canada pursues international agreements as a way of securing an American commitment to deal with the sources of what are necessarily common problems.

The other side of this relationship has its logic too. Given the large US population and industrial base, the sheer amounts of both air and water pollutants in the United States are enormous. Thus in both cases the costs of any potential clean-up on the US side are considerable. Secondly, at least some, and perhaps much, of the benefit of reduced US emissions accrues not to the American environment but to the Canadian. Thus, for both reasons – high costs and limited benefits – there is almost inevitably strong opposition to action within the US political system. Moreover, the extent of transboundary pollution from Canada into the United States is generally so small, comparatively, that there is little potential benefit to be derived from any reductions undertaken on the Canadian side. For the US, therefore, bilateral agreements are less attractive and the Administration is relatively slower to act on many transboundary pollution issues. But they are not always so.

Ironically, the Reagan Administration moved extremely quickly in late 1986 and early 1987 to conclude an international air quality agreement with Mexico. Why the contrast? The fundamental difference between the Canada-US and Mexico-US cases is that in the latter it is the United States who is the major recipient of transboundary pollution. The major air pollution problem along the Mexican-American border is a new, very large, Mexican smelter: it is thus a problem of air pollution *flowing into* the United States. And it is thus a problem on which the Reagan Administration found little research was needed and on which action was taken immediately.[42]

When the Great Lakes Water Quality Agreement was first being negotiated, the Canadian side was trying to extract greater American commitments on the nutrient problem; it was the *demander*, with little to offer in return, and in the end had to settle for whatever the Americans were willing to do. The dynamics of the negotiation of an air quality accord were essentially the same. The main difference is that an informed and aroused Canadian public made it clear to government that a weak compromise on acid rain with the United States would not be tolerated. Canada held out for a promise of the reductions it had long sought.

What did and did not happen in Canadian-American environmental relations in recent years, then, as well as in domestic environmental policy formation with respect to water pollution and acid rain, can be substantially explained by the politics of environmental dependence. Without a massive and sustained clean-up program in the United States, this fundamental structural reality of transboundary pollution will remain. One implication of this fact is that both the timing and content of Canadian domestic and bilateral environmental policies – not to mention the results obtained – depend at least as much on American domestic politics as on events in Canada itself.

FOR FURTHER READING

John E. Carroll, *Acid Rain: An Issue in Canadian-American Relations* (Washington, DC: Canadian-American Co., 1982).

Fitzhugh Green, 'Public Diplomacy and Acid Rain', *Toledo Law Review* (17), Fall 1985.

Don Munton, 'Great Lakes Water Quality: A Study in Environmental Politics and Diplomacy', in O.P. Dwivedi, ed., *Resources and the Environment: Policy Perspectives for Canada* (Toronto: McClelland and Stewart, 1980).

Jurgen Schmandt, *Acid Rain and Friendly Neighbors: The Policy Dispute between Canada and the United States* (Duke University Press, 1988).

Neil Swainson, 'Developing the Columbia', in Don Munton and John Kirton, eds, *Cases in Canadian Foreign Policy* (Toronto: Prentice Hall, 1991).

Ernest J. Yanarella and Randal H. Ihara, *The Acid Rain Debate: Scientific, Economic and Political Dimensions* (Boulder: Westview, 1985).

CHAPTER 12

The Multilateral Dimension

Canada in the International System

ROBERT BOARDMAN

Canada has been a consistently active participant in multilateral developments in environmental issues.[1] If we add to the federal government's
role – of representing Canada in intergovernmental forums and collabo-
rating with other states in international technical programs – the transnational activities and concerns of Canadian environmental groups, as
well as the role of provincial governments in deliberations on external
policies and on their implications for programs under their jurisdiction,
it is evident that the multilateral dimension is an intrinsic, substantial,
and growing feature of environmental policy in Canada. Just as the issue
of acid rain vividly underscored the facts of ecological as well as economic
interdependence in Canadian-American relations, so those issues characteristic of the early 1990s – protection of the ozone layer, and the complex
policy questions arising from the hypothesis of climate change – increasingly situated Canadian approaches to environmental policy within global
frameworks.

Their recurrent air of novelty notwithstanding, international environmental issues have in fact enjoyed a lengthy history on Canadian agendas.
The UN Conference on the Human Environment (UNCHE), held in
Stockholm in 1972, began the process. Its impact had been foreshadowed
in Canadian debates of the international implications of pollution problems, particularly in the context of Great Lakes water quality. And though
the term 'environmental' was not then part of the vocabulary, the Canada-
US migratory bird protection arrangements instituted from 1917 were a
still earlier forerunner. Yet attention to environment questions generally,
and within these to their international aspects more particularly, has been
marked by a succession of high and low points. In two respects, the late
1980s and early 1990s saw a significant resurgence of interest on the part
of governments and attentive publics.

First, the multilateral aspect of environmental policy became a much
more prominent theme of discussions in Canada. The same was true of

most western countries. As *The Economist* put it in 1991: 'More and more, the environment harm that ministers discuss is global or regional, not national. Acid rain and marine pollution hurt neighbouring countries; ozone depletion and global warming threaten the entire planet.'[2] Secondly, the growing preoccupation of Canadian and other governments of the Organization for Economic Co-operation and Development (OECD) countries with environment-economy linkages gave environmental issues a new political legitimacy. Ironically, it also fed disenchantment on the part of some environmental groups unaccustomed to see traditional economic policy goals being used as the rationale for environmental action. The process has transformed what Jim MacNeill has called the 'standard agenda' of environmental issues (focused on environmental pollution, natural resources, and urban settlements) into alternative agendas of sustainable development. This concept embraces all of these, he suggests, but also 'integrates them with the issues of growth, development, employment, energy, trade, peace, and security'.[3]

Viewed through these kinds of lenses, environmental issues are, almost by definition, primarily international in character. Canada's efforts are to be seen in the larger context of what other nations, and the international community collectively, are doing about the planet's ecological ailments. Such an approach, however, also risks pushing environmental thinking, redefined as the holistic basis for a 'policy on everything', into the hinterlands populated by escapists and doomsayers. That this has not happened is significant. The present chapter examines the reasons for the prominence of international questions in Canadian approaches to environmental policy.

THE DOMESTIC–INTERNATIONAL NEXUS

While they cannot be ignored, it is easy to exaggerate the importance of international developments. If left entirely to its own devices, without external constituencies to fret about or multilateral forums to cultivate, would Canada have an environmental policy regime significantly different from the one it has? Probably not. Without Canadian input, could the international community devise workable and effective schemes for handling global environmental problems? In most instances, yes. Would the same be true if formal intergovernmental organizations such as the United Nations ceased to exist? Probably. These questions, however, reflect a naïvely cynical rather than a realistic frame of mind. In practice, several sets of connections link the domestic and the international levels of Canadian environmental policy.

First, the international setting defines a variety of obligations. Given the anarchic character of the state system, however, and the voluntarist principles underlying international law and organization, these are obligations only if Canada chooses to regard them as such. International environmental rules are in the last resort enforced only by the states that wish to see them enforced within their respective jurisdictions. States need not sign, or if they do so need not ratify, international conventions. Even assuming completion of these steps, the political will to comply may dissipate. The national enforcement of international rules is in itself a complex political process, separate from that of engaging in the multilateral negotiations that produce and define them. It is also a process that requires possession of adequate regulatory capabilities. For many countries, implementation through domestic law and administration may accordingly never occur.[4]

There are, however, substantial pressures on states, including practical considerations of national self-interest, to observe the rules (and the results) of the game. Such rules include at the minimum participating in multilateral forums, taking seriously the tasks of negotiating new international instruments, and accepting the broad consensus-forming procedures of international meetings. Substantive policy concerns on many environmental issues, combined with a larger foreign policy commitment to the continued viability of intergovernmental organizations, have made Canada a leader in the task of constructing a new global environmental order.

Secondly, the international level is a germination area for environmental policy ideas. Only a small minority of the proposals aired at international meetings ever find their way into international law or the programs of governments. But some set the themes of national environmental debates. The first version of the *World Conservation Strategy* (1980), for example, and still more so the report of the World Commission on Environment and Development (the Brundtland Commission) of 1987, each figured prominently in Canadian debates on environmental policy. Enterprising advocates of policy change, both within government and in environmental groups outside, have exploited such instruments as devices for pressing governments into action. Government officials also draw comparative lessons about policy formation in specific areas from multilateral encounters. For Ottawa, the meetings of the OECD environment committee have been particularly important in this regard. Critics can find in cross-national comparisons ammunition for the politics of shaming. Canadians waste more paper, and recycle less, groups have pointed out, than do the citizens of similar countries.[5]

Thirdly, the international and domestic levels are connected insofar as each is a means to solving the problems of the other. Each is also a communal source of such problems. Pollution in the north in the form of Arctic haze particles may have its origins in oil and coal combustion, and from smelters, in Europe and the Soviet Union.[6] As the Science Council expressed its view of these kinds of links in 1988:

> The ecological crisis is global in origin and extent. Not only do ecological processes operate at a global level, but all nations contribute to ecological deterioration and all nations are affected by it. Unfortunately, no international mechanisms exist for applying effective global solutions. But ... global ecological deterioration can be slowed down if each country, to the extent that it is capable on its own, puts its house in order ....[7]

International engagement thus helps promote domestic policy goals. Given the tortuous and apparently intractable character of many environmental problems, it may even be an indispensable route. Domestic programs are likewise a base for the effective pursuit of external objectives. Operating effectively outside national boundaries requires a solid and visible base of domestic activity. That this is crucial to external credibility, and hence influence in multilateral forums, was a point increasingly stressed by the federal government's environmental critics in the context of global climate change issues in the late 1980s and early 1990s.[8]

It is, though, only one factor. Delegations at international conferences are often content in practice to shelter behind the principle of the sovereign equality of nations and to overlook flaws, ambiguities, and inconsistencies in the policies of others. Turning a blind eye may avert unwelcome scrutiny of one's own faults. International conferences are also widely perceived by their supporters as tools that may eventually edge hesitant governments towards unavoidable domestic policy commitments; appreciation of this risk reinforces the natural caution of states in their approaches to such gatherings.

There are other reasons for questioning the robustness of the link between the international and the domestic levels of policy-making. Some international environmental activities undertaken by Ottawa are driven in part by extraneous considerations. Support for international organizations, particularly those associated with the UN system (and particularly those with an appropriately progressive flavour), and the concomitant pursuit of middle-power prestige and standing through such means, are long-standing features of Canadian foreign policy. The raw facts of Canada's support for many environmental initiatives (though not necessarily the vigour of this support and the nuances of its expression) could thus be adequately explained solely by reference to general foreign policy principles. International environmental policy is both an end in itself and a means towards other ends.

It could also be argued that, assuming others take action, the benefits of more effective international regulation of emissions accelerating global climate change or ozone layer depletion can in theory be gained by any state, regardless of whether its government contributed to that end. If so, participation in international organizations tackling these problems is redundant (or of value only if it serves other purposes). The classical economist's formulation of the free-rider problem, however, ignores the multiple political pressures that in practice bear on government decisions. Watching the movie without paying for admission is virtually impossible under prevailing conditions of complex interdependent governance in the western world. And the makers of Canada's environmental policies have in any case never been attracted to the lazy option.

International environmental questions are nonetheless vulnerable to a double marginalization. As environmental issues, they risk being out of touch with shifting Canadian political climates that frequently place a higher value on more traditional ideas about the management of economies; as international issues, they may fail to grip the imagination of those whose attentiveness stretches only to provincial, regional, or national borders.

By emphasizing both the international and the economic, the concept of sustainable development can be viewed as a dual attack on this problem and as a means of consolidating the shift of environmental questions from the periphery to the core of political agendas. This process of redefinition has characterized debates over 'environmental' policy from the outset. An emphasis in the 1960s on urban pollution questions (and an earlier history of concerns about wildlife, natural habitats, and national parks), gave way two decades later to preoccupations with environment-economy and global-domestic linkages. Concepts of national and international security were also increasingly redefined during the 1980s to encompass environmental aspects. Environmental security became a growing concern of Canadians in the late 1980s; as many as 85% of those polled in a 1990 survey saw the United States for this reason as a serious threat to Canada.[9] The overlapping domestic constituencies of environmental groups reinforce different sets of linkages, for example with international development, gender questions, minority rights, and aboriginal land ownership issues.

Despite all this, environmental problems, especially the longer-term ones with chronic rather than acute effects, remain notoriously easy to marginalize. The assessment of environmental risk is as much a political as a scientific exercise. As Braybrooke and Paquet have observed, 'risk is a cultural concept'.[10] In the case of environmental issues with international ramifications, solutions are clearly so dependent on the good will and capabilities of other countries that investment in multilateral problem-solving can lose much of its political glamour. Canada has nonetheless been a leading nation in this field. We will review the record, and then try to assess its significance in the overall context of Canadian environmental policy.

THE COURSE OF CANADA'S INTERNATIONAL ENVIRONMENTAL POLICIES

Institutional Multilateralism

The global and regional institutions that have some kind of environmental mandate are many and diverse, in part because of an inherent competitiveness among intergovernmental (and nongovernmental) actors, and in part because of the scope for unilateral ventures that the multiple and proliferating issues in this area give them. The functions they perform are also varied.[11] The Canadian presence reaches deep into this network.

Some of these bodies have arisen out of special-purpose conferences (as did the UN Environment Program [UNEP] as a result of UNCHE). Many, like the OECD's Environment Committee, are institutional adaptations to changing agendas. Still others service particular needs, for example the international secretariat administering the Convention on International Trade in Endangered Species (CITES). Many have changed character over the course of time. The International Union for the Conservation of Nature (IUCN), for example, became steadily more intergovernmental as its complement of state and government agency members grew.

The process of adding environmental tasks to organizational mandates has had widespread effects. Following Canadian initiatives, the North Atlantic Treaty Organization (NATO), through its Science Committee, took an early interest in ecology in the 1960s, and expanded the scope of its concerns during the following decade. The UN Economic Commission for Europe (ECE), having become an 'almost empty shell'[12] as a result of the late 1940s' cold-war division of Europe, later took environmental matters on board and became an enthusiastic gatherer of national data and a promoter of international conferences and conventions. The environmental policies of the World Bank, first developed in 1970, have been criticized by Canadian groups as ineffective and reactive; yet the sheer magnitude of the Bank's presence in development projects in the South in effect makes it one of the most significant international actors on environmental issues.[13] Sections dealing with the environment were included in the Helsinki (1975) and Madrid (1983) conferences of the Conference on Security and Co-operation in Europe (CSCE) process. Revamped in the language of sustainable development, the question has also been dealt with by the Western Economic Summits. The concept was endorsed by the Group of Seven in 1988; the following year, Canada promoted the idea of an environmental index as a common measure to judge environmental performance. Similarly the Langkawi Declaration, signed during the Kuala Lumpur Commonwealth Heads of Government Meeting in 1989, focused attention on global environmental problems and attempted to reconcile these with the economic development needs of developing countries.

These institutions hold varying degrees of significance for Canada. It is a member of all those mentioned, as well as of other UN bodies with environmental interests such as the World Health Organization (WHO), the World Meteorological Organization (WMO), the Food and Agriculture Organization (FAO), and the Educational, Scientific, and Cultural Organization (UNESCO). Even obscure non-governmental organizations provide opportunities for demonstrating environmental leadership, as in Canada's 1986 hosting of the International Ornithological Congress. The juggling of expected returns against the investment of resources, however, has led to a fairly consistent policy focus on two since the early 1970s: the environmental work of the OECD, the twenty-four-member organization based in Paris which brings together the western industrialized nations; and UNEP, more globally oriented and, from the late 1970s, increasingly tuned to the problems of blending economic development in the South with promotion of a healthy natural environment.

Founded in 1970 in the context of a flurry of intergovernmental activity on environmental questions, the OECD's environment committee has been more a forum for the exchange of ideas and for comparative note-taking than a policy-making organization. Its original terms of reference reflect the OECD's primary concern with broader questions of economic policy. They include 'investigating the problems of preserving or improving man's environment, with particular reference to their economic and trade implications', and 'proposing solutions for environmental problems that would as far as possible take account of all relevant factors including cost effectiveness'.[14] Early technical work on air and water pollution — and endorsement of the 'polluter pays' principle — has been followed by examination of a variety of questions, for example on chemicals (largely as a result of the OECD goal of reducing trade barriers between member-nations) and wide-ranging discussions of global environmental questions, including the impact of western policies and multinational corporation activity on developing countries. Canada's growing interest in this work both encouraged and reflected the OECD's sharper focus during the early 1980s on linkages between environmental and economic questions. These assessments influenced in turn the orientation of the Brundtland Commission, and as a result played a crucial role in focusing Canadian attention on these questions in the late 1980s.

Many environmental groups, by contrast, tended to be critical of prescriptions which appeared to legitimize traditional philosophies of economic management, and to be more sympathetic to the aspirations of UNEP as a more globally representative forum. Canada has been a consistent supporter of UNEP from the outset. The organization is the only intergovernmental body dealing with environmental problems at a global level. Its Governing Council comprises states representative of the mix of wealth, ideologies, and ecological circumstances found in the real world. The founding conference at Stockholm in 1972, moreover, articulated a number of the basic principles of international environmental co-operation that Canada has since promoted and internalized. One of these—the principle that, while states had the sovereign right to develop their own resources, no country should undertake action within its borders causing environmental damage to another country—had obvious implications for relations with the US, and was described in 1988 by a senior official of Environment Canada as 'the basis for all our international environmental policies'.[15]

There have also been strains in the relationship. Like other parts of the UN system, UNEP came under fire from Canada, as it did from other western countries, in the 1980s for a variety of alleged failings. These ranged from lack of budgetary stringency to ineffectual management and program co-ordination. Yet UNEP's accumulated background of experience on global problems also made the organization a primary focus of Canada's initiatives in this area, for example in the Montreal ozone-layer conference of 1987, the Toronto global-warming conference of 1988, and the subsequent work of the Intergovernmental Panel on Climate Change (IPCC), a forum sponsored by UNEP and the WMO. Canada has also been a long-standing defender of UNEP's technical and data collection programs.[16]

The Development of International Environmental Law

One function of intergovernmental bodies has traditionally been to lay the foundations for the expansion and strengthening of international law, particularly by way of treaties and conventions. The number of environmental conventions in existence is partly a taxonomic problem. It depends on the definition of the term 'environment' being used. One UN estimate is that there are presently more than one hundred multilateral legal documents of various kinds which relate to issues of environmental protection;[17] of these 44 have been defined as environment-related conventions of interest to Canada.[18]

Partly for historical reasons, and the involvement of IUCN in the 1970s in pressing for this kind of action by governments, a significant proportion of these relate to various aspects of wildlife, heritage, and natural area conservation. Several are clustered in the area of marine pollution. Others deal with a range of topics from transboundary pollution to protection of the ozone layer. A looser definition takes in a wider variety of instruments, such as the 1985 FAO Code on the export and import of pesticides. The network continues to evolve. In the early 1990s a degree of government attention unprecedented in the international environmental policy area centred on production of the global climate change convention. For the most part, the creation and continuing life of these kinds of agreements attract minimal public interest in Canada outside environmental agencies of government and some environmental groups. They nonetheless provide an element of continuity in the international environment regime, and are important as possible models for future innovations. Canada has been active in many of them.

Much of the politics of CITES, of which Canada was a signatory in 1975, centres on the regular meetings of the states that are party to the agreement. The underlying principles of the convention, and the placing of different species of flora and fauna on the agreement's Appendices, are debated at these sessions. A typical example can be drawn from the 1987 meeting. The Canadian delegation supported Ecuadorian and United States proposals to shift hummingbirds and North American pitcherplants to Appendix II (a less stringent trade control device than that governing the endangered species listed in the first Appendix).[19] Much of this detail appears arcane. But there are hidden agendas, and real interests to be protected. Canada has had, in the form of European pressures against the eastern harp seal harvest and the fur trade, first-hand experience of the wider political and economic consequences of some forms of international species politics. Also in 1987, Canada success-fully resisted a Dutch initiative designed to tighten restrictions on the use of walrus populations. Canada has for similar reasons also been active in an international committee of seven countries (through the International Organization for Standardization) seeking harmonized international standards on humane trapping.

Thus Canada has a complex blend of interests when approaching many international environmental agreements. One has been the protection of traditional hunting rights. This has led to support for more 'user' participation in the management of the 1973 international polar bear convention.[20] Like the US and a number of other western countries, Canada has also shied away from signing the 1979 Bonn convention on the conservation of migratory species, on the grounds that the definitions and commitments contained in the agreement are too broad-ranging, and that the management issues are better tackled by existing conventions to which Canada is a party, particularly the Canada-US arrangements which date back to the early years of the century.

Other international conventions reinforce domestic programs. Cana-da's national parks and protected area system would still exist in the absence of any international agreements in this area. Specific instruments, however, for example on wetlands (the Ramsar Convention) and on the protection of world heritage, have influenced the evolution of the system by sharpening the criteria for selection of sites, creating an external constituency for their continued good management, and bolstering the arguments of domestic groups. Canada signed the Ramsar convention in 1981 and proceeded to list 17 sites in the next five years. World heritage sites nominated by Canada include Wood Buffalo National Park, Kluane

National Park, and Nahanni National Park. Canada is a major actor in such enterprises if only because of the sheer size of the areas involved. Canadian nominations for inclusion on the world wetlands list, for example, constitute about one-half of the total area designated by all countries.[21] Conventions thrive on a mixture of concrete obligations and voluntarist spirit. Canada has been energetic not only at substantive policy levels, but also procedurally and politically as a member of the World Heritage Committee and in the executive bodies and working group structures related to other key conventions.

During the 1980s, international environmental issues began to take on more of the flavour of high politics as a result of the growing prominence first of the issue of ozone layer deterioration, and then of the prospects of global climatic change brought on by a combination of industrialization and urbanization processes and of large-scale deforestation in the tropics. As Jake Epp, Minister of Energy, Mines and Resources, put it in 1989 with understandable hyperbole, the 'issue of global warming is changing the entire policy agenda around the world'.[22] The success of the Montreal conference of September 1987, which produced a detailed protocol to the 1985 Vienna convention on ozone layer protection, represented a high point of Canadian global change diplomacy, and stimulated a series of related moves on world climate issues. These focused on development of a framework convention by the early 1990s on climate change, dealing particularly with the various greenhouse gases viewed as the main culprits. Preparatory work by Canada and other countries took place in a multilateral framework that began to take shape after the world climate conference of 1979. Canada hosted the major international conference on atmospheric change held in Toronto in 1988. Canadian scientists and officials were active in the IPCC.[23] Here, and in subsequent negotiations in Washington in 1991, Canada emphasized the financial requirements of developing countries, and problems of technology transfer and technical assistance, as well as the need for careful planning on the role and power of the new institutions to be created by the convention.[24]

Environmental Bilateralism

This kind of environmental diplomacy is in principle universal in scope: all states can take part. Processes are accordingly protracted, definitions of consensus are difficult to arrive at, and, usually to the frustration of Canadian environmental groups viewing events from a distance, agreements often rest upon compromises, qualifications, and exemptions that water down original goals. Much the same is true of the bilateral level. Here, however, individual governments have greater leeway for manoeuvre. Initiatives do not rely for their success on the acquiescence of a large group of bystanders.

Bilateral environmental co-operation agreements vary from packages negotiated with countries with which Canada wishes to improve relations, such as that with Mexico, to specific sectoral technical arrangements such as those on forestry that have been signed with the Soviet Union, China, and Japan.[25] Canada also has consultation and co-ordination arrangements for handling marine pollution problems in the maritime border area with Greenland.

With the exception of the relationship with the US, however, bilateralism is still a relatively novel feature of Canadian environmental diplomacy. In the case of co-operation with the Soviet Union and the European Community (EC), which we will take as examples, environmental agreements nestle in the midst of a complex political and economic relationship. Differing objectives are served simultaneously. Environmental co-operation is seen primarily — or at least by the main actors in the foreign policy community — as a building block of a larger political and economic relationship, and only secondarily as a modestly useful contribution to environmental improvement at the international level.

Common environmental problems, or complementary past experience at tackling them, were part of the rationale for the cluster of environmental and scientific agreements signed during Prime Minister Mulroney's 1989 visit to Moscow. There is a lengthy background of bilateral co-operation, for example through the Canada-USSR Arctic science exchange program, as well as in multilateral settings such as the administration of the 1973 polar bear convention. Contacts were already expanding significantly during the late 1980s, especially on Arctic issues. The main impetus for Canada, however, came from the broader foreign policy objective of fostering relations with the changing Soviet Union, and of promoting Canada's commercial and investment links. Given the magnitude of the problem of environmental deterioration in the Soviet Union, Moscow was more insistent that the implementing machinery should be clearly structured, and that its focus should be on concrete actions and not merely on the exchange of ideas and specialists. Even so, the institutional arrangements that resulted from the 1989 agreement (centring on several working groups operating under a Joint Commission) allowed for the flexible development of co-operative policy-oriented studies in the early 1990s in several areas of direct interest to Canada.

A similar blend of motivations on the Canadian side can be found in relations with the European Community. Circumstances differed, however, in that both the EC and each of its twelve member-states had in place their own extensive environmental programs, operating within political and economic systems broadly similar to that of Canada.[26] As part of the process of building relations with the EC — for a time an important foreign policy goal of the Trudeau government — an agreement of 1975 provided for environmental co-operation and consultations between Canada and the Community. This proved to be ineffectual. What few discussions there were in the 1970s had in effect collapsed by the mid-1980s. There was little impetus on either side to pursue this aspect of the relationship. The broader framework of Canada-EC exploratory discussions on joint ventures, sectoral initiatives, and other matters also failed to achieve much. Several more specific agreements — on research on wastewater treatment (1983), for example, and on the health and environmental effects of radiation (1987) — had varying results.[27]

In the second half of the 1980s, however, environmental topics were becoming more urgent in both Canada and Europe. Mounting pressures for a strengthening of political and commercial ties — particularly in the wake of the Canada-US Free Trade Agreement, and preparations for the post-1992 single European market — made the instrument of environmental co-operation more attractive again, as did the related Canadian goal of forging more effective contacts in various fields of science and technology. In addition, several contentious issues straddled the environmental and resource development areas. For a period in the mid-1980s, the eastern Canadian seal hunt was in effect the only environment-related topic on the Canada-EC agenda, particularly following the EC's 1983 ban on the import of baby seal skins (which was extended for a further four years in 1985). Other questions, particularly the fur trade, then showed a similar potential for damaging Canadian economic interests as a result of the strength of European environmental and animal-rights lobbies. The long-standing fisheries dispute between Canada and the EC, centring on catches off the Atlantic coast, also fitted into this wider picture of accumulating resource and environmental irritants.

Environmental co-operation thus became an important ingredient in a drive to improve relations in the late 1980s. At first, the environment did not occupy much space in proposals for a revitalization of the relationship.[28] Environmental issues were more an impediment requiring damage-control strategies than an opportunity for collaboration. Steps were then taken by the European Parliament to diminish these obstacles. It urged greater 'objectivity' in European public debates on issues such as Canadian fur exports and hunting methods, more understanding of native hunting rights, and more appreciation of the 'high degree of environmental awareness' in Canada.[29] Canada-EC co-operation in multilateral frameworks on global climate change also accelerated bilateral developments.

The 1989 meeting of the Canada-EC Joint Co-operation Committee (JCC) singled out the environment and health as possible areas for 'intensified co-operation' between Canada and the EC. Remote sensing in the field of environmental protection was one area identified as promising.[30] This led to what Joe Clark in May, 1990, called a 'new phase' of Canada-EC political relations.[31] It culminated in the Declaration on EC-Canada Relations issued by Prime Minister Mulroney and the EC President (then Giulio Andreotti, Prime Minister of Italy) in November 1990. The document identified environmental protection as one of several possible areas for strengthening co-operation. It also listed five areas of transnational challenges to which a high priority was assigned, one of which was environmental protection and the 'preservation of the fragile global ecosystem'.[32]

THE ENVIRONMENT AND FOREIGN POLICY:
AUTONOMY VS DEPENDENCE

Environmental questions are thus subject to elbowing and prodding from other issues that may at any time hold sway in Canada's bilateral relations with other countries, or in a variety of multilateral contexts. Quite different agendas may influence the course of an environmental policy idea through such mazes. Even allowing for the possibility of such linkage, the interests of states in relation to environmental issues themselves are rarely simple. The negotiation and implementation of international instruments often proceed at a tortoise-like pace irksome to the would-be hares of the environmental movement. An important question is the degree to which international environmental policy can be considered relatively autonomous, and the extent to which objectives, processes, and outcomes are shaped by relations of dependence on other policy areas.

The view that states acting alone cannot hope to tackle adequately the many policy problems confronting them is an old one in the theory of international relations. Environmental problems have given the argument new force. As one scientist told the House of Commons environment committee in 1989, 'international management is the only way to go in the larger scale of environmental issues, because you cannot operate inside national boundaries when you are dealing with a fluid media.'[33] At one end of the international scale, bilateral co-operation on environmental questions is 'literally forced upon Canada and the US' by the common problems the two countries face, the parliamentary Joint Committee on Canada's International Relations concluded in 1986.[34] At the other, the question of global warming can only be addressed through multilateral approaches, especially in view of the impact on global processes of large developing countries such as India, China, and Brazil.[35]

Thus environmental policy has an in-built logic that drives thinking towards the international level. Another logic, however, defines the traditional rules of prudent statecraft operating at that level. One of these is that a concentration on single issues should not deteriorate into tunnel vision. Governance requires a sense of perspective. The strategy of multilateralizing issues on the bilateral agenda with the US, for example, has at various times had attractions for Canadian policy-makers. Canada would, regardless of this consideration, have been an active participant in ECE transboundary pollution debates, but the potential of this and other multilateral forums to generate criticism of US positions added to its value. Single-minded *realpolitik*, however, can be costly. Particularly since 1984, and the Mulroney government's preference for closer US-Canadian ties, Canadian delegations to such meetings have been sensitive to the risks of appearing to gang up on Washington. This wider framework was not a significant factor in shaping the events that concluded with the Canada-US acid rain accord of 1991. Earlier attempts by Ottawa to put pressure on the Reagan and Bush administrations by multilateralization of the issue were not successful.[36]

An additional factor making for caution in approaches to multilateral encounters is that some 'international' developments tend on closer scrutiny to be largely European in character. In early 1986, for example, a major international conference on a variety of forestry-related topics, including acid rain, was attended at head of government and ministerial level by many countries; Canada's representation, by contrast, was restricted to a small official delegation since the Department of External Affairs regarded it primarily as a 'European affair'.[37] Environmental groups were quick to diagnose myopia. On the other hand, the history of international environmental co-operation since 1945 does reveal a strong element of pressure from European countries motivated primarily by regional concerns.

It is often difficult in practice to distinguish those actions which spring from a policy logic of environmental cosmopolitanism from those which reflect Canada's traditional middle-power attachment to multilateralism and institution-building at the international level. It has been argued that there is a 'preoccupation with international organizations in Canada's foreign policy that arguably exceeds anything observed' in the policies of other western states.[38] For the most part, of course, the two sources — the pursuit of domestic environmental policy goals by international means, and the promotion by way of middle-power statecraft in the environmental arena of Canada's standing in the international community — are mutually reinforcing. When we probe the mainsprings of each a little more deeply, however, some divergences come to light.

Inside the federal government, environmental actors view such activities as ends in themselves, and are largely uninterested in any pay-offs that may accrue in terms of Canada's external image, prestige, or capacity to exercise influence in other international settings (with the exception of other environmental policy settings). Some basic formulae of mutual dependence govern relations between the major players. If and when External Affairs and International Trade wishes to take a lead on an environmental issue, it is largely dependent on the expertise of other departments. Environment Canada, for its part, has much of the technical expertise (though there are often significant gaps), but it must operate internationally within a framework defined primarily by others. According to some critics, the predictable result has been gaps in Canada's coverage of international environmental issues, compounded by administrative confusion and a lack of integrated policies. There has been criticism, too, not only of the lack of relevant expertise in the Department of External Affairs, but also of its officers' reluctance to turn to the scientific community for help.[39] The need for Environment Canada to develop its own capacity to play a larger role in environmental diplomacy has been a recurring theme in these debates.[40]

CONSTITUENCY PRESSURE: DOMESTIC PUSH AND EXTERNAL PULL

All western governments are subject to a variety of domestic and external influences, in the environmental as in other policy areas. Canada is at the same time pulled along by external developments and also pushed in this direction from inside. Competing domestic forces, suspicious of the stated goals and hidden agendas of environmentalism, restrain the vigour of the push.

First, the international milieu has a dynamic of its own that exerts a variety of influences over nations. Countries can become targets of the attention of others, for example, as Canada did over polar bears in the 1960s, seals in the 1970s, and the fur trade in the 1980s. Even the most retiring of states may be compelled by such processes to develop defensive strategies. Further, even if a country were to go on automatic pilot for a while, it would still be possible for its government to produce impressive evidence of international activity. System-driven labours form a hefty component of Canada's own international environmental role. Routine maintenance of the regime is an obligation which the Canadian government takes seriously. Much of this is at the elementary level of submitting data to bodies such as the ECE or the OECD Environment Committee for their publications and meetings, or circulating information bulletins to interested Canadians. Important though this largely invisible work is for sustaining the life of international arrangements, it is at best the chore of the passive citizen. More importantly, the international level also pulls states into its orbit by forcing choices upon them. How many, and which, sites should be nominated for inclusion on the World Heritage list? To what extent should Canada's domestic regime on matters such as CFC production, greenhouse gas regulation, or pesticide use, precede agreed international measures?

External developments also contribute vocabularies and issues, and goals and criteria, to national debates. The arguments of the Club of Rome studies of the 1970s, and the US *Global 2000* report of 1980, became reference points for many Canadian debates.[41] These in turn were easily overshadowed by the response to the WCED report in the late 1980s. Though criticized in some quarters as excessively sympathetic to the requirements of economic growth (and in others as wilfully neglectful of the errors of over-regulation of the private sector), Brundtlandism nonetheless became a rallying point for many calls for government action on the environment. The report provided accessible measures of performance. As federal Environment Minister, Lucien Bouchard declared himself in support of the Brundtland goal of a protected natural area system of 12% of national territory, for example, though he also defended the need for a more cautious approach: '12% of Canada is quite a chunk of land.'[42] The 1986 visit of WCED Commissioners to Canada also led directly to the creation of the National Task Force which reported to the Canadian Council of Resource and Environmental Ministers (CCREM) in 1987, in anticipation of the Canadian contribution to the UN General Assembly debate on the Brundtland recommendations later that year.

It would be wrong, however, to see Canada as only a reactive source of responses to the outside world. Canadian officials also take proactive stances in multilateral forums. And there are more complex circular processes at work. Canadians also press for international actions that, if successful, then form part of Canada's external policy setting. Again, the WCED is a good example. The initial moves, as we have seen, can be traced to environment-economy debates in OECD meetings in the early 1980s. Canadian officials took a leading part in these, and also in later actions to foster wider UNEP support in Nairobi for the Norwegian initiative.[43] Several individuals, including Maurice Strong and Jim MacNeill, have played important roles in this process of welding together the domestic and the international dimensions of thinking about the environment.[44] Similarly, the transnational organization of scientific communities gives opportunities for internationally oriented Canadian scientists to forge linkages between different policy levels. This has been particularly true of larger policy-oriented research and data-gathering programs, such as the Man and the Biosphere Program (MAB) of UNESCO in the 1970s, and the International Geosphere-Biosphere Program (IGBP) of the 1990s.[45]

This brings us to the second factor, the push from domestic actors. Pressures from environmental groups form an important nutritional source for Canadian interest in international developments. Leadership at the international level is frequently advocated by groups as desirable in itself because of the magnitude of the world's environmental problems; as an obligation on the government of Canada; as a spur to much-needed domestic programs; and as a logical follow-up to Canada's acknowledged environmental expertise, multilateral experience, and appreciation of the special needs of countries in the South.

A diffuse concern for the global environment is an intangible factor in this kind of advocacy. It can be a powerful motivator for members of environmental groups, even those whose activities are directed mainly towards local or provincial levels. Some groups go further and use global environmental criteria for evaluating Canadian actions. What Canada should do, that is, is what is held to be needed from a planetary perspective. The ozone layer campaign of Friends of the Earth, the marine mammals advocacy of Greenpeace, and the focus of Probe International and other groups on Brazilian rainforest issues, are examples. The 'Canadian Wilderness Charter' being promoted by several groups in 1991 included specific reference to the Brundtland goal of each country protecting 12% of its national territory, and called for monitoring of progress by international bodies. Cues are picked up directly, or indirectly through transnational links with US and European groups. The news media also act as a significant connecting device between groups by giving publicity to matters such as threats to the world's coral reefs.[46]

There is also scepticism on the part of groups about multilateral developments. Bureaucrats and diplomats appear to dominate such activities. Compromises bought by 'politics' seem rife. Access is often blocked by the rules of the game. Politicians' minds, never easily focused, become distracted from urgent questions nearer home. On the other hand, as the *Greenprint* of 1989 put it, Canada's 'credibility in the international conservation community' is at stake when major international conventions are left unsigned or inadequately implemented.[47] Specific instruments occasionally become salient for environmental groups. Pressures from Canadian environmental groups in 1989 for greater protection of the African elephant in CITES produced positive responses from both External Affairs and Environment Canada. Groups sometimes bypass Ottawa in their search for environmental solutions. The Canadian Nature Federation, for example, contacted the World Heritage Committee directly over the issue of diseased bison slaughter in Wood Buffalo National Park in 1990.[48]

The relationship between governments and environmental groups on these questions is rarely smooth. It is prone to periodic bouts of alienation. This happened in the late 1970s, when groups detected a growing lack of willingness on the part of federal ministers and officials to listen and act,[49] and again during the 1980s, as a result first of budgetary cutbacks and restrictions on information and access under the first Mulroney government, and then of the protracted delays and mixed results of the government's Green Plan deliberations.

Yet the relationship is more than a one-sided flow of attempted influence. Groups are an important constituency of environmental agencies. Governments provide them with funding, for example in the financial support given to groups in 1991 by the Ontario Environmental Assessment Board to assist challenges to Ontario Hydro's expansion plans. Environmental officials and members of groups may share objectives in relation to specific conventions or international organizations. Groups, or individual experts associated with their networks, frequently have access to technical expertise of value to agencies. Co-operative projects can materialize. Environment Canada has collaborated with the World Wildlife Fund, for example, on the protection of Canadian endangered species.

Environmental groups, however, are only one element in the domestic political picture. Other voices are critical of excessive emphasis on global environmental issues. Imperial Oil, for example, in a 1990 call for more research on the consequences of anti-greenhouse measures, argued that there was 'much scientific uncertainty' about both the causes and the seriousness of global warming, and that there was a danger of damaging Canada's international competitiveness if carbon dioxide emissions were reduced unilaterally.[50] The forestry and mining sectors have been particularly critical of media coverage of international and Canadian environmental issues.[51] In 1989 Canadian exporters lobbied successfully for special treatment of the Export Development Corporation and the Canadian Commercial Corporation in the application of the government's environmental assessment guidelines. The other side of this private sector argument, increasingly evident from the late 1980s, is that a deepening application of sustainable development principles will help rather than hinder the longer-term competitiveness of Canadian resource products on international markets. There is also considerable potential for a growing Canadian niche in the world environmental protection industry, for example in relation to the export of clean-water technologies and expertise.[52]

Parliament took increased interest in global environmental matters in the late 1980s. The 1986 visit of the Brundtland commissioners to Canada, publication of the WCED report the following year, and the emergence of widespread public attention to ozone layer and climate change questions all served to accelerate this process. The traditional parliamentary constraint of lack of information and expertise has been eased to some extent by reliance on the research staff of the Parliamentary Centre for Foreign Affairs and Foreign Trade, use of occasional consultants on contract, and by extensive committee hearings which draw in representatives of the major environmental groups. Several months of 1989–90, for example, in both the environment and other Commons committees, were devoted to global warming issues. At one point the environment committee simply adopted as its own resolution a draft submitted by Friends of the Earth on the policy implications for Canada of developments in the ozone layer protection regime.[53]

FRAGMENTATION OF AUTHORITY: THE CANADIAN AND THE
INTERNATIONAL REGIMES

Canada's environmental regime, grounded in collaboration and agreed divisions of labour between federal and provincial governments, in some ways resembles international arrangements. The character of the Canadian political system is clearly qualitatively different from that of the international system; but in both, processes of divergence and convergence can be seen in the approaches of the basic units to issues of policy development and harmonization in the environmental area.

The jurisdictional division between the federal and provincial governments makes the latter to a large extent the primary environmental policy actors in Canada. While the federal government acts as Canada's representative in multilateral bodies, and as the authoritative actor for the negotiation of international environmental agreements, the provinces have responsibility for 'the implementation of international agreements where the subject matter falls within their sphere of legislative jurisdiction'.[54] Agreements between Ottawa and individual provincial governments underpin the making and implementation of environmental policy. Some provinces have their own 'international' agreements, as in the case of forest conservation arrangements with bordering states of the US. Both directly and indirectly the provinces propel Canada forward into the international environmental policy community, while at the same time acting as a brake on Ottawa's external policies. Several characteristically stress the view that pursuit of economic development goals—usually without a sustainable development coloration—should remain paramount. Competition, for example between New Brunswick and Nova Scotia in forest products, further limits in this context the appeal of constricting environmental regulatory systems.

The fact that multilateral questions fall firmly within the federal government's orbit, moreover, has given them a special significance. These are indisputably questions on which Ottawa can take the lead. They represent one of the few environmental areas in which the federal government can claim for itself a distinctive role. This suggests that Canada's international environmental activism is in part a product of the interest of the federal government—and Environment Canada's organizational stake—in shoring up what might otherwise be a precarious role in the formulation of overall environmental policy. Without at least tacit provincial acquiescence, however, Ottawa's engagement even in these areas would have a hollow ring. Its role is threatened, then, by any prospect of a deepening of trends in the 1990s towards structural decentralization of the Canadian polity.

The mechanisms for federal-provincial consultation on environment-related matters, originally set in motion in 1962, received a major boost at the start of the 1970s.[55] While the provincial premiers took the initiative to press for change, a key factor was the establishment of the federal government's own environment department. Spurring on both levels of government was the publicity surrounding UNCHE in 1972. Consensus was reached during preparations for the conference, and in the context of the creation of Environment Canada, that Ottawa was the appropriate government to take the lead in the newly emerging international area; the provinces, however, would retain authority for their respective environmental policy frameworks. The need for more effective federal-provincial collaboration on environmental policy was identified by senior environmental officials from the federal and provincial governments in the immediate aftermath of the conference. Broad public support for a larger international role for Canada was also confirmed in polls.[56] A federal-provincial task force recommended in 1975, among other things, that Ottawa initiate and strengthen international agreements on migratory fish and wildlife – in effect that it support internationally the interests of the provinces. Further, Ottawa was to 'consult with provincial governments in developing its participation in activities leading to international conventions or agreements on environmental matters involving provincial jurisdiction or of mixed jurisdiction.'[57]

Occasional tensions over jurisdictional boundaries have resurfaced. The pre-eminence of the federal government in international matters has been acknowledged by the provinces. Problems arise, however, when questions of implementation are discussed. Provincial and territorial government representatives made the point forcefully when the CCREM looked at the *World Conservation Strategy* in 1981. Although they approved in principle the general objectives of the Strategy, it was agreed that appropriate responses could best be made by individual jurisdictions. The federal-provincial task force on carbon dioxide controls in 1988–89 similarly encountered substantial objection from several provincial governments to restrictions – views criticized by Stephen Lewis, former ambassador to the UN, as those of 'provincial ostriches burrowing in the sand'.[58] Opposition centred particularly on the 20% reduction goal around which consensus was then growing in Canada and internationally. The late 1980s were marked nonetheless by institutional improvements in the ability of the Canadian Council of Ministers of the Environment (CCME) to handle discord on international questions.

Provincial governments and the Territories become engaged in such questions according to their respective interests. The Atlantic provinces, for example, have little interest in international wildlife trade matters. With one exception (Newfoundland in 1985), none of the governments of the region attended any of the four intergovernmental meetings on CITES convened by Ottawa in the period 1980–85.[59] Ontario, by contrast, has had a major stake in the convention by virtue of its regulation of fur shipments passing through the province. The Ontario Ministry of Natural Resources (OMNR) has been especially active compared with other provinces' agencies in checking consignments originating in, or destined for, the US, Europe and elsewhere. Indeed the routine contacts of Ontario officials with the US Fish and Wildlife Service on enforcement questions have meant that Ottawa, formally the responsible authority, has sometimes been sidestepped, with US government enquiries going direct to OMNR instead of to the CITES Administration in Ottawa.[60]

Of all the issues that can be classed under the heading 'environmental', the provinces have been especially zealous in protecting their regulatory roles in relation to wildlife management. Many international instruments directly or indirectly touch on such questions. However, these often spring from different management philosophies. The contrasting viewpoints have surfaced at the regular federal-provincial-territorial wildlife meetings. At the 1987 meetings in Tuktoyaktuk, for example, criticisms were voiced that 'The administration of [CITES] has gone astray, and the convention is being misused.'[61] It was argued that it did not yield any substantive conservation benefits for North American species, and was inefficient and costly. Further, difficulties with the convention 'cause suspicion of international agreements and bring disrepute to conservation agreements in general'. Provincial and Territorial critics also put on record their view of the 'embarrassment value' and 'political' character of the Ramsar convention.

CONCLUSIONS

Environmental issues have demonstrated remarkable stamina on the agendas of international politics. The 1992 UN Conference on Environment and Development marks the twentieth anniversary of their arrival. Distant from the more immediate questions confronting governments and publics, they have nonetheless also occupied an increasingly prominent place in the domestic politics, policy-making processes, and administrative programs of Canada and of other OECD nations. Asked to rank five international environmental issues (global warming, toxic waste, acid rain, ozone depletion, and water pollution) in terms of their seriousness in a 1990 survey, 30% of respondents identified depletion of the ozone layer as the highest priority.[62]

Environmental questions have had in Canada a special resonance with traditional approaches to international questions. They fit snugly into thinking about institution-building at the international level and about new ways to exploit the repertoire of mediatory and problem-solving skills in Canada's middle-power arsenal. This combination has facilitated Canadian leadership in environmental diplomacy. At the CSCE Summit in Paris in November 1990, Prime Minister Mulroney called for more environmental co-operation among its members, in association with existing organizations, 'to meet newer, more unconventional threats to our common security'. The conventions of national sovereignty were 'becoming too narrow a base from which to resolve the broadening global and regional problems of environmental deterioration, debt, drugs, population growth, and human rights'.[63]

Many actors have honed their roles on these stages. As in the 1982 UNEP 'Special Character' session and in the Western Economic Summits of the late 1980s, the opportunity to pronounce on global environmental questions appears to have a peculiar fascination for heads of government and foreign ministers. We should not jump from this observation to the conclusion that the international level is merely a declaratory, or rhetorical, one. There are substantive, if often subtle, implications for national environmental policy agendas. The generally less-publicized arena of intergovernmental organizations, or of the meetings of parties to international environmental conventions, is, by the early 1990s, sufficiently well established for it to be regarded as a normal part of the process by which Canadian governments formulate environmental policy.

FOR FURTHER READING

Fenn Osler Hampson, 'Climate Change: Building International Coalitions of the Like-Minded', *International Journal* 45 (Winter, 1989–90): 36-74.

Patrick Kyba, 'International Environmental Relations: Twenty Years of Canadian Involvement', Paper presented at the Annual Meeting of the Canadian Political Science Association, Victoria, May 1990.

Doug Macdonald, *The Politics of Pollution* (Toronto: McClelland and Stewart, 1991), Ch. 16.

Jim MacNeill, 'The Greening of International Relations', *International Journal*, 45 (Winter 1989–90): 1-35.

David G. LeMarquand and Anthony Scott, 'Canada's International Environmental Relations', in O.P. Dwivedi, ed., *Resources and the Environment: Policy Perspectives for Canada* (Toronto: McClelland and Stewart, 1980), 77-103.

Gwyn Prins, 'Politics and the Environment', *International Affairs* 66, 4 (1990): 711-30.

Jan Schneider, *World Public Order of the Environment: Towards an International Ecological Law and Organization* (University of Toronto Press, 1979).

CHAPTER 13

Comparing Canadian Performance in Environmental Policy*

GEORGE HOBERG

When then Environment Minister Lucien Bouchard introduced the *Green Plan* discussion paper in early 1990, he proclaimed that the primary goal of the government's effort was 'to make Canada, by the year 2000, the industrial world's most environmentally friendly country'.[1] How much work must be done to achieve this goal? This chapter evaluates the performance of Canadian environmental policy by comparing it to other advanced industrial democracies, focusing especially on the United States. The comparative perspective is a valuable one, because rather than comparing performance with some abstract standard, we can compare Canada's activities to what other countries have done within similar constraints, be they technical, economic, social, or political. The focus on the US is also particularly relevant to Canada. Perhaps because Canadian perceptions of US environmental policy have been dominated by acid rain, many Canadians seem to have adopted an attitude of environmental superiority towards the giant neighbour to the south. This chapter will explore whether that attitude is justified.

A substantial body of literature on comparative environmental policy exists, although it has focused on comparisons between the US and Europe, and to a lesser extent Japan, and largely overlooked Canada.[2] If there is one theme pervading this literature, it is that the regulatory processes differ significantly in different countries, a variance that David Vogel has aptly characterized as 'national styles of regulation'. Most studies have focused on these differences in process, and have shied away from rigorous analyses of policy outcomes. The studies that have looked at policy outcomes have come up with a surprising conclusion: despite these widely divergent regulatory styles, there is a surprising amount of policy convergence. Can the same be said of Canada?

The focus of this comparison is on the content and consequences of environmental policy, and not on an evaluation of Canada's regulatory style or an examination of the reasons for Canada's performance. After a brief survey of the methodological problems involved, the financial resources, both public and private, that Canada has committed to environmental protection will be evaluated. Then the analysis turns to a detailed examination of four important areas of environmental policy: air pollution, water pollution, pesticides, and environmental impact assessment. For each policy area, the analysis will compare the applicable laws and regulations, and then whatever data are available on actual policy outcomes and their consequences. The concluding section will provide a summary assessment of Canada's environmental performance in comparative perspective. While an explanation for the observed patterns is beyond the scope of this chapter, several important explanatory forces will be given brief mention because they shed valuable light on Canada's regulatory performance to date.

METHODOLOGICAL OVERVIEW

This type of analysis is fraught with methodological pitfalls. The first difficulty is the choice of criteria for evaluation — how do we decide whether one country has a better environmental record than another? For the purpose of this analysis, we are concerned with how much environmental protection is provided, not with some more complex notion of net social welfare. But even this more narrow concern creates difficulties, in large part because different nations confront different environmental problems. The objective of environmental policy is of course to provide a desirable level of environmental quality in terms of clean air, clean water, etc. But because different nations confront different problems, it may not be appropriate merely to compare indices of environmental quality. For instance, because of Canada's relatively low population and industrial density, it can more easily take advantage of the assimilative capacities of the environment than a country with greater density. Thus, Canadians could pollute far more per capita and still have better environmental quality than their American neighbours. If Canada's regulations are weaker, that may reflect the presence of a less serious environmental threat rather than lack of environmental concern.

While taking this problem into account, this chapter will use the criteria of the *amount of environmental protection provided*. In principle, this would be measured by the difference between actual levels of environmental quality and what those levels would be in the absence of environmental protection measures. Unfortunately, such measures are simply not available. We must rely instead on the proxy indicators that are available, but even then much of the relevant data are scarce and difficult to interpret. Nations use different regulatory approaches that are frequently difficult to compare, and they frequently measure the implementation and consequences of regulations differently, if at all.

But this comparative task is too important to surrender to methodological difficulties. The analysis proceeds in the spirit of making the best of the data that are available, bearing in mind these dilemmas of comparison. The availability of data limits the scope of the analysis in two important ways. First, the analysis focuses on a comparison between Canada and the United States. Only occasional references, when comparable data are readily available, are made to other nations. Second, only four areas of environmental policy are considered, excluding such important areas as hazardous waste management, toxic substance control, endangered species protection, wilderness preservation, and policies towards global environmental problems. While the four areas surveyed here cover a broad range of environmental policy problems, there is no guarantee that these areas are representative of environmental policy generally.

RESOURCE COMMITMENTS

When we examine the level of financial resources Canada and the United States commit to environmental protection, the two countries appear to have similar levels of commitment. For purposes of our analysis, data for the fiscal year 1985–86 have been chosen. As shown in Table 13.1, at the federal level the Canadian commitment at first appears larger. Environment Canada spending was 0.46% of the total federal budget, whereas US Environmental Protection Agency spending was 0.32% of the total US federal budget.[3] But the analysis is complicated by the fact that Environment Canada's jurisdiction is more expansive than EPA's—for instance, it includes the parks branch, which in the US is included in another department.[4] When the parks branch is removed from Environment Canada's budget, environmental spending makes up 0.21% of total federal spending, less than the US amount. If, however, we leave the parks branch in Environment Canada, and add the National Park Service to EPA's budget, Canada's fraction is slightly higher, 0.46% vs 0.41%.

The analysis of government spending is greatly complicated by the fact that much of it occurs at the sub-national level. Here the problem of consistent jurisdiction is magnified, because it is impractical to compare the scope of responsibilities of so many sub-national agencies. In the United States, the state governments spent 1.46% of their total budgets on the environment during the 1986 fiscal year. In the same year, the four largest Canadian provinces spent 0.89% of their total budgets on the environment. This difference is quite surprising, given Canada's reputation for being more decentralized. Again, these figures must be qualified by possible jurisdictional differences similar to those mentioned above, between Environment Canada and EPA.

When added together, the federal and state/provincial totals give us a better idea of total financial commitments of each government. In the US, environment spending comprises 0.65% of total government spending if you exclude the National Park Service. In Canada, it comprises 0.49%

**TABLE 13.1   GOVERNMENT SPENDING ON THE ENVIRONMENT
1986 FISCAL YEAR, MILLIONS OF DOLLARS**

	US	Canada
Federal Environment Budget		
Parks Included	$4,451[1]	520[2]
Parks Excluded	3,446	231
Total Federal Budget	1,072,773	111,227
Per cent Environment of Total		
Parks Included	0.41%	0.46%
Parks Excluded	0.32%	0.21%
Subnational Environment Spending	5,283[3]	699[4]
Subnational Total	361,897	78,513
Per cent Environment of Total	1.46%	0.89%
National Environment Total		
Parks Included	9,734	1,219
Parks Excluded	8,729	930
National Budget Total	1,434,670	189,740
Per cent Environment of Total		
Parks Included	0.68%	0.64%
Parks Excluded	0.61%	0.49%

1. Figures for EPA and total US budget from Executive Office of the President, Office of Management and Budget, *Historical Tables — Budget of the U.S. Government: Fiscal Year 1988* (Washington, D.C.: Government Printing Office, 1987). Figures for the National Parks Service are for 1985, and are from Norman Vig and Michael Kraft, eds, *Environmental Policy in the 1990s* (Washington, DC: CQ Press, 1990), appendix 3.

2. Canadian figures for total federal budget and Environment Canada budget are from *Public Accounts of Canada*, FY 85-6. The figure for Environment Canada excludes the Atmosphere Environment Service. Amount of AES and Parks comes from *Environment Canada Annual Report, 1986*.

3. Spending by the states derived from Council of State Governments, *Resource Guide to State Environmental Management* (Lexington, Ky: Council of State Governments, 1988).

4. Provincial spending on the environment includes the ministries of Environment in Ontario, Quebec, Alberta, and British Columbia. Figures derived from Public Accounts of the individual provinces.

if you exclude parks at the federal level. If federal parks programs are included in both estimates, US environmental spending is 0.68% of total government spending, and Canadian environmental spending is 0.64%. Thus, the comparison is highly sensitive to how you measure budgetary commitments, but whatever differences there are, they are relatively small.

However, government spending is an extremely indirect indicator of society's commitment to environmental protection. When governments rely on the instrument of regulation to protect the environment, government expenditures are only a weak reflection of environmental concern because the costs of environmental protection are borne by the private sector, and the administrative costs to government are quite small in comparison. For that reason, a more appropriate measure of commitment is how much business spends on environment clean-up. For instance, in the US, government regulation and monitoring makes up only 2% of total pollution control expenditures. When direct government pollution abatement is included, such as municipal sewage treatment, the fraction increases to 22%.[5]

While they are done with different methodologies, and care must therefore be taken in how they can be compared, both nations have developed estimates for the fraction of new capital investment that is spent on pollution control. In the US, approximately 2.0% of new plant and equipment expenditures by US non-farm business was dedicated to pollution abatement over the period 1985–1987. In Canada, about 0.7% of total capital expenditures over the period 1985–7 was spent on pollution control. Comparing these two measures, the US resource commitment to the environment is nearly three times greater than that in Canada. When the analysis if restricted to the manufacturing sector, the gap narrows somewhat — 4.0% for the US and 1.9% for Canada — but it is still substantial.[6]

AIR POLLUTION

Our first substantive area of environmental policy for comparison is air pollution. There are two types of air pollution regulations: ambient air quality standards, which place limits on the concentration of various pollutants in the air, and emission standards, which place limits on the amount of various pollutants emitted by a particular source, such as smokestacks or cars.

There are significant differences between the two countries' regulatory frameworks for air pollution controls. In the US, air pollution control occurs largely through the federal Clean Air Act of 1970, amended in 1977 and 1990.[7] The Clean Air Act requires the federal government to establish binding National Ambient Air Quality Standards (NAAQS) for a specified list of important pollutants. These standards are supplemented by the Prevention of Significant Deterioration (PSD) program, which is designed to maintain air quality in areas where the air is already cleaner than the national standards. In effect, the combination of NAAQS and PSD creates a bewildering patchwork of air quality standards, in which the NAAQS provides a national maximum, but the PSD limits impose more stringent standards in clean air areas. The states are responsible for implementing regulations to achieve the standards, but they do so under close federal supervision, backed by the threat of financial sanction. In its most stringent section, the US Clean Air Act directly establishes federal emission standards for cars and trucks. The Act also requires EPA to establish stringent federal emission standards for new sources of pollution, called New Source Performance Standards, and emission standards for new and existing sources of especially toxic air pollutants.

In Canada, the federal government plays a much smaller role in air pollution control. The Canadian Clean Air Act, passed in 1971, gives the federal government authority to set non-binding guidelines;[8] binding air quality standards and the regulations to achieve them are issued by provinces. However, the federal statute does authorize the federal government to establish national emission standards for pollutants that 'pose a significant danger to the health of persons', but this provision has only been used four times in 20 years.[9] Virtually all emission standards are set by the provinces. The major exception is standards for automobile emissions from new vehicles, which are established by the federal Minister of Transportation under the Motor Vehicle Safety Act.[10]

Thus, American air pollution regulation is far more centralized than it is in Canada, and far more of the substance of the regulations is specified in US legislation. When combining provincial and federal statutes, however, there is little difference in the extent of regulatory authority over air pollution in the two countries.

The record on policy outcomes in the air pollution area is quite mixed, but it seems that Canada has had marginally more success than the US. A comparison of four provinces shows that Canadian ambient air quality standards are either equivalent to or more stringent than American National Ambient Air Quality standards.[11] However, when the US Prevention of Significant Deterioration program is included, the US air quality standards could be considered more stringent.

In the case of emissions from automobiles, the US government has been a world leader, but just recently Canada has caught up. Prior to the 1988 model year when new Canadian regulations took effect, Canadian emission standards lagged far behind American standards. Previously, Canadian standards had been between three and seven times less stringent, depending on the pollutant in question.[12] Both governments are currently in the process of tightening their regulations significantly. The

1990 Amendments to the US Clean Air Act require much more stringent standards to be implemented between 1994 and 1996. In Canada, an intergovernment agreement announced in 1989 would tighten Canadian auto emission standards to a comparable level by about the same time.[13]

The case of acid rain involves the opposite pattern. During the 1980s acid rain was a major irritant in Canadian-American relations. While pollutants flow across the border in both directions, the greater amount of US emissions carried by prevailing winds ensures that Canada is far more affected by American-generated acid rain than vice versa. It is estimated that 50% of the acid rain falling in Canada comes from American sources, whereas a much smaller fraction, between 10% and 15%, of US acid rain originates in Canada.[14] In 1982, the Canadian government proposed an agreement whereby both nations would reduce sulphur dioxide by 50%. However, the Reagan administration, which at that time refused to formally admit that acid rain was a human-made phenomenon, adamantly rejected the proposal. Facing a recalcitrant Reagan Administration, Canada shifted its strategy to emphasizing unilateral reductions. In March, 1985, Prime Minister Brian Mulroney and Eastern Canadian premiers announced that Canada would reduce its emissions of sulphur dioxide by 50% by 1994.[15]

With the 1990 Amendments to its Clean Air Act, the United States finally introduced a stringent new acid rain reduction program. The statute requires that sulphur dioxide emissions be reduced by 10 million tones below 1980 levels by the year 2000. Both countries have presented slightly manipulated figures. Taking actual 1980 emission levels as a common baseline, the Canadian program requires a 37% reduction by 1994, and the US program requires a 39% reduction by the year 2000.[16]

Thus, while the US performance in the area of acid rain has undergone a dramatic improvement, it still lags behind the Canadian program by six years. While Canadians deserve credit for addressing the problem earlier, the American program has three features which make it somewhat more stringent than its Canadian counterpart. First, the American program is nationwide, whereas the Canadian program only includes provinces from Manitoba east. Second, the American program places a 'cap' beyond which sulphur dioxide emissions cannot rise, whereas the Canadian program permits future growth. The hard-fought reductions achieved by Canada between 1985 and 1994 could be lost as a result of future population or industrial growth. *Canada's Green Plan*, announced in December 1990, proposes to rectify both of these flaws, but that depends on provincial co-operation. Third, American officials face a more difficult task to achieve similar objectives. There are only 10 major sources of sulphur dioxide in Canada, whereas the 1990 Clean Air Act Amendments directly control emissions from 111 major sources.

When actual trends in air quality and emissions are examined, the

TABLE 13.2   NORTH AMERICAN AIR QUALITY TRENDS

		Canada	US
Sulphur dioxide	(ppb)		
	1975	11	15.4
	1987	5	8.4
	% change	−55%	−45%
Carbon monoxide	(ppm)		
	1975	1.9	11.96
	1987	1.0	6.88
	% change	−47%	−42%
Ozone	(ppb)		
	1979	15	142
	1987	16	129
	% change	+7%	−9%
Nitrogen dioxide	(ppm)		
	1977	31	29
	1987	21	25
	% change	−32%	−14%
Total Suspended Particulates	(μg/m^3)		
	1975	65.9	61.9
	1987	48.0	49.4
	% change	−27%	−20%
Lead	(mg/m^3)		
	1975	.00055	1.04
	1987	.00010	0.12
	% change	−82%	−88%

Methodological note: Different measurement methods are used. All Canadian figures, and US figures for nitrogen dioxide and sulphur dioxide, are annual arithmetic means. US figures for carbon monoxide are based on the second highest readings for 8-hour periods; those for TSP are annual geometric means; ozone counts are the second highest daily one-hour maximums; and figures for lead are maximum quarterly averages.

Canadian record appears to have a marginal edge over the US one. Table 13.2 displays trends in air quality in Canada and the United States. Because of differences in measurement methods, the air quality measures reported cannot be directly compared across the two nations. While the methodological differences may affect the rates of change as well, the percentage change figures are a reasonably reliable comparative indicator. Canadian progress in improving air quality from the mid-1970s to the mid-1980s surpassed US progress in four out of six commonly measured pollutants. When analysing the separate measure of emissions (the amount of pollution being released, rather than its concentration in the air) over the period 1980–1986, Canada had more success in reducing emissions of sulphur dioxide, but the US has had more success than Canada in reducing nitrogen oxides.[17]

In comparison to other advanced industrial countries, both the US and Canada seem to have very strong air pollution records. For instance, the major European countries are significantly behind North America in automobile emission standards. In 1989, the European Commission finally adopted standards that would move member countries to adopt standards by 1992 that were in place in both the US and Canada by 1988. By that time, North America will be well on the way to meeting much more stringent standards. Lead in gasoline, effectively banned in North America by 1990, is still used in several European countries. Finally, European nations have not gone as far as the US and Canada in addressing acid rain. A recent British program will reduce sulphur dioxide emissions by only 14% by 1997 — both North American programs go farther faster.[18]

WATER POLLUTION

The overall regulatory frameworks for water pollution control in the two jurisdictions have some important similarities. Both are federalist in nature, involving shared responsibilities between the national and subnational governments. The principal regulatory mechanism is basically the same: waste discharges are prohibited without a permit from the government. Despite the overall similarity in approach, however, there are important differences between the two jurisdictions' regulatory framework, reflecting each nation's institutional make-up and regulatory style.

Water pollution control in the United States is based upon the Federal Water Pollution Control Act of 1972 (FWPCA).[19] While it was amended in 1977 and 1987, the basic structure of the statute, as it applies to industrial effluents, has remained essentially the same. The 1972 statute announced extremely ambitious goals (not subsequently attained): the nation's waters were to be 'fishable and swimmable' by 1983, and the discharge of pollutants into navigable waters was to be eliminated altogether by 1985.[20]

To implement these goals, two major programs were established, one for industrial sources, one for municipal sewage disposal. The US Environmental Protection Agency was charged with issuing technology-based effluent standards for industrial plants. Polluters were required to install the Best Practicable Technology by 1977 and the more stringent Best

Available Technology (BAT) by 1984. In addition, new sources brought on line after 1973 were required to meet an even more stringent standard, the New Source Performance Standard.

To implement these standards, permits are issued to each source of discharge. It is this permit that formally establishes the allowable quantity and quality of effluent the plant can emit. The Act gives EPA the authority to delegate the permitting and enforcement responsibility to state governments. These authorities have been delegated to thirty-three states. These states thus have primary responsibility for permitting and enforcement, although EPA actively monitors these activities. For those states that do not have their own programs, EPA performs the permitting and enforcement functions itself.

The 1972 statute also contained an elaborate program for municipal sewage treatment. The Act required almost all municipalities to install 'secondary' treatment of municipal wastes by 1977. To encourage them to do so, the federal government created an $18-billion construction grant program that would pay for 75% of the costs of constructing new sewage treatment facilities. The 1977 Amendments extended the deadline to 1983 (it was later extended again to 1988), and continued the authorization of huge sums of money. The construction grant program has become America's second largest public works program, after the highway system.[21]

As in the case of air pollution, Canadian water pollution regulation is much more decentralized. There is a strong basis for federal power under the Fisheries Act, which prohibits emissions of any 'deleterious substance of any type in water frequented by fish' (section 33[2]). Exemptions are allowed if the discharge is authorized by regulation. The federal government has issued regulations for six industries, but with one exception they only apply to new plants. Enforcement of these standards has for the most part been delegated to provincial regulators, although the federal government reserves the right to take enforcement action in the case of inadequate provincial action. The principal mechanism for water pollution control is thus permits for specific facilities that are issued by provinces.[22]

Federal water pollution regulation is also authorized by the Canada Water Act of 1970. Part II of the Act authorizes unilateral federal action in 'interjurisdictional waters', and only if water quality has become a matter of 'urgent national concern' and efforts to reach a co-operative solution with the provinces have failed. Despite the expansive authorities for water quality management in this part of the Act, it has never been used. However, Part III of the statute, now incorporated into the Canadian Environmental Protection Act, authorized regulation of phosphates in detergents.[23]

Thus, as in the case of air pollution, water pollution control in Canada is far more decentralized than in the United States. Regulatory performance is not as easily measured in the case of water pollution. Ambient standards are not used, and while both countries monitor water quality, data have not been compiled in comparable terms. Certainly the American regulatory system seems more developed. For instance, under the FWPCA the US federal government has issued effluent standards for a mind-boggling 642 industrial subcategories. The pulp and paper mill regulations alone are divided into 25 subcategories. US leadership in water pollution is reflected by the fact that Ontario, typically the most progressive province environmentally, is revamping its regulatory system, using the US statute as a model.[24]

The comparable measures that do exist suggest that the US has a better record on water pollution control. For instance, the elaborate, statutory-based programs on municipal sewage treatment seems to have paid off. By 1988, 71% of the US population was served by municipal wastewater treatment, while only 58% of the Canadian population was. When analysed by level of treatment, the US record is even more favourable. Of the US population, 58% is served by facilities with at least secondary treatment, whereas only 37% of the Canadian population is served by similar facilities.[25] It should be noted that Quebec has lagged far behind other provinces in this area, and facilities currently under construction in Quebec should significantly improve the sewage treatment record in Canada.

One area where there has been substantial co-operation between the two nations is water pollution in the Great Lakes. Both nations signed the Great Lakes Water Quality Agreement of 1972, to be implemented under the auspices of the International Joint Commission. Implementation of the agreement has revealed differences in the two countries' records. As a result of its larger population and industrial activity, the US contributes far more pollution to the Great Lakes than does Canada. But the US has been significantly more aggressive in trying to control its effluents. For example, the US states' limit for phosphorus in detergents, a major source of Great Lakes pollution, is more than four times more stringent than the comparable Canadian standard.[26] Pulp mills in the US are required to have secondary effluent treatment, whereas mills in Ontario are not. As of April, 1989, only six of 27 Ontario mills had secondary treatment.[27] The US has more rigorous and comprehensive requirements for the pre-treatment of industrial wastes discharged into municipal systems.[28]

Data on water pollution also provide an opportunity to test one of the most common criticisms of American environmental programs. Analysts have repeatedly denounced the 'implementation gap' in American regulation—the gap between regulatory requirements and the actions of polluters.[29] However, the record suggests this characterization is more myth than fact, at least when compared to Canada. In the Great Lakes area, US compliance rates for both municipal and industrial sources are approximately 90%. In contrast, Canadian municipal compliance rates are between 40% and 50%, and industrial compliance rates are even worse, between 30% and 40%.[30] Differences in compliance definitions make only the most general comparisons possible with these aggregate figures. But when the Great Lakes Water Quality Board analysed an indicator for which there was consistent data — compliance with the Agreement's phosphorus effluent benchmark — the same disparity emerged. Forty-eight per cent of US sources met the benchmark, compared to 29% in Canada.[31]

Thus, while Canada's record on air pollution seemed marginally better than the US one, the US water pollution control record surpasses Canada's by a larger margin.

PESTICIDES

The basic structure of pesticide regulation in Canada and the US is similar. In both nations, pesticides are regulated through two main approaches. The 'front-end' approach is based on controlling the introduction of new products into the marketplace. In the US, the Federal Insecticide, Fungicide, and Rodenticide Act (FIFRA) prohibits the sale of pesticides unless they are registered with the federal government.[32] In Canada, a similar restriction is imposed by the Pest Control Products Act (PCPA).[33] Jurisdiction over pesticide regulation, however, is substantially different in the two countries. In the US, pesticides are regulated by the Environmental Protection Agency; in Canada, they are regulated by Agriculture Canada, although Health and Welfare Canada also plays an important role. Under a 1982 interdepartmental agreement, Health and Welfare assesses the safety of pesticides, and Agriculture determines whether the identified risks are 'acceptable'.[34]

Front-end statutes give both governments the authority to remove chemicals from the market when new information raises health, safety, or environmental concerns. In the US, FIFRA gives EPA the authority to remove pesticides from the market if they are found to present an unreasonable risk-benefit balance. Like the US statute, the Canadian PCPA allows the Minister of Agriculture to remove a product from the market when 'the safety of the control product or its merit or value for its intended purpose is no longer acceptable to him'.[35]

The second, 'back-end' approach is the regulation of food quality through restrictions on food adulteration. The 1954 amendments to the Federal Food, Drug, and Cosmetic Act require EPA to set quantitative limits, called 'tolerances', on the amount of pesticide residues in food. In Canada, similar restrictions are imposed by Health and Welfare Canada under the Food and Drugs Act.

While the regulatory frameworks in the two countries are very similar, two important differences give Canadian regulators a small theoretical advantage. First, the EPA must weigh the benefits of pesticide use against the risks, but Canadian regulators do not. While this difference in law is significant, in practice, Canadian regulators typically perform risk-benefit analyses anyway.[36] Second, Canadian manufacturers must demonstrate that their product is effective as well as safe, while US law has no such efficacy requirement. In some cases, this may lead to greater restrictions on pesticide use in Canada.

Policy outcomes in the area of pesticides show an appreciable amount of convergence between the two nations. In the 'front end' regulation of pesticide use, the two countries have taken similar actions in eight of the ten high-profile pesticide controversies since 1970. In the other two cases, the US has gone further on one and Canada has gone further on another.[37] However, a slight edge can be granted to the US because it acted first in seven cases, with Canada responding. In one case (dinoseb) the timing was nearly identical. In the other two cases (captan and alachlor) Canada took action before the US; both cases arose early in the Reagan Adminis-tration when the pesticide regulatory machinery was in its early stages.[38]

When evaluating the back-end of pesticide regulation—limits on the amount of pesticide residues in food—there is also a large amount of convergence, but in this case a definite edge for regulatory stringency goes to Canada. Of the 775 cases where the two countries limit the same pesticide in the same food, for example alar on apples, Canadian and US tolerances are equivalent in 465, or 60% of the cases. Canadian tolerances are more stringent in 298, or 38.5% of the cases, while American toler-ances are more stringent in only 12, or 1.5% of the cases.[39] While the US record on front-end pesticide regulation is among the world's strongest, it is out of step with that of most other advanced countries, where residue limits are more similar to Canada's.[40]

ENVIRONMENTAL IMPACT ASSESSMENT

The US National Environmental Policy Act, enacted in 1970, is renowned throughout the developed world for its rigorous requirements for environ-mental impact statements (EISs). Section 102(2)(C) requires that an EIS be performed for 'every recommendation or report on proposals for legislation and other major Federal actions significantly affecting the quality of the human environment'. Citizens have the right to sue the government to enforce compliance, and courts have rigorously enforced the requirement. In the early 1970s, the standing joke in the halls of the US bureaucracies was that when Moses needed to cross the Red Sea, God would agree to part the waters only after Moses performed an environmental impact assessment.[41]

Until recently, Canadian impact assessment requirements have been far less rigorous. Although attracted to the NEPA model of environmental impact assessment, Canadian governments consistently rejected the accompanying legalism. The federal government, for instance, historically opposed placing EIA requirements into a statute, because they thought it would undermine the flexibility of the process.[42] In late 1973, the federal Cabinet in Canada established the Environmental Assessment and Review Process (EARP). In response to criticisms about the informality of the process, EARP was issued as a 'Guidelines Order' in 1984 under the authority of the Government Organization Act. However, the 1984 changes failed to address many of EARP's perceived shortcomings. In particular, the legal status of the Guidelines was questionable; it was generally assumed that they 'had no legal force to ensure compliance from intransigent departments'.[43]

As a result of a combination of events in recent years, the EARP process is undergoing profound changes. In two recent cases, at the request of environmental groups Canadian courts have intervened to block the construction of dams because the federal government did not follow its own Cabinet guidelines on environmental impact assessment. As a result of the legal uncertainty generated by these cases, and strong public pressures for more rigorous environmental assessments, the federal government tabled legislation in June 1990 to incorporate EIA into a statute. If passed, Canada's impact assessment requirements may become as stringent as those south of the border.

Comparing policy outcomes under the two systems is extremely difficult. It would seem that many more full-blown impact assessments are performed in the US than in Canada, even when taking into account the larger size of the US. US federal agencies perform approximately 424 formal environmental-impact statements each year.[44] Since 1973, Canada has completed a total of 35 panel reviews under the auspices of the Federal Environmental Assessment Review Office (FEARO).[45] Many more initial environmental assessments are performed by individual agencies in Canada, but these are typically not nearly as elaborate and formal as NEPA statements. While the impact on policy decisions of these different systems is uncertain, the American impact assessment requirements thus far certainly have been more rigorous, and appear to have generated more assessment activity.

CONCLUSION

These four areas of environmental policy reveal a complex pattern. There are no major differences in the two nations' legal authority to regulate the behaviour causing environmental problems, despite fundamental differences in regulatory style. Certainly there are important differences in regulatory frameworks, with the Canadian system being both more decentralized and discretionary. In many cases, Canadian regulators are simply granted regulatory authority, whereas American statutes specify the rules themselves, or explicitly require regulators to take particular actions. For example, Canadian auto emission standards are established by the Minister of Transport under a broad grant of authority by the Motor Vehicle Safety Act, while in the US the standards are actually written into the legislation by Congress in the Clean Air Act.

When analysing what the two nations do with that authority — the policy outcomes — the picture becomes far more complex. In the air pollution case, there has been recent convergence in auto emission standards and acid rain programs, but Canada has been marginally more successful at reducing emissions and improving air quality. In the area of water pollution, the US record appears to be substantially stronger. In the case of pesticides, the US has been slightly stronger on front-end regulation, and Canada stronger in the regulation of food residues. On environmental impact assessment, American requirements historically have been more rigorous.

Given these differences, it is hard to describe the overall pattern as one of convergence, although there are some striking examples of that phenomenon. It would be more accurate to conclude that there is an *absence of patterned divergence*. In some cases, the US has gone further, in others Canada has. Based on these four areas, on balance, the two countries' environmental records seem to be roughly comparable. Of course, there are a number of additional areas of environmental policy that need to be compared before a more confident assessment can be made. It is possible that after a more comprehensive analysis, one country's record may emerge as more favourable.

The task of this analysis was to compare records, not explain the observed patterns. But it is useful to mention briefly several of the most important explanatory forces because they do have implications for the overall assessment. First, because of Canada's lower population density and smaller number of important sources of pollution, in some respects its regulatory task is easier. For example, Canada has had more success in reducing air pollution despite the fact that its regulatory requirements have not been more stringent, and, in fact, historically have been far less stringent in the notable case of automobile emissions. Canadian regulators attribute this difference to the fact that it has been much easier for them to target the small number of large, poorly controlled sources, and even to provide them with financial assistance if necessary.[46] This difference in the severity of the environmental problem is perhaps the major reason why US industry spends far more on pollution control than Canadian industry, but has not been comparatively more successful in reducing pollution. In economic terms, the marginal costs of achieving a given level of environmental quality are apparently significantly higher in the US than in Canada.

Second, one of the most important forces behind Canadian environmental regulation is in fact the influence of American environmental regulation. Despite the fears of environmental critics of the Free Trade Agreement, US influence on Canadian environmental regulation has on notable occasions been very positive. For instance, the US-dominated North American automobile market has encouraged Canada to adopt the more stringent US emission standards, producing one of the most notable cases of convergence between the two nations. Another prominent example is the pesticide alar, used as a growth regulator on apples but found to cause cancer in laboratory animals. The product was removed from the Canadian market, against the wishes of Canadian regulators, largely because of the regulatory scandal that erupted in the US in early 1989.[47]

While there are many more explanatory factors at work, these two factors strengthen the American record. Some of Canada's notable successes result from the fact that it confronts a comparatively easier regulatory problem. If Canada committed the same level of economic resources as its neighbour to the south, its environment would be much cleaner. Moreover, some of the cases of convergence are also examples of American leadership and influence on Canadian policy. Thus, the Canadian environmental record is strong in some cases *because* the American record is strong.

One final fact should be mentioned. While the two factors noted above create a more favourable image of the American record, Canada has been forced to suffer environmental harm from pollution generated in the United States far more so than vice versa, with acid rain and Great Lakes water pollution being the most prominent cases. This is unquestionably a major flaw in the US record. However deserving of criticism, US culpability in Canadian environmental damage should not make Canadians complacent about their own contributions to the degradation of the shared environment. In particular, the US appears to have been more aggressive in addressing Great Lakes water pollution.

How does Canada's environmental performance compare with the US? Certainly, Canadians have nothing to be ashamed of; this comparison suggests that the Canadian environmental record compares favourably with the American record in some areas. But the analysis also reveals areas where the US performance exceeds Canada's. The pervasive Canadian perception of environmental superiority towards the US is clearly unjustified. Even when compared to the benchmark of US policy, there is a still a great deal of room for improvement in Canada's environmental performance. Canada must redouble its efforts if it intends to become 'the industrial world's most environmentally friendly country' by the turn of the century.

FOR FURTHER READING

Terry Fenge and L. Graham Smith, 'Reforming the Environmental Assessment and Review Process', *Canadian Public Policy* 12 (1986): 596-605.

George Hoberg, 'Reaganism, Pluralism and the Politics of Pesticide Regulation', *Policy Sciences* 23 (1990): 257-89.

————, 'Risk, Science, and Politics: Alachlor Regulation in Canada and the United States', *Canadian Journal of Political Science* 23 (June 1990): 257-78.

————, 'Sleeping with an Elephant: The American Influence on Canadian Environmental Protection', *Journal of Public Policy* 10, 1 (1991): 107-32.

Thomas Ilgen, 'Between Europe and America, Ottawa and the Provinces: Regulating Toxic Substances in Canada', *Canadian Public Policy* 11 (1985): 578-90.

R. Shep Melnick, *Regulation and the Courts: The Case of the Clean Air Act* (Washington, DC: Brookings, 1983).

Peter Nemetz, 'Federal Environmental Regulation in Canada', *Natural Resources Journal* 26 (1986): 552-608.

Norman Vig and Michael Kraft, eds, *Environmental Policy in the 1990s* (Washington, DC: CQ Press, 1990).

David Vogel, *National Styles of Regulation* (Ithaca: Cornell University Press, 1986).

Contributors

HERMAN BAKVIS is a Professor of Political Science and Public Administration at Dalhousie University. He has written extensively on postmaterialist politics, federalism, and public policy. His most recent publication is *Regional Ministers: Power and Influence in the Canadian Cabinet* (Toronto: University of Toronto Press, 1991).

ROBERT BOARDMAN is Chair of the Department of Political Science, and a Professor of Resource and Environmental Studies, at Dalhousie University. His publications include *Global Regimes and Nation-States: Environmental Issues in Australian Politics* (Ottawa: Carleton University Press, 1990).

M. PAUL BROWN is Associate Professor in the School of Public Administration at Dalhousie University. His most recent research has concentrated on administrative decentralization for environmental quality protection, and on the environmental industry. He has had an Executive Interchange with Environment Canada and consulting assignments on opportunities for the environmental industry in Atlantic Canada.

GEOFFREY CASTLE recently completed a Master's degree in Environmental Studies at York University. The title of his thesis was 'Canada in International Environmental Politics: The Cases of Acid Rain and Global Warming'. Mr Castle is currently involved in environmental policy research at the University of British Columbia's Sustainable Development Research Institute.

RAY CÔTÉ is Associate Director of the School of Resource and Environmental Studies and Co-Director of the Marine Affairs Program at Dalhousie University. His research interests are in environmental policy formulation, management of toxic substances, and marine environment assessment and protection. He has been an advisor to federal and provincial governments on environmental matters including pesticide control and harbour clean-up. He formerly worked with Environment Canada for 15 years in a number of management positions on a wide range of environmental issues. Mr Côté has a BSc in biology and chemistry and an MSc in environmental biology.

LINDA F. DUNCAN is Assistant Professor of Law at Dalhousie University, and Legal Advisor to the Indonesian Ministry of Population and Environment. She was formerly chief of enforcement and compliance, Environment Canada, and both founder and Executive Director of the

Environmental Law Centre. She is also currently a member of the Canadian Environmental Advisory Council.

GREGOR FILYK has bachelor degrees in Business Administration from the University of Manitoba, and in Environmental Biology from Macdonald College of McGill University. He has recently completed a Master of Environmental Studies degree at Dalhousie University. His interests lie in the application of environmental policy in the public and private sectors, particularly in ecological conservation. Mr Filyk is currently employed as a project administrator with Wildlife Habitat Canada in Ottawa.

FREDERICK J. FLETCHER is Professor of Political Science and Environmental Studies at York University. He recently served as Research Coordinator, Media and Elections, Royal Commission on Electoral Reform and Party Financing, and he is author or co-author of numerous publications on the media and politics, including *The Newspaper and Public Affairs*.

GEORGE HOBERG is an Assistant Professor of Political Science at the University of British Columbia. He is author of *Pluralism by Design: Environmental Policy and the American Regulatory State* and a number of scholarly articles. He is currently writing a book comparing Canadian and American environmental policy.

PAUL KOPAS is a doctoral student in Political Science at the University of Toronto. He completed BA and MA degrees at the University of British Columbia. His PhD dissertation is on the bureaucracy and environmental policy.

VAUGHAN LYON is a Professor of Political Science at Trent University, Peterborough, Ontario. His major interest is the development of democratic politics and the role of various institutions in this. His published research is on parties and political participation.

DON MUNTON is in the Department of Political Science at the University of British Columbia and is a research associate at the UBC Sustainable Development Research Institute. He has published articles on Canada-US environmental politics and foreign policy, especially dealing with Great Lakes water pollution and acid rain, and is currently completing a book on the politics of acid rain. He taught previously at Dalhousie University and was in 1981–85 the Director of Research at the Canadian Institute of International Affairs.

NEIL NEVITTE is a Professor of Political Science and Director, Research Unit for Public Policy Studies, at the University of Calgary. His publications include *New Elites in Old States: Ideologies in the Anglo-American Democracies*, with Roger Gibbins (Toronto: Oxford University Press, 1990).

TED SCHRECKER is now completing a doctorate in political theory at the University of Western Ontario. He has more than twelve years' experience as a legislative researcher, consultant, and university teacher in the environmental policy field.

GRACE SKOGSTAD is a Professor of Political Science at the University of Toronto. Her research interests focus on the interplay of federalism, organized interests, and public policy. She is the author of *The Politics of Agricultural Policy-Making in Canada*, and co-editor of *Policy Communities and Public Policy in Canada* and *Agricultural Trade: Domestic Politics and International Tensions*.

LORI STAHLBRAND has worked for most of the past decade as a reporter and current affairs host for CBC radio in locations across Canada. She is currently working towards a master's degree in Environmental Studies at York University.

DAVID VANDERZWAAG is Associate Professor of Law at Dalhousie University, and formerly Co-Director of the Marine Affairs Program. He has published extensively in the fields of environmental law and the law of the sea.

JEREMY WILSON is an Associate Professor of Political Science at the University of Victoria, where he has taught since 1975. He is engaged in ongoing research on wilderness and forest policy in British Columbia.

Abbreviations and Acronyms

ACOA	Atlantic Canada Opportunities Agency
BAT	best available technology
BRCG	Bilateral Research Consultation Group
CCE	Cabinet Committee on Environment
CCF	Co-operative Commonwealth Federation
CCME	Canadian Council of Ministers of the Environment
CCREM	Canadian Council of Resource and Environment Ministers
CEAA	Canadian Environmental Assessment Act
CEAC	Canadian Environmental Advisory Council
CEARC	Canadian Environmental Assessment Research Council
CEIA	Canadian Environmental Industries Association
CEN	Canadian Environmental Network
CEPA	Canadian Environmental Protection Act
CFCs	chloro-fluorocarbons
CITES	Convention on International Trade in Endangered Species
CNF	Canadian Nature Federation
CSCE	Conference on Security and Co-operation in Europe
CSM	control, sampling, and monitoring
CWF	Canadian Wildlife Federation
DFO	Department of Fisheries and Oceans
DRI	Data Resources Incorporated
DRIE	Department of Regional Industrial Expansion
EAB	Environmental Assessment Board (Ontario)
EAITC	External Affairs and International Trade Canada
EARP	Environmental Assessment and Review Process
EC	European Community / Environment Canada
ECC	Economic Council of Canada
ECE	Economic Commission for Europe (UN)
EIA	environmental impact assessment
EIS	environmental impact statement
EISI	Environmental Industries Sector Initiative
EPA	Environmental Protection Agency (US)
EPS	Environmental Protection Service
ERDAs	Economic and Regional Development Agreements

FAO	Food and Agriculture Organization (UN)
FEARO	Federal Environmental Assessment Review Office (Can.)
FEDC	Federal Economic Development Council
FIFRA	Federal Insecticide, Fungicide, and Rodenticide Act (US)
FIRA	Foreign Investment Review Agency (Can.)
FOE	Friends of the Earth
FPAC	Federal-Provincial Advisory Committee
FWPCA	Federal Water Pollution Control Act (US)
IGBP	International Geosphere and Biosphere Program
IJC	International Joint Commission (Great Lakes)
IOS	International Organization for Standardization
IPCC	Intergovernmental Panel on Climate Change
IRPP	Institute for Research on Public Policy
ISTC	Industry, Science, and Technology Canada
IUCN	International Union for the Conservation of Nature
JCC	Joint Co-operation Committee (Can./EC)
LRCC	Law Reform Commission of Canada
MAB	Man and the Biosphere Program (UNESCO)
MPM	materialist-postmaterialist index
MSERD	Ministry of State for Economic and Regional Development
MSSD	Ministry of State for Social Development
MSST	Ministry of State for Science and Technology
NAAQS	National Ambient Air Quality Standards (US)
NAPAP	National Acid Precipitation Assessment Program (US)
NDP	New Democratic Party
NEP	National Energy Policy (Can.)
NEPA	National Environmental Protection Act (US)
NGO	non-governmental organization
NIRB	Nunavut Impact Review Board
NTA	nitrilotriacetic acid
OECD	Organization for Economic Co-operation and Development
OMB	Office of Management and Budget (US)
OMNR	Ontario Ministry of Natural Resources
OWMC	Ontario Waste Management Corporation
PCBs	polychlorinated biphenyls
PCO	Privy Council Office
PCPA	Pest Control Products Act (Can.)
PEMS	policy and expenditure management system

PMO	Prime Minister's Office
POGG	peace, order, and good government
P&P	Priorities and Planning
PR	Proportional Representation
PSD	prevention of significant deterioration (US)
R&D	Research and Development
SCC	Science Council of Canada
TFN	Tungavik Federation of Nunavut
UNCHE	United Nations Conference on the Human Environment
UNEP	United Nations Environment Program
UNESCO	United Nations Educational, Scientific, and Cultural Organization
VOC	volatile organic compound
WCED	World Commission on Environment and Development (Brundtland Commission)
WCWC	Western Canada Wilderness Committee
WHC	World Heritage Committee
WHO	World Health Organization (UN)
WMO	World Meteorological Organization
WWF	World Wildlife Fund

Notes

BOARDMAN

[1]Jim MacNeill, 'The Greening of International Relations', *International Journal* 45, 1 (1989–90): 1-35.

[2]OECD, *Environmental Policies for Cities in the 1990s* (Paris: OECD, 1990).

[3]Cf. *Constitution of the Canadian Greens*, Article 5.

[4]Don Munton, 'Changing Conceptions of Security: Public Attitudes in Canada', *The 1990 CIIPS Public Opinion Survey* (Ottawa: Canadian Institute for International Peace and Security, 1990), 8.

[5]See for example David Braybrooke, 'Limits to Risk', *Transaction. Social Science and Modern Society* 28, 3 (March-April 1991): 23-7.

[6]Robert Paehlke, *Environmentalism and the Future of Progressive Politics* (New Haven: Yale University Press, 1989), 144-5.

[7]Ibid., 3.

[8]Daniel H. Henning and William R. Mangun, *Managing the Environmental Crisis: Incorporating Competing Values in Natural Resource Administration* (Duke University Press, 1989), 2.

[9]Linda Starke, *Signs of Hope: Working Towards Our Common Future* (Oxford: Oxford University Press, 1990), 28.

[10]Cf. John Robinson, et al., 'Defining a Sustainable Society: Values, Principles and Definition', *Alternatives* 17, 2 (1990): 36-47.

[11]Wendy Holm, ed., *Water and Free Trade: The Mulroney Government's Agenda for Canada's Most Precious Resource* (Toronto: James Lorimer, 1988), xii.

[12]Ed Struzik, 'The Last Buffalo Slaughter', *The Canadian Forum* (November 1990): 6-11.

[13]Moira Jackson, 'Industry and the Environment: More than a Matter of Perception', *CRS Perspectives* 31 (November 1989): n.p.

[14]Ted Schrecker, 'Resisting Environmental Regulation: The Cryptic Pattern of Government-Business Relations', in Robert Paehlke and Douglas Torgerson, eds, *Managing Leviathan: Environmental Politics and the Administrative State* (Peterborough: Broadview Press, 1990), 169, 185.

[15]G. Bruce Doern, 'Getting It Green: Canadian Environmental Policy in the 1990s', in G. Bruce Doern, ed., *The Environmental Imperative: Market Approaches to the Greening of Canada* (Toronto: C.D. Howe Institute, 1990), 5.

[16]Thomas H. Birch, 'The Incarceration of Wildness: Wilderness Areas as Prisons', *Environmental Ethics* 12, 1 (Spring 1990): 3-26.

[17]Koula Mellos, 'The Conception of 'Reason' in Modern Ecological Theory', *Canadian Journal of Political Science* 21, 4 (December 1988): 716.

[18]P.R. Hay and H.G. Haward, 'Comparative Green Politics: Beyond the European Context?', *Political Studies* 36 (1988): 437. See further Ferdinand Muller-Rommel, ed., *New Politics in Western Europe: The Rise and Success of Green Parties and Alternative Lists* (Boulder: Westview, 1989).

[19]Thomas O. Hueglin, 'The Politics of Fragmentation in an Age of Scarcity: A Synthetic View of Welfare State Crisis', *Canadian Journal of Political Science* 20, 2 (June 1987): 237.

[20]William F. Sinclair, 'Controlling Effluent Discharges from Canadian Pulp and Paper Manufacturers', *Canadian Public Policy* 17, 1 (March 1991): 86-105.

[21]See for example Gwyn Prins, 'Politics and the Environment', *International Affairs* 66, 4

(1990): 711-30; and David P. Newsom, 'The New Diplomatic Agenda: Are Governments Ready?', *International Affairs* 65, 1 (1989): 29.

²²Steven A. Kennett, 'Federalism and Sustainable Development: The Institutional Challenge in Canadian Water Resource Management', *Alternatives* 17, 3 (1990): 32-9.

²³Kathryn Harrison and George Hoberg, 'Setting the Environmental Agenda in Canada and the United States: The Cases of Dioxin and Radon', *Canadian Journal of Political Science* 14, 1 (March 1991): 24.

²⁴O.R. Young, *Resource Regimes: Natural Resources and Social Institutions* (Berkeley: University of California Press, 1982), vii.

VANDERZWAAG AND DUNCAN

*The authors would like to acknowledge the research assistance of Andrea Smillie, Dalhousie Law School, Class of 1991.

¹R.S.C. 1985, c. 16 (4th Supp.), *as amended by* S.C. 1989, c. 9.

²R.D. Lindgren, 'Toxic Substances in Canada: The Regulatory Role of the Federal Government', in D. Tingley, ed., *Into the Future: Environmental Law and Policy for the 1990's* (Edmonton, Alberta: Environmental Law Centre, 1990) 37, at p. 38.

³Government of Canada, *Canada's Green Plan* (Ottawa: Minister of Supply and Services Canada, 1990) xii.

⁴Linda F. Duncan, Submission to the Parliamentary Committee on Bill C-78, December 1990, p. 1.

⁵For a review of roundtable activities, see G. Gallon, 'Sustainable Development: the Brundtland Commission and Round Tables in Canada' (Toronto: Environmental Economics International, February 1991). Recent important task force reports include: 1) the Final Report of the Public Review Panel on Tanker Safety and Marine Spills Response Capability, which made 107 recommendations including the proposal that Canada should require all tankers entering its waters to be double-hulled within ten years; and 2) the Final Report of the Pesticide Registration Review Team, which recommended among other things the creation of a new Pest Management Regulatory Agency responsible for registering pesticides in Canada instead of the present process where the Minister of Agriculture determines acceptability for registration purposes. Public Review Panel on Tanker Safety and Marine Spills Capability, *Protecting Our Waters* (Ottawa: Minister of Supply and Services, 1990) and Pesticide Registration Review Team, *Recommendations for a Revised Federal Pest Management Regulatory System: Final Report* (Ottawa: Communications Branch, Agriculture Canada, 1990).

⁶SOR/84-467.

⁷R.S.C. 1985, c. F-14.

⁸1982, c. 11 (UK), R.S.C. 1985, Appendices, No. 44, Schedule B.

⁹For a listing of various US states having environmental or natural resource rights in the constitution, see note 'Constitutional Law and the Environment: *Save Ourselves Inc. vs Louisiana Environmental Control Commission*' (1985), 59 *Tulane Law Review* 1557, at 1559, n. 8.

¹⁰30 & 31 Victoria, c. 3 (U.K.), R.S.C. 1985, Appendices, No. 5.

¹¹R.S.C. 1985, c. F-14.

¹²R.S.C. 1985, c. N-22.

¹³R.S.C. 1985, c. A-12.

¹⁴R.S.C. 1985, c. N-25.

¹⁵R.S.C. 1985, c. M-7.

¹⁶R.S.C. 1985, c. I-20.

[17]For a summary of provincial management regimes, see Michael I. Jeffery, *Environmental Approvals in Canada Practice and Procedure* (Toronto: Butterworths, 1989), ch. 1.

[18]A Law Reform of Canada report lists the British Columbia Waste Management Act as an example of a trend towards legislative consolidation. The Act requires anyone wishing to introduce a waste (air contaminants, litter, effluent, and refuse) into the environment to obtain a permit. K. Webb, *Pollution Control in Canada: The Regulatory Approach in the 1980's* (Ottawa: Law Reform Commission of Canada, 1988). Alberta has proposed new legislation, the Alberta Environmental Protection and Enhancement Act, which would integrate approval processes recognizing the interdependence of air, water, and land and would increase public participation. Alberta Environment, *A Guide to the Proposed Alberta Environmental Protection and Enhancement Legislation* (1990).

[19]A.R. Lucas, 'National Resource and Environmental Management: A Jurisdictional Primer', in D. Tingley, ed., *Environmental Protection and the Canadian Constitution* (Alberta: Environmental Law Center, 1987) 31, at 33.

[20]Ibid., at 34.

[21]Ibid., at 35.

[22]See (1990) 20, No. 5 *Environmental Policy and Law*, 161-2.

[23]Government of Canada, *supra*, note 3, p. 61.

[24]Ibid., p. 41.

[25]*A.G. Canada vs A.G. Ontario* [1937] A.C., 326 (P.C.).

[26]J.S. Fiegel, 'Treaty Making and Implementing Powers in Canada: The Continuing Dilemma', in B. Cheng and E.D. Brown, eds, *Contemporary Problems of International Law: Essays in Honour of George Schwarzenberger on his Eightieth Birthday* (London: Stevens & Sons Ltd, 1988) 333, at p. 338.

[27][1977] 2 S.C.R. 134, 7 n.r. 477.

[28]Ibid., at 171, 7 N.R. at 511-12.

[29]J.S. Fiegel, *supra*, note 26, at 339.

[30](1969), 8 I.L.M. 679, Art. 27.

[31]See *Environmental Protection Amendment Act, 1989*. S.O. 1989, c. 30, and *Ozone Depleting Substances — General Regulation*, O. Reg. 394/89.

[32](1987) 17 *Environmental Policy and Law*, 256-7.

[33]1929 S.C.R. 200, [1929] 2 D.L.R. 481.

[34]Justice Duff indicated the great breadth of federal power in these words:

We must, as best we can, reconcile the control by the provinces of their own assets . . . with the exercise by the Dominion of its exclusive powers. . . . This can only be accomplished by recognizing that the proprietary rights of the provinces may be prejudicially affected, even to the point of rendering them economically valueless, through the exercise by the Dominion of its exclusive and plenary powers of legislation . . . (1929 S.C.R. at 219, [1929] 2 D.L.R. at 489-90).

[35][1980] 2 S.C.R. 292, 32 N.R. 541.

[36][1980] 2 S.C.R. at 301, 32 N.R. at 550.

[37](1980), 2 N.R. 230.

[38]Ibid., at 241.

[39]Ibid., at 243.

[40][1984] 2 W.W.R. 699 (B.C.C.A.).

[41]A.R. Lucas, *supra*, note 19, at 37.

[42](1988) 1 S.C.R. 401.

[43]S.C. 1974–75-76, c. 55, s. 4(1).

[44]A.R. Lucas, *R. vs Crown Zellerbach Canada Ltd* (1989) 23 U.B.C.L. Review, 355, at 356.

[45]*Supra*, note 42, at 431-2.

[46]Ibid., at 436.

[47]The Court indicated that in 'determining whether a matter has attained the required

degree of singleness, distinctiveness and indivisibility that clearly distinguishes it from matters of provincial concern it is relevant to consider what would be the effect on extra-provincial interests of a provincial failure and to deal effectively with the control or regulation of the intra-provincial aspects of the matter.' Ibid., at 432.

[48]Ibid.

[49]L.A. Willis, 'The *Crown Zellerbach* Case, on Marine Pollution: National and International Dimensions' (1988), 26 *Can. Yearbook of International Law*, 235, at 244.

[50]R.S.C. 1985, c. E-10.

[51]R.S.C. 1985, c. 16 (4th Supp.), s. 15.

[52]Ibid., s. 12. The initial Priority Substances List named 44 substances for assessment including effluents from pump mills using bleaching and chlorinated wastewater effluents. *Canada Gazette*, Part I (11 February 1989), 543-5.

[53]R.S.C. 1985, c. 16 (4th Supp.), s. 33.

[54]Ibid., s. 34.

[55]Ibid., s. 113(p). That is for an indictable offence. Upon summary conviction a person would be subject up to a $300,000 fine or imprisonment up to six months, or both. Ibid., s. 113(o).

[56]*Canada Gazette*, Part I (11 February 1989), 543.

[57]*Supra*, note 53, s. 14.

[58]Ibid., s. 96.

[59]SOR/90-582.

[60]*Supra*, note 53, 5.34(1). It should be noted that the province must have in place similar provisions granting citizen rights to compel the investigation of an offence.

[61]Ibid., s. 34(5)(6).

[62]See A. Lucas, 'Jurisdictional Disputes: Is "Equivalency" a Workable Solution', in D. Tingley (ed.), *supra*, note 2.

[63]*Supra*, note 53, 98. As of 10 April 1990, no federal-provincial agreements on administration had yet been signed. Draft agreements with Nova Scotia and New Brunswick were in preparation. (Personal communication with Ms Beverly Hobby, Legal Counsel, Federal Environmental Assessment Review Office.)

[64]*Supra*, note 53, s. 61.

[65]Ibid., s. 63(3). The Minister of the Environment and the government of a province would have to agree in writing.

[66]Proposal was defined as 'any initiative, undertaking or activity for which the Government of Canada has a decision-making responsibility'. SOR/84-467, s. 2.

[67]Ibid., s. 6.

[68]Initiating department was defined as 'any department, that is, on behalf of the Government of Canada, the decision-making authority for a proposal'. Ibid., s. 2.

[69]Ibid., s. 3.

[70]Ibid., s. 13.

[71]Ibid., s. 12(c).

[72]Section 33 provided that the initiating department, in co-operation with any other department, agency, or board of the Government of Canada to whom the Panel recommendations are directed, would have to decide the extent to which recommendations should become requirements.

[73]SOR/84-467, s. 5.

[74]Other projects, of course, have also displayed great controversy and uncertainty in environmental decision-making processes. For example, Hydro-Québec's proposed $12.6 billion Great Whale hydroelectric project has involved months of public feuding between Energy Minister Lise Bacon, responsible for Hydro-Québec, and Environment Minister Pierre Paradis, over the adequacy of environmental impact studies. See 'Great Whale May be Killed by Delays, Supporters Say', *Globe and Mail* 12 April 1991: B3. The federal

Minister of the Environment, Mr Robert de Cotret, was accused of being the Monty Hall of the environment by playing 'Let's Make a Deal' with Quebec in negotiating a joint panel review with two separate mandates, one to review the infrastructure and one to review the project. Statements of Ms Ethel Blondin (Western Arctic), *House of Commons Debate* (21 November 1990), 15520.

[75]For a detailed chronological listing of events surrounding the Rafferty-Alameda project, see *Environmental Digest* 1, 17 (29 October 1990): 3. The federal government's assessment role was described by Ray Robinson, Executive Chairman of the Federal Environmental Assessment Review Office, as relying upon 'an assessment undertaken by the United States government for impact on North Dakota' and doing 'some work in Manitoba in terms of attempting to get a sense of the impact likely in Manitoba'. Minutes of Proceedings and Evidence of the Standing Committee on Environment, 2nd sess., 34th Parl. 1989, Issue No. 1, at 32.

[76]*Canadian Wildlife Federation vs Canada (Minister of the Environment)* (1989), 4 C.E.L.R. 1 (F.C.A.) aff'g (1989), 3 C.E.L.R. 287 (F.C.T.D.).

[77](1989), 3 C.E.L.R. 287, at 292.

[78]Ibid., at 304.

[79]*Canadian Wildlife Federation vs Canada (Minister of the Environment)* (1989), 4 C.E.L.R. 201 (F.C.T.D.).

[80]'The Rafferty-Alameda Fiasco', *The Financial Post* 5 Feb. 1990: 13.

[81]*Canadian Water Watch* 77 (October-November, 1990). A new panel was subsequently appointed.

[82]*Agreement between the Government of Canada and the Government of the United States of America for Water Supply and Flood Control in the Souris River Basin*, Articles IV and II.

[83]'Rafferty-Alameda Project Criticized by Rawson Academy', *Eco-Log Week* 19, 10 (15 March 1991): 5.

[84]For a synopsis of the provincial reviews, see *Friends of the Oldman River Society vs Canada (Minister of Transport)* (1990), 5 C.E.L.R. 1, at 6-8 (F.C.A.), reversing (1989), 4 C.E.L.R. 137 (F.C.T.D.).

[85]The Minister of Transport had issued approval pursuant to the Navigable Waters Protection Act, and the Minister of Fisheries and Oceans, responsible for protecting fish habitats under Section 35(1) of the Fisheries Act, did not invoke his authorization or study powers.

[86]*Minutes of Proceedings and Evidence of the Standing Committee on Environment* 2nd sess., 34th Parl., 1989, Issue No. 1, at 1:35.

[87]*Supra*, note 84.

[88]*Supra*, note 81, at 75. 'Manitoba Government Intervenes in Oldman River Case', *Eco-Log Week* 19,7 (22 February 1991): 4. The case was heard in February 1991.

[89]See 'Missing the Point at Aconi', *The Chronicle-Herald* (Halifax) 22 Sept. 1990: A6 and L. Corbett, 'The Point Aconi Struggle', *Probe Post* 8 (Spring, 1990), at 10.

[90]Nova Scotia Environment Control Council, *Report and Recommendations to the Minister Regarding the Environmental Assessment Report for the Proposed Point Aconi Electrical Generating Station* (23 February 1990), at 49.

[91]'Point Aconi: Environment Loses to Politics (Again)', *The Sunday Daily News* (Halifax) 18 March 1990: 15.

[92]*Cantwell vs Canada (Minister of the Environment)*, Ct. No. T-2975-90 (F.C.T.D.) (18 January 1991), 6-9.

[93]*Minutes of Proceedings and Evidence of the Standing Committee on Environment*, 2nd sess., 34th Parl., 1989–90, Issue No. 60 (1 November 1990), pp. 60:9 and 60:33.

[94]*Nova Scotia House of Assembly Debates* (13 March 1990), p. 764-5.

[95]*Supra*, note 92, at 32. The case was subsequently appealed and the decision upheld.

[96]Bill C-78, 2nd sess., 34th Parl., 1989–90.

[97]Such enforcement powers, however, are only granted for certain projects, for example, a project likely to cause serious adverse environmental effects in another province or a project likely to cause serious adverse environmental effects on federal lands or to Indian lands.

[98]*Supra*, note 96, s. 20.

[99]For a comprehensive critique of the proposed Bill, see Environmental Assessment Caucus, *Reforming Federal Environmental Assessment: Submission of the Environmental Assessment Caucus on the Canadian Environment Assessment Act, Bill C-78* (November, 1990).

[100]Section 55(2) allows the Governor in Council to set out in regulations a list of projects or classes or projects exempt from an environmental assessment, where in the opinion of Cabinet an assessment would be inappropriate.

[101]*Supra*, note 96, s. 55 (1)(b)(d).

[102]Project is defined as ' a physical work that a proponent proposes to construct, operate, modify, decommission, abandon or otherwise carry out or a physical activity that a proponent proposes to undertake or otherwise carry out'. Ibid., s. 2(1).

[103]When the Minister of the Environment tabled the Act in the House of Commons on 18 June 1990, the Minister unveiled a non-legislated related package of reforms including a government commitment to assess all new proposals requiring Cabinet decisions and a participant funding program. The failure of the Act to include a legislated guarantee of Cabinet policy review has been noted by various critics. See, e.g., statement by Mrs Marlene Cutterall (Ottawa West), *House of Commons Debates* (26 June 1990), 13138.

[104]The Canadian Bar Association, at its mid-winter meeting on 26 February 1991, passed a resolution calling for an independent review agency with actual authority to grant or deny approval of initiatives. *West Coast Environmental Law Research Foundation Newsletter*, 5, 6 (14 March 1991): 2.

[105]S.C. 1991, c. 1, s. 10.

[106]See, e.g., Department of Fisheries and Oceans, Pacific Region, *Habitat Prosecution Procedures* (November, 1986); *Regional Working Agreement between Environment Canada (EC) and the Department of Fisheries and Oceans (DFO) for Administration of Section 33 of the Fisheries Act in New Brunswick, Nova Scotia, Prince Edward Island and Newfoundland* (January, 1988); the Alberta Law Foundation, *Enforcement of the Federal Fisheries Act* (September 1984); and L.B. Heustis, *Policing Pollution: The Prosecution of Environmental Offenses* (1984).

[107]Copy attained by the authors through the office of Jim Fulton, MP Skeena, House of Commons. The leaked memo was described in 'Pollution Law "Immunity" Claimed', *Vancouver Sun* (1 December 1989): A1.

[108]'Boat Harbour Guidelines Released', *The Chronicle-Herald* (Halifax) 12 April 1991: A20.

[109]J. Swaigen and G. Bunt, *Sentencing in Environmental Cases* (Ottawa: Law Reform Commission of Canada, 1985), p. 50.

[110]1982, c. 11 (U.K.), R.S.C. 1985, Appendices, No. 44, Schedule B.

[111]M. Jackman, 'Rights and Participation: The Use of the Charter to Supervise the Regulatory Process' (1990) 4, *Cdn. J. of Admin. L. & Practice*, 23.

[112]C.P. Stevenson, 'A New Perspective on Environmental Rights After the Charter' (1983), 21, Osgoode Hall, L.J. 390.

[113](1989) 68 O.R., 2d, 449, 37 Admin. L.R.1., 58 D.L.R., 4th, 513, leave to appeal to S.C.C., refused (1989), 102 N.R. 399 (note) (S.C.C.).

[114]R.S.C. 1985, c. N-28.

[115]Section 15(1) provides: 'Every individual is equal before and under the law and has the right to the equal protection and equal benefit of the law without discrimination . . .'.

[116]The actual success of the section 15 arguments is highly speculative given the Supreme Court of Canada's trend towards restricting discrimination for section 15 purposes to disadvantaged groups in Canadian society. See *R. vs Turpin*, [1989] 1 S.C.R. 1296.

[117]A.R. Lucas, *supra*, note 19, at 40.

[118]*Operation Dismantle vs The Queen* (1985), 59 N.R. 1 (1985), 18 D.L.R. 4th, 481 (S.C.C.).

[119]A.R. Lucas, *supra*, note 19, at 40.

[120]*Waste Not Wanted Inc. vs R.* (1987), 2 C.E.L.R. (N.S.) 24.

[121]*Dywidag Systems International Canada Ltd vs Zutphen Bros Construction Ltd.* (1990), 97 N.S.R., 2d, 181 (S.C.C.).

[122]For cases upholding governmental search and seizures, subject to section 8 Charter challenge, in the environmental and resource conservation fields, see *Regina vs Burton* (1983), 1 D.L.R., 4th, 152 (Nfld C.A.), Re Eagle Disposal Systems and Minister of the Environment (1983), 44 O.R., 2d, 518 (Ont. H.C.) and *R. vs Betram S. Miller Ltd* (1986), 1 C.E.L.R. 16 (F.C.A.). Environmental offenses that combine absolute liability with imprisonment provisions may also be struck down. A.R. Lucas, *supra*, note 19, at 41. For a recent case finding that a Court order requiring a corporation to publicly apologize for depositing oil in fisheries waters contrary to section 36(3) of the federal Fisheries Act may violate the principles of fundamental justice in section 7 of the Charter, see *R. vs N.W.T. Power (1990)*, 5 C.E.L.R. (N.S.) 67.

[123]For the potential scope of aboriginal water rights, see R.H. Bartlett, *Aboriginal Water Rights in Canada: A Study of Aboriginal Title to Water and Indian Water Rights* (Calgary: Canadian Institute of Resources Law, 1988).

[124]Section 35(2) further defines aboriginal peoples of Canada to include the Indian, Inuit, and Métis peoples of Canada.

[125][1990] 1 S.C.R. 1075.

[126]Ibid., at 1110.

[127]Ibid., at 112.

[128]Ibid., at 1113.

[129]Ibid., at 1114-17.

[130]Ibid., at 1119.

[131]The Court indicated the government's minimal objection in these rather ambiguous words: 'The aboriginal peoples, with their history of conservation-consciousness and interdependence with natural resources, would surely be expected, at the least to be informed regarding the determination of an appropriate scheme for the regulation of the fisheries.' Ibid.

[132]For a case involving Indian treaty rights to fish and manage fisheries along the Pacific Northwest Coast of the United States and judicially sanctioned tribal self-regulation in some circumstances, see *United States vs Washington*, 384 F. Supp. 312 (W.D. Wash. 1974).

[133]Editeur officiel du Québec, *The James Bay and Northern Quebec Agreement* (1976). Federal legislative approval of the agreement may be found in James Bay and Northern Quebec Native Claims Settlement Act, S.C. 1976–77, c. 32.

[134]For brief reviews of the Agreement, see Samuel V. Stevens, 'Indian Rights to Environmental Protection: A Constitutional Basis', in D. Tingley, *supra*, note 19, at 46-47 and R.H. Bartlett, *supra*, note 123, at 220-2.

[135]The regimes are set out in sections 22 and 23 of the Agreement, respectively.

[136]*The James Bay and Northern Quebec Agreement*, *supra*, note 67, s. 8.1.3.

[137]Department of Indian Affairs and Northern Development, *Inuvialuit Settlement Agreement* (1984).

[138]For a further discussion of the Agreement see M. Valencia and D. VanderZwaag, 'Maritime Claims and Management Rights of Indigenous People: Rising Tides in the Pacific and Northern Waters', (1989) 12 Ocean & Shoreline Management, 125 at 138-40 and R.H. Bartlett, *supra*, note 123 at 222-4.

[139]Indian and Northern Affairs Canada, *Agreement-in-Principle Between the Inuit of the Nunavut Settlement Area and Her Majesty in Right of Canada* (1990).

[140]Ibid., art. 12, ss. 12.2.1 - 12.2.2. If NIRB rejects a project proposal, the federal or territorial Minister having jurisdictional responsibility for authorizing a project to proceed may override the determination because of a project's importance in the national or regional interest. Ibid., s. 12.5.7.(d).

[141]Environmental Impact Review Board, *Public Review of the Gulf Canada Resources Limited Kulluk Drilling Program 1990–1992* (1990).

[142]Ibid., at 16. Gulf's inability to provide a liability estimate was based on refusal to make assumptions on three variables: area of impact, shoreline response, and standards for clean-up. Ibid., at 20.

[143]Canadian Petroleum Association, 'Back to Basics', *Arctic Petroleum Review* 13 (Winter 1990): 6.

[144]See *supra*, note 19, at 57-98 for a detailed discussion on federal-provincial co-operative measures including mirror legislation, environmental accords, and delegation of administration.

[145]*Agreement Between the Government of Canada and the Government of Nova Scotia Relating to Oil and Gas Resource Management and Revenue Sharing* (2 March 1982), subsequently replaced by the *Canada - Nova Scotia Offshore Petroleum Resources Accord* (26 August 1986).

[146]*The Atlantic Accord: Memorandum of Agreement Between the Government of Canada and the Government of Newfoundland and Labrador on Offshore Oil and Gas Resource Management and Revenue Sharing* (11 February 1985).

[147]For a discussion of the agreements, see Leo Barry, 'Offshore Petroleum Agreements: An Analysis of the Nova Scotian and Newfoundland Experience', in J.O. Saunders, ed., *Managing Natural Resources in a Federal State* (Calgary: Carswell, 1986) at 177.

[148]*Supra*, note 3 at 133.

[149]For a critique of the traditional regulatory offence approach, see K. Webb, 'On the Periphery: The Limited Role for Criminal Offenses in Environmental Protection', in D. Tingley, *supra*, note 2, at 58.

[150]*Supra*, note 3, at 53.

[151]See, e.g., '$6-8 Million, Five–Year Cleanup Set for N.B. Sites', *The Chronicle-Herald* (Halifax) 11 April 1991: A13.

[152]*Supra*, note 3, at 120.

[153]*Cooperation Agreement on Sustainable Economic Development Between the Government of Canada and the Government of the Province of Nova Scotia* (18 March 1991).

[154]See M.I. Jeffery, 'Ontario's Intervenor Funding Project Act' (1990), 3 C.J.A.L.P. 69 and J. Keeping, 'Intervenors' Costs' (1990), 3 C.J.A.L.P. 81.

[155]Environmental Rights Act, S.N.W.T. 1990, c. 38.

[156]Ibid., s. 3.

[157]Ibid., s. 4.

[158]Ibid., s. 5.

[159]Ibid., s. 6. Compensation for damage to property would be recoverable by the plaintiff himself or herself.

[160]Ibid., s. 7.

[161]Environment Ontario, *Environment Information* (December, 1990). Various model bills had already been debated over the last 10 years. See, e.g., An Act Respecting Environmental Rights in Ontario, Bill 12, 2nd sess., 34th leg., Ontario (1989).

BROWN

[1]John Dryzek, 'Don't Toss Coins in Garbage Cans: A Prologue to Policy Design', *Journal of Public Policy* 3 (1983): 354.

[2]See Peter Aucoin, 'Portfolio Structures and Policy Coordination', in G. Bruce Doern and Peter Aucoin, eds, *Public Policy in Canada* (Toronto: Macmillan of Canada, 1979), 213-38, and Donald J. Savoie, *The Politics of Public Spending in Canada* (Toronto: University of Toronto Press, 1990), 64.

[3]See Donald J. Savoie, 'ACOA: Something Old, Something New, Something Borrowed, Something Blue', in Katherine Graham, ed., *How Ottawa Spends 1989–1990, The Buck Stops Where* (Ottawa: Carleton University Press, 1989), 107-30.

[4]Fritz W. Scharpf, 'Policy failure and institutional reform: why should form follow function?' *International Social Science Journal* 38, 108 (1986): 180.

[5]See Hubert L. Laframboise, 'Here come the program-benders!' *Optimum* 7, 1 (1976): 40-7.

[6]Paul Sabatier and Daniel Mazmanian, 'The Implementation of Public Policy: A Framework of Analysis', *Policy Studies Journal* 8 (1980): 542.

[7]The departmental title has varied over the years. The latest designation, Environment Canada, will be use throughout for sake of clarity.

[8]See O. P. Dwivedi, 'The Canadian Government Response to Environmental Concern', in O. P. Dwivedi, ed., *Protecting the Environment:Issues and Choices – Canadian Perspectives* (Toronto: Copp Clark, 1974), 175-7.

[9]Canada. *Environmental Quality Strategic Review: A Follow-On Report of the Task Force on Program Review* (Ottawa: Ministry of Supply and Services, 1986), Annex A, 'Acts of the Department of the Environment (Extracts)', 135.

[10]Laframboise, 41.

[11]Environmental Quality Strategic Review, 38–9.

[12]Ross H. Hall, 'Why We Need an Alternative to Environment Canada', *Probe Post* (Spring, 1986): 26-9.

[13]R. Brian Woodrow, 'Resources and Environmental Policy-Making at the National Level: The Search for Focus', in O.P. Dwivedi, ed., *Resources and the Environment: Policy Perspectives for Canada*, 42.

[14]"Pollution problem serious, 72% agree', *The Toronto Star* 19 June 1989: A1, A11.

[15]Anthony Downs, 'Up and Down with Ecology – The "Issue-Attention Cycle" ', *The Public Interest* 28 (1972): 38-50.

[16]André Raynauld, 'Protection of the Environment: Economic Perspectives', in O. P. Dwivedi, ed., *Protecting the Environment*, 77.

[17]Woodrow, 'Resources and Environmental Policy-Making', 43.

[18]Webb, 50. See also Allan Schnailberg, 'The Retreat from Political to Technical Environmentalism', in Augustine Brannigan and Sheldon Goldenberg, eds, *Social Responses to Technological Change* (Westport, Conn.: Greenwood Press, 1985), 22-6.

[19]The use of this argument has been called 'job blackmail'. See, for example, Richard Kazis and Richard L. Grossman, *Fear At Work: Job Blackmail, Labor and the Environment* (New York: The Pilgrim Press, 1982) and Ted Schrecker, 'Resisting Environmental Regulation: The Cryptic Pattern of Business-Government Relations', in Robert Paehlke and Douglas Torgerson, eds, *Managing Leviathan: Environmental Politics and the Administrative State* (Toronto: Broadview Press, 1990), 168-71.

[20]Woodrow, 'Resources and Environmental Policy-Making', 25. It is instructive, for example, that while all Throne Speeches between 1967 and 1970 referred to the environment, a listing by Doern and Phidd of major themes in throne and budget speeches for selective years from 1970 to 1982 contained no allusions to environmental quality concerns at all. See G. Bruce Doern and Richard W. Phidd, *Canadian Public Policy: Ideas, Structure, Process* (Toronto: Methuen Publications, 1983), 237-43.

[21]David Bercuson, et al., *Sacred Trust? Brian Mulroney and the Conservative Party in Power* (Toronto: Doubleday Canada Limited, 1986), 47.

[22]Scharpf, 181.

[23]*Environmental Quality Strategic Review*, 4, 29.

[24]Dale Gibson, 'The Environment and the Constitution: New Wine in Old Bottles', in O.P. Dwivedi, ed., *Protecting the Environment*, 106.

[25]Even the Nielsen Task Force, for example, was at pains to stress that any amendments to strengthen Environment Canada's legislative base be 'crafted so as to minimize unfounded provincial suspicions that the federal government is attempting to arrogate more power to itself', *Environmental Quality Strategic Review*: 17.

[26]Sabatier and Mazmanian: 546.

[27]M. Paul Brown, 'Environment Canada and the pursuit of administrative decentralization', *Canadian Public Administration* 29, 2 (1986): 222.

[28]Laframboise, 44.

[29]Stephen Hazell, 'An Environmental Auditor', *Policy Options*, 9,3 (1988): 9.

[30]See *Environmental Quality Strategic Review*, Annex C, 157-70.

[31]Kernaghan Webb, *Pollution Control in Canada: The Regulatory Approach in the 1980s* (Ottawa: Law Reform Commission of Canada, 1988), 25.

[32]*Environmental Quality Strategic Review*, 25.

[33]Ibid., 26.

[34]For an excellent discussion of PEMS, see Donald J. Savoie, *The Politics of Public Spending in Canada* (Toronto: University of Toronto Press, 1990), 60-70.

[35]The Nielsen Task Force commented, for example, that because Environment Canada's funding 'usually [came] from the social development reserve in competition with other social initiatives. . .its argumentation [had] therefore [to] be socially oriented', *Environmental Quality Strategic Review*, 76.

[36]Doern and Phidd, 272.

[37]Ibid., 285.

[38]In consultation with officials.

[39]'Pollution problem serious, 72% agree', *The Toronto Star* 18 June 1989: A1, A11.

[40]Herman Bakvis and Neil Nevitte, 'The Greening of the Canadian Electorate: Environmentalism, Ideology and Partisanship', a paper presented to the Annual Meeting of the Canadian Political Science Association, University of Victoria, Victoria, British Columbia, 28 May 1990: 2.

[41]Bakvis and Nevitte report, for example, that in the 1988 election survey, 64.5% of respondents mainly agreed with the statement 'Protecting the environment is more important than creating jobs', 3.

[42]Ted Schrecker, 'Resisting Environmental Regulation: The Cryptic Pattern of Business-Government Relations', 165.

[43]See Bakvis and Nevitte, 3-4.

[44]For a useful discussion on these themes see Schrecker, 'Resisting Environmental Regulation', 174-9.

[45]Gro Harlem Brundtland et al., *Our Common Future* (Oxford: Oxford University Press, 1987), 46.

[46]Canadian Council of Resource and Environment Ministers, *Report of the National Task Force on Environment and Economy* (Downsview, Ont.: CCREM, 1987), 1.

[47]Ibid., 6.

[48]So declared David Buzzelli, Chairman and President Dow Chemical Canada Inc., and the Minister of Environment Canada, respectively, ibid., 3.

[49]Alistair Crerar, 'Brundtland Bettered: A Review', *Policy Options* 8, 9 (1987): 28.

[50]Schrecker, 185.

[51]*Environmental Quality Strategic Review*, 120.

[52]Environment Canada. Canadian Environmental Protection Act, 'Enforcement and Compliance Policy', 1988, 13-14.

[53]See Wayne Bond and Peter LeBlanc, 'Incorporating Sustainable Development into Eco-

nomic and Regional Development Agreements: Atlantic Region Example', a case study for the National Round Table Symposium on Decision-Making Practices for Sustainable Development, October, 1990, 4.

[54]*Environmental Quality Strategic Review*, 71.

[55]Bond and LeBlanc, 5. This process was greatly assisted by the enthusiasm of the most senior FEDC, Jaffrey Wilkins in Nova Scotia, for environment-economy linkages and the strong working ties which developed between him and senior Environment Canada officials in the region.

[56]Bond and LeBlanc, 13.

[57]Government of Canada. *Canada's Green Plan for a Healthy Environment* (Ottawa: Ministry of Supply and Services, 1990), 159, 161.

[58]For a useful summary of these arguments, see G. Bruce Doern, 'Getting It Green: Canadian Environmental Policy in the 1990s', in G. Bruce Doern, ed., *The Environmental Imperative: Market Approaches to the Greening of Canada* (Toronto: C.D. Howe Institute, 1990), 15-16.

[59]Canadian Press Release, 'Environment Estimates', 4 April 1989: 2.

[60]Canada. Federal Environmental Assessment Review Office. 'Fact Sheets: Federal Environmental Assessment Reform,' June 1990, 1.

[61]'Major Cabinet Shakeup', *Ottawa Letter* 19, 6 (6 February 1989): 40. The incumbent, Tom McMillan, had been defeated in the November, 1988, election.

[62]'Deputy under fire on "action plan": controversy swamps Environment Ministry's stalled strategy', *Financial Post Daily* 3 (27 February 1990): 15.

[63]*Report of the National Task Force on Environment and Economy*, 8.

[64]Office of the Prime Minister. 'Background Paper on the New Cabinet Decision-making System', 30 January 1989: 2.

[65]Office of the Prime Minister. 'New Cabinet: Press Highlights', 30 January 1989: 1.

[66]The others were (1) Economic Policy, (2) Cultural Affairs and National Identity, and (3) Human Resources, Income Support, and Health.

[67]'Background Paper on the New Cabinet Decision-Making System', 1.

[68]'New Cabinet: Press Highlights', 2.

[69]*Canada's Green Plan for a Healthy Environment*, 9.

[70]For a good description of the work of MSSD and MSERD, see Peter Aucoin and Herman Bakvis, 'Regional Responsiveness and Government Organization: The Case of Regional Economic Development Policy in Canada', in Peter Aucoin, ed., *Regional Responsiveness and the National Administrative State* (Toronto: University of Toronto Press, 1985) 64-82.

[71]'Deputy under fire on "action plan" ', 15.

[72]Bakvis and Nevitte, 2.

[73]On attempts to secure an industrial development strategy, see Douglas Brown and Julia Eastman, *The Limits of Consultation: A Debate among Ottawa, the Provinces, and the Private Sector on an Industrial Strategy* (Ottawa: Science Council of Canada, 1981) and Richard French, *How Ottawa Decides: planning and industrial policy making, 1968–1984* (Toronto: Lorimer, 1984).

SKOGSTAD AND KOPAS

[1]Alastair R. Lucas, 'The New Environmental Law', in Ronald L. Watts and Douglas M. Brown, eds, *Canada: The State of the Federation 1989* (Kingston: Institute of Intergovernmental Relations, Queen's University, 1989) 168, 170.

[2]Andrew R. Thompson, *Environmental Regulation in Canada* (Vancouver: Westwater Research Centre, 1980), 24.

[3]Kenneth McRoberts, 'Unilateralism, Bilateralism and Multilateralism: Approaches to

Canadian Federalism', in Richard Simeon, *Intergovernmental Relations*, Research Report Vol. 63 (Toronto: University of Toronto Press, 1985), 111.

[4]O.P. Dwivedi, 'The Canadian Government Response to Environmental Concerns', in O.P. Dwivedi, ed., *Protecting the Environment* (Toronto: Copp Clark, 1974), 186.

[5]Peter Nemetz, 'Fisheries Act and Federal-Provincial Environmental Regulation: Duplication or Complementarity?', *Canadian Public Administration* 29 (Fall, 1986): 401-24; L.J. Lundqvist, 'Do Political Structures Matter in Environmental Politics? The Case of Air Pollution Control in Canada, Sweden, and the United States', *Canadian Public Administration* 17 (Spring, 1974): 119-42.

[6]Alastair R. Lucas, 'Harmonization of Federal and Provincial Environmental Policies: The Changing Legal and Policy Framework', in J. Owen Saunders, ed., *Managing Natural Resources in a Federal State* (Agincourt: Carswell, 1986), 35.

[7]A primary reason for the relative lack of influence of provincial governments was that the provinces did not speak with one voice. British Columbia refused to participate on the ground that the federal regulations infringed on provincial jurisdiction; Quebec was willing to go along with the regulations once old mills were exempt and after Ottawa agreed the provinces could administer them; and Ontario wanted stronger federal regulations to bring them up to the provincial standard and thereby avoid the possibility of industry feeling an obligation to satisfy only the less stringent federal requirements. See James W. Parlour, 'The Politics of Water Pollution Control: A Case Study of the Canadian Fisheries Act Amendments and the Pulp and Paper Effluent Regulations, 1970', *Journal of Environmental Management* 13 (1981): 143.

[8]Lucas, 'Harmonization of Federal and Provincial Environmental Policies', 40.

[9]G. Bruce Doern, 'Regulations and Incentives: The NO_x-VOCs Case', in G. Bruce Doern, ed., *Getting It Green: Case Studies in Canadian Environmental Regulation* (Toronto: C.D. Howe Institute, 1990), 101; William D. Coleman, *Business and Politics: A Study of Collective Action* (Kingston and Montreal: McGill-Queen's University Press, 1988), 212.

[10]Norman C. Bonsor, 'Water Pollution and the Canadian Pulp and Paper Industry', in G. Bruce Doern, ed., *Getting It Green*, 156.

[11]James W. Parlour, 'The Politics of Water Pollution Control', 141. This conclusion is also based on information gleaned in interviews of federal officials by Paul Kopas.

[12]One attempt between 1974 and 1977, and another in 1982, to strengthen the Regulations on technical and legal grounds failed. The pulp and paper industry, having put substantial effort into the first round only to have it fail owing to intragovernmental limitations, was unwilling to co-operate with a second revisionist effort.

[13]Lorne Giroux, 'Delegation of Administration', in Donna Tingley, ed., *Environmental Protection and the Canadian Constitution* (Edmonton: Environmental Law Centre, 1987) 84-92.

[14]Lucas, 'Harmonization of Federal and Provincial Environmental Policies', 48.

[15]G. Bruce Doern, 'The Federal Green Plan: Assessing the "Prequel"', *Commentary* (Toronto: C.D. Howe Institute) 17 June 1990, 4, lists a number of other consultative vehicles.

[16]Wyn P. Grant, 'Forestry and Forest Products', in William D. Coleman and Grace Skogstad, eds, *Policy Communities and Public Policy in Canada* (Toronto: Copp Clark Pitman, 1990), details the role of the Canadian Council of Forest Ministers and the National Forest Sector Strategy, 121-36.

[17]Lucas, 'Harmonization of Federal and Provincial Environmental Policies,' 34-5. He further states that a Canada Environment Act that would regulate toxics on a national scale in the early 1980s was scuttled by unease about its constitutional appropriateness.

[18]Lundqvist, 'Do Political Structures Matter. . .?'

[19]Robert Gibson explains Ontario's slowness in ordering abatement action on acid rain as the consequence of polluting companies being able to negotiate abatement requirements

with government officials. Ontario government officials in the 1970s and early 1980s believed that stringent abatement requirements would be unfair to Ontario polluters, whose competitors elsewhere were not subject to these requirements. The Ontario companies, as a result, would likely threaten economically and politically undesirable cutbacks or closures. See Robert B. Gibson, 'Out of Control and Beyond Understanding: Acid Rain as a Political Dilemma', in Robert Paehlke and Douglas Torgerson, eds, *Managing Leviathan: Environmental Politics and the Administrative State* (Peterborough: Broadview Press, 1990), 250.

[20]Tom Conway, 'Taking Stock of the Traditional Regulatory Approach', in Doern, *Getting It Green*, 36.

[21]Giroux, 'Delegation of Administration', 89, 85.

[22]Nemetz, 'Fisheries Act and Federal-Provincial Environmental Regulation'.

[23]Lundqvist, 'Do Political Structures Matter . . .?' 134 ff.

[24]See *Soil at Risk*, A Report on Soil Conservation by the Standing Committee on Agriculture, Fisheries, and Forestry to the Senate of Canada (Ottawa: Senate of Canada, 1984), 21-3; G.C. Van Kooten, 'A Socio-Economic Model of Agriculture: A Proposal for Dealing with Environmental Problems in a Rural Economy', *Prairie Forum* 12 (1987): 160, cites the mechanization and specialization of farming as responsible, with the former having been fuelled by government policies stressing 'production and ever-higher yields . . . instead of conservation and stewardship'.

[25]These other factors are DOE's 'inability to establish and carry out rigorous compliance procedures', 'an overtaxed and declining scientific and investigative capacity', and 'a lack of economic and legal literacy'. See Tom Conway, 'Taking Stock of the Traditional Regulatory Approach', in Doern, *Getting It Green*, 34–5.

[26]G. Bruce Doern, 'The Federal Green Plan: Assessing the "Prequel" ', *Commentary* (Toronto: C.D. Howe Institute), 17 June 1990; G. Bruce Doern, ed., *The Environmental Imperative: Market Approaches to the Greening of Canada* (Toronto: C.D. Howe Institute, 1990), 11-12.

[27]*Regina vs Crown Zellerbach Canada Ltd, et al. (1988)*, 3, *Canadian Environmental Law Reports*, (N.S.) 1(S.C.C.) at 49, 52, and 47, respectively.

[28]Peter H. Russell notes that the political effects of judicial rulings are often more important than the legal results. See 'The Supreme Court and Federal-Provincial Relations: The Political Use of Legal Resources', *Canadian Public Policy* 2, 2 (1985): 161-70.

[29]Robert Paehlke and Douglas Torgerson, 'Environmental Problems and the Administrative State: The Case of Toxic Waste Management', in O.P. Dwivedi and R. Brian Woodrow, eds, *Public Policy and Administrative Studies*, Vol. 2 (Guelph: University of Guelph, 1985), 118, notes provinces have taken key responsibility for the disposal of toxic wastes, while Environment Canada has concentrated on research and regulating their inter-provincial transport.

[30]Lucas, 'The New Environmental Law', 176, 182-3 states that the use of POGG to justify federal jurisdiction over the environment has left the provinces apprehensive. The court drew on international agreements and studies to conclude that marine pollution was a matter of national interest. Lucas suggests that this opens up the possibility for Canadian international activities and obligations to justify a federal authority for a host of particular environmental subjects. 'Large chunks of the broad "environment" subject now appear to be fair game for federal legislators.'

[31]Tamsin Carlisle, 'Bouchard's moves arouse provincial ire', *Financial Post*, 17 February 1990. In its response to the draft CEPA, the province of Saskatchewan expressed its concern that the act would 'inadvertently cede to the federal government' provincial rights over the control and use of provincial resources. 'How the province develops its resources is its own business.'

[32]Alberta proceeded with construction of the Oldman River Dam, as did Saskatchewan with

the Alameda and Rafferty dams. In late 1990, Saskatchewan mounted a politically heated challenge to the right of an EARP panel to stop a provincial resource development. Regarding the Alpac project in Alberta, the Getty government optimistically struck its own panel to deliver another verdict on the environmental effects of the proposed kraft mill; its report warned of the adverse environmental effects. And Nova Scotia declared its intent to ignore the report of any future EARP review of its proposed Point Aconi coal-fired electricity generating plant.

[33]See 'Quebec calls hearings on James Bay II', *Montreal Gazette* 5 April 1990: A5; Louis-Gilles Francoeur, 'Baie James: Québec va de l'avant sans le fédéral', *Le Devoir* 5 avril 1990: 1.

[34]The concept and virtues of competitive federalism are outlined by Albert Breton, 'The Theory of Competitive Federalism', in Garth Stevenson, ed., *Federalism in Canada: Selected Readings* (Toronto: McClelland and Stewart, 1989), 457-502.

[35]Alberta released a draft Alberta Environmental Protection and Enhancement Act in June 1990 which introduces comprehensive environmental impact assessment legislation for the first time in Alberta. It was accompanied by Bill 52, the Natural Resources Conservation Board Act, which allows for a board to review the environmental impact of projects affecting the natural resources of Alberta. Details of the legislation are given in *Newsletter*, Environmental Law Centre, Edmonton, 5, 3 (1990). The opening of a new waste disposal and treatment facility in Swan Hills, Alberta, in 1987 was preceded by a process of wide consultation with the Alberta public. See Barry G. Rabe, 'Hazardous Waste Facility Siting: Subnational Policy in Canada and the United States', unpublished paper, 1989.

Kernaghan Webb notes that the Manitoba Environment Act, promulgated in 1987, contains specific legislation to inform and involve the public in the drafting of regulations, approval of licences, and ensuring of enforcement. See Kernaghan Webb, 'Between Rocks and Hard Places: Bureaucrats, Law and Pollution Control', in Robert Paehlke and Douglas Torgerson, eds, *Managing Leviathan* (Peterborough: Broadview Press, 1990), 219.

Robert Paehlke and Douglas Torgerson observe that the Ontario Waste Management Corporation has recently altered its policy regarding public participation; it is now 'not only to be allowed, but promoted . . . in each critical stage'. See Robert Paehlke and Douglas Torgerson, 'Toxic Waste and the Administrative State: NIMBY Syndrome or Participatory Management?', in Paehlke and Torgerson, op.cit., 274.

[36]CCME, *Statement on Interjurisdictional Co-operation on Environmental Matters*, n.d., 3.

[37]Unlike the Cabinet Guidelines, which require that projects that might affect an area of federal jurisdiction must be reviewed, the new legislation gives the federal government the discretion to determine which federal projects require EARPs. Regulations, rather than the Canadian Environmental Assessment Act, will dictate which federal statutes and federal projects are affected by the CEAA.

[38]Albert Breton, 'The Theory of Competitive Federalism', pp. 465-6. The limitations of co-operative federalism are well delineated by Donald Smiley in 'An Outsider's Observations of Federal-Provincial Relations Among Consenting Adults', in Richard Simeon, ed., *Confrontation and Collaboration: Intergovernmental Relations in Canada Today* (Toronto: The Institute for Public Administration, 1979), 105-13.

[39]Such jockeying has been very visible throughout the controversy over whether construction of the Oldman River Dam should proceed prior to the recommendation of a federal EARP. It is worth noting that the Government of Canada did not respond to dam opponents' request that Ottawa force a stoppage of work on the dam and/or lay charges in connection with its construction. By contrast, opponents of the Rafferty-Alameda dams in southern Saskatchewan were somewhat more successful in obtaining the public support of the federal Minister of the Environment.

'Opponents of Diversion Seek Review', *Winnipeg Free Press* 29 March 1990: 2, reports a group of environmentalists, cattle producers, and grain farmers requesting Ottawa to conduct a full environmental review to stop a water diversion project. The groups are reported to have said they would drop their request if the Manitoba Clean Environment Committee, which had not yet had a say, recommended that a licence not be issued for the project.

[40]As quoted in Jeb Blount, 'A blurred blueprint for the environment', *Financial Times of Canada* 25 June 1990.

[41]Doern states that officials and ministers in line departments; Finance; Industry, Science and Technology; and the Privy Council Office blocked attempts to require environmental considerations to be incorporated into all government policies and decisions, both in terms of CEAA and the 1990 Green Plan. See G.Bruce Doern, 'The Federal Green Plan: Assessing the "Prequel" ', 6.

[42]For example, new legislation in Alberta in 1990 to provide environmental impact reviews of major projects fell under the Energy Minister's portfolio. See Vickie McGrath, 'Klein loses lead role in legislation', *Calgary Sun* 16 May 1990: 2.

[43]The amendments were also intended to clarify the technical specifications for traditional pollutants; cover the previously excluded polluting dioxins, furans, and related chemicals; and regulate all pulp and paper mills, including older mills previously excluded.

[44]A concertation relationship is one in which industry and government make policy in isolation from the influence of other relevant publics. Jeremy Wilson uses the term 'contested concertation' to describe the assault on this closed policy process as environmental groups have gained expertise and demand a right to have their (differing) views and goals incorporated into government policy. See Jeremy Wilson, 'Wilderness Politics in BC: The Business Dominated State and the Containment of Environmentalism', in Coleman and Skogstad, 141-69.

[45]Bonsor, 'Water Pollution and the Canadian Pulp and Paper Industry', 185.

[46]Kenneth McRoberts, 'Unilateralism, Bilateralism and Multilateralism', 120.

FILYK AND CÔTÉ

*This chapter is based largely on thesis research by Gregor Filyk: 'The Influence of Advisory Groups on Environmental Policy in Canada', Master of Environmental Studies thesis, Dalhousie University, 1991.

[1]A. Paul Pross, *Group Politics and Public Policy* (Toronto: Oxford University Press, 1986), ch. 5.

[2]Ibid. See also the discussion of advisory bodies in Robert J. Jackson, Doreen Jackson, and Nicolas Baxter-Moore, *Politics in Canada: Culture, Institutions, Behaviour and Public Policy* (Scarborough: Prentice-Hall, 1986), 373-6.

[3]For more detailed references, see Filyk, 'The Influence of Advisory Groups'. The main sources are Mort Grant, 'The Technology of Advisory Committees', *Public Policy* 10 (1960): 92-108; David S. Brown, 'The Public Advisory Board as an Instrument of Government', *Public Administration Review* 15 (1955): 196-204; David S. Brown, 'The Management of Advisory Committees: An Assignment for the '70s', *Public Administration Review* 32 (1972): 334-42; Thomas E. Cronin and Norman C. Thomas, 'Educational Policy Advisers and the Great Society', *Public Policy* 18 (1970): 659-86; Norman N. Gill, 'Permanent Advisory Committees in the Federal Government', *Journal of Politics* 2 (1940): 411-25; Thomas B. Smith, 'Advisory Committees in the Public Policy Process', *International Review of Administrative Sciences* 43, 2 1977: 153-66; Michael Whittington, 'Environmental Policy', in G. Bruce Doern and V.S. Wilson, eds, *Issues in Canadian*

Public Policy (Toronto: Macmillan of Canada, 1974): 203-27; George T. Sulzner, 'The Policy Process and the Uses of National Governmental Study Commissions', *Western Political Quarterly* 24 (1971): 438-48.

[4]Guy P.F. Steed, 'Alerting Canadians: The Scope and Use of Policy Research in the Science Council of Canada', *Technology in Society* 10 (1988): 165-83.

[5]Cassia Spohn, 'The Role of Advisory Boards in the Policy Process: An Analysis of the Attitudes of HEW Board Members', *American Review of Public Administration* 16, 2/3 (1983): 185-94; Cronin and Thomas, 'Educational Policy Advisors'; Philip L. Gianos, 'Scientists as Policy Advisors: The Context of Influence', *Western Political Quarterly* 27 (1974): 429-56.

[6]Steed, 'Alerting Canadians'.

SCHRECKER

[1]M. Jeffery, *Environmental Approvals in Canada: Practice and Procedure* (Toronto: Butterworths, 1989), 5.5 (para. 5.13). Jeffery served until recently as chairman of Ontario's Environmental Assessment Board.

[2]Statutes of this kind are not strictly a contemporary phenomenon. 'The statute books of New Brunswick and the United Province of Canada are littered with statutory attempts to deal with the problem of [lumber] mill waste in the waters of those jurisdictions' in the nineteenth century. J. McLaren, 'Closing Remarks', in L. Duncan, ed., *Environmental Enforcement: Proceedings of the National Conference on the Enforcement of Environmental Law* (Edmonton: Environmental Law Centre, 1985), 156-7.

[3]For more detailed discussions see P. Elder, 'Environmental Protection through the Common Law', *University of Western Ontario Law Review* 12 (1973): 113-42; J. McLaren, 'The Common Law Nuisance Actions and the Environmental Battle — Well-Tempered Swords or Broken Reeds?', *Osgoode Hall Law Journal* 10 (1972): 505-61; D. Estrin and J. Swaigen, *Environment on Trial* (Toronto: Macmillan, 1978), 399-413.

[4]M. Horwitz, *The Transformation of American Law, 1780-1860* (Cambridge, Mass.: Harvard University Press, 1977), 71.

[5]H. Hovenkamp, 'The Economics of Legal History', *Minnesota Law Review* 67 (1983): 670-90; H. Scheiber, 'Regulation, Property Rights and the Definition of "The Market": Law and the American Economy', *Journal of Economic History* 41 (1981): 103-11; G. Schwartz, 'Tort Law and the Economy in Nineteenth-Century America: A Reinterpretation', *Yale Law Journal* 90 (1981): 1717-75; A. Simpson, 'The Horwitz Thesis and the History of Contracts', *University of Chicago Law Review* 46 (1979): 533-601.

[6]J. Nedelsky, 'Judicial Conservatism in an Age of Innovation: Comparative Perspectives on Canadian Nuisance Law 1880-1930', in D. Flaherty, ed., *Essays in the History of Canadian Law* vol. 1 (Toronto: University of Toronto Press, 1981), 308; see generally 295-312.

[7]*Black vs Canadian Copper Co.* (1917), 12 *Ontario Weekly Notes* 243, at 244 (emphasis added).

[8]Nedelsky, 'Judicial Conservatism', 308; McLaren, 'The Common Law Nuisance Actions', 556-8.

[9]McLaren, 'The Common Law Nuisance Actions', 547-60.

[10]Nedelsky, 'Judicial Conservatism', 303.

[11]*McKie et al. vs The K.V.P. Co. Ltd* (1948), 3 *Dominion Law Reports* 201; aff'd (1949) *Supreme Court Reports* 698.

[12]G. Morley, 'The Legal Framework for Public Participation in Canadian Water Management', in P. Elder, ed., *Environmental Management and Public Participation* (Toronto: Canadian Environmental Law Research Foundation, 1975), 47-8; see also A. Bryant, 'An Analysis of the Ontario Water Resources Act' in Elder, ed., *Environmental Manage-*

ment, 165. Interestingly, the Premier of the day accepted a directorship of K.V.P. following his retirement from politics.

[13]Bryant, ibid. This seems less clearly part of a Horwitzian pattern than the K.V.P. case, until one acknowledges the crucial role of municipalities' ability to provide serviced land in stimulating industrial and commercial development.

[14]J. Nedelsky, 'From Common Law to Commission: The Development of Water Law in Nova Scotia', in *Water and Environmental Law*, Proceedings of a Conference at Dalhousie University, 14-16 September 1979 (Halifax: Institute of Resource and Environmental Studies, Dalhousie University, 1981), 98.

[15]Ibid., 99-108; see generally D. Percy, *The Framework of Water Rights Legislation in Canada* (Calgary: Canadian Institute of Resources Law, 1988).

[16]J. Benidickson, 'Private Rights and Public Purposes in the Lakes, Rivers and Streams of Ontario 1870-1930', in D. Flaherty, ed., *Essays in the History of Canadian Law* vol. 2 (Toronto: University of Toronto Press, 1983), 368-78.

[17]For a considerably more detailed discussion, see A. Roman, 'Locus Standi: A Cure in Search of a Disease?', in J. Swaigen, ed., *Environmental Rights in Canada* (Toronto: Butterworths, 1981), 13-18; Estey, 'Public Nuisance and Standing to Sue', *Osgoode Hall Law Journal* 10 (1972): 563-82; McLaren, 'Common Law Nuisance Actions', 511-16.

[18]McLaren, ibid., 511.

[19]Estey, 'Public Nuisance', 567.

[20]Horwitz, *Transformation*, 76–8.

[21]*Canada Paper vs Brown* (1922), 63 *Supreme Court Reports* 243; discussed in considerable detail by Nedelsky, 'Judicial Conservatism', 295-8.

[22]*Hickey et al. vs Electric Reduction Co. of Canada Ltd* (1971), 21 *Dominion Law Reports* (3rd Series) 368.

[23]See, e.g., Elder, 'Environmental Protection'; P. Elder, 'An Overview of the Participatory Environment in Canada', in Elder, ed., *Environmental Management*, 370-3.

[24]L. Boden et al., 'Science and Persuasion: Environmental Disease in U.S. Courts', *Social Science and Medicine* 27 (1988): 1019–29; T. Brennan and R. Carter, 'Legal and Scientific Probability of Causation of Cancer and Other Environmental Diseases in Individuals', *Journal of Health Politics, Policy and Law* 10 (1985): 33-80; S. Shindell, 'Evidentiary Problems in Pollution-Engendered Torts', *Cato Journal* 2 (1982): 137-55.

[25]L. West, 'Mediated Settlement of Environmental Disputes: Grassy Narrows and White Dog Revisited', *Environmental Law* 18 (1987): 131-50. The history of this episode is related in W. Troyer, *No Safe Place* (Toronto: Clarke, Irwin, 1977) and A. Shkilnyk, *A Poison Stronger than Love: The Destruction of an Ojibway Community* (New Haven: Yale University Press, 1985), 179-230.

[26]M. Jeffery, 'Science and the Tribunal', *Alternatives: Perspectives on Society, Technology and Environment* 15, 2 (April/May 1988): 24-30.

[27]*Palmer et al. vs Nova Scotia Forest Industries* (1983), 60 *Nova Scotia Reports* (2nd Series) 271. For commentary on the case see E. Foley, 'Rising from the Ashes', *Environmental Law Centre Newsletter* 1, 2 (Winter 1984): 1-3 (Edmonton: Environmental Law Centre); also P. Donham, 'Next moves unclear in wake of spraying verdict', *Financial Post* 24 September 1983: 6.

[28]D. Trezise, 'Alternative Approaches to Legal Control of Environmental Quality in Canada', *McGill Law Journal* 21 (1975): 405.

[29]Hon. J. Sauvé, in *Minutes of Proceedings and Evidence*, House of Commons Standing Committee on Fisheries and Forestry, xx Parl., x Sess. (no. 16, 11 April 1975), 6.

[30]For a discussion of the ineffectiveness of the *Environmental Contaminants Act*, see J. Castrilli, 'Control of Toxic Chemicals in Canada: An Analysis of Law and Policy', *Osgoode Hall Law Journal* 20 (1982): 322-401; R. Demayo, 'New Chemicals Notification

and Regulation Under the Environmental Contaminants Act', in *New Chemicals Workshop*, EPS 3-EP–83-4 (Ottawa: Environment Canada, 1983).

[31]*Re Pim and Minister of the Environment et al.* (1978), 9 *Canadian Environmental Law Reports* 54.

[32]S.O. 1976, c. 49 as cited in ibid., 54-6.

[33]D. Henley, 'The Advocacy Approach', in Duncan, ed., *Environmental Enforcement*, 151.

[34]R.S.O. 1980, c. 141, s. 14(1); R.S.C. 1985, c. F-14, ss. 36(3) and 36(4); see also s. 35(1).

[35]P. Emond, 'Environmental Law at the Limits of Incremental Development', in P. Finkle and A. Lucas, eds, *Environmental Law in the 1980s: A New Beginning* (Calgary: Canadian Institute of Resources Law, 1982), 8.

[36]For illustrations see J. Castrilli and C. Lax, 'Environmental Regulation-Making in Canada', in Swaigen, ed., *Environmental Rights*, 338-45; J. Castrilli and T. Vigod, *Pesticides in Canada: An Examination of Federal Law and Policy* (Ottawa: Law Reform Commission of Canada, 1987), 41-117; D. Lees, 'Club Lead', *Toronto Life* (December 1986), 43-45; J. Parlour, 'The Politics of Water Pollution Control', *Journal of Environmental Management* 13 (1970): 127-49; W. Sullivan, 'An Overview of the Background and Development of the Canadian Mercury Chlor-Alkali Emission Regulation', paper presented at Annual Meeting, Air Pollution Control Association (Montreal, 1980).

[37]Castrilli and Lax, 'Environmental Regulation-Making', 345; see generally 345-7.

[38]Ibid., 347-56; R. Gibson, *Control Orders and Industrial Pollution Abatement in Ontario* (Toronto: Canadian Environmental Law Research Foundation, 1983), 9-42.

[39]See generally M. Rankin and P. Finkle, 'The Enforcement of Environmental Law: Taking the Environment Seriously', *University of British Columbia Law Review* 17 (1983): 35-57.

[40]Gibson, *Control Orders*, 65–73; P. Victor and T. Burrell, *Environmental Protection Regulation, Water Pollution and the Pulp and Paper Industry*, Regulation Reference Technical Report no. 14 (Ottawa: Economic Council of Canada, 1981). On the most infamous recent case, involving Kimberly-Clark of Canada Ltd's Terrace Bay plant, see M. Keating, 'Kimberly-Clark told it must cut toxic waste', *The Globe and Mail*, 26 January 1987: A9; K. Noble, 'Pulp mill test of new pollution policy', *The Globe and Mail*, 26 January 1987: B1-B2; S. Oziewicz, '1,600 jobs preserved as Terrace Bay mill gets pollution reprieve', *The Globe and Mail*, 31 January 1987: A4.

[41]R. Kazis and R. Grossman, *Fear at Work: Job Blackmail, Labour and the Environment* (New York: Pilgrim Press, 1982). On this tactic in the Canadian context see T. Schrecker, 'The Political Context and Content of Environmental Law', in T. Caputo et al., eds, *Law and Society: A Critical Perspective* (Toronto: Harcourt Brace Jovanovich, 1989), 180-2. Observations of the inhibiting effects of such economic dependency on public policy are not a new phenomenon. In *Canada Paper vs Brown*, Justice Anglin argued that most people living around the Canada Paper plant were 'so dependent upon the operation of the defendant's mills for their support that they are quite prepared to submit to some personal annoyance rather than jeopardize their means of livelihood. The inaction of the municipal authorities is no doubt ascribable to similar influences'. 63 *Supreme Court Reports* 243, at 256.

[42]A. Thompson, *Environmental Regulation in Canada* (Vancouver: Westwater Research Centre, University of British Columbia, 1981), 33. See also M. Rankin and P. Finkle, 'The Enforcement of Environmental Law: Taking the Environment Seriously', *University of British Columbia Law Review* 17 (1983): 37-43.

[43]L. Giroux, *Enforcement Practices of Environment Canada* (Ottawa: CEAC, 1987), 5-6.

[44]L. Huestis, 'Policing Pollution', [Draft] Working Paper, Protection of Life Project (Ottawa: Law Reform Commission of Canada, mimeo, 1984).

[45]'Inconsistent Application of the Fisheries Act', memorandum from O. Langer, Head, Habitat Management Unit, Fraser River, Northern BC and Yukon Division to F. Fraser, Area Manager, Department of Fisheries and Oceans. My thanks to Jim Fulton, MP, for providing a copy of this material.

[46]Both factors add to the bargaining resources of polluters, since 'a regulatory agency faces the possibility not of a handful of violators that it could reasonably and effectively handle, but of tacit noncompliance by large segments of an industry.' F. Anderson, *Environmental Improvement Through Economic Incentives* (Baltimore: Johns Hopkins University Press for Resources for the Future, 1977), 16.

[47]Rankin and Finkle, 'The Enforcement of Environmental Law', 55.

[48]Huestis, 'Policing Pollution', 100.

[49]Private prosecutions under the Fisheries Act have been successfully undertaken, but the citizen organizations in question were the beneficiaries of official support either informally, by way of the provision of legal advice and technical support, or formally, by way of charges laid by the relevant government agencies following the initiation of private prosecutions; see Huestis, 'Policing Pollution', 65-7. Consequently, these instances do not seriously undermine the assertion that, in general, access to the evidence-gathering capabilities of the state is virtually essential for access to the judicial remedies available, if indirectly, by way of private prosecution.

[50]R. Bourassa, 'Sentencing in Environmental Cases: A View from the Bench', in Duncan, ed., *Environmental Enforcement*, 101; D. Saxe, 'Fines Go Up Dramatically in Environmental Cases', 3 *Canadian Environmental Law Reports* (New Series) 1988, 104; Trezise, 'Alternative Approaches', 407.

[51]Trezise, ibid., 410.

[52]R. Kagan, 'On Regulatory Inspectorates and Police', in K. Hawkins and J. Thomas, eds, *Enforcing Regulation* (Boston: Kluwer-Nijhoff, 1984), 53-4.

[53]Saxe, 'Fines Go Up', 104; the case was *R. vs Cyanamid Canada Inc.* (1981), 11 *Canadian Environmental Law Reports* 31-4. To be precise, rainbow trout placed in aquaria filled with cooled effluent from the plant died within 51 seconds. Fish in aquaria filled with water taken from upstream of the effluent source 'lived for many hours'.

[54]11 *Canadian Environmental Law Reports* (1981), 41.

[55]M. Kansky, 'Private Prosecutions from the Public's Perspective', in Duncan, ed., *Environmental Enforcement*, 108-10.

[56]A. Picard, 'Polluters get off lightly in Quebec, study finds', *The Globe and Mail*, 20 March 1989: A4.

[57]Saxe, 'Fines Go Up', 105, 108-10; see 112-121 for a detailed inventory of such cases, most of which are otherwise unreported.

[58]A systematic national data base on frequency of charging and conviction, or on sentences following conviction, simply does not exist in the environmental field. (Neither, for that matter, does it exist in most other areas of law enforcement.) The problem is compounded by the fact that most environmental cases involve provincial statutes and are 'unreported': that is, data on the disposition of the case are available only by consulting actual court records or local press reports.

[59]Such as *R. vs Suncor Inc.* (1985), Alberta Provincial Court, summarized in *Environmental Law Centre Newsletter* 3 (no. 2, 1985), 3-4 ($15,000 fine on each of two charges under the Fisheries Act); *R. vs FibreCo* (1991), BC Provincial Court, summarized in *West Coast Environmental Research Foundation Newsletter* 15 (no. 3, 21 January 1991): 1 ($5,000 fine per day for each of 40 days during which a violation of BC's Waste Management Act continued); and *R. vs Canadian Marine Drilling Ltd.* (1983), Territorial Court of the Northwest Territories, summarized in *Environmental Law Centre Newsletter* 1 (no. 2, 1984), 4 ($20,000 fine on a charge under the Fisheries Act). The latter case is interesting in that the sentencing judge subsequently explained his rationale in some detail, focusing on the problem of relating fines to the cost savings from non-compliance and arguing that in future judges should use the powers given them by many environmental statutes to order actions necessary to prevent the commission of further such offences. See Bourassa, 'Sentencing in Environmental Cases'.

[60]Ibid., 110-11; L. McCaffrey, 'The Ontario Special Prosecution Team', in Duncan, ed., *Environmental Enforcement*, 80–2.

[61]Saxe, 'Fines Go Up', 106.

[62]Emond, 'Environmental Law at the Limits of Incremental Development'.

[63]Elder, 'Environmental Protection', 163-70.

[64]Roman, 'Locus Standi', 13.

[65]R.S.O. 1980, c. 140. On the implementation of the *Act* during its first decade of existence see R. Gibson and B. Savan, *Environmental Assessment in Ontario* (Toronto: Canadian Environmental Law Research Foundation, 1986); R. Pushchak, 'The Political and Institutional Context of Environmental Impact Assessment in Ontario', in J. Whitney and V. Maclaren, eds, *Environmental Impact Assessment: The Canadian Experience* (Toronto: Institute for Environmental Studies, 1985), 75-88.

[66]Jeffery, *Environmental Approvals*, chapter 2. Since 1981, provincial legislation has provided for hearings by a 'joint board' composed of members of EAB and the Ontario Municipal Board when hearings on a project may be required under both the Environmental Assessment Act and a variety of land-use planning statutes. M. Jeffery, 'Consolidated Hearings: An Interim Report Card', *Advocates' Quarterly* (1986): 286-311.

[67]Jeffery, *Environmental Approvals*, 2.2-2.5 (paras. 2.6-2.17), chapter 3, 5.27–5.34 (paras. 5.59-5.83).

[68]R.S.O. 1980, c. 140, s. 29; the precise wording of the section permits exemption when Cabinet believes 'that the exemption is in the public interest having regard to the purpose of this Act and weighing the same against the injury, damage or interference that may be caused to any person or property by the application of this act to any undertaking'. For discussion see Gibson and Savan, *Environmental Assessment*, 29–48.

[69]See generally Jeffery, *Environmental Approvals*, ch. 3.

[70]Gibson and Savan, *Environmental Assessment*, 222-8.

[71]Hon. J. Bradley (Ontario Minister of the Environment) as quoted by J. Temple, 'Province allows logging in Temagami wilderness', *Toronto Star* 18 May 1988: A1.

[72]Pushchak, 'The Political and Institutional Context', 81-2.

[73]Gibson and Savan, *Environmental Assessment*, 223. The first EAB hearing under the *Environmental Assessment Act* was not held until four years after the passage of the act: Jeffery, *Environmental Approvals*, 2.12 (para. 2.45).

[74]The history of this proposal is illustrative of the expanding role of the Board. OWMC was originally created in 1979 as a response to intense public and opposition party criticism of industrial waste disposal practices in the province, and its activities were exempted by Cabinet from the application of the *Environmental Assessment Act*. In 1985, a newly elected government quickly revoked the exemption.

[75]M. Jeffery, 'Ontario's Intervenor Funding Project Act', *Canadian Journal of Administrative Law and Practice* 3 (1989): 69-80.

[76]This is true not only with respect to the application of the Act, but also with respect to changes in the Board's Cabinet-appointed membership. Jeffery, *Environmental Approvals*, 2.6 (paras. 2.20-2.23). Although 'its early membership had strong ties with former civil servants and elected members of the legislature' (ibid.) it is now chaired by a former staff lawyer with the Canadian Environmental Law Association, a Toronto-based advocacy group.

[77]42 United States Code 4321 *et seq*. The text of NEPA is available in many critical works on the Act, e.g. L. Caldwell, *Science and the National Environmental Policy Act* (Birmingham: University of Alabama Press, 1982), 152-8.

[78]Comment: 'The National Environmental Policy Act: How It is Working, How It Should Work', *Environmental Law Reporter* 4 (1974): 10003; K. Murchison, 'Does NEPA Matter?', *University of Richmond Law Review* 18 (1984): 562-3.

[79]The legislation did establish the President's Council on Environmental Quality (CEQ),

but its role was confined to policy advice and to preparing criteria for the adequacy of environmental impact statements.

[80] J. Handler, *Social Movements and the Legal System* (New York: Academic Press, 1982), 46-8; R. Stewart, 'Regulation, Innovation and Administrative Law', *California Law Review* 69 (1981): 1274-77.

[81] *Calvert Cliffs' Coordinating Committee vs U.S. Atomic Energy Commission* (1971), 449 *Federal Reporter* 2nd series 1109 (D.C. Circuit). The case involved the application of NEPA to the Commission's power reactor licensing requirements, and is discussed at length by F. Anderson, *NEPA in the Courts* (Baltimore: Johns Hopkins University Press, 1973), 247-71 and Murchison, 'Does NEPA Matter?' 563-6.

[82] *Robertson vs Methow Valley Citizens' Council* (1989), 19 *Environmental Law Reporter* 20743, at 20747.

[83] Caldwell, *Science and the National Environmental Policy Act*, 71-2.

[84] The most useful recent studies of the impact of NEPA are: D. Bear, 'NEPA at 19: A Primer on an "Old" Law with Solutions to New Problems', 19 *Environmental Law Reporter* (1989), 10060; Caldwell, *Science and the National Environmental Policy Act*; S. Fairfax and H. Ingram, 'The United States Experience', in T. O'Riordan and W. Sewell, eds, *Project Appraisal and Policy Review* (London: John Wiley, 1984); V. Fogelman, 'Threshold Determinations under the National Environmental Policy Act', *Boston College Environmental Affairs Law Review* 15 (1987): 59-103; R. Liroff, 'NEPA Litigation in the 1970s: A Deluge or a Dribble', *Natural Resources Journal* 21 (1981): 315-30; Murchison, 'Does NEPA Matter?'; S. Taylor, *Making Bureaucracies Think: The Environmental Impact Statement Strategy of Administrative Reform* (Stanford: Stanford University Press, 1984). For an argument that NEPA, at least in the 1970s, 'turned energy, attention and effort away from a redefinition of agency authorities and spent it on proliferating paper', see S. Fairfax, 'A Disaster in the Environmental Movement', *Science* 199 (1978): 743-8, but compare the comment that: 'It is hard to dismiss as ineffectual a statute which the [U.S. Army] Corps of Engineers says caused it to drop 24 projects, temporarily or indefinitely delay 44, and significantly modify 197 more'. Comment, 'The National Environmental Policy Act', 10004.

[85] Task Force on Environmental Impact Policy and Procedure, 'Final Report: An Environmental Impact Policy and Procedure', Final Report (Ottawa, mimeo, 1972) 6-11.

[86] Environmental Assessment and Review Process Guidelines Order (1984), SOR/84-467. For historical background see M. Bowden and F. Curtis, 'Federal EIA in Canada', *Environmental Impact Assessment Review* 8 (1988): 97-106; R. Cotton and P. Emond, 'Environmental Impact Assessment', in Swaigen, ed., *Environmental Rights*, 251-5, 261-3; T. Fenge and G. Smith, 'Reforming the Federal Environmental Assessment and Review Process', *Canadian Public Policy* 12 (1986): 596-605.

[87] P. Emond, *Environmental Assessment Law in Canada* (Toronto: Emond-Montgomery, 1978), 6.

[88] The major criticisms of EARP are outlined in FEARO, 'Improvements to the Federal Environmental Assessment and Review Process', Discussion Paper (Ottawa, mimeo, 1983); Fenge and Smith, 'Reforming'; W. Rees, 'EARP at the Crossroads', *Environmental Impact Assessment Review* 1 (1980): 355ff; W. Rees, 'Environmental Assessment of Hydrocarbon Production from the Canadian Beaufort Sea', *Environmental Impact Assessment Review* 4 (1983): 539-56; W. Rees and P. Boothroyd, 'Background Paper on EARP Reform: Process and Structure' and 'Background Paper on EARP Reform: Activities' (both Ottawa: Rawson Academy of Aquatic Science, 1987).

[89] Task Force on Environmental Impact Policy and Procedure, 'Final Report', 17 (emphasis added).

[90] *Canadian Wildlife Federation Inc. vs Canada (Minister of the Environment)* (1989), 3 *Canadian Environmental Law Reports* (New Series) 287, aff'd on appeal (1989) 4 *Canadian*

Environmental Law Reports (New Series) 1; *Canadian Wildlife Federation Inc. vs Canada (Minister of the Environment) (1989)*, 4 *Canadian Environmental Law Reports* (New Series). 201; *Friends of the Oldman River Society vs Canada (Minister of Transport) (1989)*, 4 *Canadian Environmental Law Reports* (New Series) 137, rev'd on appeal (1990) 5 *Canadian Environmental Law Reports* (New Series) 1. For a comment on the *Canadian Wildlife Federation* decision, see M. Bowden, 'Damming the Opposition: EARP in the Federal Court', 4 *Canadian Environmental Law Reports* (New Series) 227.

91 3 *Canadian Environmental Law Reports* (New Series) 287, 292-304; 5 *Canadian Environmental Law Reports* (New Series) 1, 16-21.

92 *Friends of the Oldman*, 5 *Canadian Environmental Law Reports* (New Series) 1, at 16-21.

93 See in particular the decision of Mr. Justice Muldoon in *Canadian Wildlife Federation*, 4 *Canadian Environmental Law Reports* (New Series) 201.

94 Bowden, 'Damming the Opposition', 236; R. Howard and D. Roberts, 'Rafferty dam goes ahead', *The Globe and Mail* 13 October 1990: A1. It should also be noted that news reports of two subsequent cases (not yet reported) involving the application of the EARP Guidelines indicate that the Federal Court has rejected the arguments of environmentalist litigants: 'EARP Cases in the Courts', *West Coast Environmental Law Research Foundation Newsletter* 15 (no. 3, 21 January 1991).

95 *The Proposed Alberta-Pacific Pulp Mill: Report of the EIA Review Board* (Edmonton: Alberta Environment, March 1990). Alberta was the only province with which the federal government had concluded (in 1986) an agreement for the environmental assessment of projects covered by both federal and provincial jurisdiction — an agreement which facilitated the rapid establishment of the Alberta-Pacific review panel.

96 D. Fagan, 'Energy export applications in for environmental scrutiny', *The Globe and Mail* 20 February 1990: B3.

97 For a detailed commentary on the bill see T. Schrecker, 'The Canadian Environmental Assessment Act: Tremulous Step Forward, or Retreat into Smoke and Mirrors', 5 *Canadian Environmental Law Reports* (New Series) (1991), 192-246. To give just one example, the categories of regulatory and licensing decisions which brought the Rafferty-Alameda and Three Rivers Dams under the provisions of EARP are excluded from the application of the draft legislation unless specifically brought under its provisions by regulation.

98 Estrin and Swaigen, *Environment on Trial*, 458-81; P. Muldoon, 'The Fight for an Environmental Bill of Rights', *Alternatives: Perspectives on Society, Technology and Environment* 15 (no. 2, April/May 1988): 33-9; J. Sax, *Defending the Environment: A Strategy for Citizen Action* (New York: Random House, 1970); J. Swaigen and R. Woods, 'A Substantive Right to Environmental Quality', in Swaigen, ed., *Environmental Rights*, 195-241.

99 Muldoon, 'The Fight for an Environmental Bill of Rights', 35.

100 Swaigen and Woods, 'A Substantive Right', 204.

101 Sax, *Defending the Environment*, 58–60.

102 Muldoon, 'The Fight for an Environmental Bill of Rights', 35-6.

103 Swaigen and Woods, 'A Substantive Right', 204.

104 See C. Hunt, 'The Public Trust Doctrine in Canada', in Swaigen, ed., *Environmental Rights in Canada*, 151-94.

105 Bill 172, 'An Act respecting Environmental Rights in Ontario', 2nd Sess., 33d Leg., Ontario (1st Reading 10 December 1986); Bill 13, 'An Act respecting Environmental Rights in Ontario', 1st Sess., 34th Leg., Ontario (1st Reading 9 November 1987). The two bills are exactly identical in wording.

106 Ibid., s. 4(1).

107 Ibid., s. 4(3).

108 Ibid. ss. 12(1) - 12(4).

109 Muldoon, 'The Fight for an Environmental Bill of Rights', 38.

[110]Hunt, 'The Public Trust Doctrine', 187-8.

[111]P. Gorrie, 'Environmental law to list public's rights', *Toronto Star* 14 December 1990.

[112]Bill C-74, 2nd Sess., 33rd Parl., 1987 [enacted with minor modifications in 1988]; Hon. T. McMillan, 'Notes for a statement at a news conference announcing the proposed Environmental Protection Act' (Ottawa: Environment Canada, mimeo, 18 December), 1 (emphasis added).

[113]Comments of P. Muldoon (Counsel, Energy Probe), in *Minutes of Proceedings and Evidence*, House of Commons Legislative Committee on Bill C-74, 33rd Parl., 2nd Sess. (no. 5, 10 December 1987), 6-14; 'Submissions by the Canadian Environmental Law Association', in *Minutes of Proceedings and Evidence*, House of Commons Legislative Committee on Bill C-74, 33rd Parl., 2nd Sess. (no. 9, 19 January 1988), A1-A33; Comments of K. Millyard (National Affairs Researcher, Pollution Probe), in *Minutes of Proceedings and Evidence*, House of Commons Legislative Committee on Bill C-74, 33rd Parl., 2nd Sess. (no. 10, 20 January 1988), 8-19; Canadian Environmental Advisory Council, *Review of the Proposed Environmental Protection Act* (Ottawa: CEAC, March 1987), 27-9; A. Lucas, 'Legal Review of the Proposed Environmental Protection Act', in CEAC, ibid., 63-4.

[114]The principal changes involved legislative provisions (a) enabling citizens to request the establishment of Boards of Review to examine certain regulatory decisions related to toxic substances, fuel additives, and ocean dumping, and (b) enabling any 12 citizens to apply to the Minister of the Environment for an investigation of an alleged offence under the Act. Bill C-74, ss. 81-89, 100-102. However the scope of such investigations, like the establishment of Boards of Review, was entirely at the discretion of the Minister without right of appeal. In addition, no provision was made for establishment of Boards of Review to inquire into government *inaction* on environmental matters: see Lucas, 'Legal Review', 59-60. In addition, persons who had suffered loss or damage as a result of violations of the Act were empowered to recover damages as well as to seek an injunction prohibiting the violation. Bill C-74, s. 128. This is a less important provision than it would at first appear, since in practice conviction under the Act would appear to be a precondition for the recovery of such damages; the possibility of recovery is thus subject to the vagaries of federal enforcement policy, as well as to the evidentiary problems discussed earlier in the chapter.

[115]Hon. T. McMillan, in *Minutes of Proceedings and Evidence*, House of Commons Legislative Committee on Bill C-74, 33rd Parl., 2nd Sess. (no. 1, 24-25 November 1987), 25.

[116]Hon. T. McMillan, in *Minutes of Proceedings and Evidence*, Legislative Committee on Bill C-74, 33rd Parl., 2nd Sess. (no. 14, 3 February 1988), 14-16.

[117]C. Forget (President, Asbestos Institute), in *Minutes of Proceedings and Evidence*, House of Commons Legislative Committee on Bill C-74, 33rd Parl., 2nd Sess. (no. 3, 3 December 1987), 12.

[118]J. Garon (Director of Socio-economic Research, Conseil du patronat du Québec), in *Minutes of Proceedings and Evidence*, House of Commons Legislative Committee on Bill C-74, 33rd Parl., 2nd Sess. (no. 7, 16 December 1987), 13.

[119]On this point see generally Schrecker, 'The Political Content and Context of Environmental Law'.

[120]Muldoon, 'The Fight for an Environmental Bill of Rights', 36.

[121]R. Inglehart, *Culture Shift in Advanced Industrial Society* (Princeton: Princeton University Press, 1990); R. Inglehart and J. Rabier, 'Political Realignment in Advanced Industrial Democracies', *Government and Opposition* 21 (1986), 456-79; Bakvis and Nevitte, this volume.

[122]McLaren, 'The Common Law Nuisance Actions', 559.

[123]C. Sunstein, '*Lochner*'s Legacy', *Columbia Law Review* 87 (1987): 873-919. Lawrence Tribe makes a similar point about 'the manipulable concept of a "natural" social order,

providing a backdrop to state action'; 'The Curvature of Constitutional Space', *Harvard Law Review* 103 (1989): 15; see generally 1-39.

[124]Dworkin, *Taking Rights Seriously* (Cambridge, Mass.: Harvard University Press, 1974), 127.

[125]D. Hartle, *Public Policy Decision-Making and Regulation* (Montreal: Institute for Research on Public Policy, 1978), 82.

[126]R. Dahl, *A Preface to Democratic Theory* (Chicago: University of Chicago Press, 1956), 129-30.

[127]Full-line forcing refers to the ability of candidates (or parties, in the context of Westminster systems) to combine policies on various issues in the attempt to maximize electoral support. Voters are offered only a choice among policy packages. The degree of choice offered voters with respect to specific policy options as a result has been illustrated with the example of a hypothetical supermarket which stocked a multitude of items, but made them available to shoppers only in two or three carefully preselected market baskets. We would be very sceptical about appeals to the concept of consumer sovereignty in such a situation!

[128]E. Schattschneider, *The Semisovereign People* (Hinsdale, Illinois: Dryden [1960] 1975), 34-5.

[129]S. Holmes, 'Precommitment and the Paradox of Democracy', in J. Elster and R. Slagstad, eds, *Constitutionalism and Democracy* (Cambridge: Cambridge University Press, 1988), 195-240.

[130]F. Zemans, 'Legal Mobilization: The Neglected Role of the Law in the Political System', *American Political Science Review* 77 (1983): 690-703.

WILSON

[1]Claude Galipeau, 'Political Parties, Interest Groups, and New Social Movements: Toward New Representations?' in Alain G. Gagnon and A. Brian Tanguay, eds, *Canadian Parties in Transition: Discourse, Organization, and Representation* (Scarborough: Nelson Canada, 1989), 404-26; and Warren Magnusson, 'Critical Social Movements: De-Centring the State', in Alain G. Gagnon and James P. Bickerton, eds, *Canadian Politics: An Introduction to the Discipline*, (Peterborough, Ontario: Broadview Press, 1990), 525-41.

[2]These estimates are from Rob Macintosh, co-ordinator of the Pembina Institute's preparation of a new directory of Canadian environmental groups (interview, 29 November 1990). He stresses the dependence of any estimate on what is defined as a group, and emphasizes the difficulties involved in arriving at a precise estimate.

[3]Michael Manolson (Executive Director, Greenpeace Canada), interview, 20 November 1990; and Canadian Wildlife Federation, *1989-90 Annual Report*, 3. The CWF total includes direct members, those who donate money but choose not to take out memberships, and members of the CWF's twelve provincial and territorial affiliates.

[4]Canadian Nature Federation, *1989 Annual Report*; Friends of the Earth, *Annual Report 1989-90*, 2; 'Wilderness: Newsletter of the Western Canada Wilderness Committee', Fall/Winter 1990; and Pollution Probe, personal communication, December 1990.

[5]Margaret Munro and Anne McIlroy, 'Green Revolution Favored in Poll', *The Vancouver Sun* 2 October 1989: A6.

[6]Ken Lay (Director, WCWC), interview, 18 July 1990; and WCWC, 'Wilderness Committee Memo', 26 October 1990.

[7]Jeffrey M. Berry, *Lobbying for the People: The Political Behavior of Public Interest Groups* (Princeton: Princeton University Press, 1977), 36-44.

[8]Peter B. Clark and James Q. Wilson, 'Incentive Systems: A Theory of Organizations', *Administrative Science Quarterly* 6 (1961): 146, cited in Berry, *Lobbying*, 42.

[9]Michael McCann, *Taking Reform Seriously: Perspectives on Public Interest Liberalism* (Ithaca, New York: Cornell University Press, 1986), ch. 4; and Berry, *Lobbying*, ch. 3.

[10]Roger Gibbins, *Conflict and Unity: An Introduction to Canadian Political Life*, 2nd ed. (Scarborough: Nelson Canada, 1990), 304.

[11]Ducks Unlimited Canada, *1989 Annual Report*, 22; and World Wildlife Fund Canada, *1990 Annual Review*, 2-3.

[12]Canadian Nature Federation, *1989 Annual Report*; and Friends of the Earth, *Annual Report 1989–90*, 7.

[13]Friends of the Earth, 7, 10; Canadian Nature Federation; and Western Canada Wilderness Committee, 'Wild: Wilderness is the Last Dream'. The latter figures are based on the WCWC's estimated 1988–89 revenues.

[14]From statements of 1989 revenues and expenditures filed with the British Columbia Registrar of Companies under the terms of the BC Societies Act.

[15]Manolson interview.

[16]Peter Bahouth and Andre Carothers, 'In defense of junk mail: mailbox as public square', *Utne Reader* 42 (Nov./Dec. 1990): 55-6.

[17]Canadian Wildlife Federation, *1989 Annual Report*, 27; Western Canada Wilderness Committee, *Wild*.

[18]Eva Schacherl (Executive Director, Canadian Environmental Network), interview, 1 November 1990.

[19]For example, in 1990 the Ontario Environmental Assessment Board ordered Ontario Hydro to pay $21.5 million to groups intervening at hearings on the utility's expansion plans. The largest grant ($2.8 million) went to the Coalition of Environmental Groups. See Martin Mittelstaedt, 'Challengers given money to fight', *Globe and Mail* 26 December 1990.

[20]World Wildlife Fund Canada, *1990 Annual Review*, 26.

[21]Ibid.

[22]Ibid., 15.

[23]Elizabeth May, 'Political Realities', in *Endangered Spaces: The Future for Canada's Wilderness*, ed. Monte Hummel (Toronto: Key Porter Books, 1989), 84.

[24]John Broadhead, 'The All Alone Stone Manifesto', in *Endangered Spaces*, 59-60.

[25]Elizabeth May (National Representative, Sierra Club and Executive Director, Cultural Survival), interview, 12 November 1990.

[26]Arlin Hackman (Director, Endangered Spaces Program, World Wildlife Fund Canada), interview, 22 October 1990.

[27]Julie Gelfand (Communications and Programs Manager, Canadian Wildlife Federation), interview, 25 October 1990.

[28]Adele Hurley and Michael Perley (Canadian Coalition on Acid Rain), CBC *Morningside* 20 November 1990.

[29]Hackman interview; Kevin McNamee (Parks and Protected Areas Coordinator, Canadian Nature Federation), interview, 25 October 1990.

[30]David Israelson, *Silent Earth: The Politics of Our Survival* (Markham, Ontario: Viking, 1990), 233-5.

[31]Elizabeth May, *Paradise Won: The Struggle for South Moresby* (Toronto: McClelland and Stewart Inc., 1990), 171-2, 196-200, 212-16.

[32]Ibid., 212-14.

[33]McNamee interview.

[34]On the concept of policy community and the distinction between the sub-government and attentive public parts, see A. Paul Pross, *Group Politics and Public Policy* (Toronto: Oxford University Press, 1986), 97-107, 145-54, 173-5.

[35]Ibid., 149-54.

[36]Among the groups publishing magazines are the Canadian Nature Federation (*Nature*

Canada), the Canadian Parks and Wilderness Society (*Borealis*), and the Canadian Wildlife Federation (*International Wildlife*, along with *Ranger Rick* and *Your Big Backyard* for children.)

[37]Pollution Probe, 'Program Highlights 1989/90. Information and Education'.

[38]Conservation Council of New Brunswick, 'Current Publications'.

[39]Lay interview.

[40]Broadhead, 'All Alone Stone', 54.

[41]For example, Western Canada Wilderness Committee, 'Carmanah Valley Campaign: Phase II', (Summer 1990); and 'Tatshenshini: Ice Age Wilderness', (Spring 1990).

[42]Michael M'Gonigle and Wendy Wickwire, *Stein: The Way of the River* (Vancouver: Talon Books, 1988); Islands Protection Society, *Islands at the Edge: Preserving the Queen Charlotte Islands Wilderness* (Vancouver: Douglas and McIntyre, 1984); and Cameron Young and Adrian Dorst, *Clayoquot — On the Wild Side* (Vancouver: Western Canada Wilderness Committee, 1990).

[43]Broadhead, 'All Alone Stone', 54.

[44]Western Canada Wilderness Committee, *Carmanah: Artistic Visions of an Ancient Rainforest* (Vancouver: Western Canada Wilderness Committee, 1989).

[45]André Picard, 'Patron saint of white whales seeks converts to beluga's cause', *Globe and Mail* 14 August 1989.

[46]Robert Hunter, *Warriors of the Rainbow: A Chronicle of the Greenpeace Movement* (New York: Holt, Rinehart and Winston, 1979).

[47]André Picard, 'Activists chained to track', *Globe and Mail* 24 October 1990.

[48]Jeff Keller, 'Mind Games', *Equity* (September 1990): 20.

[49]Rowe Findley, 'Will We Save our Own?' *National Geographic*, 178, 3 (September 1990): 114-15.

[50]W. Lance Bennett, *TV News: The Politics of Illusion* 2nd ed. (New York: Longman, 1988).

[51]Jeremy Wilson, 'Wilderness Politics in BC: The Business Dominated State and the Containment of Environmentalism', in William Coleman and Grace Skogstad, eds., *Policy Communities and Public Policy in Canada: A Structural Approach* (Mississauga: Copp Clark Pitman Ltd., 1990), 141-69.

LYON

*I am indebted to Professors Robert Paehlke and Peyton Lyon for their constructive comments on an earlier draft of this paper.

[1]Robert Heilbroner, *An Inquiry into the Human Prospect* (W.W. Norton: New York, 1974), 99-124. For a critique of the ideas of Heilbroner and others sharing his views, see R. Paehlke, 'Democracy, Bureaucracy, and Environmentalism', *Environmental Ethics* 10, 4 (Winter, 1988): 291-308.

[2]Both Liberal and NDP members of the Ontario legislature have proposed an 'environmental bill of rights' which would allow citizens the legal standing they require to sue polluters. See Linda Hossie, 'Environment minister hints of big changes', *Globe and Mail* 5 November 1990.

[3]Herman Bakvis and Neil Nevitte, 'The Greening of the Canadian Electorate: Environmentalism, Ideology and Partisanship', Paper presented at the annual meeting of the Canadian Political Science Association, 2 May 1990: 2-3.

[4]Peter Howell, '86% say they'd pay to save environment national poll finds', *Toronto Star* 28 December 1988.

[5]Bakvis and Nevitte, 1.

[6]Alex Davidson and Michael Dence, *The Brundtland Challenge and the Cost of Inaction*

(Halifax: The Royal Society and The Institute for Research on Public Policy, 1988), xxvi-xxvii.

[7]David Rapport, 'Impressions from the Workshop on the Brundtland Challenge', in Davidson and Dence, 127.

[8]Giovanni Sartori, *Democratic Theory* (New York: Praeger, 1965), 120.

[9]See Jeffrey Simpson, *The Spoils of Power* (Toronto: Collins, 1988).

[10]The point is developed in, and I am indebted to, E.E. Schattschneider, *Party Government* (New York: Holt Rinehart and Winston, 1967).

[11]Kay Lawson, ed., *Political Parties and Linkage* (New Haven: Yale University Press, 1980), 23.

[12]Bakvis and Nevitte, 7.

[13]Bakvis and Nevitte, 7.

[14]Lynn McDonald, 'Can the NDP Become the Green Party of Canada?' *Canadian Forum* December 1989: 13-14.

[15]'Those closer to the NDP are somewhat less supportive of environmental issues, and any move toward creating a sharper environmental profile may well be resisted by them. The category of moderate identifiers, incidentally, constitutes almost half of all NDP identifiers' (Bakvis and Nevitte, 9). It is instructive that the leader of the Quebec NDP during the 1989 election, while elected to that office on an environmental platform, was, according to him, forced by his executive to campaign on other issues. He resigned from the leadership and the party (André Picard, 'Marxist members blamed for Quebec NDP's demise', *Globe and Mail* 27 September 1989).

[16]I recall listening to a soon-to-be-forgotten cabinet minister who had been very effective and, partly for that reason, stayed out of the public limelight, complain about the prominence of his successor who was gaining fame solving, in a very public way, crises of his own creation.

[17]For an account of the dilemmas facing the new party see Vaughan Lyon, 'The Reluctant Party: Ideology versus Organization in Canada's Green Movement', *Alternatives* (December 1985): 3-9.

[18]For a good account of the German Greens see Werner Hulsberg, *The German Greens* (London: Verso, 1988).

[19]In the 1988 national election the Greens ran 68 candidates who received approximately 27,000 votes (1/3 of 1% of the total votes cast). *Globe and Mail* 2 May 1990.

[20]One student of Canadian parties finds their support base even more volatile than that of parties in the US and UK. Joseph Wearing, *Strained Relations: Canadian Parties and Voters* (Toronto: McClelland and Stewart, 1988), 84.

[21]The usual pattern at the federal and provincial levels is for financial aid to be limited to parties which get more than 15% of the popular vote. See Wearing, 125-6.

[22]Anne McIlroy, 'Green party hopes for rosier future', *Toronto Star* 18 October 1990.

[23]The classic account of the movement of the CCF/NDP from radical movement to middle-of-the-road party is found in Walter Young's *The Anatomy of a Party: The National CCF 1932–61* (Toronto: University of Toronto Press, 1969).

[24]Murray Bookchin, *Remaking Society* (Montreal: Black Rose Books, 1989), 160.

[25]Cited in A.H. Hanson, 'The Purpose of Parliament', *Parliamentary Affairs* 17 (1984): 279-96.

[26]Bakvis and Nevitte, 8.

[27]For a discussion of this point see Murray Edelman, *The Symbolic Uses of Politics* (Urbana: University of Illinois Press, 1964).

[28]For a full discussion of this point see Harold D. Clarke et al., *Absent Mandate: The Politics of Discontent in Canada* (Toronto: Gage Publishing Limited, 1984).

[29]Wearing, 225.

[30]Wearing, 95. Also see Wearing, 199, for comments on how policy advisers to the federal caucuses of the parties regard convention policy positions.

[31]Wearing, 198.

[32]Lawson, 21.

[33]For a recent evaluation of the Liberal attempt see Lorna Marsden, 'The Party and Parliament: Participatory Democracy in the Trudeau Years', in Thomas S. Axworthy and Pierre E. Trudeau, eds, *Towards a Just Society* (Markham, Ontario: Viking, 1990), 262-81. On the CCF/NDP see Evelyn Eager, *Saskatchewan Government* (Saskatoon: Western Producer Prairie Books, 1980), ch. 11. The story of the Progressives' (United Farmers of Alberta) attempt to make party government democratic is told in C.B. Macpherson, *Democracy in Alberta: Social Credit and the Party System* (Toronto: University of Toronto Press, 1953). A synthesis and analysis of the party democracy phenomenon in Canada is found in Vaughan Lyon, 'Democracy and the Canadian Political System', PhD dissertation, University of British Columbia, 1974.

[34]Lawson, 21.

[35]Dalton Camp, 'The Limits of Political Parties', in H.V. Kroeker, ed., *Sovereign People or Sovereign Governments* (Montreal: Institution for Research on Public Policy, 1981), 150.

[36]'Pro–environment respondents are only marginally more likely to be members of a political party and somewhat less likely to acquire a strong partisan identity'. Bakvis and Nevitte, 8.

[37]Robert C. Paehlke, *Environmentalism and the Future of Progressive Politics* (New Haven: Yale University Press, 1989), 193.

[38]Paehlke, 279.

[39]For an extended discussion of this point see Joseph Tussman, *Obligation and the Body Politic* (New York: Oxford University Press, 1966).

[40]'Canadians are deeply worried about the environment, but most are unwilling to make major changes in their lives to do something about it.' Margaret Polanyi, 'Canadians balk at altering lives to aid environment, poll shows', *Globe and Mail* 6 June 1990.

[41]See William Irvine, *Does Canada Need a New Electoral System?* (Kingston: Queen's University Institute of Intergovernmental Relations, 1979).

[42]With good reason, Canadian voters have now come to believe that less stable minority government is more responsive to its needs and demands than majority government. See the Gallup Polls on the subject, 25 and 28 April 1983. For an extended discussion of changing public attitudes toward minority government at the federal level see Lawrence LeDuc, 'Political Behaviour and the Issue of Majority Government in Two Federal Elections,' *Canadian Journal of Political Science* 10 (1977): 311-39.

[43]Paehlke, 'Democracy, Bureaucracy, and Environmentalism', 308.

[44]Various versions of the community assembly idea have been advanced in recent years. For a US proposal see James Barber, *Strong Democracy* (Berkeley: University of California Press, 1984) and for Canada, Philip Resnick, *Parliament vs People* (Vancouver: New Star Books, 1984). A summary description of my own model, which I argue is much more realistic than either of the other two, is presented below. A somewhat more extended discussion of the model is found in Vaughan Lyon, 'Houses of Citizens', in Cliff Scotton, ed., *People Taking Part* (a collection of reprints from *Policy Options*, The Institute for Research on Public Policy, n.d.).

[45]Constituencies might be divided into wards of 1000 voters each electing a community parliament member. Approximately 17,500 members would be elected across Canada. The basic task of these representatives would be to give government 'roots' from which it could draw authority and inspiration.

[46]Joseph Schumpeter, 3rd ed., *Capitalism, Socialism and Democracy* (New York: Harper and Row, 1950), 253.

BAKVIS AND NEVITTE

*We are much obliged to Lori Galbraith, Research Associate with the Research Unit for Public Policy Studies at the University of Calgary, for advice on statistical procedures and for carrying out the data analysis. The 1988 Canadian national election survey was conducted by the Survey Research Centre, Institute for Behavioural Research, York University. Principal investigators were André Blais, Henry Brady, Jean Crête, and Richard Johnston. An earlier version of this paper was presented at the Annual Meeting of the Canadian Political Science Association, University of Victoria, May 1990.

[1]P.R. Hay and M.G. Haward, 'Comparative Green Politics: Beyond the European Context?', *Political Studies* 36 (1988): 433-48.

[2]See Neil Nevitte, Herman Bakvis and Roger Gibbins, 'The Ideological Contours of "New Politics" in Canada: Policy, Mobilization and Partisan Support', *Canadian Journal of Political Science* 22 (1989): 475-503.

[3]Gallup Canada, 'Fears of Economic Downswing Preoccupy Canadian Public', *Release* (Toronto: 5 February 1990); Gallup Canada release, 'Environment and Taxation Most Concern Canadian Public' (Toronto: 31 July 1989).

[4]Gallup Canada, 'Canadians Increasingly Concerned about Dangers of Pollution' (Toronto: 19 June 1989).

[5]We borrow this distinction from Robert Rohrschneider, 'The Roots of Public Opinion toward New Social Movements: An Empirical Test of Competing Explanations', *American Journal of Political Science* 34 (1990): 1-30.

[6]Robyn Eckersley, 'Green Politics and the New Class: Selfishness or Virtue?' *Political Studies* 37 (1989): 205.

[7]Claus Offe, *Contradictions of the Welfare State* (Cambridge, Mass.: MIT Press, 1985).

[8]Ronald Inglehart, 'Post-Materialism in an Environment of Insecurity', *American Political Science Review* 75 (1981): 881.

[9]See Herman Bakvis and Neil Nevitte, 'In Pursuit of Postbourgeois Man: Postmaterialism and Intergenerational Change in Canada', *Comparative Political Studies* 20 (1987): 357-89.

[10]J.A. Laponce, *Left and Right: The Topography of Political Perceptions* (Toronto: University of Toronto Press, 1981).

[11]The regional categories do disguise considerable variation. Thus within the Atlantic region, Newfoundland is lowest in support of the environment over jobs (52.2%) and PEI highest (71.4%). For the prairies the variation is only in the order of 3%.

[12]Rohrschneider, 'The Roots of Public Opinion toward New Social Movements'.

[13]See Ronald D. Lambert, James E. Curtis, Steven D. Brown, and Barry J. Kay, 'In Search of Left/Right Beliefs in the Canadian Electorate', *Canadian Journal of Political Science* 19 (1986): 541-63.

[14]The six postmaterialist items include: 'ideas count', 'free speech', and 'beautiful cities/nature'. The materialist items include: 'strong defence forces', 'fight rising prices', and 'economic growth'. For details such as the full wording of the items and the computation of MPM scores see Inglehart, *The Silent Revolution: Changing Values and Political Styles Among Western Publics* (Princeton: Princeton University Press, 1977), 59, note.

[15]The low response rate on this item is puzzling. In the 1984 national election survey over 55% of respondents were able to place themselves on a seven point left-right scale. In the 1988 charter rights survey, which used a three stage question, 42% were able to place

themselves. It appears the initial filtering question, which is different from the ones used in the other surveys, may well be responsible for the low response rate in 1988.

[16]The logistic regression procedure enters independent predictor variables in an order determined hierarchically in terms of goodness of fit (Chi Square) through successive data sweeps. See Laszlo Engelman, 'Stepwise Logistic Regression', in W.J. Dixon et al., eds, *BMDP Biomedical Computer Programs* (Berkeley: University of California Press, 1983), 941-69. In our analysis MPM clearly emerged as the best predictor in the model (significant at .0001) followed, in order, by education (.0140), age (.0334), and left-right (.0515).

[17]Ronald Inglehart, *Culture Shift in Advanced Industrial Society* (Princeton: Princeton University Press, 1990).

[18]Ibid., 336-42.

[19]For example, see David Butler and Donald Stokes, *Political Change in Britain: Forces Shaping Electoral Choice* (Harmondsworth: Penguin, 1971); Samuel H. Barnes and Max Kaase, eds, *Political Action: Mass Participation in Five Western Democracies* (Beverly Hills: Sage, 1979).

[20]Russell J. Dalton, 'The Environmental Movement and West European Party Systems', (Florida State University: Environmental Movements in Western Democracies, Project Report 8, 1988), 14; see also Herbert Kitschelt, 'Organization and Strategy of Belgian and West German Ecology Parties: A New Dynamic of Party Politics in Western Europe?', *Comparative Politics* 20 (January 1988): 127-54.

[21]Dalton, 'The Environmental Movement and West European Party Systems'.

[22]See Wolfgang Rüdig and Philip D. Lowe, 'The Withered "Greening" of British Politics: a Study of the Ecology Party', *Political Studies* 34 (1986): 262-84.

[23]Robert Paehlke, *Environmentalism and the Future of Progressive Politics* (New Haven: Yale University Press, 1989).

[24]See 'Neither left nor right', *Green Policy Seeds: Official Publication of Canadian Greens, Rocky Mountain Region Association*, 1, 2 (March/April 1990): 2.

[25]'B.C. NDP averts public rift over logging issue', *Globe and Mail*, 12 March 1990): A9.

[26]In the tripartite division of respondents into pure postmaterialists, mixed and pure materialists, the preponderance (75%) of the sample fell into the mixed category, in other words those who likely hold both types of values in rather uneasy balance. And again, despite a clear majority of respondents (65%) choosing environment over jobs, only 6% indicated this as the single most important issue in the 1988 election.

[27]Gallup Canada release, 'Canada's Frail Economy Viewed As Most Important Problem' (Toronto: 14 January 1991).

BROWN

[1]Charles E. Lindblom, 'The Science of "Muddling Through" ', *Public Administration Review* 2 (Spring 1959): 79-88.

[2]George D. Greenberg, et al. 'Developing Public Policy Theory: Perspectives from Empirical Research', *American Political Science Review* 71, 4 (December, 1977): 1533.

[3]Henry Mintzberg and Jan Jorgensen, 'Emergent strategy for public policy', *Canadian Public Administration* 30, 2 (Summer 1987): 217.

[4]Richard B. Simeon, 'Studying Public Policy', *Canadian Journal of Political Science* 9, 4 (December, 1976): 555.

[5]Leslie A. Pal, *Public Policy Analysis: An Introduction* (Scarborough: Nelson Canada, 1989), 29.

[6]Simeon, 551.

[7]Greenberg et al., 1542.

[8]Graham Molitor, 'The Hatching of Public Opinion', *Corporate Planning Review* 28 (July 1977): 4-5.

[9]Ibid., 5, 6.

[10]Greenberg et al., 1540.

[11]Henry Mintzberg and Jan Jorgensen, 'Emergent strategy for public policy', *Canadian Public Administration* 30, 2 (Summer 1987): 227.

[12]See, for example, Peter Aucoin, 'Public Policy Theory and Analysis', in G. Bruce Doern and Peter Aucoin, *Public Policy in Canada: Organization, Process, and Management* (Toronto: Macmillan of Canada, 1979) 14-16.

[13]See, for example, A. Paul Pross, *Group Politics and Public Policy* (Toronto: Oxford University Press, 1986), esp. chapter 5, 'Types of Groups' and 8, 'The Interior Life of Groups'.

[14]See, for example, Dale H. Poel, 'The Diffusion of Legislation among the Canadian Provinces: A Statistical Analysis', *Canadian Journal of Political Science* 9, 4 (1976): 605-26 and Virginia Gray, 'Innovation in the American States: A Diffusion Study', *American Political Science Review* 67, 3 (1973): 1174-85. For an interesting revisitation to Poel's article, see James M. Lutz, 'Emulation and Policy Adoptions in the Canadian Provinces', *Canadian Journal of Political Science* 22, 1 (1989): 147-54.

[15]See Patrick Lennon, 'Canadian Environmental Business Opportunities', in *The Proceedings: Environment and Economy, Partners for the Future — A Conference on Sustainable Development* (Winnipeg, 1989), 159.

[16]Industry, Science and Technology Canada was actually formed under Bill C-3, passed on 23 February 1990. It incorporated among other responsibilities the industrial expansion component of the old Department of Regional Industrial Expansion (DRIE). Since the reorganization was not germane to the emergence of environmental industry policy, the department is referred to as ISTC throughout.

[17]Canada. Industry, Science and Technology Canada. *Environmental Industries Sector Initiative: Workplan for 1989–90*, 30 June 1989: 1. The widespread dissemination of this workplan by ISTC officials was itself a highly unusual consultative step in the development of a strategy for the industry.

[18]Organization for Economic Co-operation and Development, *The Macro-Economic Impact of Environmental Expenditure* (Paris, France, 1985), 35.

[19]Michael G. Royston, *Pollution Prevention Pays* (Oxford: Pergamon Press, 1979), 67.

[20]Data Resources Incorporated concluded, for example, that as a result of pollution controls there would be a net increase of some 524,000 jobs in 1987 as compared to 1970. Another study by the Bureau of Economic Analysis identified similar employment benefits for the US economy. Data Resources, Inc., *The Macroeconomic Impact of Federal Pollution Control Programs* (Washington, DC: The Council on Environmental Quality and the US Environmental Protection Agency, 1975), 2. Bureau of Economic Analysis figures are cited and assessed in *The Status of Environmental Economics: The 1984 Update*. Report from the Environment and Natural Resources Policy Division of Congressional Research Service, Library of Congress, for the Senate Committee on Environment and Public Works (Washington: US Government Printing Office, 1984), 47, 54.

[21]Royston, 68.

[22]Richard Kazis and Richard L. Grossman, *Fear at Work: Job Blackmail, Labor and the Environment* (New York: The Pilgrim Press, 1983), 24-5.

[23]'Jobs and the Environment: Some Preliminary Number Crunching', a report by Corpus Information Services, Don Mills, Ontario, 1987, 4-14. This information was subsequently published as William M. Glenn, 'Jobs and the Environment: Some Preliminary Number Crunching', *Alternatives* 14, 3 (1987): 18-30. Another study placed employment estimates in the water pollution control industry alone at 49,000 yearly through 1980–82. See R. Laikin and J. A. Donnan, 'Expenditures on Environmental Protection in Canada, 1980–84', in G. D. Riggieri, *The Canadian Economy: Problems and Policies*, 3rd ed., (Toronto:

Educational Publishing House, 1987), 241. The latter noted that 'there are no data available. . .on the number of people employed by the Canadian air pollution control industry, by private waste disposal companies, or in the operation and maintenance of installed pollution control equipment.'

[24]Organization for Economic Co-operation and Development, *Biotechnology and the Changing Role of Government* (Paris, 1988), 36-8.

[25]See Monica E. Campbell and William M. Glenn, *Profit from pollution prevention: a guide to industrial waste reduction and recycling* (Toronto: Pollution Probe Foundation, 1982).

[26]Robert Collison, 'The Greening of the Boardroom', *Report on Business Magazine* (July 1989): 44.

[27]Canadian Council of Resource and Environment Ministers, *Report of the National Task Force on Environment and Economy* (Downsview, Ont.: CCREM, 1987), 4.

[28]In fact, MacNeill while at OECD commissioned a series of studies to determine whether environmental protection was a drag on the economy, and found that 'overall. . .the impact was to stimulate innovation and productivity', Collison, 44-5.

[29]Collison.

[30]James F. MacLaren Limited, *Potential for Expansion of the Pollution Equipment Manufacturing Industry in Canada* (Willowdale, Ontario, 1979).

[31]See, for example, Bill Glenn, 'Pollution Abatement Creates Employment', *Probe Post* 4, 5 (March, 1982): 19-22.

[32]Canada. Minister of State for Science and Technology. *Report: Task Force on Environmental Protection Technologies* (Ottawa, 1983), cited in *Defining The Environmental Protection Industry* (Ottawa: Institute for Research on Public Policy, 1987), 1-2.

[33]In order of appearance these were *The Environmental Economic Sector in Nova Scotia* (Halifax: Nolan Davis and Associates, 1988), The Asia Pacific Initiative Advisory Committee, *Export Market Capabilities of the British Columbia Environmental Industry* (Vancouver: Price Waterhouse, 1988), and *Study of the Ontario Environmental Protection Industry* (Toronto: Environment Ontario, 1989).

[34]One example of which was K. J. De Waal and W. J. Van Der Brink, eds, *Proceedings of the Second European Conference on Environmental Technologies* (Boston: Martinus Nijhoff Publishers, 1987).

[35]This was the Environmental Monitor.

[36]National Task Force on Environment and Economy, 16.

[37]Molitor, 6.

[38]*Export Market Capabilities of the British Columbia Environmental Industry,* 5. The IRPP also detected 'little [environmental] industry association activity' and attributed this to the 'nature of the industries and commodities', in that many of the goods and services involved were 'produced by companies for whom environmental protection is only a portion of their business, and not unique to environmental protection applications'. *Defining the Environmental Protection Industry,* 35–6.

[39]These being the Ontario Society of Environmental Management, Ontario Liquid Waste Carriers Association, Canadian Water Systems Manufacturers Association, Association of Consulting Engineers of Canada, Recycling Council of Ontario, Ontario Pollution Control Equipment Association, Air Pollution Control Association (Ontario Section), Ontario Waste Management Association, Pollution Control Association of Ontario, Canadian Association of Recycling Industries, and the Environmental Industries Council (US).

[40]For example, the Alberta Special Waste Management Association was also trying to establish a national presence by recruiting members in Ontario, New Brunswick, Nova Scotia, and Newfoundland.

[41]Molitor, 6.

[42]In consultation.

[43]See Royston, 81-2, 142.

[44]Cynthia P. Shea, 'Protecting the Ozone Layer', in Lester R. Brown, ed., *The State of the World, 1989* (New York: Worldwatch Institute, 1989), 92.

[45]See Claudine Schneider, 'Hazardous Waste: The Bottom Line is Prevention', *Issues in Science and Technology* 4, 4 (Summer 1988): 77-8, and also Darrell W. Ditz, 'The Phase-out of North Sea Incineration', *International Environmental Affairs* 1, 3 (Summer, 1989): 189-90.

[46]The responsible project officer reported to the Director of Machinery and Electrical Equipment in the Surface Transportation and Machinery Branch which, in turn, came under the ADM for Industry and Technology.

[47]Canada. Industry Science and Technology Canada. *The Environmental Industries Sector Initiative: An Overview and Progress Report for 1989–90* (June 1990): 1-2.

[48]Canada. Industry, Science and Technology Canada, *Environmental Science and Technologies to Support Canadian Industries: Early Options.* Volume 1: Action Report, 1990: 35-6.

[49]*The Environmental Industries Sector Initiative*, 5, 6.

[50]Lennon, 163.

[51]*The Environmental Industries Sector Initiative*, 2-3.

[52]Ibid., 3. For a fascinating practitioner's discussion of this kind of horizontal management, see Peter LeBlanc, 'Managing Towards Sustainable Development: A Manager's Perspective', in *The Proceedings: Environment and Economy—Partners for the Future*, 269-76.

[53]Bruce A. Fenton, *The Canadian Water Resources Equipment Industry: Opportunities for Research and Manufacturing* (Ottawa: Science Council of Canada, 1989), 3. Two of the countries showing the greatest percentage increase in their share of the Canadian markets were West Germany and the Netherlands (loc. cit. 21).

[54]*Study of the Ontario Environmental Protection Industry*, 59–60. In 1986, for example, Canada showed huge deficits in trade with the US with respect to industrial control equipment ($122 million of imports versus $10 million in exports), electrical measuring/testing instruments ($134 million in imports versus $23 million in exports), physical properties testing equipment ($96 million in imports versus $10 million in exports), and thermal measuring control equipment ($12 million in imports versus $1 million in exports).

[55]C.D. Howe Institute has, for example, acknowledged the presence of a 'growing environmental industries sector (suppliers and consultants)'. See G. Bruce Doern, 'Getting It Green: Canadian Environmental Policy in the 1990s', in G. Bruce Doern, ed., *The Environmental Imperative: Market Approaches to the Greening of Canada* (Toronto: C.D. Howe Institute, 1990), 10.

[56]Fenton, 3.

[57]For a useful summary of this debate, see Stephen Brooks, *Public Policy in Canada: An Introduction* (Toronto: McClelland & Stewart, 1989), 202-5. The Science Council of Canada for which Fenton wrote is, of course, one of the chief proponents of the view that Canadian development is best served by an aggressive industrial R&D policy.

[58]*Study of the Ontario Environmental Protection Industry*, 44. This discovery tends to lend credence to Glen Williams' complaint that 'where significant product or process innovation has been developed by the subsidiary, the decision as to whether production for export would be carried out in Canada has been made by the corporate parent'. See his *Not For Export: Towards a Political Economy of Canada's Arrested Industrialization*, updated edition (Toronto: McClelland and Stewart Inc., 1986), 111-12.

[59]See 'Newsletter: The Voice of the Canadian Environment Industry', March 1990: 1.

[60]As of 1990, 'support for a national industry association' had been identified as one of the important steps in the EISI, *Environmental Science and Technologies to Support Canadian Industries*, 36.

[61]According to Richard Van Loon and Michael Whittington, 'reverse' pressure groups may be created by government itself as, among other things, a means of 'communication with

an otherwise poorly organized portion of the public'. *The Canadian Political System: Environment, Structure, and Process, 4th ed.* (Toronto: McGraw-Hill Ryerson Ltd., 1987), 409.

[62] The definitive work on business associations is William D. Coleman, *Business and Politics: A Study of Collective Action* (Montreal: McGill-Queen's University Press, 1988). See especially the chapter on 'Business and Democracy', 261-85.

[63] For example, firms in the Atlantic Canadian environmental industry can access Atlantic Canada Opportunities Agency financial support for business planning studies and marketing and feasibility studies in support of innovation. However, the maximum federal share is 50% for the former and 75% for the latter. While not insignificant, this level of commitment compares poorly with that historically available to firms pursuing development of clean technologies in places like the Netherlands and France.

[64] Schneider, 80.

[65] Kurt Yeager, 'Clean Coal: A Prototype for R&D Collaboration', *Forum for Applied Research and Public Policy*, 4, 1 (Spring 1989): 4.

[66] Government of Canada, *Canada's Green Plan for a Healthy Environment* (Ottawa: Ministry of Supply and Services Canada, 1990), 151-2. The Technology Development Branch of Environment Canada, which has traditionally been a lead federal agency in the development of pollution control technology from the environmental impact perspective, is expected to be heavily involved in this effort.

FLETCHER AND STAHLBRAND

[1] J.W. Parlour and S. Schatzow, 'The Mass Media and Public Concern for Environmental Problems in Canada, 1960–72', *International Journal of Environmental Studies*, 13 (1978): 12.

[2] See for example Robert B. Gibson, 'Out of Control and Beyond Understanding: Acid Rain as Political Dilemma', in Robert Paehlke and Douglas Torgerson, eds, *Managing Leviathan: Environmental Politics and the Administrative State* (Peterborough: Broadview Press, 1990): 248.

[3] David Taras, *The Newsmakers: The Media's Influence on Canadian Politics* (Toronto: Nelson Canada, 1990), Ch. 1.

[4] Ted Schrecker, 'Resisting Government Regulation: The Cryptic Pattern of Government-Business Relations', in Paehlke and Torgerson, op. cit., 179; Joyce Nelson, *Sultans of Sleaze: Public Relations and the Media* (Toronto: Between the Lines, 1989) ch. 6.

[5] Michael J.L. Clow, 'The Limits to Debate: Canadian Newspapers and Nuclear Power', PhD dissertation, York University, 1989; ch. 6.

[6] Alan Gregg and Michael Posner, *The Big Picture: What Canadians Think About Almost Everything* (Toronto: MacFarlane, Walter and Ross, 1990); 92.

[7] John Allen Lee, 'Seals, Wolves, and Words: Loaded Language in Environmental Controversy', *Alternatives* 15,4 (1988): 26; Richard V. Ericson, Patricia M. Baranek and Janet B.L. Chan, *Negotiating Control: A Study of News Sources* (Toronto: University of Toronto Press, 1989): 377.

[8] Parlour and Schatzow, op. cit., 14.

[9] Ibid., 12; Frederick J. Fletcher and Robert Drummond, *Canadian Attitude Trends, 1960–1978* (Montreal: Institute for Research on Public Policy, 1979): 63-5.

[10] Gregg and Posner, op. cit., 95.

[11] R.H. MacDermid, Marie-Christine Chalmers, and H. Michael Stevenson, 'Public Opinion on Environmental Issues', paper presented at the Canadian Political Science Association Annual Meeting, Kingston, 1991: 1-3.

[12] Gregg and Posner, op. cit., 95.

[13]MacDermid et al., op. cit., 3, 12-22.

[14]Schrecker, op. cit., 178.

[15]In selecting our respondents, we decided to omit the most influential journalist/commentator in this field in Canada: David Suzuki. As a newspaper columnist and host of *The Nature of Things* on CBC television, Suzuki is a passionate and compelling voice warning of the dangers of environmental degradation. It was our view that he was more a media star and advocate than a journalist. He is not subject to the same constraints and dilemmas.

[16]Parlour and Schatzow, op. cit.

[17]For a useful discussion of media coverage of the accident, see Dan Nimmo and James E. Combs, *Nightly Horrors: Crisis Coverage in Television Network News* (Knoxville: University of Tennessee Press, 1985), ch. 2.

[18]On these points see Ericson et al., op. cit., and Nelson, op. cit.

[19]Gaye Tuchman, *Making News: A Study in the Construction of Reality* (New York: Free Press, 1978), ch. 2; Richard V. Ericson, Patricia M. Baranek and Janet B.C. Chan, *Visualizing Deviance: A Study of News Organization* (Toronto: University of Toronto Press, 1987), Part III.

[20]Tuchman, op. cit., ch. 5.

[21]Joyce Nelson, *The Perfect Machine: TV in the Nuclear Age* (Toronto: Between the Lines, 1987): 133.

[22]Richard V. Ericson et al. (1989): ch. 1.

[23]See for example Clow, op. cit.

[24]Nelson, op. cit. (1989), ch. 6.

[25]Nelson, op. cit. (1987), 98-104.

[26]Gabriel Kolko, *The Triumph of Conservatism: A Re-interpretation of American History* (New York: Free Press, 1963).

[27]Mark Langdon, 'Media Agenda Setting for Provincial Political Elites', paper presented at the Canadian Political Science Association Annual Meeting, Kingston, 1991.

[28]Parlour and Schatzow, op. cit. 12-14.

[29]Nelson, op. cit. (1989), chs. 1, 6.

[30]Parlour and Schatzow, op. cit., 15.

[31]Michael Greenberg et al., 'Risk, Drama and Geography in Coverage of Environmental Risk by Network TV', *Journalism Quarterly* (Summer 1989): 275-6; Gregg and Posner, op. cit., 101.

MUNTON AND CASTLE

*This chapter is in part an adaptation and revision of a number of earlier articles by the authors. Their research in this essay on the Great Lakes Water Quality Agreement was made possible by a leave fellowship from the Social Sciences and Humanities Research Council, and by part of a collective grant to the Centre for Foreign Policy Studies at Dalhousie University by the Donner Canadian Foundation. The acid rain research was assisted by a grant to the Institute of International Relations at the University of British Columbia, also from the Donner Canadian Foundation. Diane Pothier and Danielle Wetherup provided invaluable research assistance at Dalhousie. Nancy Mina helpfully word-processed the revised manuscript at the UBC.

[1]International Joint Commission, *Final Report of the International Joint Commission on the Pollution of Boundary Waters*, Washington, DC, 1951.

[2]International Lake Erie Water Pollution Board and International Lake Ontario – St Lawrence River Water Pollution Board, *Report to the International Joint Commission on the Pollution of Lake Erie, Lake Ontario and the International Section of the St Lawrence River*, Ottawa, 1969.

[3]On the Arctic Waters Pollution Prevention Act, see Franklyn Griffiths, ed., *Politics of the Northwest Passage* (Kingston: McGill-Queen's University Press, 1987). On the Canada Fisheries Act and the Canada Water Act, see Don Munton, 'Canadian Laws and Institutions', in D. Misener and G. Daniel, eds, *Decisions for the Great Lakes*, Great Lakes Tomorrow and the Purdue Foundation, 1982, 143-52.

[4]The consensus of senior Nixon Administration officials interviewed by the author was that the President was personally indifferent, but probably not opposed, to more effective pollution control measures. For a defence of the Nixon administration's policies, see John Quarles, *Cleaning Up America: An Insider's View of the Environmental Protection Agency* (Boston, 1976); and John D. Whitaker, *Striking a Balance: Environmental and Natural Resources Policy in the Nixon-Ford Years* (Washington, DC, 1976).

[5]For a discussion of these speeches, see Don Munton, 'Dependence and Interdependence in Transboundary Environmental Relations', *International Journal* 36, 1 (1980–81): 139-84.

[6]Memorandum for the President, Russell Train, Chairman, Council on Environmental Quality, 'Task Force on the Improvement of the Effectiveness of Water Quality Control on the Great Lakes – Final Report', 24 September 1970, Department of State files (declassified).

[7]Without such an agreement, the federal government could not be sure that the Canadian commitments in the prospective bilateral agreement would be met. This situation was precisely the bind that the Diefenbaker government had gotten itself into with respect to the Columbia River Treaty of 1961 when the province of British Columbia insisted on a different financing arrangement. See Neil Swainson, 'Developing the Columbia', in Don Munton and John Kirton, eds, *Cases in Canadian Foreign Policy* (Toronto, Prentice Hall, 1991).

[8]See Canada and the United States, *Great Lakes Water Quality Agreement of 1972*, International Joint Commission, Ottawa and Washington, 1974.

[9]For the texts of the 1972 and 1978 Agreements, see Canada and the United States, *Great Lakes Water Quality Agreement of 1972*, International Joint Commission, 1974, and Canada and the United States, *Great Lakes Water Quality Agreement of 1978*, International Joint Commission, 1978. For the background to the negotiation of the 1972 and 1978 Agreements, see Don Munton, 'Great Lakes Water Quality: A Study in Environmental Politics and Diplomacy' in O.P. Dwivedi, ed., *Resources and the Environment: Policy Perspectives for Canada* (Toronto: McClelland and Stewart, 1980).

[10]Established by the 1909 Boundary Waters Treaty. The Commission is headed by a six-member executive. Three commissioners are appointed each by the United States and Canada.

[11]*Annual Report*, International Joint Commission, Ottawa and Washington, 1978.

[12]One must keep in mind here the distinction between legally specified effluent standards (e.g., the amount of a particular pollutant allowed to be present in the effluent produced) and whether or not these standards are in fact enforced. Some critics of US practice point out that while American law specifies tough standards in terms of how much pollutant is allowed, these standards are rarely rigidly enforced on a case-by-case basis. In both countries, industries are given a period of time to comply, during which, of course, they are not meeting the standard.

[13]See Canada and the United States, *Great Lakes Water Quality Agreement of 1978*, International Joint Commission, Ottawa and Washington, 1978.

[14] Eventually published at the end of 1985 as *The Great Lakes Water Quality Agreement: An Evolving Instrument for Ecosystem Management*, the RSC-NRC report was privately funded by grants from the William H. Donner Foundation (New York) and the Donner Canadian Foundation (Toronto).

[15] International Joint Commission, 1986. *Third Biennial Report Under the Great Lakes Water Quality Agreement of 1978*, Ottawa, Canada and Washington, DC.

[16] Ross Howard, 'Industrial Pollutants "Time Bomb" LeBlanc Warns', *Toronto Star*, 21 June 1977: B2. The first mention by a Canadian politician of acid rain as a problem — in Sweden — seems to have been by then Environment Minister Jack Davis during his November 1969 Columbia University speech.

[17] Acidity is conventionally measured on the pH scale with low values being highly acidic. Given that rain, snow, and dry particles can all deposit these acidic compounds, the term 'acidic deposition' is more descriptive. Given that other substances, particularly toxic chemicals, are also emitted and transported long distances through the atmosphere, and pose significant environmental hazards, the term 'long-range transport of air pollution' might also be used.

[18] Some pioneering research on rainfall acidity had actually been done in Canada and the United States in the decades preceding 1960 (e.g., M. Katz, F.A. Wyatt and H.J. Atkinson, in *Effects of Sulphur Dioxide on Vegetation*, No. 815, Ottawa: National Research Council, 1939). These studies, however, were isolated exceptions.

[19] Phil Weller and the Waterloo Public Interest Research Group, *Acid Rain: The Silent Crisis*, (Kitchener, Ontario: Between the Lines, 1980).

[20] While the 21 June article did not cite LeBlanc personally as having provided this estimate of relative contributions, a 23 October 1977 article in the same newspaper does so cite him.

[21] Winnipeg *Free Press* 7 February 1978.

[22] The BRCG's work was not, however, the first such joint effort by Canadian and American experts. Both the IJC's Great Lakes Water Quality Board and its Science Advisory Board had discussed the problem of acid rain in their 1979 reports even though the Great Lakes themselves are not vulnerable to the effects of acid rain.

[23] Canada-United States Research Consultation Group on the Long-Range Transport of Air Pollutants, 'The LRTAP Problem in North America: A Preliminary Overview', (Ottawa, Canada, Washington, DC: 1979).

[24] The largest single point source of sulphur dioxide in North America was, at the time, the 'superstack' at the Inco smelter outside of Sudbury. On the other hand, the combined emissions of the power plants and other industries in a number of mid-west US urban centres, including St Louis, Cincinnati, and Pittsburgh, were each greater than Inco's.

[25] And studied they were. By early 1980, the RCG had been asked to prepare a second report, President Carter had designated $10 million for acid rain research, Congress had authorized $68 million for similar purposes, and the Clark government had promised to increase Canadian funding of acid rain research. By autumn 1980, the opportunity provided in Ottawa for bureaucratic expansion — what some within have referred to as '1960s-style empire building' — had been fully realized and a four-department, $41 million increase in acid rain-related expenditures was approved by Cabinet. See the publicly released Cabinet discussion paper: Canada, Departments of Environment, Fisheries and Oceans, National Health and Welfare, and External Affairs, 'Discussion Paper: Long Range Transport of Air Pollutants', 30 May 1980.

[26] These documents were made available to, among others, Don Sellar of the *Ottawa Citizen* 7 February 1980.

[27] During testimony at Congressional hearings on the conversion proposal it was pointed out by witnesses or Congressmen that the $400 million provided for pollution control would not be nearly sufficient for all the power plants involved, that many of the plants in

urban areas did not have the physical space to install control devices, that the controls were not mandatory, that nitrogen oxides were not covered, and that the utilities were not even required to spend money from the $400 million fund for air pollution control equipment. See United States, House of Representatives, Committee on Inter-State and Foreign Commerce, Subcommittee on Oversight and Investigations, *Hearings on Acid Rain*, Ninety-sixth Congress, Second Session (Washington: US Government Printing Office, 26 and 27 February 1980), Serial No. 96-150; United States, Senate, Committee on Environment and Public Works, Subcommittee on Environmental Pollution, *Hearings on Environment Effects of the Increased Use of Coal*, Ninety-Sixth Congress, Second Session (Washington: US Government Printing Office, March 19 and 21 and 24 April 1980), Serial No. 96-H45.

[28]EPA official Lowell Smith was quoted in Harrowsmith Staff Report, 'The Acid Earth', *Harrowsmith* 4, 27 (April 1980): 32-41, 93.

[29]One official of the National Coal Association when interviewed on television conceded that some rain was indeed acidic but would not agree that coal was at fault or that there was any proven effect on lakes or possible danger to human health. See William H. Megonnell, 'Atmospheric Sulphur Dioxide in the United States: Can the Standards be Justified or Afforded?', *Journal of Air Pollution Control Association*, 25 (1975) 9-15. See also the testimony of utility company representatives at the above noted Congressional hearings. On the economic pressures US utilities are now facing, see Sheldon Novick, 'Electric Power Companies: How to Pay More For Less', *Environment* 18, 8 (1976): 7-12.

[30]US Senate, op. cit., 187.

[31]*Toronto Star* 16 October 1979.

[32]'The Urgency of Controlling Acid Rain', speech by the Honourable John Roberts, Minister of Environment Canada, to the Air Pollution Control Association, Montreal, 23 June 1980, *Statements and Speeches*, No. 80/8, Department of External Affairs, Ottawa.

[33]*Globe and Mail* 6 August 1980: 1.

[34]John L. Sullivan, 'Beyond the Bargaining Table: Canada's Use of Section 115 of the United States Clean Air Act to Prevent Acid Rain', *Cornell International Law Journal* 16, 1 (Winter 1983): 193-227; D.R. Wooley, 'Acid rain: Canadian Litigation Options in US Court and Agency Proceedings', *University of Toledo Law Review* 17 (Fall 1985): 139-51; and Carol Garland, 'Acid Rain over the United States and Canada: The DC Circuit Court Fails to Provide Shelter under Section 115 of the Clean Air Act while State Action Provides a Temporary Umbrella', *Boston College Environmental Affairs Law Review* 16, 1 (1988): 1-37.

[35]Ernest J. Yanarella and Randal H.Ihara, *The Acid Rain Debate: Scientific, Economic and Political Dimensions* (Boulder, Col.: Westview Press, 1985) 40. A second report by the BCRG was also released in the fall of 1980. Updating and going beyond the first, this version dealt less with the aquatic effects of acid rain and more with the damage caused to agriculture and forestry.

[36]The views of the first administrator of the Reagan EPA are to be found in Anne M. Burford (Gorsuch), with John Greenya, *Are You Tough Enough?* (New York: McGraw-Hill, 1986).

[37]Fitzhugh Green, 'Public Diplomacy and Acid Rain', *Toledo Law Review* 17 (Fall 1985): 136.

[38]Philip Jessup, 'Strategies for Reducing the Cost of Acid Rain Controls: Electricity Demand-Side Management and Clean Coal Technologies', Environmental and Energy Study Institute, Washington, 1988.

[39]Personal interview, Washington, DC, 14 October 1987.

[40]Lois Ember, 'Acid precipitation program head resigns', *Chemical and Engineering News*, 12 October 1987: 15.

[41]For an overview largely, but not entirely, from an American social science perspective of

a term and literature developed by Latin American Marxist scholars, see James Caporaso, ed., 'Dependence and Dependency in the Global System', (special issue) *International Organization* 32, 1 (1978).

[42]The 'Agreement of Co-operation between the United States of America and the United Mexican States Regarding Transboundary Air Pollution Caused by Copper Smelters on their Common Border' was negotiated as a result of American concern over a new copper smelter in Nacozari, just south of the Rio Grande. The document is carefully worded so as not to contradict US Administration positions on the 'uncertainties' of long-range transport, and instead focuses on environmental problems 'in the border area'.

BOARDMAN

[1]The term 'active participant' is part of the useful classification of types of state engagement in intergovernmental organizations developed by Sewell. See James P. Sewell, *UNESCO and World Politics: Engaging in International Relations* (Princeton University Press, 1975), 7-8.

[2]*The Economist*, 26 January 1991: 14.

[3]Jim MacNeill, 'The Greening of International Relations', *International Journal* 45 (1989–90): 14-15.

[4]On the last point, see Inis L. Claude, Jr, 'Myths about the State', *Review of International Studies* 12 (1986): 5.

[5]*Intervenor (Newsletter of the Canadian Environmental Law Association)* 14, 4 (July-August 1989): 6.

[6]*Environmental Issues in Canada: A Status Report* (Ottawa: Environment Canada, 1985), 31.

[7]*Environmental Peacekeepers: Science, Technology, and Sustainable Development in Canada*, (Ottawa: Science Council, 1988), 11.

[8]For example, comments by David Runnals, in Kenneth Bush, ed., *Climate Change, Global Security, and International Governance* (Ottawa: Canadian Institute for International Peace and Security, Working Paper 23, 1990), 36. On Canada's credibility in relation to WCED recommendations, see Canadian Environmental Advisory Council, *Canada and Sustainable Development* (Ottawa: CEAC, 1987), 27.

[9]Don Munton, *Changing Conceptions of Security: Public Attitudes in Canada. The 1990 CIIPS Public Opinion Survey* (Ottawa: Canadian Institute for International Peace and Security, 1990), 8.

[10]David Braybrooke and Gilles Paquet, 'Human Dimensions of Global Change: The Challenge to the Humanities and the Social Sciences', *Transactions of the Royal Society of Canada* 5, 2 (1987): 274.

[11]Jacobson groups the functions of international organizations into five main categories: informational, normative, rule-creating, rule-supervisory, and operational. See Harold K. Jacobson, *Networks of Interdependence: International Organizations and the Global Political System*, 2nd ed. (New York: Knopf, 1984), 81-4.

[12]William Wallace, *The Transformation of Western Europe* (London: Royal Institute of International Affairs, 1990), 9. On ECE see further Patrick Kyba, 'International Environmental Relations: Twenty Years of Canadian Involvement', Paper presented to the Annual Meeting of the Canadian Political Science Association, Victoria, May 1990: 7.

[13]Philippe Le Prestre, *The World Bank and the Environment Challenge* (Selinsgrove: Susquehanna University Press, 1989), 28-9.

[14]OECD Secretariat, 'Environment Policy in the OECD', in *ECE Symposium on Problems relating to Environment, Prague, May 1971* (Geneva: ECE, 1971), 339.

[15]Dr R.W. Slater, in *House of Commons, Standing Committee on Environment and Forestry*,

33d Parlt., 2d Sess., No. 34, 9 June 1988: 10. The reference is to Principle 21 of UNCHE (*Report of the UN Conference on the Human Environment, Stockholm, 5-16 June 1972*, UN Doc. A/CONF.48/14/Rev.1, p. 5).

[16]For example, the data-gathering and monitoring program INFOTERRA, and the work of the International Registry of Potentially Toxic Chemicals (IRPTC). For a general appraisal see Mark Allan Gray, 'The United Nations Environment Program: An Assessment', *Environmental Law* 20 (1990): 291-320.

[17]ECE, *Strategy for Environmental Protection and Rational Use of Natural Resources in ECE Member Countries*, Pt. I (Geneva: UN, 1986), 113-15.

[18]*State of the Environment: Report for Canada*, prep. Peter M. Bird and David J. Rapport (Ottawa: Environment Canada, 1986), Table 10.2, 232-3. A core list of 14 is given in *Environment Canada's Mandate*, prep. E. Wylie (Ottawa: Environment Canada, 1984), App. 1, pp. 11 ff. For summaries of twelve of the main ones see Environment Canada, *Inventory of International Activities* (Ottawa: Corporate Planning Group, Environment Canada, 1986), 38-47.

[19]Canadian Wildlife Service, *CITES Report* 15 (March 1989); and *Transactions of the 52d Federal-Provincial-Territorial Wildlife Conference, Victoria, June 14-17, 1988*, 221.

[20]*Transactions of the 51st Federal-Provincial-Territorial Wildlife Conference, Tuktoyaktuk, June 16-19, 1987*, 70–1, 214.

[21]*State of the Environment: Report for Canada*, 148.

[22]*House of Commons, Standing Committee on Environment*, (1989), No. 26 (11 December 1989): 15.

[23]For a summary of Canadian activities, see Elizabeth Dowdeswell, in *House of Commons, Standing Committee on Environment* (1989), No. 19 (31 October 1989): 23-5.

[24]*Climate Change, Global Security, and International Governance*, 24–5.

[25]*World Conservation Strategy Canada*, prep. D.F.W. Pollard and M.R. McKechnie (Ottawa: Environment Canada, 1986), 45.

[26]See further Juliet Lodge, 'Environment: Towards a Clear Blue-green EC?', in J. Lodge, ed., *The European Community and the Challenge of the Future* (New York: St Martins Press, 1989), 319-26; and 'The EC and Environmental Protection', *European File* 4 (April 1990). On earlier bilateral agreements with the EC and various member-states see further Environment Canada, *Inventory of International Activities*, 66–74.

[27]European Commission, 'Review of Canada-Community Co-operation under the Framework Agreement 1976–1988' (Brussels, June 1989), 9.

[28]For example in the meeting of Canadian and European parliamentarians of September 1986. See *Europe*, No. 4398 (29/30 September 1986), 8.

[29]European Parliament, Doc. A2-98/99, 20 April 1989 (report from the Committee on External Relations).

[30]*Report of the Canada-EC Joint Co-operation Committee, Ottawa, May 25, 1990* (Ottawa: Department of External Affairs, 1990), 5.

[31]Department of External Affairs, 'Notes for a Speech by the Hon. Joe Clark, Humber College, Lakeshore Campus, May 26, 1990', 7.

[32]*EC News* (Ottawa), 22 November 1990, 3-4.

[33]Dr Kenneth Harel, in *House of Commons, Standing Committee on Environment* (1989), No. 10, 8 June 1989: 27.

[34]*Independence and Internationalism. Report of the Special Joint Committee of the Senate and of the House of Commons on Canada's International Relations* (Ottawa, 1986), 35.

[35]On the latter point see David Brooks, IDRC, at *House of Commons, Standing Committee on Environment* (1989), No. 23, 28 November 1989: 33.

[36]Joseph T. Jockel, *Canada-US Relations in the Bush Era* (Orono: Canadian-American Center, University of Maine, *Canadian-American Public Policy*, No. 1, April 1990), 12.

[37]*Globe and Mail*, 4 February 1986.

[38]Peter Gellman, 'Lester B. Pearson, Collective Security, and the World Order Tradition of Canadian Foreign Policy', *International Journal* 44 (1988–89): 68-9.

[39]For example, David B. Brooks, 'Recreating Environment Canada', in *Canada and Sustainable Development*, Annex 4, p. 57; and comments by Harel (note 33 above).

[40]'Proposals for a Department of Environment's International Policy', report by Paul Painchaud (Ottawa: Intergovernmental Affairs Directorate, Environment Canada, 1983). It has been argued that Environment Canada, rather than External Affairs, takes the lead role in representative and technical functions. See Robert Lederman, 'The Canadian Government and International Environmental Cooperation: The UN Experience', Paper presented to the Symposium on Global Issues and the Future, Trent University, 1985, 1. The existence of other departments with international environmental responsibilities further complicates this problem.

[41]Canadian Environmental Advisory Council, *Examining Environment-Economy Linkages* (Ottawa: CEAC, Report No. 16, 1985), 1.

[42]*House of Commons, Standing Committee on Environment* (1989), No. 16, 5 October 1989: 13.

[43]*House of Commons, Standing Committee on Environment* (1989), No. 5, 25 May 1989: 7 (MacNeill).

[44]Maurice Strong was Secretary-General of UNCHE in 1972, and later served as Executive Director of UNEP and in various capacities with other bodies, including IUCN. MacNeill was Director of Environment for the OECD before serving as Secretary-General of the Brundtland Commission; he later led the environment and sustainable development program of the Institute for Research on Public Policy (IRPP) in Ottawa.

[45]For an early assessment of potential IGBP projects of interest to Canadian scientists, see Royal Society of Canada, *Global Change: The Canadian Opportunity* (1986), 13. The related work of the Human Dimensions of Global Change (HDGC) project was initiated by several bodies, including the International Federation of Institutes of Advanced Study, and the United Nations University.

[46]*Globe and Mail* 26 October 1990.

[47]*Greenprint for Canada. A Federal Agenda for the Environment* (Ottawa, June 1989), 19-20. This notes particularly the Canada-US migratory birds convention, CITES, and the Law of the Sea convention.

[48]*CNF Almanac* 5, 1 (January 1991): 3.

[49]*Reports of the 1st and 2d Meetings of Public Interest Groups with the Canadian Environmental Advisory Council* (Ottawa: CEAC, Report No. 7, 1978), 74.

[50]Ivor Shapiro, 'Cleaning Up', *Saturday Night*, November 1990, 31.

[51]See for example the complaint that media people 'reflect the anti-establishment attitudes prevalent on university campuses during the 1970s' and 'often accept and report uncritically one side of an issue' (Moira Jackson, 'Industry and the Environment: More than a Matter of Perception', *CRS Perspectives* 31 [November 1989], n.p.).

[52]*Water 2020: Sustainable Development for Water in the 21st Century* (Ottawa: Science Council, 1988).

[53]This dealt with amendments to the Montreal Protocol. See *House of Commons, Standing Committee on Environment*, (1989), No. 21, 9 November 1989: 3.

[54]*Environment Canada's Mandate*, 3. The issue arises in other areas, such as the negotiation of international trade agreements. See Grace Skogstad, 'Canada: Conflicting Domestic Interests in the MTN', in Grace Skogstad and Andrew Fenton Cooper, eds, *Agricultural Trade: Domestic Pressures and International Tensions* (Ottawa: Institute for Research on Public Policy, 1990), 45.

[55]Canadian Council of Resource Ministers, *Annual Report 1970–71*: 12; Canadian Council of Resource and Environmental Ministers, *Annual Report 1983–84*: 1-2.

[56]Reported in John T. O'Manique, 'Environment Canada in a Changing Society', (typescript, August 1975), 22.

[57]*Canada's Environment: A Framework for Action. Report prepared by the Federal-Provincial Task Force on a Canadian Action Plan respecting the Environment* (Ottawa: Environment Canada, 1975), xxii, and Ch. VI.

[58]Craig McInnes, 'Cutting Emissions of Carbon Dioxide a Major Challenge', *Globe and Mail* 30 August 1989.

[59]Douglas J. Hykle, 'An Evaluation of Canada's Implementation and Enforcement of CITES', Dalhousie University, MES thesis, 1988: 41.

[60]Ibid., 181.

[61]*Transactions of the 51st Federal-Provincial-Territorial Wildlife Conference, Tuktoyaktuk, June 16-19, 1987*, 70.

[62]Don Munton, *Changing Conceptions of Security: Public Attitudes in Canada. The 1990 CIIPS Public Opinion Survey* (Ottawa: CIIPS, 1990), 7-8.

[63]External Affairs and International Trade Canada, *Statements and Speeches*, 90/16, 2.

HOBERG

*Research for this chapter was funded by the Social Sciences and Humanities Research Council of Canada. I would like to thank Jeff Waatainen and Lee Tsuan Lau for research assistance, and Kathryn Harrison, Peter Nemetz, and Tony Hodge for extensive comments on an earlier draft.

[1]Ministry of the Environment, *A Framework for Discussion on the Environment* (Ottawa: Ministry of Supply and Services, 1990).

[2]Ronald Brickman, Sheila Jasanoff, and Thomas Ilgen, *Controlling Chemicals* (Ithaca: Cornell University Press, 1985); David Vogel, *National Styles of Regulation* (Ithaca: Cornell University Press, 1986); Joseph Badaracco, *Loading the Dice: A Five Country Case Study of Vinyl Chloride Regulation* (Cambridge: Harvard Business School Press, 1985); and Lennart Lundqvist, *The Hare and the Tortoise* (Ann Arbor: University of Michigan Press, 1980). For comparative analysis including Canada, see Thomas Ilgen, 'Between Europe and America, Ottawa and the Provinces: Regulating Toxic Substances in Canada', *Canadian Public Policy* 11 (1985): 578-90; Peter Nemetz, W.T. Stanbury, and Fred Thompson, 'Social Regulation in Canada', *Policy Studies Journal* 14 (1986): 580-603; and Peter Nemetz, 'Federal Environmental Regulation in Canada', *Natural Resources Journal* 26 (1986): 552-608.

[3]It should be noted that there is environment-related spending in other federal agencies in both countries.

[4]The 0.47% figure given above already excludes the Atmospheric Environment Service, which is less directly related to environmental protection.

[5]David Bratton and Gary Rutledge, 'Pollution Abatement and Control Expenditures, 1985–88', *Survey of Current Business* (November 1990): 37. Figures are for 1986.

[6]American figures are from Gary Rutledge and Nikolaos Stergioulas, 'Plant and Equipment Expenditures by Business for Pollution Abatement, 1987 and Planned 1988', *Survey of Current Business* (November 1988): 26-9. Canadian figures are from Statistics Canada, *Analysis of the Categories of Capital Investment, 1985 to 1987*, Discussion Paper, November 1989, 15.

[7]See R. Shep Melnick, *Regulation and the Courts: The Case of the Clean Air Act* (Washington, DC: Brookings Institution, 1983).

[8]In 1988, the Clean Air Act was essentially incorporated into the Canadian Environmental Protection Act.

[9]These four cases are chlor-alkali plants, asbestos mining and milling operations, secondary

lead smelters, and vinyl chloride plants. See Peter Nemetz, 'Federal Environmental Regulation in Canada', 557.

[10]Emissions from vehicles in use are still the responsibility of the provinces.

[11]M.A.H. Franson, R.T. Franson, and A.R. Lucas, *Environmental Standards*, ECA83-SP/1, Edmonton: Environment Council of Alberta, 1982, 115.

[12]Nemetz, 'Federal Environmental Regulation in Canada', 559.

[13]Information Release, Canadian Council of Ministers of the Environment, 830-335/022, Charlottetown, Prince Edward Island, 19 October 1989.

[14]Canadian House of Commons, Subcommittee on Acid Rain, *Time Lost: A Demand for Action on Acid Rain* (Ottawa, 1984), 41.

[15]Ironically, Canada made this move in part because it realized that some of its air pollution regulations were less stringent than their American counterparts. See George Hoberg, 'Sleeping With an Elephant: The American Influence on Canadian Environmental Protection', *Journal of Public Policy* 11, 1 (1991): 107-32.

[16]The Canada objective was stated as a 50% reduction below allowable 1980 levels; the number below actual levels is closer to 37%. The US emitted 25.7 million tonnes of sulphur dioxide in 1980, so the statute calls for a 39% reduction below that level.

[17]US Congressional Research Service, *Canada's Progress on Acid Rain Control: Shifting Gears or Stalled in Neutral?* 88-353 ENR, 20 April 1988, 5-7.

[18]Information on these European programs comes from David Vogel, 'Environmental Policy in Europe and Japan', in Norman Vig and Michael Kraft, eds, *Environmental Policy in the 1990s* (Washington, DC: CQ Press, 1990), 273-4.

[19]This summary is based on Helen Ingram and Dean Mann, 'Preserving the Clean Water Act: The Appearance of Environmental Victory', in Norman Vig and Michael Kraft, *Environmental Policy in the 1980s: Reagan's New Agenda* (Washington, DC: CQ Press, 1984); and Frederick Anderson, Daniel Mandelker, and A. Dan Tarlock, *Environmental Protection: Law and Policy* (Boston: Little, Brown, 1984), chapter IV.

[20]Despite the expiry of the deadline and the patent infeasibility of the 1985 zero discharge goal, it was maintained in the preamble to the statute when Congress revised the law in 1987.

[21]Walter Rosenbaum, *Environmental Politics and Policy* (Washington, DC: CQ Press, 1985), 167-73.

[22]Nemetz, 'Federal Environmental Regulation in Canada', 554-6.

[23]Ibid.

[24]Hoberg, 'Sleeping with an Elephant'.

[25]The figures are from US Council on Environmental Quality, *Environmental Quality: Twentieth Annual Report*, 454. The Canadian figures are from a memo to the author from F. Cadoret, Environment Canada, 18 January 1991.

[26]Great Lakes Water Quality Board, *1989 Report on Great Lakes Water Quality*, Report to the International Joint Commission, Presented at Hamilton, Ontario, October 1989, 35, 19.

[27]Ontario Ministry of the Environment, *Interim Pollution Reduction Strategy for Ontario Kraft Mills*, April 1989.

[28]Great Lakes Water Quality Board, *1989 Report*, 17.

[29]See for instance Keith Hawkins, *Environment and Enforcement* (Oxford: Oxford University Press, 1984), and Eugene Bardach and Robert Kagan, *Going by the Book: The Problem of Regulatory Unreasonableness* (Philadelphia: Temple University Press, 1982).

[30]Great Lakes Water Quality Board, *1989 Report*, 6-12.

[31]Ibid.

[32]7 USC. 136 *et seq.* For an overview of the US regulatory framework, see US General Accounting Office, *Pesticides: EPA's Formidable Task to Assess and Regulate Their Risks*, RCED-86-125 (Washington, DC: GAO, 1986).

[33]Pest Control Products Act, 1968–69, c. 50, s. 1. For an overview of the Canadian regulatory framework, see J.F. Castrilli and Toby Vigod, *Pesticides in Canada: An Examination of Federal Law and Policy*, Study Paper, Protection of Life Series (Ottawa: Law Reform Commission of Canada, 1987).

[34]Alachlor Review Board, *The Report of the Alachlor Review Board* (Ottawa: 1987), 23.

[35]PCP Regulations, s. 20.

[36]See for instance George Hoberg, 'Risk, Science, and Politics: Alachlor Regulation in Canada and the United States', *Canadian Journal of Political Science* 23 (June 1990): 257-78.

[37]The cases are alachlor, aldrin/dieldrin, captan, daminozide, DBCP, DDT, dinoseb, EDB, heptachlor/chlordane, and 2,4,5-T. Canada has banned alachlor and the US has not; the US has banned dinoseb and Canada has not. In the remaining cases the outcomes are highly similar.

[38]See George Hoberg, 'Reaganism, Pluralism, and the Politics of Pesticide Regulation', *Policy Sciences* 23 (1990): 257-89.

[39]Compare US Code of Federal Regulations, Volume 40, Section 180, with Canadian Food and Drug Regulations, Division 15, Table II.

[40]Based on interviews with government officials in the US and Canada.

[41]William Kennedy, 'Environmental Impact Assessments in North America, Western Europe: What Has Worked Where, How, and Why', *International Environmental Reporter* 11 (13 April 1988): 257-63.

[42]Terry Fenge and L. Graham Smith, 'Reforming the Environmental Assessment and Review Process', *Canadian Public Policy* 12 (1986): 596-605.

[43]Ibid., 603.

[44]Based on the average for 1987–89, from Council on Environment Quality, *Environmental Quality – Twentieth Annual Report* (Washington, DC: Executive Office of the President, 1990), 439.

[45]Interview, John Mathers, Pacific Western and Northern Region, FEARO, 29 January 1991.

[46]Confidential interviews, government officials. As an example of the importance of financial assistance, see the information on the smelter modernization program in House of Commons, Special Committee on Acid Rain, *Report of the Special Committee on Acid Rain*, 2nd Session, 33rd Parliament, Ottawa, September 1988.

[47]These two examples are indicative of a much larger pattern explored in Hoberg, 'Sleeping with an Elephant'.

Index